Anthropology and Development
in North Africa
and the Middle East

MONOGRAPHS IN DEVELOPMENT ANTHROPOLOGY

Under the General Editorship of
DAVID W. BROKENSHA
MICHAEL M HOROWITZ
and
THAYER SCUDDER

Sponsored by the Institute for Development Anthropology

Anthropology and Rural Development in West Africa, edited by Michael M Horowitz and Thomas M. Painter

Lands at Risk in the Third World: Local-Level Perspectives, edited by Peter D. Little and Michael M Horowitz, with A. Endre Nyerges

Anthropology of Development and Change in East Africa, edited by David W. Brokensha and Peter D. Little

Anthropology and Development in North Africa and the Middle East, edited by Muneera Salem-Murdock and Michael M Horowitz, with Monica Sella

African River Basin Development, Thayer Scudder (forthcoming)

Anthropology and Development in North Africa and the Middle East

EDITED BY

**Muneera Salem-Murdock
and Michael M Horowitz,
with Monica Sella**

LONDON AND NEW YORK

First published 1990 by Westview Press

Published 2018 by Routledge
52 Vanderbilt Avenue, New York, NY 10017
2 Park Square, Milton Park, Abingdon, Oxon OX14 4RN

Routledge is an imprint of the Taylor & Francis Group, an informa business

Copyright © 1990 by the Institute for Development Anthropology

All rights reserved. No part of this book may be reprinted or reproduced or utilised in any form or by any electronic, mechanical, or other means, now known or hereafter invented, including photocopying and recording, or in any information storage or retrieval system, without permission in writing from the publishers.

Notice:
Product or corporate names may be trademarks or registered trademarks, and are used only for identification and explanation without intent to infringe.

Library of Congress Cataloging-in-Publication Data
Anthropology and development in North Africa and the Middle East/
  edited by Muneera Salem-Murdock and Michael M Horowitz, with Monica Sella.
      p. cm.—(Monographs in development anthropology)
   ISBN 0-8133-7688-2
 1. Applied anthropology—Africa, North. 2. Applied anthropology—Middle East. 3. Rural development—Africa, North. 4. Rural development—Middle East. 5. Africa, North—Economic conditions. 6. Middle East—Economic conditions. I. Salem-Murdock, Muneera. II. Horowitz, Michael M, 1933–   . III. Sella, Monica. IV. Series.
GN397.7.A357A58 1990
307.1′412′0961—dc20   90-32325
                                                                                           CIP

ISBN 13: 978-0-367-01287-8 (hbk)

Contents

List of Tables and Figures vii
Acknowledgments xi

    Introduction, *Muneera Salem-Murdock, Michael M Horowitz, and Monica Sella*   1

1   Brokering Social Science in Development: Experiences in Morocco, *Alice L. Morton*   15

2   Slash-and-Burn Cultivation, Charcoal Making, and Emigration from the Highlands of Northwest Morocco, *Henry Munson, Jr.*   30

3   Farm Size and Agricultural Credit in Morocco: Correcting Distorted Information in the Development Process, *John Aron Grayzel*   47

4   Water-User Associations in Rural Central Tunisia, *Nicholas S. Hopkins*   74

5   Household Production Organization and Differential Access to Resources in Central Tunisia, *Muneera Salem-Murdock*   95

6   Development in Hammam Sousse, Tunisia: Change, Continuity, and Challenge, *Frederick C. Huxley*   126

7   An Anthropologist's Contribution to Libya's National Human Settlement Plan, *John P. Mason*   155

8   Developing Egypt's Western Desert Oases: Anthropology and Regional Planning, *Douglas Gritzinger*   175

9   Agricultural Development and Food Production on a Sudanese Irrigation Scheme, *Victoria Bernal*   197

10   Advocacy in a Bedouin Resettlement Project in the Negev, Israel, *Emanuel Marx*   228

11   Rural Development and Migration in Northeast Syria, *Günter Meyer*   245

12	Doing Development Anthropology: Personal Experience in the Yemen Arab Republic, *Charles F. Swagman*	279
13	Land Use and Agricultural Development in the Yemen Arab Republic, *Daniel Martin Varisco*	292
14	The World Bank and the Çorum-Çankırı Rural Development Project in Turkey, *Zülküf Aydın*	312
15	Tradition and Change Among the Pastoral Harasiis in Oman, *Dawn Chatty*	336

About the Editors and Contributors   351
Index   355

Tables and Figures

Tables

2.1	1976–77 Monthly Rainfall in Dar Chaoui	33
2.2	Distribution of Landholdings in Bni Msawwar in 1954	35
2.3	Distribution of Landholdings in the Dar Chaoui Basin in 1968	36
2.4	Distribution of Landholdings in the Commune of the Monday Market of Bni Harshan in 1977	36
2.5	Place of Permanent Residence of Adult Male Emigrants from the Commune of the Monday Market of Bni Harshan in June 1977	41
2.6	Date of Emigration of Adult Male Emigrants from the Commune of the Monday Market of Bni Harshan	41
2.7	Occupational Distribution of Adult Male Emigrants from the Commune of the Monday Market of Bni Harshan Working in Urban Morocco in 1977	42
3.1	World Bank Farm Size Breakdown	51
3.2	Estimate of Land Distribution by Size of Farm in Traditional Dryland Arable Region	52
5.1	Distribution of Private Land in Zone A of Sbeitla PPI	99
5.2	Distribution of Land in Zone B of Sbeitla PPI	99
5.3	Distribution of Land in Shraayi' PPI	100
5.4	Distribution of Land by Sector in Foussana Delegation	101
5.5	Land Use in PPI FS6, 1985	102
5.6	Summer 1985 Soil Use in Foussana PPIs	103
5.7	Land Ownership Among PPI Farm Households	114
5.8	Intrahousehold Labor Allocation by Size of Holding and Age/Sex Group	117
6.1	Distribution of the Labor Force by Sector	139
8.1	Overall Groundwater Balance for New Valley in 1980	180
8.2	Estimated 1982 New Valley Population	181
8.3	New Valley Cultivated Land, Winter 1981–1982	182
8.4	New Valley Governorate Cropping Pattern 1980–1981	183
8.5	New Valley Target Population Distribution Year 2010	185

8.6	New Valley Proposed Irrigated Land Development Program	186
8.7	New Valley Proposed Cropping Pattern	187
9.1	Shortages of Family Labor Resources Required to Cultivate Holdings, 1980–81	211
9.2	Degree of Self-Sufficiency in Sorghum Production (Reported Consumption)	215
9.3	Degree of Self-Sufficiency in Sorghum Production (Standardized Consumption)	216
11.1	Socioeconomic Structure of the Reservoir Population Before Resettlement	249
11.2	Distribution of the Reservoir Population After Resettlement in 1979	252
11.3	Socioeconomic Characteristics of the Reservoir Population by Areas of Resettlement	255
11.4	Occupation of Temporary Labor Emigrants from the Euphrates Valley Before Going Abroad for the First Time	269
11.5	Rate of Participation in Labor Emigration by Type of Land Tenure	270
13.1	Fragmentation of Farm Holdings in the YAR	302
13.2	Average Farm-holding Size in the YAR	303
14.1	Internal Terms of Trade Indexes Between Agriculture and Industry	323
14.2	Land Distribution	325

Figures

1.1	Morocco, Showing the Project Areas	19
2.1	Northwest Morocco	31
3.1	Distribution of CRCA and CLCA Loans in El Bourg	58
3.2	Distribution of CRCA and CLCA Loans in Settat	59
3.3	Distribution of CRCA and CLCA Loans in Berrechid	60
4.1	Central Tunisia, Showing Locations of Six Case Studies	80
5.1	Central Tunisia	97
5.2	Housework Allocation by Age, Sex, and Size of Holding	118
5.3	Farm Labor Allocation by Age, Sex, and Size of Holding	119
5.4	Total Labor Allocation by Age, Sex, and Size of Holding	120
6.1	The Coastline of Tunisia Including Port el-Kantaoui, Hammam Sousse, and Sousse	127

Tables and Figures

7.1	Libya	157
7.2	Potential Breakdown of Community Linkages as a Result of National Sectoral Development	165
8.1	Egypt New Valley Study Area	179
11.1	Reclamation Areas in Northeast Syria	248
11.2	New Villages of the Reservoir Population Along the Turkish Border	251
11.3	Resettlement of Families from Flooded Villages in the Reservoir Area	253
11.4	Size of Land, Cultivation, and Average Agricultural Income per Household in New Villages Along the Turkish Border	258
11.5	State Farms of the Pilot Project in the Middle Euphrates Valley	260
11.6	Origins of the Inhabitants on the State Farm Rabi'a	261
11.7	Development of Labor Emigration in the Middle and Lower Euphrates Valley Between 1966 and 1979	265
11.8	Extent of Temporary Labor Emigration Caused by Agricultural Problems in the Villages of the Middle and Lower Euphrates Valley	267
11.9	Rate of Participation in Labor Emigration by Size of Irrigated Area of Farmers Affected by Conversion of the Irrigation System	269
11.10	Temporary Labor Emigration to Saudi Arabia and Jordan by Size of Individual Farmer's Irrigated Holdings Affected by Conversion of the System	271
14.1	Çorum-Çankırı Rural Development Project Area	313
15.1	Sultanate of Oman	338
15.2	Jiddat-il-Harasiis	340

Acknowledgments

We are grateful for the assistance of IDA staff members, present and past, who spent many days in editing the manuscript. Two former senior research assistants provided careful critical readings of many of the papers submitted for the book: A. Endre Nyerges, now of the Department of Anthropology, University of Kentucky, and Douglas Gritzinger. The IDA editorial staff, Sylvia Huntley Horowitz and Vivian Carlip, assisted by Kim Munson and Vera Beers-Tyler, copyedited the entire manuscript, proofread the text, and guided its transformation into copy suitable for computer-generated typesetting.

We wish especially to thank our contributors, who took time from their busy schedules to respond to numerous revisions and requests for additional information and clarifications. They have been graciously patient in seeing this book through to completion.

Muneera Salem-Murdock
Michael M Horowitz
Monica Sella

Introduction

*Muneera Salem-Murdock, Michael M Horowitz,
and Monica Sella*

The first two regionally based monographs in this series on anthropological perspectives on rural development and change focused on sub-Saharan Africa.[1] Black Africa received the vast bulk of development anthropology attention after 1973 when the United States Congress amended the Foreign Assistance Act of 1961 and initiated a ten-year period during which projects at least rhetorically invoking participatory rural development tended to replace top-down capital-intensive interventions, creating a niche for anthropology among the development professions. Anthropologists became component members of design and evaluation teams, offering their insights on a broad variety of development interventions. In the course of this decade, anthropologists made important, even fundamental contributions to the understanding of involuntary relocation, colonization of new lands, and resettlement; the operation of the "informal" sector; the relevance within households and communities of socioeconomic differentiation—including age, class, ethnicity, and gender—in rural production, exchange, and consumption; the diversification of rural production systems and the role of wage labor migration in rural economies; the nature of urbanization and urban social organization; the structure of user associations in the distribution and control of water; the development potential of river basins; on- and off-farm rural employment generation; marketing and rural-urban linkages; the significance of open-range access in pastoral production systems on communal lands, and common property management, especially in "fragile" lands; the relevance of local organization to recurrent costs and debt repayment; natural resource management and afforestation; the nature of elites (international, national, regional, and local, governmental, corporate, military, and religious); and a host of other areas.

Anthropologists were invited into the arena of Third World development when the international development agenda favored local-level participatory interventions. They have remained active in development through recent changes that shifted the agenda to an interest in "policy-based financial assistance," including concern for exchange rates, balances of trade and payments, debt service, adjustment and structural readjustment, decreases in public-sector expenditures, privatization, trade liberalization, and programmatic rather than project funding.

As the utility of social science perspectives for understanding local communities in Africa has come to be well-established, anthropologists' contribution to the development process in other areas of the world has grown considerably—hence this volume on North Africa and the Middle East.[2] Readers familiar with the cases explored in the two preceding regional volumes in this series will be struck by how much more prosperous and, deceptively, *developed* the countries of North Africa and the Middle East appear to be. Indeed, no country in this area is included in the World Bank's list of "low-income economies," defined by very low per capita gross national product.[3] Of the 32 poorest countries in the world, with a 1987 estimated average per capita GNP of $284 (World Bank 1989), 24 are in sub-Saharan Africa, 7 (including such large countries as China, India, Pakistan, and Bangladesh) are Asian, and 1, Haiti, is American.[4] The poorest Middle Eastern country represented in the present volume, the Yemen Arab Republic, has a 1987 estimated per capita GNP of $590, Morocco has $620, Egypt $670, Turkey $1,200, Tunisia $1,210, Syria $1,640, Libya $5,500, Oman $5,830, and Israel $6,810.[5]

Yet high per capita GNP, oil, industry, wage labor migrants, and sizeable cities notwithstanding, large numbers of Middle Eastern and North African peoples remain rural and, with few exceptions, rural and agricultural development in the region since the end of colonization has been unimpressive.[6] In those countries whose economies are primarily agricultural, such as Yemen, the Sudan, Somalia, Morocco, and Mauritania, rural income levels have for the most part remained constant or have deteriorated, and the economic gaps between their rural and urban populations and between their national economies and those of the northern industrial countries (often former colonial powers) remain large (World Bank 1989:17).

Despite some modest increases in agricultural production during the late 1960s and early 1970s, most rural regions have been unable to produce the agricultural surpluses necessary to meet the food requirements of their countries' rapidly growing populations, and as of the early 1980s, the world's most rapidly growing food-deficit area was the Middle East (Paul 1982:3–6; Weinbaum 1982:3–6).[7] This is the outcome, in part, of government development policies biased toward industry and urban populations—policies that had their origin before political independence. Although often achieving rapidly rising incomes for urban residents, such policies have discriminated strongly against agriculture and have forced many to leave the farms, thus sapping the rural area of the vital labor to maintain food production. Even when assistance has been directed toward agriculture, it has often been highly capital intensive and thus, inevitably, geared toward more affluent farmers, thereby exacerbating existing inequities. For example, because of the heavy burden of agricultural equipment and fertilizer imports on foreign

Introduction

exchange earnings, public credit institutions all too often have been unwilling to distribute loans to any but the more commercially oriented farms.

In some countries, such as Tunisia, Sudan, and Syria, the state intervened in the agrarian sector either directly or through the agency of parastatal corporations, transforming large numbers of formerly independent smallholders into tenants or wage laborers on big, often export-oriented, schemes. In others, including Syria, actual reforms were introduced, with the goal of appropriating large farms from affluent holders and redistributing them to small producers. But even these land reforms and agrarian support services, carried out first in Egypt in 1952, then in Syria and Iraq in 1958, and later in Algeria, Jordan, and Iran, have had fewer positive impacts than initially anticipated. In Egypt, the 1952 and 1961 land laws succeeded at least initially in narrowing the gap between the poorest and wealthiest rural farmers, but failed over the long run to prevent the concentration of arable land among middle farmers. Similarly, the 1958 land legislation in Syria, though particularly progressive in its provision for rights of tenants and agricultural workers, as well as for the redistribution of land, was eventually ignored in many areas as wealthy farm units reintegrated and private holdings exceeded size limits. Successful land redistribution in Iraq and Iran was severely hindered by the economically unviable size of parcels, which often were neither able to employ all family members, nor, for that matter, to generate the necessary funds for land improvements. And in Jordan, in an attempt to promote larger, more efficient farms, the post-1959 land legislation tended to overlook family ownership concentration in the valley. Common to most of the reforms have been political and bureaucratic motivations and policies that have failed to assure farmers access to farm inputs and markets or to provide them with basic support services.

For those accustomed to working in sub-Saharan Africa, most immediately apparent in North Africa and the Middle East is the relative ease of travel and communications, evidence of the region's massive expenditures on industry and infrastructure. Hard-surfaced roads link even the smaller towns; telephones tend to function; and telex and even telefax machines are widely available. One of the consequences of the ease of communication is that in the Middle Eastern state, compared with its sub-Saharan African counterpart, the government appears to be ubiquitous, with much of its apparatus located in rural as well as in urban areas. The state maintains frequent and intense contact in the Middle East between the capital city, the secondary cities and towns, and the rural hinterlands, whereas in rural Black Africa, the state is often conspicuous by its general absence.

Less obviously apparent, but perhaps more significant to an understanding of rural economies, is the much wider penetration of commodity relations of production in North African and Middle Eastern rural areas. Without embracing the thesis that the crisis of African agriculture is a function of the *under*development of capitalism south of the Sahara (Hyden 1986; Hart 1982), we can observe that the Middle East has both a far more intense separation of agrarian labor from ownership of land and a much larger capital investment at the level of the individual farm. Agricultural tenancy and an agrarian proletariat are more common in the Middle East, though the presence of a dominant landholding class is perhaps less-developed there than in Latin America and in parts of Asia.

> There exists in the Middle East a chasm between those in the rural areas who are able to profit from the increased productivity of the land and others without the means to extract a decent living from their land or labor. Classic distinctions between cultivating and appropriating classes are by no means inappropriate to the Middle East. But the advantages of the privileged are not found solely or even primarily in their direct exploitation of tenants and wage laborers; the relative prosperity of a region's surplus farmers is frequently a result of their differential claims on the state's resources. Where modernization, mobilization, and commercialization have had their heaviest impact on rural life, there emerge two agricultural societies, one commercially oriented and favored, the other composed of either neglected or administratively oppressed subsistence farmers and agricultural workers (Weinbaum 1982:51).

In sub-Saharan Africa, the typical smallholding is farmed by those whose rights of access are defined by membership in a landholding community (whether a tribe, village, or lineage). In the Middle East, other than in pastoral areas where communal access to the range is normal, farms are more likely to be registered with individual owners, and persons with no effective jural rights to productive fields form a landless class.

This wider separation of agrarian labor from ownership of land can be attributed partly to the markedly greater capital investment on Middle Eastern farms.[8] African farms classically use low energy, being exploited in the main by simple tools: the hoe and the machete remain the major implements of production; animal traction is relatively rare; and tractors are found only on large, often white-owned, commercial or parastatally managed farms. Middle Eastern farms, on the other hand, have known traction for a long time, and they consume chemical fertilizers and other inputs (selected seeds, irrigation water, pesticides, herbicides) to a degree unknown in most of sub-Saharan Africa.

The explosion of Middle Eastern urban centers, of craft production and trade, and of state formation throughout the region in the centuries following the Muslim conquest would not have been possible without the accompanying investment in productivity-increasing techniques and technologies in the agricultural sector.

> Beginning with the eighth century, the Islamic countries underwent an agricultural revolution that entailed changes in plants and plant strains, in farming practices, and in hydraulic technology. This revolution issued in a great expansion of colonization and recolonization. The agricultural sector yielded increasing surpluses, which were plowed back into agricultural intensification and underwrote an expansion of commerce and town life (Wolf 1982:103).[9]

Thus, what anthropologists have sometimes termed the "domestic," "communal," "kin-ordered," and "lineage" modes of production (Meillassoux 1981; Wolf 1982), strong in much of sub-Saharan Africa, survive more weakly in the agrarian Middle East. Not only are the factors of production in the Middle East and North Africa overwhelmingly commoditized, but production itself is heavily market oriented. Whereas much small-scale farming in Africa is aimed at directly sustaining the producers, in the Middle East more of the product is shipped to urban markets and exported to other countries.[10]

In short, where the domestic mode of production continues to characterize rural areas of Africa, a consequence of what has been labeled the "asymmetrical" development of capitalism (Amin 1973), Middle Eastern and North African agriculture, and therefore rural society, are more fully and directly incorporated into the world economy. These differences are, of course, matters of degree, and the commoditization of land and labor in Africa is also intensifying. But that process lags considerably behind North Africa and the Middle East.

We do not wish to convey a sense of homogeneity among the societies and states of Southwest Asia and North Africa. Within the region there is an extraordinary diversity. Even the almost universal commitment to Islam hardly serves to unify the area, as conflicts between Iran and Iraq, between Libya and its neighbors, and between more secular and more fundamentalist Muslims, amply demonstrate. The states of the region differ politically, with some regimes based on parliamentary forms, some on dynastic monarchical succession, some on theocratic rule, and still others on military juntas who seized power in coups d'états. Economically, they include some states with an active industrial sector, some whose economies rest almost entirely on agriculture, and some for whom oil exports play an important role.[11] These latter include nations with very large populations, like Iran and Algeria, and nations with relatively small populations, like Libya and the Gulf States. In such countries as Algeria, Syria, and Israel, the state and parastatal agencies play central economic roles. In others, like Jordan and Morocco, an active private sector is encouraged. Socially, the region includes countries in which legal slavery was practiced until very recently, and countries where it has not existed for centuries. It includes states in which effective citizenship is denied to all but privileged ethnic groups, and states that have been more receptive to outsiders. It includes some societies in which the position of women has deteriorated in recent years and others in which the political regime has embraced a more progressive policy. Above all, the states of the Middle East and North Africa do not stand in a fixed relationship to the world economic system or to each other. The region "does not constitute a well-bounded area with its own core and periphery or with its own distinctive type of social formation, political behavior or mode of cultural expression" (Asad and Owen 1983:4).

As the chapters in this volume amply demonstrate, anthropology and its sister social sciences have a good deal to contribute to the understanding of more fully commoditized as well as communal and domestic economies. They document the increasingly important function of social science analyses in the identification, design, implementation, and evaluation of development programs and projects in ten Middle Eastern and North African countries, and, by extension, in other middle-income economies in the region and throughout the world. They reveal once again that local rural production systems must be understood before regional or national development can take place. Most importantly, these case studies demonstrate that sustainability cannot be achieved independently of or in opposition to the interests of the rural poor. Environmentally sound development must be predicated on increased real income, greater surplus retention, for small producers. As long as wealth continues to be appropriated from the poor in such gross disproportion as it is today in most parts of the Middle East and North Africa, and indeed, throughout the developing world, the poor will be unable to make the kinds of investments in land, labor, and capital that will help reverse the rapid deterioration of environmental conditions (watershed degradation, soil loss, deforestation, overgrazing, and overfishing) (Blaikie and Brookfield 1987). Sustainable improvements in the health of the earth require prior and parallel improvements in the economic health of the poor, especially the agrarian proletariat and smallholders.

The sequence of chapters is based on geography, moving from the westernmost extension of the region, Morocco, across North Africa (Tunisia and Libya) to Egypt, moving southward to the Sudan, then northeast to Israel, Syria, and Yemen, and concluding with contributions from Turkey and the Sultanate of Oman. The authors are anthropologists, regional planners, and geographers experienced in the application of their science to humane and sustainable development in the rural Third World.

Alice Morton's chapter, "Brokering Social Science in Development: Experiences in Morocco," explores problems of integrating indigenous social scientists in national development activities. She documents a conflict unforeseen when the project was designed: the expatriate agronomists (in this case from the United States) and the Moroccan social scientists disagreed in their assessments of the research required for increasing farmer productivity. Part of the problem stemmed from the special culture of the donor organization, the United States Agency for International Development, a culture that has both a world view and a social organization alien to host country personnel. Morton trenchantly presents the cultural dissonance that may pervade projects that laudably involve host government personnel and institutions in the development process, and she provides useful insights, as do several of the other chapters in this book, into the role of the anthropologist as broker or mediator, who sorts through conflicting interests of local, national, and foreign organizations.

Henry Munson, Jr., in "Slash-and-Burn Cultivation, Charcoal Making, and Emigration from the Highlands of Northwest Morocco," suggests that peasants are more in tune with their environments than is often thought. Their familiarity with and dependence on local resources induces them to adopt production strategies that do not degrade the environment, and when ecological imbalances do occur the peasants are at least as much the victims as they are the causes of environmental decline. Munson evidences this claim by identifying the conditions that led to serious problems of deforestation and erosion in the Jbalan highlands in the late 1970s. He documents the consequences of government measures to prohibit traditional practices of swidden cultivation and charcoaling, and demonstrates the importance of undertaking socioeconomic and ecological analyses in rural areas before attempting to alter local practice.

Munson attributes deforestation and erosion to environmental, locational, and land-tenure factors. Violent rains on steep slopes lead to soil losses, yet farmers are forced onto the hillsides because of the very limited amount of arable land available to them in the valleys. The peasants argue that given the unavailability of alternative lands, slash-and-burn agriculture is an environmentally sound way of maintaining soil fertility over the long run, while the government opposes it as a destructive practice. Indeed, the government's prohibition of slash-and-burn has led to accelerated erosion, as farmers have had little choice but to plow the steep slopes. At the same time, the cleared brush is no longer available for charcoaling. The declining capacity of the land to support the population results in high rates of emigration.

In the last of the chapters dealing with Morocco, "Farm Size and Agricultural Credit in Morocco: Correcting Distorted Information in the Development Process," John Grayzel argues that anthropologists are in a unique position to influence applied studies because of their longstanding concern with identifying and, at times, mediating discrepancies that exist in all facets of development. He describes an AID-funded rural-credit project whose planned activities and long-term policy concerns were modified following an appraisal of country characteristics and needs. Grayzel shows that the general understanding of Morocco's agricultural sector, as in government and donor documents, was severely flawed, showing ignorance especially of the degree of social differentiation among farmers. His analysis leads him to suggest a beneficiary group, "farmers in transition," a group that had largely been excluded from access to credit because of inaccurate data on farm size and distribution, but that constituted the one segment of rural producers who were both capable of reimbursing loans and of achieving desired increases in productivity.

"Water-User Associations in Rural Central Tunisia" stems from work undertaken as part of the Institute for Development Anthropology's (IDA's) long-term socioeconomic research in Kasserine Governorate. In that chapter, Nicholas Hopkins reminds us that sustainable development must be based on effective local management as well as on appropriate material interventions. Hopkins has been advising the Central Tunisia Development Office on the institutionalization of water-user associations in the region since 1983, a response to the previously poor performance of top-down government efforts to meet the water needs of dispersed rural households. These associations are now functioning, responsible for controlling access to new deep-water points and for covering the recurrent costs of their operation and repair.

IDA's work in Kasserine Governorate has been directed jointly by the editors of this book. In "Household Production Organization and Differential Access to Resources in Central Tunisia," Muneera Salem-Murdock argues that inter- and intra-household access to resources is paramount in the determination of production strategies and disparities in wealth levels. In addition to such material resources as land, water, labor, livestock and other capital, and access to markets, Salem-Murdock shows the saliency of less tangible resources—kinship, tribal affiliation, and social and political position. Her findings reveal further that differential access to resources also exacerbates the social differences between richer and poorer farmers. She offers this telling example: on the public irrigation schemes, where water is often scarce, poorer farmers who cannot afford the costs of irrigation either abandon irrigation altogether or substantially restrict its use, making more water available to those who can afford it and thereby increasing the yields of the richer tenants. Salem-Murdock also demonstrates that within households gender makes a great difference in resource access.

Frederick Huxley, in "Development in Hammam Sousse, Tunisia: Change, Continuity, and Challenge," documents the evolution of socioeconomic development in a Tunisian town over a thirty-year period. Using a political economic approach, Huxley links current developments in the town to its tradition of social cohesiveness and collective actions and sentiments, and to its active political participation in the struggle for independence from the French. He incorporates into the study an account of the various forms of social organization and their relationship to one another and to community development.

The critical role of the anthropologist, with specialized knowledge of a region or country, as mediator between the planning impulses of donor and government personnel and the needs of local people, is forcefully portrayed in John Mason's chapter, "An Anthropologist's Contribution to Libya's National Human Settlement Plan." So too are the resistance and constraints faced by anthropologists and other social scientists seeking to have their recommendations inform integrally on project design.

Few American social scientists have carried out work in Libya since Colonel Muammar el-Qaddafi's accession to power in 1969. In 1977–1979 Mason was part of an interdisciplinary team asked to design a national settlement plan based on a spatially and socially equitable distribution of resources. Mason's task was to reconcile planning with existing social and cultural conditions. Background knowledge of Libya's people, of her numerous ecological regions, of the division of labor, and of trade patterns linking dispersed communities revealed an opportunity for a strategy of social integration where human needs would be met by encouraging movement and the exchange of goods and ideas. The marketplace was seen as the focal implementing institution, and the agricultural village as the productive beneficiary of the program.

Introduction

Mason's recommendations met with stiff opposition both from the team manager, who preferred using imported models rather than locally based understandings, and from government officials. He frankly assesses his work as only partially successful, but the chapter will prove instructive in its insights into the workings of project bureaucracy.

Douglas Gritzinger, in "Developing Egypt's Western Desert Oases: Anthropology and Regional Planning," points out how the lack of in-country experience among expatriate planners, an overriding commitment to use excessively sophisticated mathematical modeling procedures, and a determination to come up with a definitive plan produced largely inappropriate and inflexible results. He suggests that field-informed anthropological inputs regarding the limitations and potentials of existing farm systems and comparative analyses of similar regions and production systems would generate more useful planning.

Development projects, whose objectives are frequently defined by narrow interests, all too often actually worsen the living conditions of local populations. This outcome is reinforced by research efforts limited to evaluating the extent to which project objectives have been met, for they fail to investigate further into the implications of such objectives for the lives of local people. Victoria Bernal's study of the Blue Nile Irrigation Scheme, "Agricultural Development and Food Production on a Sudanese Irrigation Scheme," indicts both the Sudan's agricultural development strategy and the bulk of development-related research so far carried out in that country. She shows that the Sudanese government and the donors contributed to the food crises of the 1980s by prioritizing irrigated cotton production, and that most research efforts, by adopting project performance as their scope of inquiry, dealt only peripherally with the project's impact on the quality of life of the scheme's tenants.

Bernal carefully examines the effects of the Blue Nile Scheme on the lives of farmers in the village of Wad al Abbas. She demonstrates that management's control of inputs, services, research, land, and labor effectively restricts households' food production capacities and results not only in making tenants more vulnerable to food shortages, but in severely inhibiting the national ability of the Sudan to achieve food security.

Emanuel Marx, in "Advocacy in a Bedouin Resettlement Project in the Negev, Israel," returns to the theme of the anthropologist as broker: how the anthropologist can exert his or her influence in a powerful state bureaucracy. He describes his advocacy on behalf of a community of 5,000 Bedouin in the northern Negev following the 1979 peace treaty between Israel and Egypt, when an Israeli airbase was built in the Negev to compensate for one turned over to Egypt in the Sinai. The action forced the relocation of Bedouin whose grazing lands had been in the area of the base. Marx was invited by both sides to serve as intermediary between the Abu Jwe'id tribe and the government planning team.

Marx concludes that advocates working within the state system often find their initial successes compromised as their policy recommendations are increasingly ignored by bureaucratic interest groups. He nevertheless feels that anthropologists are both qualified and morally obligated to assume the role of advocate when requested to do so by members of the communities among which they have conducted research.

Large-scale agricultural resettlement schemes have elicited a good deal of anthropological attention, as most recently shown in Muneera Salem-Murdock's *Arabs and Nubians in New Halfa: a Study of Settlement and Irrigation* (Salt Lake City: University of Utah Press, 1989), and in Victoria Bernal's and Zulkuf Aydin's chapters in this book. Geographer Günter Meyer examines the Euphrates Scheme, a huge capital-intensive irrigated project, in "Rural Development and Migration in Northeast Syria." The largest development project in the country, the Euphrates Scheme has failed to meet its objectives of improving the rural economy and markedly increasing agricultural yields. The economic status of households relocated onto the scheme has, in general, not improved, and chronic underemployment among most households has led to either a resumption of pastoral nomadism or migration for wage labor to other parts of the country and the region. Meyer points out that remittances from absent wage earners have not been reinvested in productive activities, but have been used for domestic consumption and bride-price. A major cause of the scheme's poor performance at the household level is that farmers have had to bear heavy managerial costs. The lessons learned from Meyer's analysis of this project are relevant to other countries in which large-scale irrigated settlement schemes with centralized management have been installed.

Charles Swagman, in "Doing Development Anthropology: Personal Experience in the Yemen Arab Republic," returns our attention to the anomalous position of the anthropologist on an interdisciplinary development team. On the one hand, as a member of the team the anthropologist is supposed to articulate the goals of the development organization, whether it be a host government, a funding bilateral or multilateral agency, or a contractor employed to design or implement a project. On the other hand, the anthropologist's special task is to assure that the proposed activity is socially sound, that it conforms to the socioeconomic, cultural, and increasingly the environmental realities within which the local population lives. In these often opposing requirements is a recurrent potential for the anthropologist to assume an adversary relationship, to be seen as a "nay-sayer" rather than as a "team-player."

Based on his experiences in two projects, one dealing with the establishment of a local fuelwood industry and the other with the provisioning of improved health services, Swagman exposes some of these problems and indicates possible approaches to a resolution. Most important, he says, is prior agreement among all parties concerned as to precisely what the role of the social scientist is to be.

In "Land Use and Agricultural Development in the Yemen Arab Republic," Daniel Varisco corrects a general deficiency in Yemeni development: its misunderstanding of and minimal interest in the Yemeni farmer. He catalogs

Introduction

and describes land-use patterns and their relevance to agricultural development, distinguishing among different types of land ownership (private, state, communal, and *waqf*) and tenancies (sharecropping, cash rentals), and indicating what land-use factors must be taken into account in the design and implementation of rural development projects. He signals the critical importance of women in agriculture, especially as large numbers of Yemeni men migrate for wage labor to Saudi Arabia and the oil sheikhdoms.

Varisco expands on the role of the anthropologist in development, pointing out that the social analysis is often necessarily superficial, given the short time allotted to it, and the superficiality then reinforces the perception that such analyses are not really needed, that they do not contribute to the ultimate success of the intervention. The fault is not only that of those who employ anthropologists, but also of the anthropologist him/herself who agrees to an unrealistic scope of work. Reaffirming a point made by Swagman and others, Varisco feels that anthropologists must communicate their analyses and recommendations in a language that is readily understood by other development professionals.

Zülküf Aydın demonstrates that because of the planners' failure to consider the effects of social, economic, and political forces, the World Bank's Çorum-Çankırı Rural Development Project in Turkey was only minimally successful in its aims of increasing agricultural production and eliminating poverty among poor rural households. The project was flawed at the start because of the planners' assumption of economic homogeneity among the beneficiary population. They assumed erroneously that these farmers had equal access to land, labor, and capital, and that therefore all would benefit from the same interventions. The project in fact intensified preproject inequities; Çorum-Çankırı advantaged more affluent farmers and further impoverished the others. Aydın concludes that a detailed socioeconomic study prior to the intervention might have alerted planners to the socioeconomic differentiation that characterized the region, and enabled them to implement a more appropriate project.

Dawn Chatty, in "Tradition and Change Among the Pastoral Harasiis in Oman," closes the book with a discussion of the process of transformation to full commoditization of a herding economy based on a communal mode of production. Beginning in the early 1950s, rangelands previously exploited uniquely by nomadic sheepherders attracted the attention of the Omani Government, which was interested in the region's oil-producing capacity. This interest was manifested in new wage-earning opportunities, the introduction of social services, roads, and wells, and the rapid acquisition of motor vehicles. Chatty shows how the old political structure of the tribe was unprepared to accommodate the changing situation and was challenged by new contractual-type relationships. She suggests that the transformations are most profoundly felt not in the economic sphere but in what she refers to as identity, in which for the first time, and for certain purposes, it became useful for some Harasiis to see themselves in a national, Omani, context rather than a regional or tribal one. Rather than the one completely replacing the other, tribal consciousness continues to operate in the sphere of pasture and water for livestock; but credit, leasing arrangements for vehicles, wage labor opportunities, and access to social and governmental services are negotiated contractually, invoking relationships that do not reaffirm the tribal structure of decision making. The implication is that over time commoditization will assume greater and greater pertinence in the structuring of private and public activities.

Notes

1. *Anthropology and Rural Development in West Africa*, Michael M Horowitz and Thomas M. Painter, eds., Boulder and London: Westview Press, 1986; *Anthropology of Development and Change in East Africa*, David W. Brokensha and Peter D. Little, eds., Boulder and London: Westview Press, 1988. A third volume in the Monographs in Development Anthropology Series published by Westview, *Lands at Risk in the Third World: Local-Level Perspectives*, Peter D. Little and Michael M Horowitz, eds., 1987, is worldwide in scope.

2. In this book, the term "Middle East," which originates in British Foreign Office usage, includes all countries in Southwest Asia and North Africa, and is synonymous with "Near East," the term preferred by the U.S. Department of State. We have somewhat arbitrarily included the Sudan in this book because of its intermediate position between Africa and the Middle East. Unlike most of the other countries in the region, however, but like the Yemen Arab Republic and the People's Democratic Republic of Yemen, Sudan has one of the world's poorest and least-developed economies. Its 1987 estimated per capita gross national product was $330 (World Bank 1989).

3. In no sense do we share the World Bank's emphasis on average per capita GNP as the prime measure of development, since such a figure tells us nothing about how wealth is distributed within the country. A comparison of China and Brazil is instructive, with estimated 1987 per capita GNPs of $290 and $2,020 respectively (World Bank 1989:15, 17). Yet China shows far more favorable indexes of caloric consumption, infant mortality, life expectancy, and scholarization, indicating a more equitable distribution of wealth and a greater public investment in social services.

4. The *World Development Report* (World Bank 1988:222) lists 33 countries in the low-income category, but because 1987 per capita GNP for Burma is not available it is omitted. Without China and India, whose large populations influence the figure heavily, average per capita GNP falls to $247.

5. Both Oman and Libya have experienced substantial declines in GNP in the past few years, a consequence of the general fall in the price of oil. In 1986 the World Bank (1986:181) estimated Oman's 1984 per capita GNP at $6,490 and Libya's at $8,520, and grouped them with the high-income "oil exporting economies."

6. According to some critics, urban and industrial development has not been spectacular either: "For despite massive expenditures on industrial and infrastructural projects, on schools and on health facilities . . . the development effort in the Arab world in general suffers from major shortcomings and the results are, indeed, modest, far below expectations" (Abu-Laban and Abu-Laban 1986:5).

7. "Optimism has largely waned that the region's increasing food consumption can be met by the Green Revolution. The relatively easy gains from improved seed-cum-fertilizer and water application were realized in many countries in the late 1960s

and early 1970s. Cereal yields rose between 1961–1965 and 1969–1971 by a regional average of 6 percent, and this improvement climbed to 10 percent between 1969–1971 and 1976–1978. There was, however, little consistency or uniformity in the performance of most countries. Of the seven countries that registered substantial increases in cereal yields by 1969–1971, only four were able to maintain these impressive rates during the 1970s. Many countries like Tunisia and Libya remained far behind in relative productivity. Others—namely, Algeria, Sudan, and Jordan—appear to have been bypassed entirely by the Green Revolution in cereals. The performance of the region as a whole has been unimpressive in terms of both yields attained and comparative rates of growth. In every period, the Middle East yield averages rank ahead only of Africa, and by the late 1970s they were far behind Latin America, the Far East, all developing countries, and the world average (Weinbaum 1982:6)."

8. For a penetrating analysis of the agricultural sector in one North African country, see Thami El Khyari (1987).

9. There is an enormous literature on Middle Eastern and North African urbanization. Two recent collections are Bouhdiba and Chevallier (1982), and Rivlin and Helmer (1980).

10. Stating that African production is oriented mainly to on-farm and local consumption does not mean that we distinguish "subsistence crops" and "cash crops," as is commonly done in the development literature. ". . . [A]t the level of the small farm, subsistence crops often are cash crops. Small farmer reluctance to make a full commitment to export sector production may reflect not only a risk-averse strategy, but also sound judgment as to where the net economic advantage lies. An individual smallholder may most effectively increase net cash income through a concentration on production for local consumption, both on the farm and in local markets, particularly under conditions where 'export' crops are purchased by state marketing boards at depressed price levels" (Little and Horowitz 1987:254). Nor are we postulating the existence of two parallel but independent economies, one traditional and agrarian, the other modern and industrial. As Meillassoux (1981:98) states: "We will . . . be exploring not the destruction of one mode of production by another, but the contradictory organization of economic relations between these two sectors (the capitalist and domestic), one of which preserves the other to pump its substance and, in so doing, destroys it."

11. ". . . the enormous increase in oil wealth accruing to thinly populated and militarily weak states on the periphery of the Arab world after the nationalizations and price rises of the early 1970s had a considerable effect on inter-Arab relations, shifting financial power to the more conservative regimes and encouraging a much closer Arab economic integration based on the exchange of migrant workers for remittances and other large flows of funds" (Asad and Owen 1983:8).

References

Abu-Laban, Baha, and Sharon McIrvin Abu-Laban, eds.
  1986 The Arab World: Dynamics of Development. Leiden: E. J. Brill.

Amin, Samir
  1973 Le Développement inégal. Paris: Les Editions de Minuit.

Asad, Talal, and Roger Owen, eds.
  1983 Sociology of "Developing Societies": The Middle East. New York, NY: Monthly Review Press.

Blaikie, Piers, and Harold Brookfield
1987 Land Degradation and Society. New York, NY: Methuen.

Bouhdiba, Abdelwahab, and Dominique Chevallier, eds.
1982 La ville arabe dans l'Islam: histoire et mutations. Université de Tunis, Centre d'Etudes et de Recherches Economiques et Sociales. Tunis: Imprimerie Al Asria.

Hart, Keith
1982 The Political Economy of West African Agriculture. Cambridge: Cambridge University Press.

Hyden, Gören
1986 The Anomaly of the African Peasantry. Development and Change 17(4):677–704.

Khyari, Thami El
1987 Agriculture au Maroc. Mohammedia, Morocco: Editions Okad.

Little, Peter D., and Michael M Horowitz
1987 Subsistence Crops *Are* Cash Crops. Human Organization 46(3):254–258.

Meillassoux, Claude
1981 Maidens, Meal and Money: Capitalism and the Domestic Community. Cambridge: Cambridge University Press.

Paul, Jim
1982 Perspective on the Land Crisis. MERIP Reports 99:3–6. (Middle Eastern Research and Information Project Reports.)

Rivlin, Helen Anne B., and Katherine Helmer, eds.
1980 The Changing Middle Eastern City. Binghamton, NY: State University of New York at Binghamton Program in Southwest Asian and North African Studies.

Weinbaum, Marvin G.
1982 Food, Development, and Politics in the Middle East. Boulder, CO: Westview.

Wolf, Eric R.
1982 Europe and the People without History. Berkeley, CA: University of California Press.

World Bank
1986 World Development Report 1986. New York, NY: Published for the World Bank by Oxford University Press.

1988 World Development Report 1988. New York, NY: Published for the World Bank by Oxford University Press.

1989 World Tables, 1988–1989 Edition: From the Data Files of the World Bank. Baltimore, MD: The Johns Hopkins University Press.

1

Brokering Social Science in Development: Experiences in Morocco

Alice L. Morton

Introduction

Anthropologists have given a good deal of thought to the roles they play in international development, including that of broker or representative for the generally unempowered potential beneficiaries or losers in development projects. One issue concerns the ability of foreign anthropologists from the First World adequately to understand the cultures they study and to speak in their defense. Related to this is a concern about the role of the indigenous anthropologist vis-à-vis the development process in his or her own country (cf. Asad 1975; Fahim 1979). A move toward enhancing indigenous social-science involvement has been made, especially in Latin America and in South Asia, and the question of the role of expatriate anthropologists and related foreign funding permeates debate among Africanists and those working in the Middle East. In North Africa, a number of local social scientists have expressed their aversion even to involvement with such organizations as the Social Science Research Council (SSRC) and the Ford Foundation (Zghal 1986).

From the mid-1970s on, anthropologists at the Agency for International Development (AID), which at that time had just hired a new cohort of noneconomist social scientists, became especially concerned about these matters (see Hoben 1980; Horowitz 1980; *Practicing Anthropology* 1980–1981: inter alia). While they gave most weight to the values and ethics questions of participation by Western anthropologists in development, they also looked for ways in which indigenous anthropologists could be integrated into the process. Where this was actually done, it was frequently at the initiative of an individual social scientist in AID, whether at the Washington headquarters or in the field. One example of an attempt at an institutional level to enhance local social-science capacity, however, comes from two projects funded by the AID Mission in Morocco.

Background

The projects in question, Dryland Agriculture Applied Research (DAARP) and the Agronomic Institute Project, were both early examples of AID foresight in attempting to involve local social scientists in agricultural and rural development. The relationship between the two projects has varied over time, as has the tenor of relations between their respective host-government counterparts, l'Institut National de Recherche Agronomique (INRA) for DAARP and l'Institut Agronomique et Vétérinaire Hassan II (IAV) for the "Institute" project. Since 1973, AID has provided, through the University of Minnesota, funds for faculty and institutional development at IAV. Junior faculty from IAV were trained in the United States in agricultural sciences and research techniques, and a few social-science-oriented faculty trainees were also included. The goal was to develop a U.S. land-grant type of institution along Moroccan lines.

DAARP, whose design began in 1976, preceded a later move in AID in the 1980s to design farming systems projects that integrated some social-science input with agronomic research and extension (see Cernea and Guggenheim 1985). The project goal was "to develop a permanent applied research program aimed at increasing farmer productivity" (USAID/Rabat 1977). This included establishing a dryland agronomic research program within INRA to identify suitable farming equipment for small farmers, and establishing a socioeconomic research program at IAV to provide a better understanding of the current behavior of dryland farmers and, thus, a basis for more effective research and extension programs. DAARP also included a substantial component for training Moroccans from INRA in agricultural sciences in the United States. The socioeconomic research program was implemented under a separate grant to IAV's Department of Human Sciences.

By early 1982, IAV had finished carrying out an initial round of studies under the DAARP-funded grant. Due to contracting delays, the research agronomists, fielded by the MidAmerica International Agriculture Consortium (MIAC) with the University of Nebraska as lead institution, had only just arrived. Thus, for once, the social scientists were ahead of the game and had begun producing results that were supposed to provide background to the agronomists as they began to design their experiments on-station and on-farm.

Despite this seemingly favorable situation, the non-French-speaking MIAC agronomists indicated no interest in the IAV socioeconomic research results. Among those members of the AID staff in charge of monitoring the grant, a suspicion arose that this might be because the research somehow was not being done right, or presenting the right kind of results. In part, this was caused by a pervasive lack of French language skills among the AID personnel, but those who did scan the French language reports felt that what they were reading was some sort of foreign social science, not the analogue of American agricultural economics and rural sociology that they had expected.

The Basis of the Broker Role

As a result of this concern, the USAID Mission's Agriculture Office asked me to review the results and revise the scope of the socioeconomic research component of the DAARP. Under the same five-month contract, I was also asked to develop a beneficiary profile, based on these data, for a potential new project to be located elsewhere in Morocco. I returned in 1983 with other contractors to evaluate and redesign the entire project so that it could be extended for another five years. At the same time, I led a team to evaluate and redesign the institute project with IAV, thus becoming familiar with the other departments there and with Institute senior management. Subsequently, I worked on the design of the extension of that project (1983) and a special evaluation of that extension (1988). This combination of contracts has permitted me to follow the social-science and institution-building dimensions of a series of AID-sponsored interventions over six years but always as a "proximate outsider" rather than as a permanent official of either of the governments concerned.

Before I was given the first contract in 1982, I was taken to IAV to meet Professor Paul Pascon, then head of the Department of Human Sciences, who had collaborated in developing the scope of work for the IAV socioeconomic research with AID. This fairly unusual step for a USAID mission to take—I was clearly there to pass his inspection—indicated the respect in which the mission staff held Professor Pascon, a French-born social scientist who took up Moroccan citizenship at independence (and who has died recently). While I passed muster sufficiently to be given the contract, it was not until I returned to Morocco on the successive contracts that I felt I had achieved some credibility with Professor Pascon and his colleagues.

The Socioeconomic Research Program

The recommendation for the IAV socioeconomic research program had been included in the project-design study carried out by a first MIAC team, including a senior rural sociologist from the University of Missouri. This team had recommended a broad outline for socioeconomic studies and suggested that a U.S. sociologist be dispatched to Morocco to assist IAV in developing the program. The team was expressing its awareness that research methodologies and standards were likely to be different at IAV from those common at U.S. universities, especially regarding quantification of research results.

The mission did not accept this recommendation, partly at least because of strong objections from IAV, which felt that an American presence in the Department of Human Sciences was neither necessary nor appropriate—this, despite their willingness to have U.S. academic technical assistance from the University of Minnesota in other departments under the Agronomic Institute Project. The "human scientists," however, appeared strongly to resent the implication that they should do social science research à l'américaine, and that they needed help to do so. This situation persists today (USAID/Rabat 1988).

Funding for the program took the form of a grant rather than a contract. In AID's terms, this meant that IAV—and especially Professor Pascon as Principal Investigator—had broader latitude in managing the activity than would have been the case under a contract.[1] As the language of the grant was quite general, the AID mission tended to rely, de facto, on Professor Pascon and his colleagues to define the methodology to be applied. This was especially true as there was no social scientist in the AID mission. From 1980 to early 1982, then, the mission exercised only very limited supervision over the grant, making little effort to assess the direction the research was taking.

In fact, by 1982 Professor Pascon had developed a team approach to the work, and had involved some young researchers from outside IAV, as well as a number of Third Cycle (roughly M.S. level) students. As part of their course requirements, these students were to carry out original research where possible, and the AID funding provided much-needed support for these efforts. By 1986 some 23 students had received partial funding for their degrees under the DAARP grant (Winrock 1986).

The broad range of studies included both qualitative and quantitative approaches. On the more qualitative side was a study of rural employment and migration. At the more quantitative end was a survey of nearly 2,000 households that was intended to lead to the development of a data-based typology of farms in the project area. Also included were several soil-mapping efforts, which took a holistic approach to understanding the area and its inhabitants. These studies, together with other efforts funded separately by the Institute, became known as Projet Chaouia, as they were concentrated in the Haute Chaouia region (see Figure 1.1).[2]

The core element of Projet Chaouia, a longitudinal study of 50 farms drawn from the initial sample of 2,000, was intended to describe and analyze changes in the whole-farm system, and thus to examine in detail what risks these farm families faced and how they coped with them. The study was under way by 1982, and from IAV's point of view, the socioeconomic research program was generally going well. Students and faculty were engaging in what they saw as relevant applied research in the field, using a variety of techniques and exploring a broad range of topics. Relatively modest funding was being used to support a large number of junior researchers at what was, after all, essentially a teaching institution.

The reports were slow in arriving at AID, however, and the mission felt exposed. On the one hand, they suspected that IAV might be carrying out its own agenda under the grant, while at the same time the MIAC scientists couldn't assess the work for the mission because of the language barrier. The kind of close association between counterparts that had been envisaged by the MIAC project designers was clearly not taking place.

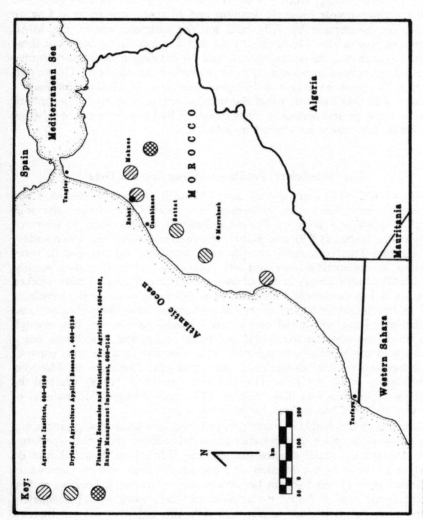

FIGURE 1.1
Morocco, Showing the Project Areas. *Source:* AID/Washington.

Bringing in the U.S. Social Scientist

In order to address some of these concerns, the Agriculture Officer contracted with me, a social scientist with considerable experience translating academic anthropology from French to English, to assess the data generated by the socioeconomic research program and to synthesize them in English for further assessment by AID, and for the ultimate use of the MIAC agronomic researchers. My contract provided five months to carry out these tasks, to conduct a literature review, and to develop a beneficiary profile for a future rainfed-agriculture project elsewhere in Morocco. Given AID practice, five months was a rather generous amount of time for such a contract, a further indication that the mission was taking the socioeconomic aspects of the project seriously, even though it had begun to doubt whether this would ultimately be a good investment.

The Beneficiary Profile—Looking for the Data

When I arrived to carry out my scope of work under this contract, I was presented with photocopies of twelve IAV Third Cycle theses, the soils mapping studies, a copy of Professor Pascon's encyclopedic two-volume study of the Haouz (1979), and some fugitive literature on Moroccan society and culture. This contrasted sharply with my prior experiences in other missions, where social science and other literature had been in short supply. The USAID/Rabat library is one of the best mission libraries I have worked with, for it has consistently ensured, over the years, that local journals as well as books published in and outside Morocco have been obtained and maintained. Thus, my initial belief that I would have more than enough data lulled my concern that I did not have Arabic and that I was not a specialist in the Maghreb. In the past, I had become familiar with some of the better-known English-language anthropological literature on Morocco, especially the work of Gellner (1969) and Geertz et al. (1979). (Part of the subsequent problem was that I continued to seek *ethnographic* material of this sort for the Chaouia and neighboring regions.)

Armed with U.S. and U.K. training in sociology and anthropology, including field research, six years of experience as an AID officer, and prior experience with international social science through the SSRC, I felt that I should do all right as long as the mission and the local social science community continued to help me become better informed. Further, it seemed at first that some amount of "rapid reconnaissance" field work would adequately complement the secondary source material, although the mission director had initially stressed that the effort was to be mainly literature based.

Soon after beginning to read, I became extremely uneasy, for the more I read, the less information I found to answer the questions framed in my scope of work. And yet, the scope of work seemed to be fairly sensibly put together from an anthropological point of view. It asked for some social history of the area, some data on kinship and other dimensions of social organization on women, and on social mobility. Surely, I thought, in all this wealth of documentation, I should be able to find the data to weave into my beneficiary profile. So I kept reading.

When unease turned into anxiety, I went to see Professor Pascon. Explaining that I did not seem to be finding any ethnographic data, I asked him to suggest sources other than those I already had. We discussed what I meant and what I thought I needed, and he gave me access to his index of materials and, essentially, to his library. I was still somewhat at a loss, for nothing I read met the needs created by the scope of work or by my own definitional schema. I next went to the National Library to see what some of the older French colonial sources might provide. Short of coming on an unexpected wealth of new materials, however, I felt I would definitely have to renegotiate and narrow my scope of work. Ultimately, the scope of work was revised to restrict the beneficiary profile to Haute Chaouia (see Morton 1982).[3]

As the weeks passed, I continued to look for other data in the IAV reports (which covered the territory from household food consumption through regression analysis of the relation between land tenure and average farm size), and I began to ask to go to the field. Obligingly, I was invited along on various field trips, including to Settat, the main site of project DAARP itself, housing the new *Aridoculture* (dryland agriculture) Center being constructed with project funds for INRA and expatriate agricultural research staff. I usually traveled with USAID staff and other contractors, but sometimes with IAV staff either with or without AID personnel. Some of the more memorable visits were to other areas of the country, since the idea was to give me a fairly broad exposure that would, in a sense, complement the literature review and the initially broad scope of work to which I was responding. I did not, however, visit any farmers. When I asked the USAID Agriculture Officer the reason, he replied that traditional Moroccan male farmers would not talk to a woman. This was despite known and published fieldwork by expatriate women social scientists.

Finally, one of the IAV senior staff arranged for me and an AID colleague to visit a large "modern" farmer near Fez. Since I had been reading a long and informative thesis on agricultural mechanization (Zagdouni 1981), I was very pleased to be able to see some in action at this large farm, which produced cereals for sale as well as doing seed multiplication. Better yet, all the various types of land tenure and sharecropping arrangements that I had been reading about were represented on land managed by this one farmer and his sons. Things were looking up. The local representatives of the Ministry of Interior dropped by for tea, and a lively discussion ensued about the future of agriculture in Morocco, and on how the American agricultural revolution had occurred. This gave me an immediate sense of the integration of the local power structure and its views on agriculture, the big cooperatives, and production problems. The orientation seemed definitely toward following the U.S. example of mechanization, larger farm units, and modernization. I determined to create a beneficiary profile that might bring some of this to life for the Chaouia area, but first I had to turn my attention to redesigning the socioeconomic research component of the DAARP in consultation with the IAV and MIAC teams and USAID's Agriculture Office.

Brokering the Social Science Research Process and Its Results

As the weeks went by and as I was able to convey the content of the Projet Chaouia studies to the Agriculture Office staff, I became the de facto broker for the DAARP socioeconomic research component in the mission. Discussions were held, leading to an agreement that what IAV was doing was inadequate in terms of their scope of work and the real needs of the agronomic research team. This conclusion led to additional discussions about ways in which AID could help IAV do a more relevant job.

One idea was to find a way to provide the services of a U.S.-trained agricultural economist to the Department of Human Sciences and the Projet Chaouia team at IAV. As a first step, still in 1982, I would provide in my review more concrete and detailed guidance on research design and methodology for an amendment to the DAARP Project Paper. To carry out this task, I worked as closely as possible with the mission economists. We recommended that the rural economist member of the IAV team be sent for short-term training in English and in quantitative research methods at the earliest opportunity. Later, in writing the project paper amendment, we included a position for a rural sociologist and one for an agricultural economist on the expanded MIAC team (USAID/Rabat 1982, 1983). Thinking that the question of interpretation of disciplines had been resolved, we continued to discuss directions for the project as a whole, including the IAV socioeconomic component.

A locally available, U.S.-trained, agricultural economist was hired on a short-term contract to develop a microcomputer farming-systems model into which the considerable amount of data on Chaouia farms available from student papers could be programmed. It was a first step in gaining the agreement of the Department of Human Sciences to accept an outsider financed by AID. Things really seemed to be improving.

Institutional Development and New Departures

In the process of amending the DAARP, given the somewhat renewed faith of the mission in the Projet Chaouia concept and output, we met with Professor Pascon to discuss other development-related research possibilities. IAV, as part of the institutional strengthening component of the Agronomic Institute Project, had been encouraged to adopt a modified U.S. land-grant university model, with a director for instruction, one for research, and one for development (Extension and Outreach). Professor Pascon took on the latter position and began to discuss ways in which the research in Chaouia could become oriented to more action and outreach. He was particularly engaged by a concept he called a "Centre de Conjoncture" (ultimately translated by us as an Agricultural Economics Information Center). It would, he hoped, be a small unit, based at the DAARP field headquarters at Settat, that would gather data useful for farmers on prices, climate, and technology, and would eventually disseminate this information in a variety of forms, in association with a later Farming Systems/Extension Project to be developed with AID.[4]

With young researchers and technicians in the field in this kind of active research and dissemination role, the relationships between farmers, IAV researchers, and the U.S. agriculturalists would be strengthened. Farmers would begin to see a positive output from the project. If this experiment worked, it might provide a model for a new approach to extension at the grass-roots level. As a corollary, the MIAC rural sociologist and agricultural economist were to be located at Settat where they could be in close touch with the rest of the MIAC team, nearer to the farmers, and able to help broker the results of the IAV socioeconomic research to their agronomist counterparts, both U.S. and Moroccan. They were also supposed to be able to help guide the IAV research, analysis, and presentation of results.[5]

In redesigning the DAARP in 1982 and later in 1983, I was only one of a number of people from AID and IAV who were trying to make sure that the socioeconomic and agronomic research programs would be more closely linked so that the applied agronomic research results would be economically and socially appropriate for adoption by the small farmers of the project area. The newly appointed MIAC team leader seemed willing, IAV's social scientists appeared less reluctant than before to accept outside technical assistance, and the USAID mission hoped that the redesigned DAARP—in combination with a complementary Farming Systems/Extension Project that would intervene in the same econo-ecological zone—would be able to generate results that would increase agricultural production among Morocco's small dryland farmers.

By 1983–1984 the mission was beginning to show some interest in providing U.S. training to the M.S. level in sociology and agricultural economics under the institute project with Minnesota. The DDR (Direction de Développement Rural) was beginning to do some contract work for the Ministry of Agriculture and Agrarian Reform and for other donors. Despite several false starts, then, USAID/Rabat had been able to make a worthwhile contribution to the development of an applied research capacity in the social as well as agricultural sciences in Morocco.

The major motivation for this support was to ensure that U.S.-style economics and agricultural economics would be taught and practiced at IAV. AID and other donors would then have access to results that they could use, given their own worldview and bureaucratic requirements. As may be seen from recent documents from the Institute Project and DAARP, Phase III, neither the AID mission nor the Government of Morocco has resolved the question of where this capacity should really be housed. INRA and IAV are still debating their respective roles in socioeconomic research as part of a broader debate on which agency will ultimately control the research agenda as a whole.

At the same time, the Department of Human Sciences and the DDR at IAV are engaged in a similar debate about the appropriate type and role of social scientists at the Institute and in the sector. U.S. social scientists on MIAC's team at Settat have largely rejected the terms of this debate at IAV, and are instead seeking to build a U.S.-style agricultural economics department at the National Agricultural School at Meknes. At heart, the debate among the social scientists at IAV concerns quantification, modeling, the ideological underpinnings of economic enquiry and analysis, and the appropriate role for social science at the Institute and in the agriculture sector. These are genuine and complex issues, and their resolution is unlikely to be simple or speedy.

Mismatched Agendas and Where They Have Led

The founder of IAV was an agronomist who recognized the value of including the human sciences in the curriculum from the outset, and whose deputy was a rural economist. In attempting to build a genuinely Moroccan teaching and research institution, the founding staff of IAV, including Professor Pascon, were attempting at the same time to create a Moroccan applied social-science research capability that would facilitate agricultural development and agrarian reform.

For Professor Pascon specifically, to empower the beneficiaries of development to participate in the design as well as in the result of what would otherwise be an externally determined—and therefore "colonialist"—process, was a critical purpose of rural sociology. In discussing the role of this discipline in Morocco (and elsewhere), he described the rural sociologist as more a "transporter" of knowledge than an analyst (Pascon 1986:63), given that one of the first functions of the activity is to transport facts from the country to the cities, from the dominated to the dominating (Pascon 1986:65).

Pascon was wary of the political implications of collection and compilation of data that would eventually reside outside the rural area, of translation from the vernacular into French or classical Arabic, of the creation of partial intellectual constructs on the basis of data taken out of context, and finally of the use of rural sociology as a means of political repression. Still, he was optimistic enough to train a number of researchers and students, in part with the assistance of AID funding, to carry out painstaking and highly detailed rural research. It was to some extent the detail itself that was an indicator both of the quality of the research and of its probity in Pascon's world view. In retrospect, I believe that this premise of Pascon's method was never really grasped by USAID, but also was what annoyed them most. They are still asking, where is the analysis? Nor was Pascon able to articulate it to American bureaucrats, whose understanding of social-science ideology and methodology he felt was questionable. He lacked an interlocutor on the USAID side, but while perhaps sensing the gap, he was sufficiently wary of American "intervention" in IAV research to discourage USAID's attempts to fill it.

Unsurprisingly, various members of the staff of USAID/Rabat over the years became impatient with what appeared to them to be a dysfunctional level of detail in the collection of data, and avoidance of analysis in favor of exhaustive description. Similarly, they could not understand why IAV consistently rebuffed their offers to send the most senior of the DDR's young research team to America to learn English—so that they could benefit both from English-language social-science literature and from further short-term training in quantitative methods.

With the benefit of hindsight, I am convinced that there were really at least two different and in some senses opposed research agendas in uneasy coexistence under the umbrella of Projet Chaouia and the DAARP. Some of the USAID staff who became involved with the socioeconomic research program under the project certainly sensed this intermittently. They tended to summarize their discomfort, however, in terms of some intangible perceived difference between American and French research approaches. A good deal was said within the mission about French sociology and how narrative and unquantitative—and impractical—it was. Publicly, the main question asked was whether the results of the Projet Chaouia would be useful for applied agronomic research or for AID.

What AID usually wants in connection with agricultural project design and implementation is analysis cast in a format that coincides with Anglo-American traditions of applied agricultural research, whether it is done by agricultural economists or rural sociologists. Occasionally, as in the instance under discussion here, there is also a feeling that some anthropological analysis is likely to be useful to inform development decision making. Here, the end user in AID is the agricultural economist, the project manager, the mission director, or the AID/Washington generalist or technician.

In the case of the DAARP, as opposed to the Agronomic Institute Project with IAV, the institution-building emphasis was initially implicit only, except in the sense of "bricks and mortar" for the Aridoculture Center and participant training in agronomic sciences in the U.S. This may be one reason why AID did little to encourage INRA to make good on its stated intention to hire more social scientists so that this perspective could be integrated into agronomic research programs from their inception.

Yet, if institution building and the integration of socioeconomic and agronomic sciences were not overtly high on the list of priorities of what was actually a very ambitious project, at the same time, as amended in 1984, DAARP set out to support some genuine institutional innovation. In agreeing to fund the Centre de Conjoncture experiment, AID in fact went a considerable way toward reorienting the DAARP project by stressing the Moroccan small farmer as a more immediate potential end-user of data collected and disseminated by social as well as agronomic scientists. The design of this portion of the expanded project indicated that these social scientists, who were to be teamed with agriculturalists, would become communicators between the project and the intended beneficiaries. This was to be one step toward creating a model for a less "top-down" extension service for Morocco—one that might become, in a sense, "demand driven."

Perhaps because the project design recognized this as a specifically Moroccan experiment, the U.S. social scientists who joined the expanded MIAC team did not meet sufficient encouragement for them to join in the effort. Even were this not the case, the problem of language proficiency would have proved a handicap to direct participation with farmer-consumers of the center's output. The designers did, however, envisage these social scientists as brokers between the Moroccan socioeconomic team, the team from the center, the MIAC and INRA agronomic researchers, and the farmer beneficiaries. On the basis of information provided in the Winrock evaluation report (1986), it seems that at least one facet of this brokering role has indeed been exploited. The U.S. social scientists have been able to provide information about Moroccan agricultural (and cultural?) practices to their agronomist colleagues that the latter see as relevant and useful.

What is less clear is why and how so much hostility toward the IAV socioeconomic team developed on the part of the MIAC social scientists. In fact, they seem to be actively trying to discourage their INRA colleagues from reinstating the socioeconomic research component with IAV. That INRA has finally hired a Moroccan sociologist to work on the Settat team may be a relevant factor. Perhaps the U.S. technical assistants see themselves as protecting their counterpart and his "turf" from outside encroachment.

At the same time, the Memorandum of Agreement among AID, INRA, and IAV still exists, although AID cut off funding in 1987. While it has been the AID mission's view that no further funding should be provided until INRA and IAV agree on a socioeconomic research agenda, the hesitation seems to reside more with the Americans than with the Moroccans. This hesitation may be irrelevant or it may indicate a real schism in concepts of institutional development as well as those of disciplinary and methodological appropriateness. If so, this is a matter in which the relevant AID mission staff have only just begun to be aware of the key role they have played in misconstruing the terms in which the Moroccans construe the issues and their resolution.

Conclusion

In carrying out the assignments described here, I was acting as a proximate outsider to the AID mission, and to INRA and IAV, trying for a total of about ten months to play the role of translator and broker. By most definitions, including my own at the beginning, I wasn't "doing anthropology." Rather, I was working as an AID contractor, specializing in rural development and evaluation, and "doing development." I was seen as someone with training in anthropology, but my main role was as a former AID direct-hire officer who knew something about project design as well as the methods and content of social-science research. In retrospect, I am no longer certain whether, had I been a Maghreb specialist who had done field work in Morocco, I would have been more or less effective in carrying out the tasks I was assigned. Certainly, I would have known the ethnographic and historical literature. I would probably have known either Arabic or a Berber dialect and would thus have been able to make a more successful bid to do some fieldwork—however "quick and dirty." On the other hand, to be frank, I might have been less willing to accept the initial scope of work offered, since from a purely social-science perspective, it was too diffuse. Nor might I have been offered it.

From the standpoint of some of the social scientists at IAV, I think that my AID-relatedness was first perceived as a liability, but from the standpoint of the AID mission, it was probably my major asset. The IAV staff who were directly involved with Projet Chaouia could view me as a fellow social scientist and former academic. Or, they could regard me as a somehow sympathetic adjunct to the regular USAID staff. Since AID is notably poor at explaining its motives and goals to its host-country counterparts, it was also occasionally useful for IAV that I had the appropriate AID bona fides, and could explain things.

Although I am now a contractor rather than a direct-hire officer, I realize that AID has remained my culture of reference. In practicing anthropology in development, most often I try to establish some fit between that culture and others—those of the private-sector company of which I am a part, the host-government institutions with which I am involved, and the one or more population groups within a particular country who will experience the development we design, implement, and evaluate.

To have the opportunity to work with host-country social scientists is both a benefit and a challenge. It makes it even less easy than usual to accept the conventional wisdom about development as an essentially economic process, and certainly tends to reduce hubris. At the same time, the AID-related social scientist is encouraged to make every effort to demystify the institutional culture of the donor agency. At what point this becomes appropriate depends to a great extent on the situation, country, and individuals in question. In the short term, regrettably, there may be relatively few countries and development settings in which the individuals are at liberty to accept it.

Notes

Work described in this article was performed under the following contracts with AID: USAID/M-PSC-136-S-00-2006-00; PDC-1496-I-16-1138-00; PDC-1406-I-19-1138-00; and a subcontract with the University of Minnesota under Contract No. AID/PRO-AG-608-0160-001. The points made are the author's and do not necessarily reflect the views of the Agency for International Development. I thank the staff of Projet Chaouia and IAV for the great courtesy they have extended me and the time and effort spent in helping me become literate about Morocco in general and Chaouia in particular.

1. The recipient of a grant generally has more discretion about implementation than does a contractor, and AID usually funds research under grants.

2. Over the years, a number of changes have been made in the definition used by AID of the project area and, thus, the target population. IAV, however, essentially stuck to what is known as the Haute Chaouia, a cereal-producing plateau region typical of rainfed areas with 200–400 mm annual rainfall. This corresponded to other IAV objectives to carry out intensive social, agronomic, economic, and geophysical studies of a number of areas of the country in sequence. Thus, they had already begun what they called Projet Chaouia before the AID grant was received under DAARP.

3. Later attempts by other social scientists to write a more general profile for AID for the still-amorphous rainfed project were not notably more successful (Riddle 1983).

4. For a number of reasons, this companion project design was never completed. Now, five years later, the World Bank is talking about funding a "Training and Visit System" project to strengthen the Government of Morocco's extension service.

5. Because of start-up delays and a severe drought between 1981 and 1984, very few agronomic research results were available for dissemination by the time the DAARP project was redesigned and extended in 1984. The extension of the project included a separate Memorandum of Understanding (MOU) with the new DDR at IAV to continue Projet Chaouia and start the Centre de Conjoncture. Under the terms of the MOU, IAV was supposed to hire additional researchers to staff the center and replicate the 50-farm survey and the market price study outside Chaouia but in another part of the DAARP project zone. This was never done. Instead, junior technicians from the provincial extension staff were assigned to the center; they have had little supervision or link with the MIAC team, according to all informants (Winrock 1986:46, 62).

References

Asad, Talil
   1975   Anthropology and the Colonial Encounter. New York, NY: Humanities Press.

Cernea, M. M., and S. E. Guggenheim
   1985   Is Anthropology Superfluous in Farming Systems Research? In Farming Systems Research. Kansas State University Research Series 4(9).

Fahim, Hussein, ed.
   1979   Indigenous Anthropology in Non-Western Countries. Durham, NC: Carolina Press.

Geertz, Clifford, Hilda Geertz, and Lawrence Rosen
   1979   Meaning and Order in Moroccan Society. Cambridge: Cambridge University Press.

Gellner, Ernest
   1969   Saints of the Atlas. London: Weidenfeld and Nicolson.

Hoben, Allan
   1980   Agricultural Decision Making in Foreign Assistance: An Anthropological Analysis. In Agricultural Decision Making: Agricultural Contributions to Rural Development. P. Bartlett, ed. Pp. 337–369. New York, NY: Academic Press.

Horowitz, M., ed.
1980 The Workshop on Pastoralism and African Livestock Development. AID Program Evaluation Report No. 4. Washington, DC: Agency for International Development.

Morton, Alice L.
1982 A Beneficiary Profile of Haute Chaouia. Rabat: USAID.

Pascon, Paul
1979 Le Haouz de Marrakech. 2 volumes. Rabat: Centre Universitaire de Recherche Scientifique (CURS), Centre National de Recherche Scientifique (CNRS), L'Institut Nationale Agronomique et Vétérinaire (INAV) (later IAV Hassan II).

1986 La Sociologie rurale pour quoi faire? Bulletin économique et social du Maroc, No. 155–156. Pp. 59–70. Janvier.

Practicing Anthropology 3(2)
1980–1981 Winter.

Riddle, Richard
1983 Rainfed Agriculture Beneficiary Profile. Rabat: USAID.

USAID/Rabat
1977 Project Paper—Dryland Agriculture Applied Research Project.

1982 Project Paper Amendment Draft.

1983 Project Paper Amendment Draft.

1988 Midterm Evaluation Report, Agronomic Institute Project.

Winrock International
1986 The Dryland Agriculture Applied Research Project (Evaluation Report). Morrilton, AR: Winrock International.

Zagdouni, Larbi
1981 La Méchanisation Agricole. Vol. I and II. Rabat: IAV Hassan II.

Zghal, A. K.
1986 Personal communication, Tunis.

2

Slash-and-Burn Cultivation, Charcoal Making, and Emigration from the Highlands of Northwest Morocco

Henry Munson, Jr.

Introduction

Deforestation and erosion are serious problems in the Jbalan highlands of northwestern Morocco, as they are throughout that country (Dressler 1982; Fay 1984:3; SOMET-SOGETHA 1967:II, 303). After Morocco regained its independence in 1956, the government implemented a number of measures to resolve these problems, notably the prohibition of slash-and-burn cultivation and of charcoal making (Maurer 1968:37–38). But these two activities provided the basic livelihoods of most peasants in the northern Jbalan highlands near Tetouan and Tangier (see Figure 2.1). Their prohibition has been among the factors inducing many Jbala (literally, "Mountain People") to emigrate to the cities, especially Tangier, where most of them have joined the ranks of the marginally employed urban poor.

Thus, although a primary goal of the government's antierosion program was to reduce rural-urban migration and the economic and political problems it poses (de Mas 1978:216; Munson 1986), in fact the program has increased the exodus of rural people and exacerbated the already serious problem of urban congestion (see Escallier 1984:295–299; Fadl Allah, Birryan, and Birrada 1983; and Munson and LeCamus 1986). This untoward side effect has arisen because the antierosion campaign was undertaken without adequate preliminary analysis of the local ecological, economic, and social structures of the Jbalan highlands and other regions where erosion is a major problem.

In this chapter, I analyze these factors on the basis of eighteen months of fieldwork conducted in 1976–1977 in the Jbalan *qabila* of Bni Msawwar and in the city of Tangier. I focus primarily on the district (*commune* or *jama'a*) of the Monday Market of Bni Harshan, which includes most of the

The Highlands of Northwest Morocco

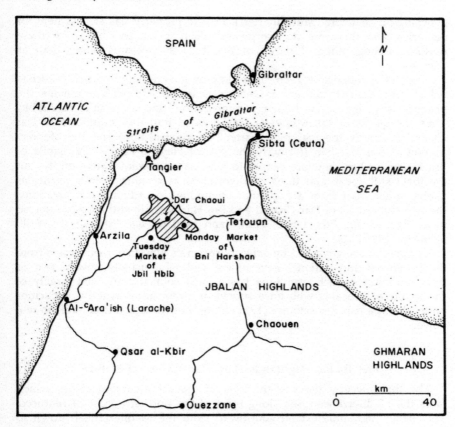

FIGURE 2.1
Northwest Morocco

The hatched area is the *qabila* of Bni Msawwar. Prepared by Steve Bicknell, University of Maine.

qabila of Bni Msawwar south and east of the town of Dar Chaoui (see Figure 2.1). The district covers about 140 square kilometers and in 1977 had a population of 6,361 according to a census undertaken with the cooperation of local authorities.

On Qabilas and Communes

The Arabic word *qabila* (plural, *qaba'il*) is normally translated as "tribe." This poses problems in the context of the Jbala and all other sedentary agriculturalists in Morocco because the qaba'il in these areas are territorial entities whose populations are not linked in terms of any recognized genealogical structure (Munson 1981). Private property has existed here for centuries, and there are no "corporate" descent groups (ibid.). For these reasons, among others, I speak of the Jbala as peasants rather than as tribesmen.

After independence in 1956, the Moroccan government divided Morocco's qaba'il into districts known as *communes* in French (which remains the primary language of the higher administration) and as jama'at in Arabic. Thus the qabila of Bni Msawwar was divided into the communes of Dar Chaoui (formerly the *rba'*, or "quarter," of Hayt al-Sifli) and the Monday Market of Bni Harshan (formerly the rba' of Hayt al-Fuqi).[1] The qabila of Bni Msawwar has therefore ceased to exist as an administrative entity, but the Jbala still speak and think of themselves as coming from a particular qabila rather than from a particular commune. In ordinary conversations, the two communes of Dar Chaoui and Bni Harshan are still usually referred to as *Hayt al-Sifli*, "the Lower Wall," and *Hayt al-Fuqi*, "the Upper Wall" (Munson 1981:251).

Communes are governed by *qaids*, bureaucrats who take their orders from the provincial and national government and who usually govern two or three communes. Each commune has a local council composed largely of the wealthier peasants who once served in minor administrative capacities under the Spanish Protectorate (1912–1956), but these councils have no real power.

The Jbalan Highlands: The Constraints of Nature

The Jbala occupy the western hills of the Rif mountain chain, which faces the Mediterranean Sea along most of the northern coast of Morocco. The Jbalan highlands extend southward from the Mediterranean down to the hills around Ouezzane (see Figure 2.1). Elevation gradually increases from the western foothills several hundred meters high near the Atlantic littoral to eastern peaks of over 1,500 m near the Ghmaran highlands (Mikesell 1961:14). The highest mountain in the qabila of Bni Msawwar is 915 m high (El Gharbaoui 1981:39). Jbalan villages are generally on mountain slopes at elevations from 300 to 600 m, with the valleys devoted primarily to plow agriculture. In the eastern Jbalan mountains near Chaouen, villages can be found at elevations as high as 1,000 meters (Fay 1984:5).

Like most of the Mediterranean region, northern Morocco has cool wet winters (late October through late March) and hot dry summers, but with considerable local variation. The high peaks of the central Rif chain block the passage of the wet winds from the Atlantic, so that most of the Jbalan and Ghmaran regions receive over 800 mm (31.2 in.) of rain a year, while the far more arid eastern Rif generally receives less than half this amount (Mikesell 1961:16; Seddon 1981:196). To put these differences in perspective, we might compare them with San Diego, Los Angeles, and San Francisco, all situated in a Mediterranean environment, which have annual rainfalls of 264, 373, and 528 mm respectively (Showers 1973:459, 463). A minimum

TABLE 2.1
1976-77 Monthly Rainfall in Dar Chaoui

Month	Rainfall (mm)
October	152.6
November	23.5
December	507.7
January	234.8
February	152.2
March	38.8
April	0
May	7.3
June	18.4
July	0
August	0
September	9
Total	1,144.3

Source: Centre de Travaux Agricoles, Dar Chaoui.

of at least 250 mm (and preferably 400 mm) is generally believed to be necessary for the unirrigated plow cultivation of wheat, which is the main food crop of the Jbala (Bates and Rassam 1983:8).

These figures are all averages, however, and thus obscure an important characteristic of rainfall in Mediterranean climates—its irregularity both from year to year and within the rainy season (Oram 1979:197). The town of Dar Chaoui, for example, at an elevation of 210 m in the main valley of Bni Msawwar, had 389 mm of rain in 1972–1973 and 1,144 in 1976–1977 (Centre de Travaux Agricoles, Dar Chaoui). In 1976, 152.6 mm of rain fell on Dar Chaoui in October, followed by 23.5 mm in November and 507.7 mm in December (see Table 2.1). The torrential December rains washed away much of the wheat sown after the first rains of October, as did some of the violent rains of January and February 1977. Then, not a single drop of rain fell in April, so that most of the wheat remaining after the winter rains succumbed to the spring drought. As is common in northwestern Morocco, there was no rain in June and July (El Gharbaoui 1981:83–84). Admittedly, 1976–1977 was a particularly bad year, but a study of agriculture in Tetouan Province, which includes the northern Jbalan region, estimates that "on the average, rainfall is favorable to the autumn and spring crops only one year out of every five" (SOMET-SOGETHA 1967:I, 27).

While the lack of rain is a basic environmental constraint throughout the Middle East and North Africa, the Jbalan hills suffer violent winter downpours coupled with spring and summer droughts. The winter rains fall with tremendous force in short periods of time. For example, 300 mm (12 in) of rain fell on Chaouen (elevation 630 m) within 24 hours in January 1963 (SOMET-SOGETHA 1967:I, 27), more rain than most of the Middle East gets in a year (Eickelman 1981:15). Such downpours wash away not only crops, but also topsoil. Coupled with the steep slopes of the hills and the nature of the soils, the compressed force of the winter rains is a major contributing cause of erosion (Fay 1984:9). There are, however, other causes related to demographic pressures and the structure of the Jbalan economy.

Mediterranean Agriculture

The classic system of production in the Jbalan hills, as in most of the Mediterranean basin, has been the complex of productive techniques often referred to as "Mediterranean agriculture." Its four basic components are:

- rainfed cereal cultivation by animal-drawn plow, primarily of hard wheat but also barley and sorghum;
- animal husbandry, primarily of goats but also sheep and cattle;
- irrigated garden cultivation of vegetables, primarily tomatoes, green peppers, and potatoes; and
- arboriculture, primarily of figs, apples, and plums (see Grigg 1974:123–151).

Plow agriculture, with wheat as the main crop, seems to have played a central role in the Jbalan economy at least since the period when the Romans controlled the lowlands of northwestern Morocco from the first century B.C. through the fourth century A.D. (Brignon et al. 1967:23–44; El Gharbaoui 1981:96, 122–123), but plow agriculture is difficult on the steep, rocky slopes of the Jbalan highlands. Only about 20 percent of the commune of the Monday Market of Bni Harshan is arable valley land, while the hills are largely covered by scrub forest (*matorral*) and, on a much lesser scale, full-fledged forests at higher elevations. (Scrub forest is usually less than two meters high.) Arable valley land is thus scarce, and it becomes even scarcer at the higher elevations further east (Maurer 1968:28). Until the late 1950s, the Jbala adapted to this scarcity principally by engaging in slash-and-burn cultivation and charcoal making (Munson 1980:166–173). To understand the rationale of these activities, we must first examine land tenure in the Jbalan highlands.

Land Tenure

Land tenure in the Jbalan highlands has for centuries taken three main forms:

- *mulk*, private property bought and sold for cash by individuals;
- *ard al-jama'a*, communal village land; and
- *hbus*, inalienable religious endowments donated by individuals for the maintenance of mosques, shrines, and other religious institutions (Munson 1981:252).

In addition to these forms of tenure, full-fledged forests and some scrub forests have been declared state domain in order to combat deforestation and erosion (Fay 1984:10).

Arable valley land, as well as the land in villages where houses are built and gardens cultivated, is predominantly private property. The religious endowments, once privately owned, also consist primarily of arable valley land and village gardens, but they include no more than 5 percent of the land in the commune of Bni Harshan. Village communal land, to which all villagers have access with the permission of the village council of adult men, consists of the less fertile hillside slopes largely covered by scrub forest (see Hart 1976:97–100 for the comparable situation in the Berber-speaking Rif).

In addition to its natural scarcity, arable valley land is owned in comparatively small units. Thus, in 1954, 65 percent of all landholdings in the qabila of Bni Msawwar were less than three ha in size, 96 percent were less than five ha, and 99 percent were less than ten ha (Table 2.2). A 1968 survey found a similar pattern in the Dar Chaoui basin (which includes much of the arable land in the commune of the Monday Market of Bni Harshan): 69 percent of the holdings were less than 1.6 ha in size, 96 percent less than 5.1 ha, and 99 percent less than 10.1 (Table 2.3). The 1977 tax records for the commune of the Monday Market of Bni Harshan also indicated that 88 percent of all landholdings were less than five ha in size, while 95 percent were less than ten ha (Table 2.4). Fay gives similar statistics for the southern Jbala near Ouezzane (Fay 1972:349–351).

These figures are significant because five hectares of unirrigated land is sometimes given as the minimum amount a household of five would need to survive in the Jbalan region without complementary resources, although some scholars believe that ten hectares would be a more accurate figure (SOMET-SOGETHA 1967:I, 97; Pascon 1977:191). Grayzel (in this volume), speaks of a minimal viable farm size of 12 to 14 ha in the more arid plains southeast of Casablanca. But even if we take the improbably low figure of five hectares as the minimal viable farm size in the Jbalan hills, it is clear that the overwhelming majority of the Jbala in the qabila of Bni Msawwar

TABLE 2.2
Distribution of Landholdings in Bni Msawwar in 1954

Categories of Size (ha)	Number	%
Less than 1	324	18
1 - 2.9	843	47
3 - 4.9	554	31
5 - 9.9	58	3
10+	16	1
Total	1,795	100

Source: de Roda Jimenez 1954:54.

TABLE 2.3
Distribution of Landholdings in the Dar Chaoui Basin in 1968

Categories of Size (ha)	Holdings No.	%	Area (ha) No.	%
0 - 1.5	783	69	313	23
1.6 - 5	299	27	627	45
5.1 - 10	34	3	157	11
10+	11	1	291	21
Total	1,127	100	1,388	100

Source: El Gharbaoui 1981:222. El Gharbaoui gives as his source the "direction provinciale de l'agriculture de Tétouan, 1968."

TABLE 2.4
Distribution of Landholdings in the Commune of the Monday Market of Bni Harshan in 1977

Categories of Size (ha)	Number	%
Less than 5	1,225	88
5 - 9	92	7
10 - 14	47	3
15 - 19	11	1
20 - 24	8	1
25 - 29	4	-
30 - 34	2	-
35+	0	-
Total	1,389	100

Source: Tax records provided by the Sheikh of the Commune in 1977.

do not own that much land and consequently must depend on other resources to survive.

In one highland village of Bni Msawwar in 1977, only 1 household out of 30 was able to grow enough wheat on its valley land to satisfy its food requirements for the year. Most families in this village owned no valley land at this time. The same pattern prevailed in all the neighboring villages and qaba'il.

The Jbala themselves say that there has "always" been a dearth of arable valley land in the Bni Msawwar region with respect to the food requirements of the local population. Considerable documentary evidence suggests that this has been true at least since the late nineteenth century (Michaux-Bellaire 1911:164, 186-187; Munson 1980:166-173).

Redistribution of arable valley land would not radically transform the situation, since even the largest landholdings in the Jbalan region are relatively small. For example, if the 291 ha in the Dar Chaoui basin belonging to the 11 peasants with holdings of over 10 ha in 1968 were distributed to the

783 peasants owning less than 1.6 ha at that time (see Table 2.3), each of the latter would receive only 0.37 ha, nowhere near enough to provide cereal self-sufficiency.

Slash-and-Burn Cultivation

The Jbala of Bni Msawwar and other nearby regions contend that slash-and-burn cultivation on village communal land has always been one of the principal options of poor Jbala with little or no arable valley land.[2] A French study published in 1911 suggests that this was true around the turn of the century, before the imposition of the Spanish Protectorate in northern Morocco in 1912 (Michaux-Bellaire 1911:187). Some more recent studies also indicate that until its prohibition after independence, hillside slash-and-burn on communal village land was the primary alternative to valley plow agriculture on privately owned land throughout the Rif chain (Fay 1972:296-303; Hart 1976:99; Maurer 1968:37-39; Pascon and van der Wusten 1983:34, 125).[3]

Fay (1972:297) describes a 3-to-5-year period of cultivation followed by 5 to 15 years of fallow among the southern Jbala near Ouezzane. Among the northern Jbala, however, cultivation was usually for two years—in rare instances three. As for fallow periods, peasants have given us estimates ranging from 5 to 20 years. Maurer contends that in the Sanhajan mountains (the highest and coldest in the Rif chain—east of the Ghmaran highlands), 10 to 20 years of fallow traditionally followed 2 years of cultivation (Maurer 1968:37). In the far more arid Rif, Hart speaks of 2 years of cultivation without specifying the length of the fallow period (Hart 1976:99).

Peasants in the northern highlands of Morocco generally do not measure time in years except for expressions such as "this year," "last year," and "next year." In speaking of the fallow periods following slash-and-burn cultivation, the northern Jbala usually say simply that they did not recultivate a field until they could see that enough scrub forest (matorral) had grown back to provide plenty of ashes to enrich the soil. Only when specifically asked for estimates in years did peasants come up with estimates ranging from 5 to 20 years. This wide range may reflect the fact that they were not used to calculating fallow time in this manner, or it could reflect site-to-site differences.

The Prohibition of Slash-and-Burn Cultivation

The Spanish prohibited slash-and-burn cultivation in most of the northern Moroccan highlands to prevent deforestation and erosion (Sanchez Cozar 1947:27). They do not appear to have actually enforced this prohibition very strictly, however, as the Moroccan government did after independence (Fay 1984:10). In the Bni Msawwar region, the local "forest rangers" have effectively eliminated slash-and-burn cultivation, although it was still being practiced (illegally) in the southern Jbalan hills in the early 1970s (Fay 1972:296).

In the commune of the Monday Market of Bni Harshan, the Jbala are unanimous in condemning the prohibition of slash-and-burn, which they contend has made it impossible for most families to survive (see Munson 1984:62-63). They deny that slash-and-burn cultivation destroys the forest, pointing out that it was usually undertaken in matorral rather than full-fledged forest and that the ashes from the burned brush enrich the soil. They contend that yields from slash-and-burn fields, especially during the first year of cultivation, are usually better than those from plowed valley fields—despite their awareness of the greater intrinsic fertility of the latter. They also stress that slash-and-burn cultivation allows the retention of roots, which prevents erosion and expedites the regeneration of the scrub forest.

One still finds some fields being cleared and burned on village lands (with special permits), with subsequent continuous cultivation by plow replacing intermittent cultivation by hoe. This occurs among both the northern and southern Jbala (Fay 1972:304). Hart describes the same sort of hybrid slash-and-burn-cum-plow agriculture in the Rif (Hart 1976:51, 99).

Some of the Jbalan arguments in favor of slash-and-burn are plausible. Ashes supply the soil with nitrogen and potash (Fay 1972:303). Slashed-and-burned hillside fields are less subject to erosion than plowed hillside fields where roots are eradicated (ibid.). And by prohibiting slash-and-burn, the Moroccan government has forced poor peasants throughout the Rif chain to clear permanently plowed (and thus rootless) fields on hillside village lands. This has apparently accelerated rather than decreased erosion. Sloping fields that were once intermittently slashed, burned, and cultivated by hoe are now often continuously cultivated by plow, and thus the fertilizing and antierosive qualities of slash-and-burn are lost. The northern Jbala contend that the yields in their plowed hillside fields are considerably lower than previously, when they used slash-and-burn techniques. Fay has often heard the same contention among the southern Jbala (Fay 1972:303).

Charcoal

Charcoal making has traditionally been the major alternative livelihood for the majority of Jbala who have little or no arable valley land of their own. This is true, at any rate, in villages at higher elevations where both forests and scrub forests are extensive. At lower elevations, there is not enough wood for charcoal making to be feasible. Thus, it has not been of major significance among the Bni Gurfet in the Jbalan foothills near the Atlantic littoral (Jacques Vignet-Zunz, personal communication). It is much more important in highlands near towns and cities—where large quantities of charcoal are needed for cooking—than it is farther away from urban centers.

Charcoal is made by covering a mound of bits and pieces of wood with leafy branches and then dirt. The branches protruding near the bottom of the mound are then fired. The fire slowly spreads throughout the leafy branches under the dirt and to the piled pieces of wood themselves. The dirt cover limits the amount of air present so that the wood is charred rather than burned. The fire smolders in this manner approximately a week, depending on the size of the mound, until all the wood has become charcoal (for similar techniques in Mexico, see Lewis 1951:163–165).

Several writers suggest that the sale of charcoal in the towns and lowlands of northwestern Morocco was a major source of income for the highland Jbala in the nineteenth century (Mouliéras 1899:706; Salmon 1904:148; Michaux-Bellaire 1911:180). A 1934 Spanish military manual concerning the Jbala declared:

> The real industry derived from wood is charcoal. In Anjera and Bni Msawwar, this occurs on a large scale, due no doubt to the easy connections between these qabilas and the towns of the Protectorate, of Tangier, and of Ceuta, for charcoal is exported to these places in considerable quantities. (Intervenciónes Militares de la región de Yebala Central 1934:102).

In 1954 the Spanish administrator of Bni Msawwar and the adjacent districts of Jbil Hbib and "Spanish" Fahs observed that "the individual who lacks land or livestock devotes himself to charcoal making, with a good market: Tangier" (de Roda Jimenez 1954:39). Thus, charcoal making, especially near towns and cities, has been a basic component of the highland Jbalan economy for at least a century and probably much longer. Like slash-and-burn cultivation, charcoal making has been a basic source of livelihood for the great majority of Jbala with little or no arable valley land.

The postindependence prohibition of charcoal making has not had as immediate an impact as that of slash-and-burn because the government has been unable to enforce it as effectively. Charcoal making is a far more surreptitious and ephemeral activity than slash-and-burn cultivation. Burning a field involves flames and large clouds of smoke visible far away, notably to the forest rangers (locally referred to as *al-wardiyya*). A field is also a long-term venture—usually lasting from October through May, giving the rangers ample time to catch anyone engaged in illegal slash-and-burn cultivation. A charcoal mound (*kosha*), on the other hand, produces only a thin whorl of smoke that may last for just three or four days. Whereas rangers can always force a village council to reveal who is cultivating a piece of village communal land (which requires the council's permission), they cannot always discover the individual responsible for a charcoal mound.

In part for these reasons, and also because of the prohibition of slash-and-burn, charcoal making continues on a greater scale than ever before. The overwhelming majority of men in the higher villages of the Bni Msawwar region have little or no arable valley land and depend on charcoal making to buy wheat and other necessities. Even relatively wealthy peasants occasionally make charcoal as a fast way to obtain cash.

The extent of illegal charcoal making in the Bni Msawwar area does not mean that the government is not trying to enforce its prohibition. The forest rangers based near Dar Chaoui constantly patrol the hills for charcoal mounds and catch charcoalmakers almost every day. This story is typical:

Si Muhammad has six goats and about a dozen chickens. Sometimes he works for the government public works program (al-Inash al-Watani) for 750 francs ($1.67) a day [in 1976–1977]. And he has a little mint garden. But mostly he depends on charcoal. He was caught by the ranger (al-wardiyya) for a second time in 1977. The judge in Tetouan made him pay 10,000 francs ($22.22). That is a fortune in the hills, where many Jbala do not see that much money in a month (Munson 1984:191–192).

Charcoal making is the last resort of poor Jbala. After being fined or jailed a few times, many of them give up trying to survive in the hills and join the ranks of the urban poor in Morocco's cities. The fact that charcoal making is widely perceived as the last step before rural-urban migration is indicated by the common phrase "Baqa al-ghabra d al-fham fi wudnu" (He still has charcoal dust in his ears), which is used to ridicule Jbala living in Tangier who try to assume the speech and manners of people born and raised in the city.

Emigration from the Bni Msawwar Highland Region

Like the rest of the Third World, Morocco has experienced massive rural-urban migration since the mid-twentieth century (Escallier 1984:159–283; Fadl Allah, Birryan, and Birrada 1983; Lahbabi 1977:195). The scale of such migration in the northern Jbalan region is particularly striking. Whereas the population of Morocco as a whole increased by 32 percent from 1960 to 1971, the population of the commune of the Monday Market of Bni Harshan increased by only 3 percent, from 6,789 in 1960 to 6,990 in 1971 (Morocco 1971:88). According to a census taken under my supervision in March of 1977, the population of this district had actually decreased to 6,361 at that time, just as, a little earlier, the populations of four neighboring communes, including that of Dar Chaoui, had decreased by 1 to 9 percent from 1960 to 1971 (El Gharbaoui 1981:136). According to a September 1982 unpublished census, the population of the Monday Market of Bni Harshan had increased to 7,155, suggesting that the 1977 results may have been too low,[4] but there is no question that the exodus from the Jbalan highlands, and from rural Morocco generally, is continuing on a massive scale (Fadl Allah, Birryan, and Birrada 1983:5, 16; Morocco 1984:5–6).

There is hardly a Jbalan highland village that does not have empty houses belonging to peasants who have emigrated to a city. Many poor peasants who remain in the commune of the Monday Market of Bni Harshan express fear that they cannot hold out in the mountains much longer, and most attribute this to the prohibition of slash-and-burn cultivation and of charcoal making.

A June 1977 survey of all male emigrants from Bni Harshan measured the extent of the exodus from the commune. With the help of the local authorities who interviewed relatives of emigrants, the survey recorded a total of 581 men aged 21 or over who had been born in the commune and were now permanently living elsewhere. In the same year, there were 1,793 men aged 21 or over living in the district. Given the virtual absence of in-

TABLE 2.5
Place of Permanent Residence of Adult Male Emigrants from the Commune of the Monday Market of Bni Harshan in June 1977

Place of Residence	Number	%
Tangier	466	80
Tétouan	90	15
Other Moroccan cities	17	3
Towns (2,000 to 9,999 pop.)	4	1
Rural areas	4	1
Total	581	100

Source: Author's survey undertaken with assistance of local authorities in June 1977.

TABLE 2.6
Date of Emigration of Adult Male Emigrants from the Commune of the Monday Market of Bni Harshan

Period	Number	%
Before Independence (1956)	119	20
1956-60	89	15
1961-65	138	24
1966-70	125	22
1971-75	91	16
1976-77	19	3
Total	581	100

Source: Author's survey undertaken with assistance of local authorities in June 1977.

migration to Bni Harshan, we can assume that these men were born there. We thus find a total of 2,374 adult men born in the commune, with 24 percent (581) of them having emigrated.

Eighty percent (466) of the emigrants had their permanent residences in Tangier, roughly 25 kilometers northwest of the commune, while 15 percent (90) had their permanent residences in Tetouan (see Table 2.5). Fifteen of the permanent residents of Tangier actually worked abroad (7 in Gibraltar, 5 in Belgium, 2 in Canada, and 1 in France). Two of the permanent residents of Tetouan also worked abroad (one in Belgium and one in France). From a total of 581 emigrants, 80 percent had emigrated since independence in 1956 and the subsequent prohibition of slash-and-burn and charcoal making (Table 2.6). Almost three-fourths of the men had joined the ranks of Morocco's irregularly employed urban poor (see Table 2.7 and Munson and LeCamus 1986).

TABLE 2.7
Occupational Distribution of Adult Male Emigrants from the Commune of the Monday Market of Bni Harshan Working in Urban Morocco in 1977 (Does Not Include Unemployed)

Occupations	Number	%
Irregularly employed urban poor earning less than 350 DH ($78) a month	367	73
Merchants and artisans with their own shops or vehicles, earning over 350 DH ($78) a month	108	22
White collar employees earning over 675 DH ($150) a month	16	3
Skilled blue collar workers earning over 350 DH ($78) a month	12	2
Total	503	100

Source: Author's survey undertaken with assistance of local authorities in June 1977.

It would be incorrect to suggest that the sole reason for the massive exodus of the Jbala has been the prohibition of slash-and-burn cultivation and charcoal making, but the people of the commune of Bni Harshan regard them as the decisive cause. The prohibitions have certainly increased the magnitude of emigration to the cities, which they were intended to decrease (de Mas 1978:216).

Conclusion

Morocco's antierosion program has been implemented without adequate understanding of the local ecological, economic, and social structure of the Jbalan highlands, and thus without awareness of the devastating impact of prohibiting slash-and-burn agriculture and charcoal making. While the long-term benefits of the ban could conceivably outweigh the short-term costs, the government does not appear to have the kinds of data needed to arrive at such a conclusion. Apparently, no attempts have been made to measure the ecological consequences of slash-and-burn and charcoal making and their prohibition. Moreover, the officials in charge of the antierosion campaign appear to be unaware of the stark contradiction between the government's goal of curbing erosion by prohibiting slash-and-burn and charcoal making on the one hand, and its goal of curbing rural-urban migration on the other. Even if one argues that massive emigration from the Jbalan highlands is ecologically necessary (and this is a plausible argument), the fact remains that the government's antierosion campaign was not intended to have this result (see de Mas 1978).

The Moroccan government deserves credit for attempting to limit deforestation and erosion, but such attempts can succeed only if they are based on detailed analyses of local ecological, economic, and social structures as well as on analyses on a national and international scale. Anthropologists and others specializing in such detailed analyses should be consulted about the local implications of conservation programs before such programs are implemented.

This is not to suggest that long-term ecological degradation be tolerated in order to provide short-term livelihoods for peasants. It is simply to suggest that local-level analysis must be undertaken—and communicated to policy makers—to determine the precise relationship between ecological degradation and the livelihoods of peasants. That relationship must then be analyzed in terms of long-term development goals. Such analysis has been neglected with respect to the prohibition of slash-and-burn cultivation and of charcoal making in the Jbalan highlands of Northwest Morocco.

I discussed the implications of these prohibitions with the qaid of the commune of Bni Harshan and several other local officials in 1979. They were familiar with the problem but stressed that they were obliged to comply with the orders sent from Rabat. In addition, I have sent an earlier version of this chapter to several scholars involved in Morocco's antierosion program, and plan to publish a translation of it in Morocco to make the appropriate policy makers aware of the plight of the highland Jbala who may have to choose between illegal charcoal making and emigration to Tangier.

Notes

My research in Morocco was undertaken from June 1976 through December 1977 and was made possible by dissertation research fellowships from the Social Science Research Council and the Fulbright-Hays program of the Office of Education. I would like to thank the Moroccan Ministry of Housing and Urbanism and the local authorities in the communes of Dar Chaoui and the Monday Market of Bni Harshan for their assistance. I would also like to thank Janet Abu-Lughod, Michael M Horowitz, Raymond T. Smith, and Jacques Vignet-Zunz for their comments on an earlier version of this paper.

1. In colloquial Moroccan Arabic, the definite article *al* is deleted before a noun modified by a following adjective; for example, the city of Qsar al-Kbir would be al-Qsar al-Kbir in literary Arabic.

2. Slash-and-burn cultivation is known as *l-zbar* or *l-zbir* among the Jbala. The term *zbir*, which refers to the brush fencing around slashed and burned fields, is also used in the Sanhajan highlands along with the Berber term *ntefersi* (Maurer 1968:37). A cognate of this Berber term, *dhifarsi* is used further east in the Rif by the Bni Wuriyaghil (Hart 1976:99). Following Sanchez Pérez, Hart translates this as "intermittent cultivation" (ibid.).

3. The juxtaposition of highland slash-and-burn with lowland plow agriculture is commonplace in Southeast Asia and Latin America (Grigg 1974:57–74; Lewis 1951:129–157; Palerm 1967). The northern Moroccan case is not mentioned, however,

in any of the standard surveys of the slash-and-burn literature (see Conklin 1961, Grigg 1974:57-74). Nor is it usually mentioned in studies of Moroccan agriculture (see Villeneuve 1971).

4. Some demographers have questioned the accuracy of the 1982 census, however. See Fadl Allah 1983:47 and Parker 1984:25-26, 36.

References

Bates, Daniel, and Amal Rassam
   1983   Peoples and Cultures of the Middle East. Englewood Cliffs, NJ: Prentice-Hall.

Brignon, Jean, et al.
   1967   Histoire du Maroc. Paris: Hatier.

Conklin, Harold C.
   1961   The Study of Shifting Cultivation. Current Anthropology 2:27-61.

de Mas, Paolo
   1978   Marges marocaines: Limites de la coopération au développement dans une région périphérique: le cas du Rif. La Haye: NUFFIC/IMWOO/PROJET REMPLOD.

de Roda Jimenez, Rafael
   1954   Estudio socio-economico sobre Beni Msawwar, Fahs, Yebel Hebib. Unpublished report by the Spanish Interventor Comercal of these three qaba'il. Collección Garcia Figueras, Biblioteca Nacional Espanola, Madrid.)

Dressler, Jurgen
   1982   The Organization of Erosion Control in Morocco. Quarterly Journal of International Agriculture 21 (March 1982):62-79.

Eickelman, Dale F.
   1981   The Middle East: An Anthropological Approach. Englewood Cliffs, NJ: Prentice-Hall.

El Gharbaoui, Ahmed
   1981   La Terre et l'homme dans la péninsule tingitane. Rabat: Travaux de l'Institut Scientifique, Série Géologie et Géographie Physique No. 15.

Escallier, Robert
   1984   Citadins et espace urbain au Maroc. Second edition. Tours: Centre d'Etudes et de Recherches URBAMA, Fascicule de Recherches No. 8.

Fadl Allah, 'Abd al-Latif
   1983   Al-taghayyurat al-zamaniyya wa al-majalliyya al-haditha li-intaj al-hubub bil-Maghrib. Majallat Jughrafiyyat al-Maghrib (Revue de Géographie du Maroc), Al-Salsala al-jadida, No. 7:21-55.

Fadl Allah, 'Abd al-Latif, Muhammad Birryan, and 'Abd Allah Birrada
   1983   Al-Taghayyurat al-majalliyya al-haditha lil-ta'mir bil-Maghrib. Majallat Jughrafiyyat al-Maghrib (Revue de Géographie du Maroc), Al-Salsala al-jadida, No. 7:3-19 (Arabic section).

Fay, Gérard
   1972   Recherches sur l'organisation de la vie rurale et sur les conditions de la production dans la basse montagne rifaine. Thèse pour le doctorat de troisième cycle, Université de Paris, UER Géographie et Sciences de la Société.

1984 Tanghaya: Un projet agro-sylvo-pastoral pour le Rif occidental. Revue de Géographie du Maroc, No. 8, Nouvelle Série:3-22.

Grigg, D. B.
1974 The Agricultural Systems of the World: An Evolutionary Approach. London: Cambridge University Press.

Hart, David M.
1976 The Aith Waryaghar of the Moroccan Rif: An Ethnography and History. Tucson: University of Arizona Press. Viking Fund Publications in Anthropology 55.

Intervenciónes Militares de la región de Yebala Central
1934 Memoria relativa a las kabilas que integran ésta regional. Tetouan: Casa Gomariz.

Lahbabi, Mohamed
1977 L'Economie marocaine, notions essentielles. Tome 1: Les Fondements de l'économie marocaine. Casablanca: Les Editions Maghrébines.

Lewis, Oscar
1951 Life in a Mexican Village: Tepoztlán Restudied. Urbana, IL: University of Illinois Press.

Maurer, Gérard
1968 Les Paysans du haut Rif central. Revue de Géographie du Maroc No. 14:3-70.

Michaux-Bellaire, Edouard
1911 Quelques tribus de montagne de la région du Habt. Archives Marocaines 17:1-538.

Mikesell, Marvin
1961 Northern Morocco: A Cultural Geography. Berkeley: University of California Publications in Geography, Volume 14.

Morocco
1971 Al-Sukan al-qanuniyyun lil-Maghrib hasab al-ihsa' al-'amm lil-sukan wa al-sukna li-sanat 1971. Rabat: Mudiriyyat al-ihsa'.

1984 Al-Ihsa' al-'amm lil-sukan wa al-sukna li-sanat 1982. Nata'ij al-uliyya hayakil al-sukan wa al-sukna ('ayyina 5 percent). Rabat: Mudiriyyat al-ihsa'.

Mouliéras, Auguste
1899 Le Maroc inconnu. Volume 2. Exploration des Djebala. Paris: Augustin Challomel.

Munson, Henry, Jr.
1980 Islam and Inequality in Northwest Morocco. Ph.D. dissertation, Anthropology Department, University of Chicago.

1981 The Mountain People of Northwest Morocco: Tribesmen or Peasants? Middle Eastern Studies 17:249-255.

1984 The House of Si Abd Allah: The Oral History of a Moroccan Family. New Haven, CT: Yale University Press.

1986 The Social Base of Islamic Militancy in Morocco. The Middle East Journal 40:267-284.

Munson, Henry, Jr., and Jack LeCamus
 1986 Al-Dradib: Hawma Sha'biyya fi Tanja. Abhath, Majallat al-'Ulum al-Ijtima'iyya.

Oram, Peter A.
 1979 Crop Production Systems in the Arid and Semi-Arid Warm Temperate and Mediterranean Zones. *In* Soil, Water and Crop Production. D. Wynne Thorne and Marlowe D. Thorne, eds. Westport, CT: EVI Publishing Co. Pp. 193–228.

Palerm, Angel
 1967 Agricultural Systems and Food Patterns. *In* Social Anthropology. Manning Nash, ed. Pp. 26–52. Handbook of Middle American Indians, Volume 6. Robert Wauchope, general ed. Austin, TX: University of Texas Press.

Parker, Richard B.
 1984 North Africa: Regional Tensions and Strategic Concerns. New York, NY: Praeger.

Pascon, Paul
 1977 Interrogations autour de la réforme agraire. *In* La Question agraire au Maroc. Volume 2. Negib Bouderbala, Mohamed Chraibi, and Paul Pascon, eds. Pp. 183–200. Rabat: Publication du Bulletin Economique et Social du Maroc, Série Documents.

Pascon, Paul, and Herman van der Wusten
 1983 Les Beni Bou Frah: Essai d'écologie sociale d'une vallée rifaine. Rabat: l'Institut Universitaire de la Recherche Scientifique and l'Institut Agronomique et Vétérinaire Hassan II (with the support of the Faculty of Social Geography of the University of Amsterdam).

Salmon, Georges
 1904 Le Commerce indigène à Tanger. Archives Marocaines 1:38–55.

Sanchez Cozar, Santiago
 1947 Ordenación de la riqueza forestal de nuestro protectorado. Africa (Madrid), No. 68:25–27.

Seddon, David
 1981 Moroccan Peasants: A Century of Change in the Eastern Rif 1870–1970. Folkestone, Kent: William Dawson and Sons.

Showers, Victor
 1973 The World in Figures. New York, NY: John Wiley & Sons.

SOMET-SOGETHA
 1967 Etude des possibilités de développement de la province de Tetouan. Unpublished study by the Société Maroc Etudes (SOMET) and the Société Générale des Techniques Hydro-Agricoles (SOGETHA), prepared for the Moroccan Ministry of Interior, Province of Tetouan.

Villeneuve, Michel
 1971 La Situation de l'agriculture et son avenir dans l'économie marocaine. Paris: Librairie Générale de Droit et de Jurisprudence, R. Pichon and R. Durand-Auzias.

3

Farm Size and Agricultural Credit in Morocco: Correcting Distorted Information in the Development Process

John Aron Grayzel

Introduction

Anthropology has throughout much of its history been concerned with the correspondence between the ideal and the real as reflected at the individual and group levels, and as expressed in the discrepancy between how people view themselves, their cultures, and their institutions, and how they actually behave. Because of this concern, anthropologists acquire a well-developed and perhaps unique skill that enables them to distinguish, with depth and facility, between the various levels of cultural realities. Such a skill can be of immense value in applied as well as academic development studies. This chapter illustrates the anthropologist's intermediary role in the dialogue between ideal and real, with a case study of an agricultural development project in Morocco financed by the Agency for International Development (AID).

In the case in point, the interplay between ideal and real is displayed in three fashions. First, the prevalent administrative and descriptive split between small and large farms is discrepant from the realities of the full spectrum of dynamic and changing Moroccan agricultural operations. Second, AID's views of the proper use of United States-financed agricultural credit, as expressed in generally stated AID policies (particularly those emphasizing help to the poorest segments of the population), is discrepant from the on-the-ground operations of such credit in the specific Moroccan context. Third, the theoretical project design is discrepant from the actual project development. It is precisely at the nexus of the real and ideal that tremendous opportunity lies for anthropologists to provide unique and valuable analytical input to development efforts.

The Real and Ideal in Project Development

Foreign development assistance is generated by and responsive to a series of agendas, often in reverse order of that publicly portrayed. An image of development assistance that is frequently conveyed by both donor agencies (e.g., AID 1975) and development anthropology manuals (e.g., Partridge 1984) is that the problems foreign assistance aims to resolve can be dealt with in a logical order: first, problems are recognized; second, they seem open to solution; so that, third, the concerned government and foreign donor study the situation; whereupon, fourth, the parties negotiate possible solutions; after which, fifth, they agree upon a course of action; which, sixth, is implemented. Purportedly, in each stage of the process objective information is obtained and used to identify problems, solutions, and consequences that are weighed against and guided by policy considerations arrived at in light of existing understandings of the long-term and fundamental development goals of the country and organizations involved.

In my experience, the reality of creating a development activity often plays itself out in a somewhat different scenario from the above ideal. Action is initiated in response to immediate political concerns, not development problem analysis. (Such concerns can be in terms of organizational or local politics and can be national or international in nature.) Convenient target areas are then looked for and possibilities are identified and judged as justifiable or not in terms of overriding policies. Unfortunately, these policies are often out of synchronization with existing circumstances, since they have evolved over time and are based upon past experience and understanding. If justification seems possible, however, an investigation of immediate circumstances is called for to determine the actual possibilities at hand and to make the case that they correspond to the already-agreed-upon parameters of action. Lastly, an attempt is made to assert precise benefits to be derived and to minimize negative consequences of the proposed activity, but this assertion is made more to fulfill bureaucratic requirements and assure that no obvious or unacceptable contravening consequences will arise than to determine the true value of the proposed plan itself.

Such a scenario as this can be frustrating to all concerned, but especially to those parties responsible for the final collection of information and the formulation of specific interventions. Such parties often find themselves at the tail end of an already well-wagged dog with little time substantially to test the operative underlying assumptions. Since this situation is very much a reflection of the present structure of development assistance, however, it is not likely to change soon, regardless of the good intentions of development personnel or the outcries of development critics. For an anthropologist working in project design, the choice is either to work within the constraints of this reality or abstain from meaningful participation.

Nevertheless, as the following case study will show, the real-world scenario of how projects develop, while it may not be many people's ideal of how things should work, does, in fact, provide a possibility to affect both short-term project design and long-term development policy. Because of the reality of already-made decisions and system inertia, the effect of new information in the short term is often limited to making minor program adjustments and damage control. In contrast, as regards long-term effects, new information can have a major influence on policy by introducing or altering the basic data and the conceptual base from which future policymakers will work.

Synopsis of Study

In 1984 AID decided to increase its assistance to the government of Morocco. This increase was to be in the form of Economic Support Funds (ESF), which are designed to contribute to development through support for a country's government and its basic economic viability. Support for Morocco was justified because of her generally pro-U.S. position and her overall moderate political stance, particularly vis-à-vis the Arab-Israeli conflict. Concomitantly, Morocco was experiencing increased need for assistance because of unfavorable terms of international trade, costly public subsidies for a wide range of goods and services, drought, and the continuing war in the former Spanish Sahara.

An appealing area for providing assistance, from the perspective of both AID and the Moroccan government, was agricultural credit. Assistance to agricultural production is a recognized priority concern for AID. From the Moroccan government's viewpoint, the provision of such loans was regarded as an important political and economic service to its indebted farmers and drought-stricken rural areas. Bureaucratically, provision of assistance through the Moroccan National Agricultural Credit Bank was attractive to the AID Mission in Morocco, since the bank was an established, relatively well-functioning organization, seen not only as deserving support and improvement but also as potentially useful in terms of future (less-crisis-oriented) programs. The bank itself needed immediate assistance since its available capital had been depleted by outstanding loans.

In designing the intervention, AID sought to follow the congressionally established policy of the U.S. Foreign Assistance Act, which stresses help to the truly needy. Existing, generally accepted figures showed Morocco's agricultural sector as divided into a very large group of subsistence farmers on small farms, and a much smaller group of larger, modernized commercial producers. This portrayal of a dual farming-sector structure was further reinforced by both Moroccan and World Bank data that indicated a significant hiatus between the value of poor and rich farms. AID therefore initially identified the poor farmers served by small local credit banks, rather than the moderately wealthier ones served by regional agricultural credit banks, as the most appropriate recipients of its proposed loans. The national credit bank, which encompasses both the local and regional banks, was amenable to this, as it is mandated politically to serve this group of poor clients.

Moroccan government loans to farmers, especially small farmers, have generally been at highly subsidized interest rates. Unfortunately, this contravened AID policy which, while supportive of assisting the neediest element of the population, states that interest on loans should be as close to market rates as possible. A major question identified by the mission was whether this targeted group could and would accept market interest rates on new loans. At the same time, project review in Washington questioned the wisdom of encouraging apparently impoverished subsistence farmers to take on new indebtedness at any rate without an indication that they would ever be able to repay, given their marginal situation. This concern was reinforced by the fact that the proposed action included no technical assistance that might increase productivity. The final project design, especially the socioeconomic analysis, was charged with the task of somehow reconciling or resolving these problems in a manner consistent with the already-reached decision to provide agricultural credit assistance.

A form of rapid rural appraisal was initiated. Given the limited time available, it was realistic only because of prior experience, sufficient existing documentation, and critical on-the-ground assistance, including the cooperation of local bank officials and local researchers and access to unpublished Moroccan credit bank reports. The findings, when reviewed in the context of existing understandings of agricultural credit in general and Morocco's agricultural situation and policies in particular, contributed to a change in the focus of planned project activities as well as to a reformulation of long-term policy concerns.

The study revealed that while the basic political and bureaucratic operating premises behind the project were sound overall, there was good reason to question the appropriateness of market-interest credit to the smallest producers. More importantly, the conception of Moroccan farm operations and size portrayed by numerous documents and used by the initial project developers was shown to be seriously flawed.

The division between small subsistence and large commercial farming operations and the associated portrayal of a skewed distribution of farms within these categories was found not to reflect the actual distribution of farm sizes, but rather the structure of banking and tax administration records and practices. These practices, in turn, seemed representative of a discernible, long-standing political strategy of both colonial and indigenous governing authorities to differentiate sharply between purported traditional/subsistence and modern/commercial agricultural producers. While the limited sample obtained was insufficient to define the actual distribution of farm size in Morocco, it demonstrated the inadequacy of much of the existing analysis and indicated the real rationale behind individual and family strategies in declaring and determining farm-holding size. It also demonstrated how evolving banking practices, premised on efficient management concerns as perceived by bank administrators, might be contributing to the demise of middle-sized farms and the evolution of a truly dual system.

In response to the demonstrated inaccuracy of the generally held view of a dual agricultural sector, an alternative perspective on Moroccan farm size based on a sliding scale of productive value and potential, which was

TABLE 3.1
World Bank Farm Size Breakdown

Farm Size (ha)	No. of Farms (000)	% of Total (%)	Cultivable Area (000 ha)	% of Total (%)	Average Size of Farms[a] (ha)
Without Cultivable Land	450.3	23.4	–	–	–
0-5	1,089.5	56.5	1,776.2	24.5	1.6
5-10	219.9	11.4	1,508.0	20.8	6.9
10-20	114.1	5.9	1,529.7	21.1	13.3
20-50	44.0	2.3	1,218.0	16.8	27.7
50-100	7.7	0.4	514.8	7.1	66.4
More than 100	2.6	0.1	703.3	9.7	278.0
Total/Average	1,928.1	100.0	7,250.0	100.0	4.9

[a] Average size of farms is calculated only for farms that have cultivable land.
Source: Kingdom of Morocco 1983:7.

determined by a combination of such factors as water availability, local climate, soil fertility, and land area, was adopted for this study. This practical alternative was possible because in Morocco such a scale already exists for purposes of certain local tax and loan valuations. Taking a second look at farm-size distribution from this perspective highlighted the existence of a previously concealed intermediate group of marginal commercial producers who were, by all indications, ill-served by the present system, while at the same time being perhaps the most appropriate clients of the proposed assistance. These producers seemed sufficiently well positioned to reject credit and continue production if they judged the terms economically unfavorable, but they were in need of and capable of using appropriately supplied credit to make a qualitative jump in technique and production. As a result, targeting this group for immediate AID-funded assistance was recommended, as well as incorporating activities to build up the institutional capacity of the bank to make future credit more flexible and responsive to middle-level producers (USAID/Rabat 1984).

The Situation as Traditionally Portrayed

Traditional Versus Modern Dichotomy in Moroccan Agriculture

Several good discussions of Moroccan agriculture exist (e.g., Van de Kloet 1975; Benatya et al. 1983),[1] but many of them (e.g., Van de Kloet 1975; MIAC 1977; World Bank 1983) foster the idea that the distribution of farmland in Morocco is highly skewed, with the vast majority of the land fragmented into small parcels under five hectares, and a concentration of large farms in the hands of a very small percentage of the total farming population. Tables 3.1 and 3.2 provide two accepted farm-size breakdowns, one from the World Bank, the other from an AID-sponsored study. Neither,

TABLE 3.2
Estimate of Land Distribution by Size of Farm in Traditional Dryland Arable Region

Arable Ha.	No. of Farms	% of Farms	Arable Land (ha)	% of Arable Land	No. of Ha/Farm
0-3	230,100	40.4	571,200	15.0	2.5
3-6	201,600	35.4	971,000	25.5	4.8
6-12	74,000	13.0	723,500	19.0	9.8
12-25	57,000	10.0	1,085,200	28.5	19.0
25-50	5,700	1.0	266,500	7.0	46.8
50 and over	1,100	0.2	190,300	5.0	173.0
	569,500	100.0	3,807,700	100.0	6.7

Source: MIAC 1977.

it should be noted, indicates how the original data were gathered or what qualifications should be applied to them. Such breakdowns are generally accompanied by an analysis that divides the Moroccan agricultural sector into two clearly differentiated production systems. The differences are characterized in terms of significant variations in labor input, cultivation practices, economic strategies, and access to and use of resources. To a significant extent the divergences are real, and a clear understanding of them is crucial to understanding how credit operates in Morocco. At the same time, as will be seen, this delineation has become both a negative self-fulfilling prophecy and an impediment to helping important numbers of farmers in their efforts to achieve higher production levels.

Traditional Farms and Farmer Strategies

Traditional farms have been characterized as varying in size from less than 1 to more than 40 hectares. Regardless of how little is actually owned, in general a minimum of 5 to 7 hectares (owned, rented, or sharecropped) is farmed (Benatya et al. 1983). In the case of the smaller traditional farms, the nature and limit of available resources seems mainly to determine farmer strategy. Conversely, on the larger of the traditional farms it seems that it is the farming strategy, and the unwillingness or inability to switch to a more modern operative style, that precludes further expansion (Zagdouni 1981). The small, five-hectare-or-less, traditional farm is the domain of the rural poor, but significant numbers of small holdings are held by people who have migrated to urban areas, or who have urban migrants in the family, and therefore possess some external income.

The existence of outside income is but one reason that the label of subsistence farming often applied to very small operations is a misnomer. Virtually all Moroccan farms, regardless of size, are integrated into the market economy with respect both to their on-farm activities and their off-farm labor and purchases. Even the poorest farmer who grows wheat for family consumption will often sell his production in the market and buy already-processed flour with the proceeds to avoid the trouble of milling. What distinguishes his operative strategy from that of better-off farmers is that his choices in production are generally not dictated by the desire to maximize profits, but rather, as will be further explained, the desire to minimize risk and assure basic family consumption needs.[2]

This risk-avoidance strategy of the smaller farmer is directly reflected in crop choice and patterns. Crops are chosen according to consumption needs of both man and animal, with an emphasis on drought resistance over yield maximization. There is a concentration on barley and hard wheat (durum) with little attention to soft bread wheat, including the high-yielding hybrid varieties introduced by development projects. Farming techniques follow a similar track, with those technologies that are believed to produce best under drought being favored, including broadcast seeding and delayed plowing. Animal production is an inherent part of the farming operation, and thus lower-yielding grain varieties may be grown, since even with little rainfall they produce more straw than high-yielding varieties, assuring an adequate supply of animal fodder during difficult times.

Almost by definition, the small, traditional farmer is poor in capital, since he consistently forgoes profit opportunities for assurances of basic needs. He thus has few or no funds to invest in farm modernization, is usually operating on an area too small to introduce technologies dependent on economy of scale, and suffers concomitant high transaction costs in relation to benefits in all transactions that require investment of time and money off the farm (e.g., traveling in search of seed, fertilizer, markets, or credit). In addition, he ordinarily possesses lower quality, less fertile land and poorer access to transport. As a direct consequence of his socioeconomic status, he has little influence to exercise to obtain a fair share of such limited resources as subsidized inputs. Mechanization is used only as necessary (usually through contract services), with human labor being used to the maximum.

Modern Farms and Modern Farming Strategy

Ownership of modern farms can be individual, cooperative, corporate, governmental, or some mixture thereof. The term is generally applied to farms that utilize, in a comprehensive fashion, such current Western technologies as intensive application of chemical fertilizer, high-yielding seeds, and mechanization. Moreover, it is because of their links to other sectors of the modern Moroccan economy (banks, commercial outlets, technical services, etc.) that modern operators are able to acquire the necessary inputs, information, and support in the quantities needed to continue operating in this fashion. Large size, as will be seen, is not an absolute prerequisite to adoption of a modernized production strategy, but farm size, value, and modernity naturally strongly correlate, since continuously available capital is needed both to acquire and to operate the technology, and since both wealth and status are primary, if not exclusive, avenues to the acquisition of limited goods and services. Most truly modern farm operations are over

100 ha. This appears to be as much a question of a management threshold as of ownership patterns. Some farm operations on almost every existing scale, from a few hectares up, are found on totally owned, shared, and rented lands. In the Settat area (the focus of this study), however, very few farms existed in the 60–80 ha range, either rented or owned. On the other hand, some farms of 100 ha and larger rented 80 percent of the land they used.

The modern farming sector in Morocco, with the exception of some government operations, is almost entirely profit oriented. Such operations eschew the diversification strategy of smaller farms, and specialize instead in one or two crops, with little mixing of cultivation within the same season and little associated livestock production. Cereal schemes are oriented to both soft and durum wheats, both with high-yielding varieties and intensive technology. Less productive barley or maize hold virtually no interest. For historic[3] as well as agronomic reasons, modern farming operations tend to be found where soils are better and in the less arid climatic zone. They have therefore experienced significantly less loss due to recurrent drought than poorer and smaller traditional operators.

The Need, Provision, and Use of Agricultural Credit

A Brief History. Agricultural credit is not a new phenomenon in Morocco but very much an established institution, well integrated into the farming system. The French introduced formal credit and extended it to rural traditional populations with the establishment in 1928 of a government-run rural banking institution called the *Société Caisse de Prévoyance* (SOCAP), which, however, was directed more toward providing limited funds for unforeseen or emergency needs than for productive investment. Informal credit probably predates colonial times, whether in the form of loans between private parties, or more importantly, of production through *association*, whereby various arrangements are made between parties to contribute land, labor, and capital and where the proceeds are divided up as mutually agreed upon after the harvest. Today, despite some government attempts to discourage it, the practice of *association* continues throughout the country. Direct private lending of funds, however, seems to have decreased significantly, especially in the last few years, as drought has hurt the basic rural economy and as alternative avenues of urban investment opportunities have expanded.

The Present Credit Structure. After independence the government created a national credit bank, the *Caisse Nationale Crédit Agricole* (CNCA). It then gradually phased out the French-created SOCAP and, under the rubric of the CNCA, established a multitiered system consisting of the CNCA (as both the overall institutional structure and the vehicle for very large loans), the present regional banks called *Caisse Régionale Crédit Agricole* (CRCA), and smaller, local bank subunits of the CRCAs, called *Caisse Locale Crédit Agricole* (CLCA). As it functioned at the time of this study, the CLCA, the lowest level, provided very limited loans to poor farmers backed primarily by obtaining cosigners (more to attest to the borrower's character than to guarantee payment). Access to the CLCA was based originally on a farm having an assessed fiscal value of less than 1,523 DH (Moroccan dirham, approximately $250), a figure later raised to 3,000 DH ($500) and, in 1984, to 6,000 DH ($1,000). Access to the CRCA was determined by having a farm valued at greater than the CLCA cutoff. The CRCA provided more substantial loans, based primarily on projected productivity, available collateral, and ability to supply a significant percentage of self-financing.

General Attitudes Toward Credit. Interviews with a broad spectrum of farmers, supported by independent Moroccan research (Lahcen 1981), indicated a shared farmer perception of formal credit and the CRCA and CLCA as a positive governmental force in rural development. (In contrast, farmers expressed dissatisfaction with such other government services as agricultural extension.) This positive attitude toward government credit was accompanied by claims that the use and availability of informal credit alternatives had decreased pronouncedly. Nobody expressed the feeling that credit per se resulted in unnecessary indebtedness, and all felt that the amounts loaned could be paid off under normal circumstances. The perception was expressed that in truly bad times the repayment of small loans would not be expected. Especially among small farmers this perception was quite realistic, as they generally obtained their loans by cosigning for each other. The result of such a system is that social pressure can effectively promote repayment by individuals when times are good, but when hard times hit everyone, as during drought, the system collapses, and widespread collection or foreclosure becomes impossible.[4]

The only strongly expressed dissatisfaction with the CLCA came from some of the small farmers in regard to two factors. The first was the requirement to make repayment shortly after the harvest when the farmers said they received the lowest price for their grain. The second concerned the limit on the amount of loan available to CLCA clients, a concern expressed mainly by the larger of the small farmers. Understandably, a desire for low-interest rates was commonly expressed, but so too was a concern that the CNCA remain a viable institution. It was when questioned on how they use credit that a significant difference between farmers appeared.

Use of Credit by Small Traditional Farmers. Given the small traditional farmers' mixed economic strategies, it is usually fallacious to ascribe a specific use to any particular bundle of borrowed capital. Many farmers borrow money annually. Whether the borrowed money goes to buy seed and they use their own harvest for food, or whether it goes to buy food, is irrelevant. Both represent obligatory expenses for survival of the production unit to which a cash loan can make a significant, but still relatively small, contribution. (This very modest use of cash loans is tied to the limits imposed by the CLCAs.) For other credit needs the small traditional farmer turns to the informal sector. Here, too, access to cash loans is usually limited to small and short-term loans. The traditional alternative is the already-mentioned system of production in *association* with another, whereby the farmer sharecrops his or her land or herd together with a partner who provides seed, animal stock, or other supplementary inputs, and with whom profits are shared based on a negotiated agreement.

Use of Credit by Modern Farmers. A distinctive feature of the use of credit in the modern sector is that the availability of credit itself induces need by creating new opportunities for investments that were not previously considered. Entire new operations may be based on newly available credit. Thus, where the traditional farmer experiences a need and then sees whether credit is available to fill it, the modern entrepreneur seeks credit opportunities for investment and then seeks a way of taking advantage of them. Unfortunately, some urban entrepreneurs procure agricultural land for the sake of obtaining access to cheaper agricultural credit, which they then plow back into urban/industrial investments.

The View from the Bank

Official Attitudes Toward Credit

Because the agricultural credit system in Morocco has been and continues to be a focal point of animated discussion and analysis (e.g., Bouarfa 1982; El Mesmoudi 1982; Masmoudi 1983), few ideas of possible change in practice and policy have not surfaced at some time and place. The direction of foreign assistance can significantly empower one position over another, or it can encourage a new alignment of positions and better collaboration between differing parties by offering a portion of support to each.

Among the limited number of bank personnel interviewed, several different positions regarding the agricultural credit system emerged. Everyone's overriding immediate concern was to recapitalize the CNCA sufficiently to permit it to meet the coming season's predicted demand. Beyond this, however, priorities differed in several ways. For top officials at the CNCA central bureau, a major concern was further to professionalize the system and to increase overall administrative capacity. This took the form of wanting, in addition to aid for loans to farmers, funds for computerizing assorted banking functions through the purchase of a substantial number of IBM personal computers.[5] The mid-level officials at the CRCA showed not only less interest in such improvements but some concern that they might, as a result of them, have to devote more time to internal management reports and less time to meeting farmer needs. While such concerns could mask another motive, such as the desire for less scrutiny, in fact CRCA officials, as revealed by both their bank dossiers and their observed interaction with customers, spent appreciable time with, and possess an appreciable knowledge about, their specific clients' affairs.[6] What CRCA staff particularly wanted were additional funds to allow them to go beyond rigidly set formulas for loan-to-capital ratios and to be able to provide loans to promising enterprises based on projected productivity alone. On the lowest (CLCA) level, the major concern of staff was to have available on time the funds necessary to meet established demand and to prevent what they expressed as the undesirable necessity of poor farmers' turning to unofficial, supposedly usurious, money lenders.

Administrative Profile of Borrowers

In order to obtain a general profile of farms accorded government credit, a random sample of 541 farms was made from the dossiers of three CRCAs and three CLCAs in the area around and to the north and south of the city of Settat. The chosen CRCAs and CLCAs were located in El Bourg (the most southern area, with the least rainfall); Settat (the central area); and Berrechid (the most northern of the sites).[7] The information obtained is presented in Figures 3.1, 3.2, and 3.3.

In assessing these data, several essential factors must be taken into consideration. First, the farms are ranked not by size but by fiscal value. Second, the value of a farm is established by the Caisse through a formula that is to some extent determined independently for each region, and includes land, crop trees, infrastructure, and, usually, animals. (Because of the severity of the drought, animals were not counted in the southernmost region of El Bourg.) Third, the ascribed value significantly underestimates true market value, especially of land. Each hectare, depending on the region and whether it was irrigated, could, at the time of this study, vary in ascribed value between $8 and $25, with much greater actual market value. While such relative standards make comparison difficult, in fact they are no less amenable to interpretation—and are probably more accurate—than the more common farm-size standard generally used. With bank records one can search back to the actual situation and standard for valuation. In contrast, the representations of data that adorn many development studies and equate one hectare of land with another while ignoring climatic zone, soil fertility, and use, approach the meaningless. In Morocco, one hectare of good irrigated land may be worth thousands of dollars, while a hectare of poor dryland in an arid region may be almost valueless.

For immediate purposes, however, questions of absolute value were of little concern. What was most striking about the distribution curve shown by the bank records was the pronounced hiatus of loans to farms valued between 1,500 DH and 3,000 DH ($250–$500). This 1,500 DH to 3,000 DH range corresponded to the most recent (3,000 DH) and previous (1,500 DH) dividing line between farms qualifying for loans from the CLCA and CRCA. The characterization of a traditional/modern division of the Moroccan farming sector did not by itself explain the apparent lack of borrowers in this range. In addition, the dossiers revealed an unexpected fact that was not evident in the distribution: the only female recipients of loans over the long term appeared in the very large (approximately 100 ha) farm category.

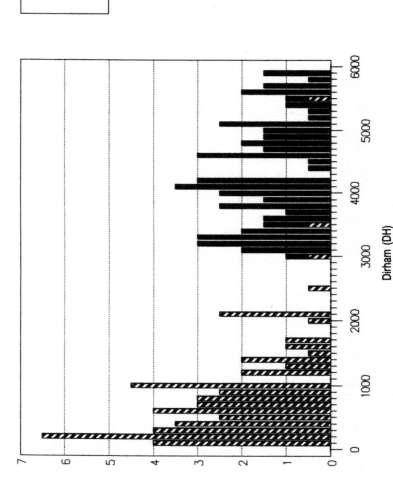

FIGURE 3.1
Distribution of CRCA and CLCA Loans in El Bourg

Frequency distribution of the declared value of 200 farms receiving credit in El Bourg (samples drawn only from a population of farms with fiscal revenue values of less than 6,000 DH). CLCA clients over 3,000 DH are new clients, denied CRCA membership under the 1983 entrance requirement of 6,000 DH. Note that El Bourg is in the lowest rainfall area of the study. Under normal circumstances farmers probably have a higher percentage of animals than in either Settat or Berrechid, but because of the severity of the drought, the Government of Morocco determined that in this area animals would not be counted for taxes.

59

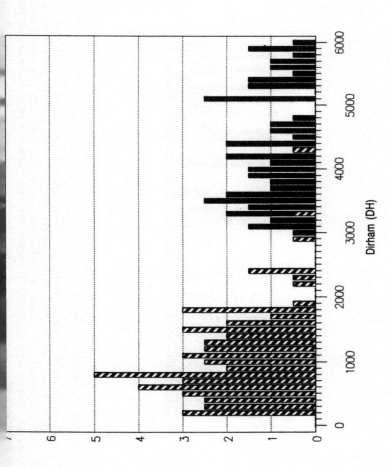

FIGURE 3.2
Distribution of CRCA and CLCA Loans in Settat

Frequency distribution of the declared value of 200 farms receiving credit in Settat (samples drawn only from a population of farms with fiscal revenue values of less than 6,000 DH). CLCA clients over 3,000 DH are new clients, denied CRCA membership under the 1983 entrance requirement of 6,000 DH. Settat is midway between El Bourg and Verrechid geographically and climatically. It has some irrigated agriculture, but much less than Berrechid. It also has a significant number of livestock that are counted for tax purposes (self-declaration of owners as to the number).

60

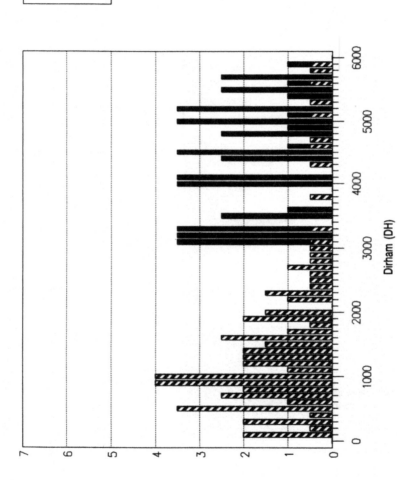

FIGURE 3.3
Distribution of CRCA and CLCA Loans in Berrechid

Frequency distribution of the declared value of 100 farms receiving credit from the Caisse Locale and 41 farms receiving credit from the Caisse Régionale (CRCA samples were weighted to equal the percentage of the 100 CLCA member sample). CLCA clients over 3,000 DH are new clients denied CRCA membership under the 1983 entrance requirement of 6,000 DH. Berrechid is the highest rainfall area of the three localities studied. It had the highest percentage of irrigated land (hard to hide from official awareness) and the lowest number of animals (at least in the immediate area).

Pursuing Reality

Research Strategy

Standard anthropological methodology is built upon a tradition of extensive collection of field data that is selectively incorporated, primarily through induction, into an explanatory theoretical construct. The severe time constraint associated with rapid appraisal provides no such luxury. At best one must shift between existing explanations and the apparent confirmation or contradictions presented by quickly retrieved data. By using selective field inquiry and highly stratified sampling, the major effort is directed toward revealing hidden factors that demand explanation, rather than attempting to obtain reliable quantification for apparent definitive resolution of outstanding questions.

Direct Survey of Farmers

Based on farmer dossiers, a representative sample that ranged from poorest to richest farmers was selected at each CRCA for field investigation. At each CLCA, I selected a random sample of farmers from among those who happened to come to the bank at that time. In both cases, bank field representatives acted as intermediaries with the loan recipients, explaining who I was and my interest, and arranging for me to accompany the various farmers back to their holdings. In addition, assisted by a local employee of an AID project in the area, I made several visits to other farms in each region. From these visits the following composite understanding of the existing situation and practices evolved.[8]

Farmers' Portrayal of the Existing Situation

Any attempt at characterizing farm types runs up against the difficulty of generalizing among many possible combinations of such variables as farmer/farm characteristics (e.g., soil fertility, water availability, family circumstances), different climatic zones (e.g., Mediterranean coastal rainfall, semiarid, arid), different production systems (e.g., irrigation, rainfed, mixed), and different product orientations (e.g., cereal, livestock, vegetables, mixed farming). Such variables shared certain consistent patterns of exploitation, however. For example, while many people had only a few hectares of land, nobody reportedly could subsist on 1 to 5 ha of rainfed land alone. Such small parcels are usually the residue of an inheritance subdivided among the heirs. The land that belonged to family members as a group could be fairly extensive. In such cases, since the members could not live off their parcels alone, they either worked elsewhere and loaned or rented their parcels to another family member or to an outsider, or, if they wished to remain farmers, augmented their parcels with additional land obtained through the same procedure. The process is consistent with the traditional Moroccan practice of farming numerous small scattered parcels, partially because of previous fragmentation through inheritance but also as a method of diversifying production in an environment where different locations and soil types yield differently, depending on the particular rainfall pattern in any given year.

With such methods in use to increase actual available land, farmers interviewed asserted that with 12-14 ha of rainfed land one could begin to make an acceptable living from farming alone, while with less land one would be obliged to supplement earnings through wage labor or assistance from others (e.g., remittances from migrant family labor). For many Moroccans, farming is a dynamic process in which an individual strives over a lifetime to build up the amount of land farmed in terms of quantity and quality to a size affording an adequate return (e.g., above 14 ha rainfed).

Farmers with 14-40 ha of land found themselves in a position of precarious but generally adequate production. The exact mix of production strategies was determined largely by the individual situation of each farmer. For example, those who had acquired the farm using earnings from other sectors tended to retain their economic involvement in the other productive sectors. In contrast, others, whose holdings reflected accumulation based primarily on agricultural production, represented the most efficient of traditional farmers who desired to concentrate more and more effort on farming and less on outside activities, as their farm capital increased. An intermediate group also existed who, after successful accumulation of farmland (e.g., up to 40 ha), would sell it at a high price during good times and then move into alternative production sectors (urban business, transport, etc.). One reason for this strategy was the already-noted qualitative difference between the larger traditional farms and truly large (90-100 ha) modern farms. The latter required almost double the land area of the largest traditional farms and a corresponding shift in management strategies from manual labor to mechanization, and from multicropping to monocropping.

As regarded agricultural credit, these middle range (14-40 ha), "potentially profitable" farms were credited under the existing system with a fiscal value of approximately 2500-10,000 DH. Thus, they found themselves straddling the cutoff point between CLCA fixed small loans and the larger CRCA credit system. At the same time, it was these producers, unlike the smaller marginal farmers, who had the minimally necessary resources to begin effective production for profit and to focus credit on specific elements that could contribute to a significant increase in production (e.g., pumps, tractors, high-yield-variety seeds). Concomitantly, such farmers seemed to have become more and more dependent on credit as a continuous resource and as part of their annual production strategy.

Analyzing Out Contradictions

The Reality Behind the Figures

Such quick surveys as that described cannot be expected (though they in fact sometimes are used) to produce such generalizable data as the real distribution of farm sizes in Morocco. What was clearly revealed, however, was that neither the hiatus in farm size shown on the CLCA and CRCA records nor the domination of the traditional sector by 1–5 hectare micro farms, shown in Tables 3.1 and 3.2, properly portrayed reality. Rather, a substantial number of middle-range farms exist in a dynamic process of growth, decay, and exchange. The immediate question was: why this divergence between reality and portrayal?

Land Tenure and Taxes

The tenure of small fragmented holdings is commonly identified as a major obstacle to improving agricultural production in Morocco. Rigid adherence to the Islamic law of inheritance is cited as the cause, exacerbated by the Moroccan tendency to have large families and the desire of many people to maintain a rural foothold for the sake of economic survival, family unity, psychological orientation, or productive investment, regardless of the actual worth of the land in question. Upon an owner's death, his holding is parceled out to his surviving spouse(s) and children, resulting in rapid fragmentation of ownership and managerial rights. Depending on how ownership claims are settled, the land itself can be divided into a number of smaller individual parcels (for use, sale, or rent); given to one party for use but not ownership; or managed as common property.

The arrangements made for use of inherited shares can be effected by either informal agreement or legal determination. Under either circumstance the potential exists for significant manipulation in terms of how the actual division of land is presented to the outside world. Thus, for example, five male sibs inheriting a 20-ha farm could present themselves to the outside world as either five 4-ha micro farms, a joint 20-ha farm, or, through official sale or lease to one of them, an individual 20-ha farm.

Such decisions have at least two appreciable consequences. First, as noted, five 4-ha farms each would qualify only for limited CLCA credit and not for larger CRCA credit, but since the division between the CLCA and CRCA clientship corresponds to liability for taxes, none of the farms would be taxed. Conversely, should the family wish access to CRCA credit, it could present the operation as a single unit, thus gaining credit at the expense of tax liability. Of course, the larger an operation the less possibility that its existence could be concealed. Such manipulation is thus limited to small- or middle-sized farms. In the case of large farms, the very nature of their management makes concealment impossible, as well as making access to substantial credit highly valuable. In fact, this seemed to be the major explanation for the existence of female clients among the largest farms serviced by the CRCA. The spouse having died, the advantage for the family was to defer any formal division among the children by keeping the entire estate in the name and trust of their mother.

Consequences for Moroccan Agricultural Policy

The situation as described raises the question of whether the perceived duality of Morocco's agricultural system represents an artificial administrative creation or a true socioeconomic division inherent in the society. To the extent the division is an artificial administrative creation, the question also arises as to whether this false portrayal has a deleterious influence on government policy, especially as regards agricultural credit. Even if it does, the question remains whether farmers have not worked out their own methods of successfully circumventing any inconveniences it seemingly creates. While no definitive answers could be given based on the limited evidence presented, viewing this situation in its historical and current sociopolitical contexts did raise issues pertinent both to the proposed project in question and to the overall strategies for the future development of the country's agricultural sector.

Historical Perspectives and Patterns

The Persistence of a Traditional Management Style. A distinctive feature of Moroccan society is the extent to which, at least for the moment, it integrates social, economic, and political systems that seem, from a Westerner's perspective, intrinsically incompatible or contradictory. Examples are: a powerful and centralized kingship with party politics and strong regional alliances; significant reliance on traditional Islamic precepts for legitimization of political and personal interests combined with the acceptance and adoption of such antithetical Western practices as consumption of alcoholic beverages, wearing of Western dress, and payment of interest on loans; the coexistence of traditional production technologies and modern industrialization; and the continued importance of regional, ethnic, and group alliances in the face of expanding urbanization and foreign migration.

Positioned at the crossroads of numerous great and often competing civilizations, and abetted by the nature of the segmentary structure of traditional tribal sociopolitical organization, Moroccan society has an old and well-developed capacity to effect the reconciliation and neutralization of counterbalancing tendencies. As is common in such segmentary systems, a major traditional mechanism for achieving stability has been to engineer repeated and opportunistic shifts in policy in order to maintain balance among opposing tendencies. Such a modus operandi can be highly effective in sustaining basic social stability as well as personal power, but it is not conducive to overall system innovation. It either encourages the maintenance of established social divisions, or it creates new divisions rather than a common union.

The Colonial Period. With colonialism the rulers changed, but in many ways the modus operandi remained the same. In the agricultural sector, when the French established colonial rule in Morocco they instituted a redivision and restructuring that persists into the present. Nomadic groups were given fixed geographic locations. Rich farmlands, especially in the coastal zones, were given to French colonists who established large and highly productive operations. The less fertile or more arid fringe and interior areas were officially assigned to members of various groups as private property for cultivation (*melk*) or as collective property primarily for livestock grazing. French strategy was to create a dynamic modern agricultural sector while providing for the indigenous population an adequate but limited subsistence base. Productive support, such as technical inputs and credits, was directed to the larger colonial farms. Support for the traditional indigenous sector was designed for political and social rather than productive reasons. In line with this was the establishment in 1928 of the already-mentioned system of Société Caisse de Prévoyance (SOCAP), which provided limited emergency loans for assorted purposes. Such loans could be used for production, but were more often used to meet sudden needs for food or medical treatment.

Post-Independence Transformations. After independence, Morocco instituted a policy of Moroccanization of French agricultural properties. Well-to-do Moroccans, with credit assistance from the government, usually procured the better French farms. These farms today represent the modern agricultural sector. The government took less desirable French lands for government operations, for the creation of farming cooperatives, or for division into small, private parcels.

The changing credit administration in this ongoing evolution of the Moroccan agricultural sector reflects the changing lending regulations of the concerned institutions. As noted, the initial cap of a fiscal value of 1,500 DH established for farms that could borrow from CLCA was later raised to 3,000 DH and, as of 1983 when this study took place, to 6,000 DH. All other clients had to use the CRCA, which provided larger loans but had significant requirements for credit history, collateral, and percent of cofinancing (e.g., 30 percent self-financing by the farmer for equipment).

The Present Situation. With the demise of the SOCAP, the only credit systems available to small and medium farmers became the CLCA and CRCA, respectively, with CLCA loans limited to 200 percent of registered fiscal value. What this meant was that while the maximum CLCA loan, as of 1983, was theoretically 12,000 DH per year, for the vast majority of its clientele the effective limit was from 600–2,000 DH ($100–$350), a sum sufficient for purchasing seeds or a few lambs for fattening, but insufficient both in amount and terms (3–4 months) for purchasing major equipment or supporting an entirely new operation (e.g., from planting through weeding to harvesting a new crop). In contrast, the CRCA, with a much larger credit line, was able to provide its clients with up to 50,000 DH for one to three years, a sum they could invest in larger fattening operations, covering the cost of both animals and feed, or in such equipment as pumps and tractors (provided they could meet the 30 percent cofinancing requirement).

In reality, therefore, by 1983 the smaller farmers were generally relegated to a system of financial assistance that helped them to survive but not to progress, while productive assistance was limited to larger operations. Though a technical opening existed for a small farmer to request a larger loan for a special project from the CRCA if he could demonstrate the financial viability of his operation, policies requiring a high percentage of cofinancing made this a difficult leap.[9] Throughout the system, differentiations seemed to function more as barriers against than as frontiers for development. Moreover, the CNCA's policy, newly established at the time of the study, of raising the amount of required fiscal revenue for CRCA participation to 6,000 DH, largely for administrative reasons, appeared destined further to exacerbate the division.

Consequences for Project Design

Conclusions and Recommendations for Project Design

Inherent in the concept of development is to change from what is perceived as a less desirable situation to a more desirable one. The change occurs in several fashions—through introducing something new, through transforming something old, or through reapportioning and repositioning existing factors within the same system. Agricultural credit can play a role in all three processes, for instance by financing the creation of new production systems (e.g., agribusiness), by financing the transformation of old production systems through the adoption of new technologies (e.g., replacing multicropping subsistence agriculture with technologically advanced specialized crop production), or by providing funds for the acquisition and operation of existing factors of production by those who otherwise lack the resources to procure or retain them (cf. Blair 1973; Gillette and Uphoff 1973; Donald 1976).

We found a group of "viable farmers in transition" suitable for assistance through the provision of agricultural credit at substantial, but still below-market, rates (e.g., 7 percent). While it was impossible to say exactly how many farmers and farms fell into this category, it seemed from the assembled information that the numbers were more than would be projected by the accepted perception of farm-size distribution (see Tables 3.1 and 3.2). On the high end of this group were those who already possessed the minimally necessary factors of production but who were stressed to the breaking point. On the low side were those who had assembled most but not all the elements required for the move from consumption to profit-oriented production (e.g., they had enough land but needed pumps or tractors, or they lacked only a few hectares, to turn the corner to profitability and permit concentrated farm management). The former needed credit to continue present profit-oriented production, the latter needed it to obtain a missing resource to cross the threshold into such production.

The best use of credit under the proposed project was seen as helping these two groups, either by aiding present agricultural producers to obtain improved technologies, or, in the majority of cases, by assisting them to maintain technologies they had already adopted but whose continued use was threatened by insufficient capitalization during the existing drought crisis. It was considered inappropriate to provide even limited subsidized assistance to those who, despite difficult circumstances, had access to sufficient reserves to continue operations on their own. Even more crucially, it was considered unwise to provide significant interest-bearing credit to those who faced a gamut of constraints on production that effectively blocked credit alone from making any substantial contribution to the ability of their production unit either to survive or to progress; the burden of interest and debt repayment might only propel them deeper into insolvency.

It was thus recommended (and accepted) that the focus of lending activity be changed from the small, poorest farms, to what the design team chose to call "viable farmers in transition." These were identified as farmers whose farms had an assigned fiscal value of 3,000–6,000 DH.

Proposals for Future Studies

Proposals for future studies made in the context of a project design are often seen as a variant of George Bernard Shaw's famous line (in *Maxims for Revolutionists*): "He who can, does. He who cannot, teaches [studies]." Studies can be the elephants' graveyard of ideas. At the same time, future changes in policy and practice depend on decision makers' accepting new ideas and studies perceived as relevant. Thus, if properly done and effectively presented, studies can influence policy. In the context of this project, in addition to specific recommendations for immediate changes in design, the following series of studies, to be done during the life of the project, was proposed:

1. *Farmers in Transition.* Since it was proposed that the major focus of credit be to help farmers for whom credit was a decisive factor in becoming or remaining profitable, a major policy concern was the extent to which those farmers were disadvantaged by policies that tended to tailor assistance to the different circumstances of two very divergent systems: the traditional small farmer and the modern large farmer. Most importantly, these policies appeared to be self-reinforcing, as taxation and loans are designed to correspond to statistics that become self-fulfilling prophesies. A specific effort therefore seemed in order to remedy this situation by identifying and demonstrating the true importance of such farm operations, their unique needs, and the extent to which current credit practices either failed to respond to, or actually aggravated, their problems.

2. *Banking Strategies for Semiarid Lands.* It is widely accepted that the traditional farmer in semiarid regions is oriented toward risk avoidance. His strategy emphasizes minimal needs rather than profit. He responds to the expectation of cyclical years of drought by storing several years' grain for both consumption and seed, for instance, and he is extremely flexible in switching his production strategy as events unfold (e.g., deciding to turn a cereal crop into fodder by allowing animals onto planted fields if rains do not seem promising). In contrast, existing banking practices required a farmer to plan ahead of time how he would use his money (e.g., a crop or animal loan); did not provide quick access to new funds if conditions changed; demanded repayment of crop loans soon after harvest when prices were usually at their lowest; required that previous loans be repaid before granting new ones, even though agricultural production activities might overlap; and charged fixed interest rates regardless of the productive situation.

None of these banking practices is inherently necessary. A special revolving fund and a limited increase in loan limit could be provided for overlapping production periods. Crop loans could be extended. An open line of credit could be given to proven clients. Even flexible interest rates that adjust with climatic conditions are a possibility. The important point is that the unique demands of arid-land agriculture should give rise to specially adapted credit policies.

3. *Regionally Appropriate Policies and Norms.* The need for the CNCA to adapt more flexible policies to its clients seemed, to some extent, related to its need to allow more discretion to its own subdivisions. Given tremendous regional variations in income level, land productivity, and production types, there seemed little justification, beyond administrative expediency, for establishing national norms for access to credit and maximum levels for individual borrowers. It was recommended that a study be conducted to identify important regional variations and to determine how practices could be modified to take them into account.

4. *Possible Uses of Credit for Land Consolidation and Reform.* In some northern European countries, credit programs have been used to help consolidate fragmented and micro farms (Ytterborn 1956). Morocco remains paralyzed in its inability to effect such needed land consolidation. A careful study of experiences in other countries and their applicability to the Moroccan situation could provide new ideas for dealing with this problem.

5. *Use of Credit for Collective Lands.* In Morocco, a significant amount of land, especially rangeland but also land under cultivation, is the collective property of one or more groups or communities. Increasingly, the productive use of such lands has been frustrated by the difficulty of establishing individual rights and obligations within a collective arrangement, and of getting people to invest in collective resources. When development of such land has taken place, often the better off and more powerful have taken advantage of the situation to expropriate an unfair share of the resources. Ways of addressing this problem other than complete privatization of the land are possible. Credit, for example for improvement of common rangeland, might be used as a mechanism for clarifying individual rights in a collective context, and for assisting poorer community members to obtain a share of the action.

6. *Credit for Micro Farms.* When all is said and done, the stark reality remains that little productive assistance is available to the smallest and poorest of farmers in Morocco. Moreover, experience has shown that single-focused interventions of credit or technical inputs that do not assure access by these operators to all the necessary components of the proposed activities, or that have not been adequately tested in their specific environment, may result in a further deterioration of the situation. Many Moroccan farmers have experienced reduced production due to the inappropriate use of a recommended fertilizer under drought conditions, for example.

Helping the micro farmer is a major challenge, and one that probably must follow applied technical and social research. A possible activity at this time would be the establishment of a system for tracking ongoing research so that an appropriate credit package could be rapidly assembled and tested as soon as new technological possibilities arise.

7. *Women in Agriculture.* As part of the proposal for the project, it was suggested that a special action be undertaken to study the role of women in Moroccan agriculture and possibilities for assisting them with credit. One indicator of the immediate need for such assistance was the very fact that the proposed project itself dealt entirely with men. The reason for this was not explicitly discriminatory practices against women by the CRCAs and CLCAs. In fact, as previously noted, the one area of somewhat substantial and continual provision of credit to women by the CRCA was in the higher category of large modern farms of 80 to 100+ ha. The predominant reason seemed to be that while women may in fact inherit property, the social and organizational realities of rural Moroccan society determine that such property be officially given to, or managed by, men, either male relatives or male renters or sharecroppers. The few women who appear on the CLCA and lower-echelon CRCA loan records took loans for only one or two years, after the death of a spouse, but thereafter apparently made other arrangements. The exceptions, as noted, were widows of large farm owners who have some adequate combination of funds to hire necessary help, the education and knowledge to manage the operation, the social influence to obtain their share of needed inputs, and children sufficiently oriented to modern urban professions that they would rather hold the farm together as a large family operation than split it into individual holdings.

Even though the lower echelon of rural women did not occupy a significant position as official titleholders or heads of families, they were a major and increasing percentage of the rural agricultural labor force, and, especially on transitional farms, appeared to be assuming more de facto daily managerial roles as male absence for urban earning activities was increasing. Thus, it seemed inadequate to consider the possibilities of more focused use of credit for farm activities without better understanding the production system from the perspective of such women. In fact, the greatest opportunities for quick and simple interventions to raise the productivity of the poorest farms may be precisely in those activities, such as poultry, that are traditionally women's responsibilities (see Mernissi 1982–1983).

The Politics of Acceptance

At the beginning of this chapter, the claim was made that the factors influencing decision making as regards the design and approval of development projects are, in reality, often different from and sometimes quite the reverse of those portrayed. If the recommenders of technical modifications in project designs are willing to work with this reality in mind, their recommendations can have a substantial positive effect.

In fact, the recommendations made in this case were accepted in the final project design. This acceptance can be explained as follows. The top priority was the immediate provision of assistance. The recommendations for change did not threaten this goal. The Moroccans themselves were predominantly concerned with acquiring a bundle of recapitalization funds from various donors and were therefore amenable to AID's directing its contribution to any particular group so long as it was a legitimate constituency in the eyes of the government. AID itself felt caught between conflicting policies that stressed aiding the poorest of the poor, requiring realistic interest on loans, collaborating with other donors, and encouraging private enterprise.

While the recommendations took exception to the originally expressed project intentions, they substituted a legitimate and acceptable series of alternative justifications that seemed able to resolve some of the outstanding contradictions. Thus, since credit to the poorest farmers really served more as social than productive assistance, it seemed legitimate to refrain from making them the focus of this particular AID effort. In addition, the suggested new orientation seemed to resolve the initially perceived contradiction between proposed EEC loans at 2 percent and U.S. loans at a recommended 7 percent, as long as EEC funds went to the poorer CLCA clients (which it was determined they would).

The suggested long-term studies represented potential openings to major policy dialogues on future activities. Since they had been generated from discussions with various bank personnel, as well as farmers, and presented possibilities for the newly revised CNCA research division, they were not seen as imposed but rather had an indigenous support constituency (though mainly among mid-level technical rather than higher-level administrative personnel). Since the studies were not to be done by independent consultants but as CNCA research with necessary outside expertise, they were perceived by bank personnel as efforts to increase the bank's sophistication rather than as remedies. Such subtle differences can be quite important. For example, several bank personnel reacted negatively to any suggestion that Morocco had much to learn about agricultural credit from sub-Saharan Africa, which they perceived as incomparably further behind Morocco in banking practices, but the idea of studying Scandinavian experience in using credit to consolidate small farms seemed interesting. Lastly, since they were to be funded from "free" U.S. grant funds, and since they were packaged as the "intellectual software" part of an institution-building effort that would include the IBM computers that CNCA central administrators wanted, the total package was acceptable.

Conclusion

Both the practice of development activities and the policies that guide and justify them inevitably involve assumption and compromise. Such assumptions and compromises are the operative representations of the dichotomy between the ideal and real that characterizes all human life. This case has shown how understanding the relationship between the ideal and real, in terms of divergences between official policies for providing agricultural credit to Moroccan farmers, and on-the-ground Moroccan farm-management strategies, was further complicated because past highly skewed portrayals of that reality had become officially accepted ideations that colored both analytical understandings and the actual rules for declaring official farm ownership. Anthropologists and anthropological approaches can play a major role in unraveling and clarifying the complexities of such interrelationships. They can have direct positive impacts on future projects and policies as long as the concerned analytical practitioners and policy implementers are willing to match their own ideations as to how development activities should be generated against the reality of how development activities are determined.

Notes

1. Particularly used in this research were various unpublished studies by Paul Pascon and his associated researchers at Morocco's Hassan II University.

2. Basic family consumption is not equatable with subsistence. For example, education for children is typically regarded by even poor farm families as a fundamental and necessary expense, though not a subsistence need.

3. In most cases these farms are found on land originally confiscated by the French during the colonial period and given to French settlers. After independence these former French farms were sold or parceled out to selected parties.

4. The CRCA agents generally shared this perception and expressed the opinion that under circumstances such as drought the problem becomes more sociopolitical than financial. Even if they wanted to collect on loans, the Ministry of Interior, to maintain civil peace, would probably—and from its perspective quite properly—not cooperate.

5. A common problem of foreign assistance is the extent to which aid is tied to the purchase of donor-country equipment. One measure of a receiving nation's sophistication in using foreign assistance is its ability to manipulate such constraints. In the case in point, AID was not as interested in contributing commodities, which could be obtained from other funding sources, as in improving the bank's basic institutional capacities through training and policy analysis. Moroccan bank managers particularly wanted money from AID for computers, however, because they wanted to establish IBM PCs as their standard system and feared that if they had to obtain funds from a European donor, they would be required to use a European manufacturer. By receiving U.S. money they would also avoid arguments with partisans of other brands by claiming they were required to buy IBM.

6. This concern is shared by mid-level personnel in most large organizations. It also indicates why institution-building exercises agreed upon by top management may often be counterproductive with respect to the actual needs of lower-echelon personnel.

7. In terms of the possibilities and usefulness of rapid appraisal, such specific, valuable information was obtainable only through the extraordinary cooperation of local bank personnel and because the research was perceived as part of a joint effort to provide positive assistance to the organization. I doubt such records would have been made available for pure research regardless of the length of stay of the researcher. On the other hand, the rapidity of the study meant that I was provided only one opportunity to request information and was unable to obtain additional information on questions that arose after subsequent analysis.

8. The methodology as practiced in this case consists of the following crucial components: (1) being introduced or accompanied by someone in whom those interviewed have confidence but by whom they are not intimidated; (2) always explaining my presence in a way that seemed to make sense but did not indicate what I might want to hear; (3) speaking to people in an environment and at a time when they feel comfortable and in control—as much as possible this meant in their own home, during and after a meal or some other form of hospitality that they have offered; (4) after any formal interviewing, engaging in some less structured situation, such as a walk around the farm during which a few additional critical questions could be asked in a very off-hand way; (5) never asking questions that were clearly too personal or sensitive given the setting; and (6) constantly trying to verify what others have said, especially if their answer was what I would have liked to hear. (This last technique also involves making clear to any person assisting you as translator that you are not as dumb as you seem when you repeatedly ask the same question.)

9. Other areas of agricultural policy hindered the effective use of credit by the small farmer. For example, agricultural research and extension in Morocco focused almost exclusively on technological matters directly relevant to the needs of modern, especially irrigated agriculture. There did not seem to be a developed technical package for small traditional farmers that could be recommended and financed with any confidence of success.

References

AID
  1975 AID Handbook 3, Part 1, Secs 4-1, 4-5, 5-11, 5A-D. September 1. Washington, DC: U.S. Agency for International Development.

Benatya, D., P. Pascon, L. Zagdouni, and O. Magoul
  1983 L'Agriculture en situation aléatoire Chaouia 1977-1982. Rabat: INAV.

Blair, H. W.
  1973 The Political Economy of Distributing Agricultural Credit and Benefits. Cornell Rural Development Occasional Paper No. 3. Pp. 39-56.

Bouarfa, M.
  1982 Fondements d'une nouvelle stratégie pour le financement par le crédit agricole de l'agriculture traditionnelle. Revue Morocaine de droit et d'économie du développement No. 2.

Donald, G.
  1976 Credit for Small Farmers in Developing Countries. Boulder, CO: Westview Press.

El Mesmoudi, T.
  1982 Le Crédit Agricole. Rabat: SMER.

Gillette, C., and N. Uphoff
  1973 Cultural and Social Factors Affecting Small Farmer Participation in Formal Credit Programs. Cornell University Rural Development Occasional Paper No.3. Pp. 1-37.

Kingdom of Morocco
  1983 Staff Appraisal Report, Fifth Agricultural Credit Project. Washington, DC: World Bank. November 22.

Lahcen, G.
1981   Le Crédit agricole en zone semi-arid: cas de Rommani. *In* Mémoire de 3ème cycle. Rabat: INAV.

Masmoudi, M. T.
1983   Rôle du crédit agricole dans le développement de l'agriculture: cas du Maroc. Revue Marocaine de droit et d'économie du développement No.2. Pp 151–160.

Mernissi, F.
1982–1983   Women and the Impact of Capital Development in Morocco. Feminist Issues 2(2) and 3(1):69–104.

MIAC (MidAmerica International Agricultural Consortium Dryland Farming Team)
1977   A Report: Applied Agronomic Research Program for Dryland Farming in 200–400 mm Rainfall Zone of Morocco Directed to the Small Farmer. Settat, Morocco: Centre Régional de la Recherche Agronomique. January.

Partridge, W., ed.
1984   Training Manual in Development Anthropology. American Anthropological Association Special Publication No. 17.

USAID/Rabat
1984   Morocco Drought Recovery Credit Project Paper. Project 608-0184. November.

Van de Kloet, H.
1975   Inégalités dans les milieux ruraux: possibilités et problèmes de la modernisation agricole au Maroc. Genève: UNRISD.

World Bank
1983   Staff Appraisal Report, Kingdom of Morocco. Fifth Agricultural Credit Project.

Ytterborn, G. R.
1956   Tenure Issues in Scandinavian Countries. *In* Conference on World Land Tenure. Land Tenure, Proceedings of the Conference. Kenneth H. Parsons, Raymond Penn, and Philip Raup, eds. Madison, WI: University of Wisconsin Press.

Zagdouni, L.
1981   Le mécanisation agricole, cas de la Haute Chaouia. Rabat: INAV.

4

Water-User Associations in Rural Central Tunisia

Nicholas S. Hopkins

The Problem

Because they have inadequate water resources, people in rural Central Tunisia must either devote considerable time and energy to hauling water to their homes or migrate seasonally or permanently from the area. USAID and Tunisian government authorities determined in 1980 that it was technically and socially possible to improve the potable water supply by both modernizing existing water points and creating new ones. Data on this process, generated through anthropologically informed research over the years, provide the basis for an analysis of conceptual and policy implications of potable water development. The issue is not only to create the necessary infrastructure but also to institutionalize the social organization needed to ensure that the dispersed rural populations have continued access to potable water. The creation of water-user associations (WUAs) that would have decision-making authority over wells and other water points was proposed by the anthropologist as the solution to this problem.

The Area

The area known administratively as Central Tunisia largely corresponds to the Governorate of Kasserine, although at various times parts of adjacent governorates have been added to this core and parts of Kasserine have been omitted. Geographically the area, called the High Steppes, is mostly south of, or astride, the Dorsal, the central range of the Tunisian Atlas that runs from southwest to northeast (see Sethom and Kassab 1981:105–123). The whole area is essentially high plateau ranging from 500 to a little over 1,000 meters above sea level, with the town of Kasserine itself at 676 meters, and other towns ranging from Sbeitla at 525 meters to Thala at 1,017 meters. Rural areas may be higher still. Tunisia's highest mountain, Jebel Chambi, at 1,544 meters, dominates Kasserine. A few streams in the area run year-round but carry little water in summer. Winter rains, conversely, often lead to floods. Annual rainfall is low, generally between 200 and 400 mm, but with considerable variation within and between years, and from one location to another. Kasserine governorate has a population of around 300,000, two-thirds of it rural, and most of this rural population lives outside "rural agglomerations" (*douars* or hamlets); it is one of the least densely populated areas of Tunisia.

Natural water points usable in the dry summer months are scarce. They consist of springs and some old wells said to be of Roman origin. In more recent times, water resources for irrigation have been developed, either by the digging of shallow wells or the drilling of deep ones; the water from these new irrigation wells is also used domestically. Some of the groundwater resources of the area have been tapped for the use of such coastal urban centers as Sfax. For instance, most of the large flow from springs near Sbeitla, which once supported a major Roman town, has been piped to Sfax since around 1910.

Before the colonial period, the people of Central Tunisia were nomadic pastoralists, specializing in sheep and goats. Their normal cycle took them into the cereal-producing lands of northern Tunisia during the summer, where they helped with the harvest in exchange for grain (Monchicourt 1913:365–389), and into the High Steppes in winter when the pasture was at its best. This cycle was interrupted by the economic and sociogeographical changes of the colonial period, particularly the appropriation of the best cereal lands by colonial farmers who introduced machinery after 1925 and so no longer needed as many extra hands to reap, thresh, and transport the wheat and barley. These changes ended the seasonal migration to the north, forced the sedentarization of the pastoralists, and obliged them to explore ways to produce their own grain under less advantageous conditions.

The local dry-farming economy is now a sometimes precarious mixture of cultivation of cereals (wheat or barley) with livestock raising (sheep, goats, and cattle), and, occasionally, tree crops. It is viable only because most households have access to other income, through government employment, commercial activity, or migration to jobs in coastal Tunisia and abroad. People remain on the land, however, and remain attached to it, often explaining that they prefer to live on their own land where they are beholden to no one and live free. That the original tribal or communal lands were progressively allocated to individuals or families also accounts for the highly dispersed settlement pattern. House sites have rarely been chosen to maximize access to water points. Instead, people typically prefer to live "on their own land" some distance away, and they also commonly choose sites on well-drained slopes rather than on the flat bottomlands where drainage may be poor but where drilled wells would be more likely to be successful. The farms are small. Zghidi (1978:25) estimated that in the Hababsa zone (Rohia delegation of Siliana governorate), 60 percent of the households held less than the level of 25 hectares of rainfed land needed to ensure household viability. In the Bnanna II zone of Foussana delegation

(Kasserine governorate), 97 percent of land titles recorded in 1974 and 1976 were for less than 20 hectares (Hopkins 1978).

The smaller holders, especially those holding under 30 or 40 hectares, are subsistence farmers oriented to strategies of low risk/low gain. The peasant household is above all interested in survival. The way to survive is to keep expenses down, and such households rarely risk investing in improved agricultural techniques. The Hababsa survey in the early 1970s found that 56 percent of the farmers had no direct expenses for agriculture at all (Zghidi 1978). Such households rarely hire labor, and in fact are likely to assign some of their members to outside wage labor, including even migratory wage labor.

Most of the people in the area under discussion belong to one of two major tribal confederations: the Majeur in the eastern part of the area and the Freshish in the west. To the north are the Ouled Ayar, and to the south the Hammama. These confederations themselves are broken into constituent parts, the *'arsh*, and these into *fariq*, both of which even nowadays generally live contiguously, though the clustering is very loose. The various levels of tribe are articulated through a patrilineal idiom. People are aware of tribal affiliations, speak of them, perhaps marry according to them, certainly reside according to them, and elect members of parliament according to them. Patterns of local cooperation among closely related households, which blur distinctions between households, are clearly a strategy of survival, since they spread the risk while sharing the work. The policy of the state since independence, however, has been to ignore tribal links, preferring to create new bases for social solidarity and cooperation. These links are part of the social patrimony of the people of Central Tunisia, but it is uncertain what would happen if an effort were made to use them as a basis for development.

Irrigation modifies the ecological base. A number of substantial irrigated perimeters in the area, under one or another form of state control, range from colonial farms taken over by the state after independence and run as state farms, to new irrigated zones created by the state on the basis of a deep well and allotted to small and medium farmers (Zghal 1967). Throughout the area private farmers have also discovered places where water is near enough to the surface to warrant a private shallow well; here they have established irrigated farms specializing in fruits and vegetables. This pattern is best established in Sidi Bou Zid, just to the south of the area considered in this study (cf. Bessis et al. 1956; Ferchiou 1985).

The Intervention

In the mid-1970s USAID began to take a special interest in Central Tunisia as a place in which to try out various approaches to rural development. Part of the rationale for doing so was an effort to find a role for USAID in a Tunisia that was rapidly becoming too prosperous in the overall sense to qualify for aid. The argument was that Central Tunisia represented the backward interior of the country, whose poverty stood in glaring contrast to the impressive developments on the coast. Calculation of per capita income for Central Tunisia showed that the level of poverty was sufficient to justify continued aid. Furthermore, it was judged politically useful to show concern for this area whose inhabitants often complained of neglect by contrast with the coastal strip.[1]

Plans were well under way by 1978, and a preliminary social-soundness analysis was carried out by anthropologist Carole Steere Ayad that summer (Ayad 1978), one of a series of studies that included one on the role of pastoral nomadism and another on the social soundness of proposed dryland farming interventions (Hopkins 1978). Also, in May 1978, a Project Paper for the "Siliana Rural Centers Water Systems" was prepared; this project in an area north of Central Tunisia in the "High Tell" geographical zone was aimed at helping the National Water Company (Société Nationale de l'Exploitation et de la Distribution des Eaux or SONEDE) in developing or improving water-supply systems in a number of small- and medium-sized communities in Siliana governorate. The intervention considered in this chapter began in May 1980, when a project paper for the "CTRD Rural Potable Water Project" was elaborated and became the basis of a USAID activity. On 10 July 1980 the agreement between the Tunisian and American governments was signed. By this time the main thrust of the project was to help the newly formed Central Tunisia Development Authority (CTDA, or, in French, Office du Développement de la Tunisie Centrale, ODTC).

The agreement between the two governments (known as the "Fifth Amendment") described the project as follows:

> This subproject is aimed at (1) improving the access to potable water of the rural, predominantly dispersed, population of the project area, including as many of the most disadvantaged as possible; (2) testing and demonstrating under Central Tunisia conditions lower-cost technologies for providing potable water to dispersed populations; and (3) encouraging the CTDA to undertake water activities at sites selected through the application of an agreed set of criteria.

The document then goes on to spell out the criteria for potable water interventions, and stresses the importance of taking health concerns into consideration.

Access to potable water was to be improved under the project by improving a certain number of existing water points—capturing springs, cleaning and motorizing old wells—and by drilling and motorizing new wells in areas where no other source of potable water is conveniently available.[2] The drilling of new wells in particular was to serve as an occasion to demonstrate the use of lower-cost technologies previously unfamiliar in Tunisia. In practice this meant the introduction of a truck-mounted drill, the TH-60, and the suggestion that well sites should be chosen with respect to population distribution and the likelihood of water being available at accessible depths, rather than solely in response to political pressures.

The elaboration of a Central Tunisia Potable Water Policy reflects the desire to apply a more rational planning methodology to the controlled use of the present and potential water resources of Central Tunisia.[3] A Potable Water Policy was prepared by the CTDA with technical assistance provided by staff from the Regional Planning and Area Development Project located at the University of Wisconsin (see University of Wisconsin 1981). The policy, designed to help the CTDA plan potable water interventions to support the regional development strategy for Central Tunisia, includes considerations to ensure water availability throughout the year, to help those with least access first, to ensure Ministry of Public Health responsibility for health education and sanitation activities, and to incorporate the CTDA as program manager. It also contains a detailed analysis of site-selection criteria, including distance/access, number of beneficiaries, cost, quantity and quality of water, drainage, proximity to other public services, accessibility, and possible damage to archaeological and historical sites. Finally a detailed site-selection methodology was spelled out to take into consideration "extant demographic, topographical and hydrogeological factors." The methodology also specified a role for beneficiaries as participants in the selection process and postulated that the selection of sites might reflect both administrative (governmental) and social (traditional social organizational) configurations to avoid rivalry over control of sites.

Most of the 48 first-phase interventions, including 18 springs, 14 shallow wells, and 16 drilled wells, were completed and brought into use in the two years following the interim evaluation of August 1983. The average number of beneficiaries appears to be over 1,000 persons per site—highest for the drilled wells, lowest for the improved springs.

My own involvement in the potable water project began with the interim evaluation of the first phase in September 1983. At that time, working with hydrologist William Turner and a team of Tunisian interviewers, I investigated the sites where work had been completed or was under way. It turned out that one of the gaps in the initial design was in the area of management of the water points that would be created or improved. Other potable water projects had attempted to use simple technology, and they often had not worked; in some cases the hand pumps had been vandalized (Potts 1983). This project foresaw the use of motors to pump water, and so would be more complicated to run, thereby making all the more necessary the encouragement of some kind of community involvement in managing these sites. Thus one of our key recommendations in the evaluation report was that the users of each water point should be organized into water-user associations that would accept some of the responsibility for running the site.

USAID and the CTDA began to put this recommendation into action by hiring a Tunisian consultant to work with the water users to create such associations. A survey of Tunisian willingness to join in water-user associations was carried out, with results indicating overwhelming support (Smith 1985). Then in 1985, I was able to return to the area with the design team for the project paper for the next phase of the project. Working with this team, and drawing on the experiences of the Tunisian consultant, I drafted more elaborate plans for the water-user associations. The task was to design a plan that would be concrete enough to satisfy funders and other skeptics, but that would leave plenty of flexibility for local initiative. This idea was readily accepted by many USAID and Tunisian officials, who had come to see this kind of decentralization as a useful experiment or model. The water-user associations did not spring into life overnight, however. For one thing, the legal institutional structure was missing; an appropriate text eventually required an act of the National Assembly and the signature of the president.

In our 1985 design, we had also called for the creation of a special office within the CTDA, which eventually became known as the Unité d'Autogestion, and which would act as a support service for the water-user associations. This office was staffed and began its work in early 1987, taking over the task from the Tunisian consultant—the first office in the CTDA specifically oriented to human relations (as opposed to engineering or agriculture). During the period since the design, I have made several visits to Central Tunisia to work with my Tunisian counterparts. In contrast to the work in 1983 and 1985 when my duty involved direct contact with the rural population to ascertain desires, needs, and likely reactions, my present assignment is to advise the Unité d'Autogestion on how to carry out its tasks of support and guidance. I have also helped design training programs for Unité members.

Overall, this involvement over a five-year period represents a case where an anthropologist, working in a team with engineers and others, was able to put forward an idea for an institutional innovation, and then to follow that idea through the early stages of its realization. Much of the information in this paper represents the early stage of this work, particularly the 1983 evaluation and the 1985 project design. Since the project is ongoing, the journey is not yet over, and this account is provisional.

Case Studies

The case studies described here clarify the reasons for the policy choices. They are selected from the completed operations included in the first phase, and include one improved well, two improved springs, and three drilled wells (see Figure 4.1). Each case has its own social and geographical features, so that the "same" intervention does not always have the same effects. The interventions affected how people hauled water as well as the hygiene of the water points. They inspired the creation of new communities of interest around newly created resources, and, indeed, changed the whole political economy of water (cf. Hopkins and Turner 1983).

1. *Bir Guerguera* is in the Rakhmat sector of Sbeitla delegation. Here an old well showing traces of Roman construction is located in a broad plain surrounded by low hills. The water table is about 65 meters below the surface. Prior to improvement, the local people drew water from the well

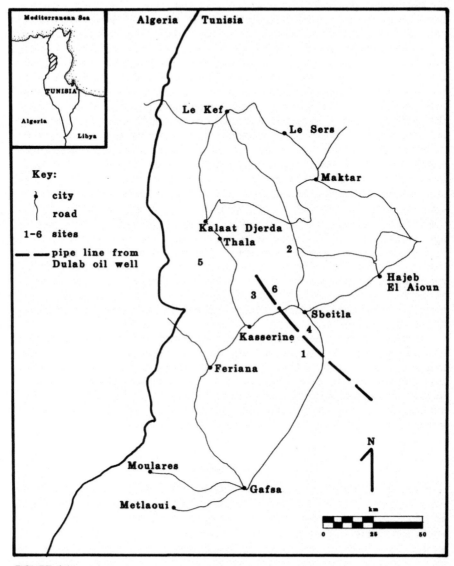

FIGURE 4.1
Central Tunisia, Showing Locations of Six Case Studies. *Source:* Adapted from Tactical Pilotage Chart (TPC), Series 2201, Sheet 3, Edition 4. US Army: September 1969. Prepared by Peter Daly.

1. Bir Guerguera
2. Ain Smiria
3. Ain Zawiyet Ben Ammar
4. Henchir Ali Majnoun
5. Um Fadgha
6. Mazreq ash-Shams

by a technique (*dellu*) in which a donkey pulls a bucket from the well using a rope run over a pulley. This laborious process required at least two people, usually men or boys. Improvement consisted in installing a motor to lift the water, adding a reservoir to store the water, and constructing a public tap and animal trough to provide public access. The initial impression of the people around this site (in 1983) was that while access to the water had been improved because of the motor, and there was an advantage in that one person could now fetch water alone, these advantages were to a great extent cancelled out by the increased crowds that the new installations attracted. Much of the water was hauled home using 500-liter mobile tanks drawn by donkeys.

By summer 1985, the other new wells in the area had been completed, and the pressure of demand was decreased at this site. One of the new drilled wells (Rakhmat) was about one kilometer away and included a standpipe suitable for filling 500- to 3,000-liter tankers, the latter tractor drawn. However, the pump operator was under instruction to collect a modest sum (intended to defray fuel costs) from people to fill their tankers, and this persuaded some to continue to use Bir Guerguera. The Rakhmat well was also pumping water to a public tap and trough (free access) on a hill some three kilometers away. In 1985 the main complaint of the Bir Guerguera pump operator was that the ground was too rocky for an irrigated garden.

2. *Ain Smiria* is a captured spring at the edge of a small wadi near Sbiba. Water is fed into a tap and animal trough about 100 meters from the spring. Most of the users, if not all, are from the settlement of Ain Smiria, and bear the lineage name of Smiri, thus forming a "natural" community. They live on a series of small ridges that run down from the mountain toward the plain of Sbiba where the irrigated perimeter is located, and the spring is in a cleft between two of these ridges. Many of the men work in the irrigated area, either as farmers or as laborers. That the community is electrified is due to its proximity to the paved road and to the town of Sbiba itself (about 3 kilometers away). Half the households interviewed here had television sets, compared with only 10 percent throughout the region.

The people of Ain Smiria took their water from the spring both before and after the intervention. In general they recognized an improvement in the quality of the water, as well as somewhat easier access, but remained convinced that the capture of the spring resulted in reduced flow. Most water was hauled by teenage girls, sometimes using donkeys, sometimes carrying a single jerrycan with a tumpline around the forehead to support the weight. The spring was definitely a "feminine" spot, and the women and girls scattered whenever a man approached it. In 1985 the spring was reportedly no longer in use.

Ain Smiria has other springs and wells, but they tend to have a minuscule flow or salty water. Some families send their teenage boys to a drilled well, almost certainly intended for irrigation in the perimeter; here the atmosphere is masculine, and water may be hauled in larger containers including mobile tanks. Women sometimes take their washing down to the irrigated area where they use water drawn from the open irrigation canals; some animals also are watered at the canals. This case illustrates the ability of people to discriminate and choose among a range of possible water sources, valued according to their usefulness for different tasks and perhaps according to whether the family has a girl or a boy available to fetch the water. Perhaps also for this reason, in 1983 Ain Smiria reported a large variety of types of containers used to fetch water.

3. *Ain Zawiyet Ben Ammar* is in the hills northwest of Sbeitla, near the border between Sbeitla and Foussana delegations. The spring stands halfway up the slope of a hill, and the users live in 45 to 50 dispersed homesteads in the valley below. There is a shrine nearby, and the government has also built some housing, a school, and a small dispensary, in the hope of collecting the population together—a vain hope, since more than half the houses remain vacant. The work here consisted in capturing the spring (or rather recapturing it, since some work had been done under the French), and feeding it into a reservoir with a single tap. Users can fill their containers here, and the overflow goes into an animal trough. As in many cases, however, the proximity of animals to the water points creates a hygiene problem. The animals include flocks of sheep and goats, and also the donkeys used to haul the water home. They inevitably produce feces and urine, which mingle with the mud caused by splashing water to make a fine mess.

The water economy here is complicated. Most users use the water from this spring only for drinking and cooking. Because the spring is on a slope, the tankers of various kinds do not have access to it. The usual method of hauling water from Ain Zawiya is thus by donkey, at 40 liters per donkey trip. The tractor-drawn tankers go to a nearby water point known as Ain Swisifa, from which they deliver loads of 3,000 liters for 6 or 7 dinars (1985) to each household cistern, to be used for washing, watering animals, and so on. Some households also have storage tanks for rainfall.

4. *Henchir Ali Majnoun* is in the Garas al-Hamra sector of Sbeitla delegation, about half a dozen kilometers from Bir Guerguera. This was the first of the drilled wells to enter into operation, and it drew users from a variety of water points in the area, including a public tap near the Oued Miaou and another at Sebbala Ouled Asker, while others were drawing water from a public irrigation system. The well is situated where a dirt track crosses a *oued*, and serves an area roughly forming a circle with a radius of several kilometers.

Because of the distance that people must go for water, most are equipped with mobile donkey-drawn tanks holding typically 500 liters. Two implications of this system are: (a) Most households have a cistern (*majen*) in the ground near the house for storing the water brought by the mobile tanks. The water consumed remains only as clean as the majen. (b) Fetching water with a mobile tank is essentially a job for men and boys. If the atmosphere at the Henchir Ali Majnoun is dominated by males, then even nearby households will be reluctant to send females to fetch water. With the new well· the average distance for hauling water was reduced from around 5–8 kilometers to around 1–4.

5. *Um Fadgha* is northwest of Foussana town in Foussana delegation. The original civil engineering works were delayed when some local people protested that to place the reservoir and public tap next to the well site would make it too far from the principal population that was to be served. As a result a two-kilometer pipeline was laid to a new site for the reservoir, somewhat closer to the houses of those who complained. The well and the reservoir sites are in a broad plain that slopes down to the Oued Hatab, and are located a few meters from a dirt track that parallels a railroad line. Traditional water points included some springs in the hills overlooking the plain, and the Oued Hatab itself. The springs are difficult of access and frequently have too many users, especially in the summer. The Oued Hatab water can be used for animals, but the people use it for themselves only as a last resort.

Because people largely obtained their water from springs located in the hills, the donkey-drawn mobile tank was not as common here in 1983 as in the two previous cases. Most people used donkeys with a pair of barrels or jerrycans. The water haulers were generally teenage girls who accompanied the donkeys, and any animals that needed to be watered, to such mountain springs as Deshrat Sidi Bou Ghanem. There in the summer time they had to use several smaller containers to fill their barrels or jerrycans, first using a dipper to fill a bucket, then climbing out of the spring area to the waiting donkey to empty the bucket into the barrel.

By 1985 the well and the pipeline were functional. The standpipe for tankers is near the well, and the reservoir was being used by teenage girls who filled barrels, then rolled them home. Cleanliness of the site was a problem because of its use for watering animals. Local users complained of the low water flow. (This well had one of the lowest flows on the project, and although it fell within the original guidelines, it apparently failed to meet local expectations.)

6. *Mazreq ash-Shams* is a drilled well on the plain northwest of Sbeitla serving a wide area of dispersed habitat. Water is normally fetched by means of 3,000-liter tractor-drawn tankers, with some 500-liter donkey-drawn tankers. At home the water is stored in cisterns. The smaller tankers are filled by means of hoses from the storage tank, while the larger ones are filled from a standpipe that functions only when the motor is running. The convention is that those who require the standpipe have to pay a small fee: sometimes they pay in fuel taken from the tractor and given to the pump operator, corresponding to the cost of pumping the water. Many of those who fetch water in this way deliver it for money in their home areas.

The sheikh for this area lives some distance away, and corresponds to the group known as Ouled Dabbab or Dabbaba, a branch of the Majeur tribe. Most users of this water point come from subgroups of the Ouled Dabbab, but some are members of other groups, such as Ouled Moussa and Haraiz. The Abidat, who live on the first slopes of the hill above the plain, are one of the subgroups of Ouled Dabbab. Their houses are strung out in a line on this slope, and they are said to number about 1,000 people. The Abidat now haul water from the new Mazreq ash-Shams well, but previously had to go much farther. The area seems relatively prosperous, perhaps because of a high proportion of migrants to Tunis and outside Tunisia as far as Iraq.

One issue here is that the well provides around 25 liters per second (l/s), a flow of water considerably above the maximum of 5 foreseen by the project, producing a "surplus." Some people use this resource to irrigate orchards or to water their flocks—the latter foreseen, the former not. The easily accessible standpipe may also be drawing tractor owners from outside the well's normal catchment area.

The Situation

The case studies reflect the kinds of problems that arise around the new or improved water points created in Central Tunisia. These problems that the new WUAs must confront and solve include cost, hygiene, management, and the resolution of conflicts arising from competition for scarce water.

Costs

Water has costs, either in money paid to a hauler or in household labor and time. Each household therefore balances off its need for water against the cash or labor it must expend to get it. The cost of paying a private hauler is often higher per cubic meter than the SONEDE price in the towns.

Uses

Every household requires a certain minimum for washing, drinking, and cooking, and the amount of water needed for these purposes remains fairly standard. Washing jobs that require a lot of water (cleaning wool or simply doing laundry) may be taken to a nearby stream or irrigation canal where there is running water. Flocks must be watered, but can be driven to a nearby water point, natural or manmade. Any surplus of water can be used to irrigate fruit trees or vegetable gardens near the home.

Getting the Water Home

The variety of ways to haul water home reflects differences in terrain, wealth, and social organization.

1. In a few areas, such as Ain Smiria, water is hauled home by people on foot (generally adolescent girls), carrying a water container on their backs. Such a container might have a volume of 20 liters.
2. More commonly, if the water point is not too far or too difficult of access, or if the people are not rich enough to afford the new technology, a donkey carries a pair of containers. Each such container has a volume

of 40 liters, for a total of 80. Here the haulers of water are likely to be adolescents of either sex—whether boys or girls depending on local social organization. A typical water point for this technology is Ain Zawiya, a spring with a low flow whose position on a slope makes it impossible for wheeled vehicles to approach; most of the users of this spring lived within a 2 kilometer radius.
3. The third technique is the use of tankers, including small ones drawn by a donkey, with a volume of around 500 liters, and large ones drawn by a tractor, with a volume of around 3,000 liters. Larger tankers are filled only at standpipes. Hoses from reservoirs created by the project fill the smaller tankers. Not surprisingly, the operators are generally men or sometimes, with the smaller tankers, boys. Many who haul water in this way sell it to customers who have no other access to water. The typical distance here is 7 to 10 kilometers, although some customers as close as a few hundred meters use this method if they desire extra water for stock or irrigation. Because the amount of water that reaches the home is much higher than by the first two methods, the paradox is that those who live farther from the water point are likely to haul more water home. They may use a larger proportion for nondomestic purposes such as watering stock. People who bring home water in large quantities must have an underground cistern for storage, whereas water brought home in smaller containers is often simply kept in those containers until used.

Hygiene

The water points established under the project, like most similar ones in Central Tunisia, present some health and sanitation problems, principally caused by poor site design and by the presence of cattle, sheep, or goats drinking from the animal trough, and of donkeys that haul water. In a poorly drained site, excrement can produce a health hazard. Donkeys are a particular problem because their owners may bring them right up to the spigots to facilitate filling their containers without unloading them. This can be alleviated by hoses. Another health problem is the use of unclean containers for the water, or the storage of water in dirty cisterns.

Maintenance

Motorization of the water points adds to the maintenance problems. Not only must the site be kept clean, but there is a constant danger that the motor will cease functioning, leaving no available water at all. Since most of these new water points are beyond telephone range, when the pump breaks down or runs out of fuel, the pump operator has to go himself in search of help. Until he finds it, if the pump is not operating, users must seek water elsewhere. The crucial problem of maintenance is complicated by the low skill level of pump operators, the isolation of the sites, and the unreliability of the government's repair services.

Conflict over Water

The establishment of a new water point creates a new resource, which can lead to a conflict between use of water for domestic purposes (including potable water) and its use for irrigation. People in Central Tunisia are very concerned about locating water to use for irrigation in order to improve their economic situation (see Hopkins 1978). Consequently the creation of a water point with additional water resources leads people automatically to think of irrigation.

In the case of the Um Fadgha drilled well, where the flow was estimated at 3 l/s, people originally hoped to use the water for irrigation, although by 1985 this had not happened. Most of the springs, like Ain Smiria, had been used for irrigation before improvement, and beneficiaries of this water tried to reestablish their claims after the improvement. In Ain Mellah (near Rohia) the farmers' desire to continue irrigating persuaded the contractor to modify his design to include an open tank, which then did not meet USAID specifications because the unprotected water was no longer potable. Those who haul water in 3,000-liter tankers may also compete for access against small-scale local users.

Several drilled wells (Henchir Ali Majnoun and Skhira el-Beida, for instance) have yielded flows of 25–35 l/s, considerably more than the amount specified in the original project documents—from 0.5 to 5 l/s. This extra water is also a resource. In Skhira el-Beida, plans were developed to pipe some of the excess water for drinking and domestic use in the community of Ramada, seat of the new delegation of El Aioun. Some water may remain even after both the local and Ramada populations have been satisfied. As expressed by the Regional Agricultural Commissioner, the official Tunisian priorities for water are: first, drinking and domestic use, then, irrigation, with people near the water point having some priority over those farther away. According to this logic, once the local people and those of Ramada have been supplied with drinking water, the remainder can be used for irrigation. The decision then arises whether this should be a government-sponsored and organized irrigation perimeter, or whether the water should be made available for small-scale, private irrigation.

In 1983, the availability of water in excess of the domestic needs of those within a reasonable radius of the water point was not recognized as a problem. The project paper, for instance, foresaw as the only effect of the project that more people would have access to better quality drinking water. The cases presented above show that conflict can arise over the question of who would determine access to even a small amount of water—the immediate neighbors (perhaps a tribal segment) of the new water point, some larger group of people, or the state. Conflict can occur between local people favoring different uses of the water, between different branches of the government, and perhaps between the bureaucratic logic and the people's plans for the use of the water.

By 1985 it appeared that the CTDA was more aware of the problem; certainly there was a more flexible attitude. What had happened in practice in those water points with a substantial "excess" was that people were indeed beginning to use the water for irrigation. Instead of building a network of canals and pipes to carry the water, however, farmers were obliged to haul water for irrigation in large animal-drawn or tractor-drawn tankers, effectively limiting irrigation to trees.

It was recommended in 1983 that any water policy for Central Tunisia should cover both domestic (potable) and irrigation water. The distinction between these two "kinds" of water exists at the bureaucratic level in that separate programs (subprojects) within the CTDA (and USAID) address the two areas—one for potable water and another for the improvement and establishment of irrigation perimeters—which includes encouraging farmers to construct and equip shallow wells. Water developed for irrigation is frequently also used for domestic purposes (Isely 1983:45). Bureaucratic distinctions between these two subprojects should not blind planners to the fact that any particular water source will probably be multifunctional.

The Proposed Solution: Water-User Associations

The landscape of Central Tunisia is littered with the remnants of earlier governmental interventions that did not work out. Cisterns to collect rainwater, wells with handpumps, and even motorized wells have either been abandoned or are not working as efficiently as planned. In some cases the technology was poor, in others the governmental intervention was "rejected" by the people—this is notably the case with handpumps, which were often vandalized. Given this sorry record, what hope is there that an even more expensive intervention—motorized deep wells—will truly deliver the benefits desired? For this dispersed population, torn between traditional affiliations and modern structures, with changing economic and social needs, and modest amounts of disposable income, some new kind of social organization around new water points must be envisaged.

The idea of water-user associations emerged from the 1983 evaluation. Our proposal at that time was to create (or encourage the creation of) associations of users around each water point, to which certain powers and responsibilities would be delegated. This administrative decentralization would improve the chances that governmental interventions would be accepted by local people. Some careful thought and continuous monitoring must be given to this process, however, for the new institution is to some extent interstitial between the poorly known patterns of local social organization and the shifting sands of bureaucracy.

Among the functions of the water-user associations are:

1. to raise money to cover operation and maintenance costs, including fuel, salary for the pump operators, basic maintenance, site sanitation, and improvements;
2. to undertake sanitation activities around the pump site, and to provide input into certain civil-works design features, such as locations of the

animal trough, the spigots where people fill their tankers and other containers, and the reservoir;
3. to undertake health education, in conjunction with the health education program of the public health service; and
4. to maintain site discipline, to organize labor inputs, and to settle disputes concerned with drawing and hauling potable water.

The two most important aspects are self-management and health, to ensure that clean water is regularly supplied in the home. Members of the WUA are those individuals or households who habitually take water from the water point. Each member of the WUA makes a contribution in money or labor to be used for operation and maintenance, repairs and improvements. Each WUA could have a managing committee including representatives of all social and economic categories in the population served. Creation of this sort of representative organization requires considerable work, as this is a new form of social organization for Central Tunisia. According to experience to date, each WUA should have a slightly different system of payment, and each WUA should be able to collect and administer its own funds, determine its own rates, keep records, and maintain an account at a local post office.

Several processes observable in Central Tunisia after 1985 suggested that the WUAs were taking root. A Tunisian consultant hired by the CTDA was successful in setting up a structure at the governorate and delegation levels that involved participation of a large number of government officials in the process of developing and caring for potable water points. The consultant encouraged the creation of a Regional Potable Water Committee corresponding to the Governorate of Kasserine, and of Local Potable Water Committees in each delegation, as well as of some 150 water-point-oriented WUAs. The Regional Potable Water Committee has above all a policy-making role in creating and managing water points in the governorate, while the Local Potable Water Committee has above all the role of visiting potable water points in order to contact the local people and encourage them to take certain actions, such as cleaning up the site.

Of the several efforts to collect money from users of the new water points, some were official: in Sbeitla delegation, the delegate set rates for large and small tankers, smaller containers being free. Other efforts were local, with fees being collected through the local branch of the Destourian Socialist Party (in these rural areas, essentially a single party). Collecting fees for water has not yet become generalized, but it seems to be fairly well accepted by the water users in these areas, who typically employ a sliding scale, with tractor-drawn tankers paying the most. Where small users are charged, it is through a fixed monthly fee rather than by the amount of water. Sometimes the user provides fuel to replace that used on his behalf. The accepted principle is that if it costs money to pump water, then the user should cover that cost. So far, however, the money collected has been used to cover only fuel costs, not maintenance.

The WUAs and the Committees require some permanent administrative support if they are to function smoothly. For this reason, the second phase of the project stipulated, as a *condition précédent*, that a Self-Management Bureau (Unité d'Autogestion) be established within the CTDA, with the task of providing technical assistance and training to the new WUAs. In the summer of 1987, this bureau was staffed by a director with a university degree in sociology, assisted by four members in Kasserine, one in Gafsa, and a driver. Most of the members had some training in social work. In addition, a Peace Corps volunteer was assigned to the Bureau. This staff was working to provide a range of services to the existing WUAs and to participate in the choice of new sites, but was stymied in its efforts to regularize the situation of the associations by the delay in preparing the authorizing statute. Itself an experiment in institutional change, the Bureau is intended to play a key part in the institutionalization of the WUAs. Let us turn now to tasks of the associations that may require some support from the Bureau.

1. *Determining the membership of the associations.* By and large, a fairly fixed list of people frequent a given water point, but Central Tunisians sometimes seek water from different water points for different purposes, or in different seasons. Thus there may be more or different users in summer than in winter; a breakdown in one water point may temporarily disperse its "members" to other points; and certain households may systematically seek water from two or more points. Determining some kind of a membership list is essential if small users are going to pay their share, since here the accepted pattern seems to be a monthly charge. This also simplifies bookkeeping. Furthermore, creating at least a core membership is necessary if health education and sanitation efforts are to work.

2. *Fixing the rates.* In principle, all public water points should charge for water, to avoid a sense of unfairness and the overuse of free water points. Each association should set its own rates, however, since the depth of the well and the number of users will vary from one water point to the next. Also, setting one's own rates is a central part of self-management. It may nonetheless be useful to establish a range for rates within each delegation or for the entire area, to avoid wide variations.

3. *Collecting money.* One problem that has arisen is to determine who has the right to collect money. Where the delegate took the initiative, he has simply instructed the pump operators to collect fees from tankers, buy their own fuel, and submit their accounts later. Where tractor owners provide fuel, the cash system is circumvented. Sometimes the party branch or a local leader takes charge, but this is regarded with some suspicion in official circles. The creation of legal water-user associations would resolve this problem. The task is to transform these various methods for collecting and spending money (or goods) into associations with a broader range.

4. *Establishing local leadership.* Probably the committee will reflect the major social categories among the users of each water point. This might be according to large and small users, according to different kinship groups, or along some other axis. It may be premature to expect women to be members of such committees, although the liaison officers should be alert

to every possibility. On many sites, children predominate among the actual users, and it is not practical to assume that they will be represented on the committee. On other sites, and especially the larger ones with a drilled well and an appreciable amount of water, men are frequent users. At these sites a committee composed of men would not be entirely a reinforcement of traditional patterns of dominance of children by parents, or of women by men, but would reflect the use pattern.

5. *Determining how rural government officials should play a role.* Another issue in the creation of these committees is to determine whether government officials assigned locally (teachers and male health workers, predominantly) should be encouraged to serve or discouraged from serving on the committees. On the one hand they possess certain useful skills, and may be neutral figures; on the other hand their membership may give the impression that this is only another way to establish lines of state power and thus discourage true self-management. Another model to be avoided is that of the town-based government official who arrives in a car, offers instructions and perhaps comments phrased as orders to whomever might be present, and then leaves. Without follow-up, the local people will not take these comments seriously, but their failure to execute the instructions and orders leaves the government officials with the idea that only a tighter control will produce results. Rural officials are dedicated and hardworking, but they start from the assumption that they provide a service to "the citizens" whose role it is to be responsive and grateful. This can produce frustration on both sides.[4]

6. *Encouraging good local leadership.* A further issue is whether the selection of local leaders will produce good results. Tunisian culture does not encourage people to seek political leadership roles openly. The kind of leader most likely to be accepted is one who is more or less drafted. When groups of men have to choose their leaders, however, they generally choose the "most respected" man, typically aged between 35 and 55. Neither the oldest nor the richest is automatically selected.[5] Most leadership is situational, and it is hard for a single individual to begin to mobilize his fellows. Once chosen, however, he can participate effectively. The style of leadership is generally one of example rather than of hierarchies of dominance. People are less likely to give orders and more likely to set an example by starting in to work or to make the first contribution themselves.[6]

7. *Facing problems of literacy.* Literacy is not widespread in Central Tunisia, even among men. Some pump operators use their sons, on school vacations, to keep records for them. The shortage of literate people may limit the choice of leaders, especially treasurers and general secretaries.

8. *Working within a legal framework.* To have a legal existence, and in particular to have the legal right to collect and spend money, WUAs must conform to government regulations, adapted from the "Water Code" approved in 1987. Local leaders are often unfamiliar with the complexities of these bureaucratic regulations, and will need the help of the Self-Management Bureau in the CTDA to comply with them.

The prognosis for the successful adaptation of the WUA model in Central Tunisia appears to be good. People (and the government) are prepared to experiment with new ways to ensure a supply of potable water for the scattered rural populations. They are willing to make a reasonable contribution in money and in labor to secure potable water for themselves and their families. From the tentative efforts to elaborate new institutions there is enough evidence to suggest that a working model will be found and negotiated among the various interested parties. The purpose of this analysis is not to lay out such a model, but simply to argue that it is conceivable. Issues of equity, leadership, and local autonomy as opposed to a top-down control system cannot be solved in a short time. Their resolution will require considerable imagination and tolerance on the part of all concerned.

Conclusion

In 1978 the most likely general pattern of development in Central Tunisia seemed to be growth centering around irrigation and some improvements in cereals and pastoralism. If this kind of growth came to pass, then some of the migrant population would be attracted home. In general this is what seems to have happened. A period of modest but real growth in the area can be measured by such indicators as plantings of trees, improved houses, additional roads, more cars and trucks, more schools, and so on. The area does not seem to have become entirely devoted to producing labor for the coastal or foreign economies, but sustains within it many economic opportunities, although the gap between the center and the coast of Tunisia remains, particularly in the general standard of living. An improved agriculture has probably contributed to this relatively positive picture for Central Tunisia, and the spread of irrigation is a major component of this agricultural growth. At the same time, the spread of infrastructure, and in particular of potable water projects, into the rural areas of the governorate has contributed toward fixing the productive activities. This does not mean that poverty has disappeared from the area. One can still see people using animals for threshing grain or women washing wool by a pool of turgid water. There are still some children with skin diseases, and diarrhea is a substantial problem in the summer. Per capita consumption of water is still often below international norms, and the relatively sparing use of water contributes to some of these health problems. Progress has been made, but more is required before the gap between the center and the coast can be significantly reduced.

This chapter has described various aspects of a development project designed to improve access to potable water for the dispersed rural population of Central Tunisia. The challenge in this project over the years has been to find ways to involve the local population in the process. By 1985 it seemed that both the Tunisian and the American officials involved had accepted the principle that some kind of users associations around the new water points offered the best chances for future development, and that the experience with these associations might serve as a model for other parts of Tunisia. In particular, the idea that the associations might raise their own funds to cover the running costs of providing water was very popular.

Indeed, some Tunisian officials clearly interpreted the word "participation" to mean only this.

The task in the next phase of this long evolution is to extend the notion of participation so that it covers local forms of self-management in general. Participation must be more than merely a way to collect money and reduce government expenses; it should increase the efficiency of management of the water points, and represent a step toward assumption of responsibility for other areas of collective life as well. Health and sanitation issues stand out as logical areas for this. Although participation is contrary to the client model of government that pervades Tunisian government official thinking, there is some support for it from Tunisian leaders. Here the anthropological imagination must be brought to bear to help create, slowly and carefully, a new set of institutions and a new way of doing things.

This process is still under way. My role as an anthropologist has been to provide accurate background for making decisions about the various phases of the program, to suggest creative solutions to the organizational problems following the establishment of the new water points, and to advise the new "social" team at the CTDA. Where matters go from here depends on many choices, made by the users and potential users of the new water points, by Tunisian government officials at all levels, and by the American personnel who must authorize and plan for future funding. At the moment one can be cautiously optimistic that something new and useful will arise in Central Tunisia.

Notes

This chapter is based on research carried out on behalf of USAID in Central Tunisia in July 1978, September 1983, and August 1985. In the latter two cases, my involvement was made possible by the Institute for Development Anthropology. My thanks to all in Central Tunisia, and in particular at the Central Tunisia Development Authority, whose cooperation made this work a pleasure. Hanan Hosni Sabea helped in the final preparation of the chapter.

1. This political judgment was then supported by the role of Central Tunisia in the riots of 1978 and of 1984, and in the 1980 attack on Gafsa; the interior has always had the reputation of not suffering central authority very easily, and even today many of the country's radical leaders are native to this area.

2. While the Fifth Amendment refers to the placement of hand pumps on both dug and drilled wells, subsequent experiences caused this idea to be abandoned in favor of generalized motorization (see Potts 1983).

3. In the second phase of the project, this desire for rational planning was furthered by a comprehensive mapping of existing water points, population distribution, the presence of water tables, and related data. The data were produced in 1987, and were to be used in site selection. See especially the report by Appleby (1987).

4. In August 1985 I went to the site of Ain Zawiyet Ben Ammar with various members of the Sbeitla Local Potable Water Committee. As soon as we arrived, a quarrel broke out between the substitute sheikh who was accompanying us and a teenage boy who was filling the casks on his donkey directly from the spigot. (The lowest-level appointed official, the sheikh is usually from the area or "secteur," but

here the sheikh had gone on pilgrimage, and so there was a substitute from another area.) The sheikh blamed the boy for the messy site; the boy said others were to blame, not he, but spoke rudely; and so soon the verbal dispute turned into a wrestling match between the man and the boy. Eventually, after a lot of free advice was offered, the health representative on the committee began to organize those present into working on some provisional improvements of the site—cleaning out the animal trough, placing rocks so as to improve drainage and prevent donkeys from getting too close. But the deficiencies of the design itself (animal trough too close to the spigot) could not be addressed. When the job was done, local people produced soft drinks, coffee, and cookies for the workers, and so we left with a feeling of accomplishment after a rough beginning.

5. These comments are based on the experience of the Community Development Foundation (CDF) in Magrouna and Ouled Boughdir. In Magrouna (Hababsa sector of Rohia delegation) the community formed a cooperative to manage a small-scale irrigation system to which the Tunisian government and the CDF have both contributed. In Ouled Boughdir (el Aioun delegation), a newly formed cooperative built a mosque and a school and worked on potable water supply. My thanks to Mondher Neji for introducing me to these sites.

6. The relationship between government officials, particularly those residing in the towns, and the "citizens" residing in the rural areas is much more likely to take on a coloring of superordination, marked by giving orders and advice without necessarily sticking around to see to the fulfillment of the instructions.

References

Appleby, Gordon
  1987 Criteria and Methodology for the Delimitation of Water-Short Areas in Central Tunisia. Working Paper No. 37. Binghamton, NY: Institute for Development Anthropology.

Ayad, Carole Steere
  1978 Social Soundness Analysis of Potable Water Interventions in the Central Tunisia Rural Development Project Zone. Tunis: USAID.

Bessis, A., et al.
  1956 Le Térritoire des Ouled Sidi Ali ben Aoun: Contribution à l'étude des problèmes humains dans la steppe tunisienne. Paris: Presses Universitaires de France.

Ferchiou, Sophie
  1985 Les Femmes dans l'agriculture tunisienne. Aix-en-Provence: Edisud.

Hopkins, Nicholas S.
  1978 Elements for a Social Soundness Analysis of the Agricultural Interventions. Tunis: USAID.

Hopkins, Nicholas S., and William M. Turner
  1983 Interim Evaluation: Rural Potable Water Subproject. Binghamton, NY: Institute for Development Anthropology.

Isely, Raymond
  1983 Small Holder Irrigation Development Subproject. Tunis: USAID.

Monchicourt, Ch.
  1913 La Région du Haut-Tell en Tunisie. Paris: Armand Colin.

Potts, Phillip W.
    1983 USAID Handpump Program in Tunisia. Washington: Water and Sanitation for Health Project, Report No. 100.

Sethom, Hafedh, and Ahmed Kassab
    1981 Les Régions géographiques de la Tunisie. Tunis: Publications de l'Université de Tunis, Faculté des Lettres et Sciences Humaines de Tunis. Deuxième série, Géographie. Vol. XIII.

Smith, Janet M.
    1985 Water Usage Patterns and Willingness to Participate in New Water Points. Report of a Survey of Central Tunisia. Tunis: USAID.

University of Wisconsin
    1981 Update. Regional Planning and Area Development Project. University of Wisconsin. Winter.

Zghal, Abdelkader
    1967 Modernisation de l'agriculture et populations semi-nomades. The Hague: Mouton.

Zghidi, Mhammed
    1978 Monographie de Hababsa (Gouvernorat de Siliana): Etude socio-économique d'un secteur rural. Tunis, Ministère du Plan.

5

Household Production Organization and Differential Access to Resources in Central Tunisia

Muneera Salem-Murdock

Background

The Government of Tunisia, in an attempt to decrease income disparities between its more affluent and developed coastal areas and the less-developed central, northwestern, and southern regions, established multisectoral *Offices de Développement* in the late 1970s, charged with managing activities to raise incomes and standards of living in their regions. The *Office de Développement de la Tunisie Centrale* (ODTC) was established in 1978 to coordinate development activities in Central Tunisia. Among the foreign donors who funneled their development assistance to the region through ODTC was the United States Agency for International Development (USAID). In 1978/1979 USAID finalized the design of the Central Tunisia Rural Development Project (CTRD), which included several subprojects: Dryland Farming Systems Research, Smallholder Irrigation, Rural Extension and Outreach, Range Management, Rural Potable Water, Urban Potable Water, and Area Development (USAID/Tunis 1983:10).

In March 1985 the Institute for Development Anthropology (IDA) under the Cooperative Agreement on Settlement and Resources Systems Analysis (SARSA), which it shares with Clark University, proposed to USAID/Tunis and ODTC a program of research and technical assistance, to be funded under the overall CTRD project. The proposal, approved in May 1985 with research to begin in June, included a field study of the socioeconomic impacts of the various USAID-funded projects on the organization of household production. This chapter is a direct outcome of that program and presents the findings of a three-month field research trip to Central Tunisia. The research had as its aim the study of household farming systems in areas where irrigation farming is practiced. It focused on the organization of household production and the differential access to resources both of individual farmers and of households in Central Tunisia.

Research Site Selection

At the time of funding, ODTC consisted of a main office in Kasserine (that housed, in addition to the President Director General, the Divisions of Planning and Evaluation, Agricultural Extension, Engineering and Irrigation, and Administration and Finances) and 17 subdivisions that corresponded to the administrative unit called *délégations*, of which 12 were in the Kasserine Governorate, 2 in Qafsa, and 3 in Siliana. USAID had project involvement in 10 of the delegations (Figure 5.1).

Several considerations were taken into account in selecting the IDA research site (délégation): USAID's presence or absence, ODTC's immediate and future development interests, earlier versus more recent development interventions, earlier versus more recent experience with irrigation, and time constraints. Accordingly, several meetings were held with ODTC officials, especially in the Planning and Evaluation and Irrigation Divisions, to discuss the different characteristics of delegations, projects, and sources of funding. In terms of implementation, all projects are administered similarly, the source of funds notwithstanding. We agreed, however, that earlier versus more recent experience with irrigation is important in defining households' adaptive strategies. Since the time allocated for the research was rather brief, it seemed important to minimize travel and to concentrate on in-depth studies of a small number of households at each site rather than to do more superficial surveys of a large number of widely distributed households.

Accordingly, we selected for initial site visits the delegations of Sbiba, Sbeitla, Foussana, Kasserine North, Firiana and Majel bel-'Abbas. On the basis of talks with the local ODTC representatives, farm households, extension agents, and further discussions with the Planning and Evaluation Division in Kasserine and the Rural Development Office of USAID/Tunis, we selected for main focus the delegations of Sbeitla and Foussana, the former with an earlier experience with irrigated agriculture and the latter with a more recent one. Both areas were within convenient driving distance from each other and from Kasserine, an important consideration in light of time constraints. Data collected were to be supplemented with materials from other ODTC areas, especially Kasserine North and Firiana.

The city of Kasserine was selected as the base of operations because it is central in the region and is the seat of ODTC headquarters, where it was felt adequate time should be spent interviewing officials, discussing preliminary findings, attending meetings, and collecting oral and written data. Accordingly, research time was divided between Kasserine and the other research sites. Travel between the various sites was facilitated by a rented vehicle, and by the kindness and hospitality of the ODTC subdivisions and Central Tunisian farm households.

We utilized several research techniques, including participant observation, formal and informal interviews, and household surveys. In each research site a nonrandom sample of households was selected for in-depth interviews. The selection was made in collaboration with the subdivision chiefs, who gave me general briefings on area households and guided the selection on

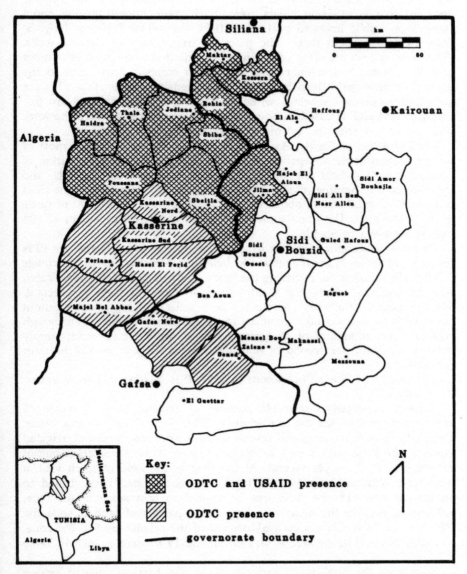

FIGURE 5.1
Central Tunisia. *Source:* Adapted from a map obtained from the Office de Développement de la Tunisie Centrale.

the basis of such criteria as land ownership, access to water, access to resources, household composition, and labor availability. It was quickly apparent that subdivision chiefs were much more knowledgeable about farmers on public irrigated perimeters (PPI, *Périmètres Publiques Irrigués*) than they were about those who practiced irrigation with shallow wells. (This uneven understanding can largely be attributed to the smaller number of PPI households and their concentration in compact areas, and to the greater attention paid them by agricultural extension agents since PPIs are government-operated schemes while shallow-well irrigated farms are privately owned and operated, although often government financed.) The work was carried out with the aid of two Tunisian research assistants.

The Delegation of Sbeitla. As in other areas in Central Tunisia, most of the population of the delegation of Sbeitla is engaged in the cultivation of dryland cereals (wheat and barley) and fruit trees (olives, almonds, and apricots), and in herding (mostly of small ruminants). According to the chief of the ODTC subdivision, about 400,000 head of sheep and 1,000 of cattle graze in the area. The population is estimated at 54,447, of whom 13,804 live in the town of Sbeitla.

Of the 472 hectares of public irrigation in Sbeitla, 313 hectares are PPIs (Sbeitla and Shraayi') and the remainder belong to *l'Office des Terres Domainiale* (OTD). The whole area, including the lands that belong to OTD, is irrigated from several deep wells that yield a total of about 45 liters per second. The equipment of already constructed new wells will bring water output up to 90 liters per second. According to the subdivision chief, even though motors run a minimum of 16 hours a day in the summer, water supply even at 90 liters per second is not sufficient to irrigate all 472 hectares properly.

The Sbeitla PPI began operations in 1971. It is divided into three zones: A, B, and C.

Zone A encompasses over 140 hectares of irrigated land, of which 95 are privately owned and the rest belong to OTD. Zone A has running water, electricity, cement housing, and several shops. It contains the oldest irrigated lands in the area, with a well in operation since 1954, the current output of which is 20 liters per second. At the time of the field research visit, a new well, with an output of 30 liters per second, had been drilled to supplement the old one. The area is reputed to host some of the most affluent farmers in the area, who have large parcels of land outside the PPI. Two of these farmers own 61 percent of the private land in the zone. In addition to OTD, the area is divided among 15 farmers as seen in Table 5.1.

Zone B of the Sbeitla PPI includes about 134 hectares divided among 63 farmers from the Oulaad bin Nouma *'arsh* (clan), as shown in Table 5.2. The farmer with more than ten hectares originally had a much larger parcel of land which, upon ODTC's strong urging, he divided among three sons, giving each five hectares. Most of the land in the zone is owned by one *fariq* (descendants of the same ancestor), the Qaasmiyya. As in Zone A,

TABLE 5.1
Distribution of Private Land in Zone A of Sbeitla PPI

Size in Ha	No. of Farmers	% of Farmers	% of Land
.00-00.99	1	6.66	0.53
1.00-01.49	4	26.66	4.74
1.50-01.99	4	26.66	6.84
2.00-02.99	0	0	0
3.00-03.99	1	6.66	3.68
4.00-04.99	2	13.33	9.47
5.00-09.99	0	0	0
10.00-12.99	0	0	0
13.00-13.99	1	6.66	13.68
14.00-26.99	0	0	0
27.00-27.99	1	6.66	28.95
28.00-29.99	0	0	0
30.00-30.99	1	6.66	32.11
	15	100	100

TABLE 5.2
Distribution of Land in Zone B of Sbeitla PPI

Size in Ha	No. of Farmers	% of Farmers	% of Land
.00-00.49	1	1.59	0.2
.50-00.99	16	25.40	9.5
1.00-01.49	8	12.70	7.9
1.50-01.99	11	17.46	15.3
2.00-02.49	19	30.16	33.9
2.50-02.99	0	0	0
3.00-03.49	1	1.59	2.6
3.50-03.99	1	1.59	3.0
4.00-04.49	2	3.17	6.7
4.50-04.99	0	0	0
5.00-05.49	3	4.76	12.5
5.50-05.99	0	0	0
6.00-06.99	0	0	0
7.00-07.99	0	0	0
8.00-08.99	0	0	0
9.00-09.99	0	0	0
10.00-10.99	1	1.59	8.3
	63	100	100

TABLE 5.3
Distribution of Land in Shraayi' PPI

Size in Hectares	No. of Farmers
0.00-0.99	0
1.00-1.49	3
1.50-1.99	19
2.00-2.49	8
	30

farmers in this zone benefit from a school, electricity, shops, and cement housing. Labor migration is a common strategy; people migrate to Libya, Algeria, France, and to other parts of Tunisia.

Zone C is 24 hectares privately held by an absentee landlord who is reported to own 300 additional hectares nearby, over and above the irrigated land. At the time of the field research, the area was not being irrigated. The ODTC subdivision had been able to shut off irrigation water flows—despite the owner's obvious affluence—because the 24 hectares were being neglected by its absentee landlord, who was not indigenous to the region, and because this small area constitutes the entire zone. The sons of the owner are disputing the measure and the possible outcome is unclear.

The Shraayi' PPI is the oldest in the Sbeitla delegation. Water was introduced in Shraayi' in 1969 through a 180-meter deep well with a water output of 35 liters per second. In 1978 water loss in this well was compensated for with a World Bank-funded 160-meter deep well with an output of 45 liters per second. Seven fariqs claimed right to the 60 hectares of land that the government put under irrigation. Disputes took place among them over who should control the land. After several negotiations with the elders, and in consultation with them, the government decided to solve the problem by dividing the land into 30 parcels to be distributed among the seven fariqs. It was agreed that two of the fariqs would receive five parcels each and the rest four each. It was then up to the different fariqs to allocate the land among their descendants on the principle of one household/one field. This resulted in a far more egalitarian distribution of land than we see in Zone B and especially in Zone A. Plot sizes range from 1.36 to 2.42 hectares, distributed among 30 households as shown in Table 5.3. Some 18 farmers supplement irrigation from the deep well in the wet season by *waadi* irrigation.

Shraayi' PPI farmers belong to the Haraahra 'arsh, represented in the area in the fariqs of the Harraathiya, the Banaajdiya, the Hamaamdiya, the Smei'iya, the Hmeishiya, the Hawaawmiya, and the Basaayriya. Constant conflicts are reported between the Harraathiya and the Hamaamdiya; the others take sides in the conflicts as suit their interests.

Most of the households own lands near the PPI, where intermittent shallow wells can also be found. Because of the population concentration

TABLE 5.4
Distribution of Land by Sector in Foussana Delegation

Sector	Area in Ha	Population
Foussana	9,555	6,053
Khmouda	10,110	5,230
Breika	8,490	3,349
Mzeir'a	8,573	4,037
Oulaad Mahfoudh	9,000	5,545
'Deira	7,000	3,594
Afraan	8,617	3,006
Haazza	7,800	3,332
Boudreisaat	8,166	1,801
'Ein Jnaan	6,509	1,336
Total	83,820	37,283

that characterizes PPIs as opposed to shallow-well areas, Shraayi' households benefit from a school, a shop, and electricity. Migration is a common strategy in the PPI. People are said to work in Tunis, Sousa, Sfax, Libya, and France. In addition to apples and peaches, the area has many olive, almond, and apricot trees.

The Delegation of Foussana. As in Sbeitla, the inhabitants of Foussana are mainly dryland (i.e., rainfed) farmers and herders. The total area is 83,820 hectares, and the population is approximately 37,300, of whom 88 percent are listed as farmers, divided among the sectors as in Table 5.4. Rain usually falls in the winter season, averaging about 250–300 mm per year; sand storms and hail are common in the summer.

PPI FS4–FS5, located 3–4 kilometers from Foussana, started operations in April 1983. Covering about 120 hectares divided among 62 beneficiaries, its plot sizes range from 1 to 5 hectares. The area is served by two deep wells, FS4 and FS5, both located in Oulaad Mahfoudh. Water cost in the PPI is 432 millimes per hour, calculated on a water output of 100 liters per second. At least two 'arsh are represented in the area: al-Firiekhi and Oulaad Mahfoudh. Before the introduction of irrigation, most of the households depended on rainfed farming, herding, and wage labor.

In the light of soil studies (undertaken before the construction of the PPI) indicating that the area was suited for fruit tree and forage cultivation, the ODTC introduced apple and pear trees from Spain, developed especially for hot climates. To encourage farmers, the government plowed the land, dug the tree holes with hired labor at 700 millimes each, and planted the trees. Small quantities of seeds were also given out to most farmers for demonstration purposes.

Farmers of PPI FS4–FS5 pay both fixed and variable costs of irrigation. Once the PPI system was set in place, farmers were expected to reimburse start-up costs over a three-year period and to cover the cost of water, seeds, seedlings, and fruit trees. Initially eight millimes per cubic meter, the price of water has since been raised twice, first to ten and later to twelve per

TABLE 5.5
Land Use in PPI FS6, 1985

	Hectares	Percent
Summer		
Arboriculture	17.5	56.9
Forage	5.5	17.9
Vegetables	7.75	25.2
Total	30.75	100.0
Winter		
Arboriculture	17.5	56.9
Forage	23.5	76.4
Vegetables	1.5	4.9
Total[a]	[42.5]	[138.2]

[a] Adds to more than 30.75 ha (and 100 percent) because of double-cropping.

cubic meter. In 1984 fruit trees were given to farmers who paid 50 percent of the cost in advance, although for amounts under 10 TD farmers were to pay the full cost upon receipt. Similarly, 50 percent of the cost of seeds and seedlings is paid on receipt, and the remainder after harvest. Farmers who receive loans have to pay them back within one-to-three years, depending on the amount.

Irrigation water from the two wells pours into a reservoir with a capacity of 1,500 cubic meters; from there it is distributed through five water lines. Each water line forms a separate water rotation: four of the lines supply participants with water once every nine days; the fifth line supplies water once every seven days. Each line has several sluices to control water distribution according to the number of plots; frequently two plots share one sluice. Farmers who have plots that are spread across two lines are treated as if they own two plots and get their water on different days.

PPI FS6 lies 8-9 kilometers from Foussana and encloses 31 hectares divided among 20 farmers; plot sizes range from 1 to 4 hectares. Water is gathered in a reservoir of 300 square meters from a deep well with an output of 60 liters per second, and is allocated according to plot size. Each hectare is accorded 1.5 hours of water per rotation, calculated on a water output of 20 liters per second. Land use in FS6 is similar to that in FS4/FS5: trees have first priority, followed by forage. Land exploitation in PPI FS6 in the summer and winter seasons of 1985 is shown in Table 5.5.

Table 5.6 shows specific crops in FS4/FS5 and FS6 grown in the summer of 1985.

PPI 3 was not operating at the time of the field research trip. The experience of PPI 3 is a classic example of what happens if proper feasibility studies are not carried out before the initiation of a project. After the completion of well drilling, canal digging, and all, it was discovered that

TABLE 5.6
Summer 1985 Soil Use in Foussana PPIs (in Hectares)

Culture	FS4/FS5	FS6
Potatoes	2.0	0.25
Tomatoes	2.5	1.5
Peppers	0.5	0.5
Watermelons	3.5	1.5
Melon	0.5	1.25
Squash	0.25	0.25
Cucumbers	0.25	0.0
Beets	0.5	0.25
Onions	2.0	1.5
Garlic	0.5	0.25
Parsley	0.5	0.25
Celery	0.25	0.0
Alfalfa	14.0	3.5
Sorghum	1.5	1.0
Corn	1.0	1.0
Apples	31.0	12.25
Pears	17.5	5.0
	78.25	30.25

the land the PPI was erected on is *waqf*, or mosque land, and therefore excluded from common use.

Farming Systems in Central Tunisia

Each of the three farming systems in Central Tunisia—dryland farming along with animal husbandry; shallow-well irrigation, largely in association with dryland farming and animal husbandry; and PPIs from deep wells, also in association with dryland farming—has its distinctive features, for example: complete dependency on rainfall in pure dryland farming, the use of irrigation with little control over water allocation on the PPIs, and the almost total control over the distribution of water in shallow-well farming.

The three activities are closely intertwined, both spatially and in terms of the practice of peasant households. Both shallow-well and PPI irrigated areas tend to be small, scattered, and intermingled with dry areas. Most households are involved in at least two of the systems, either directly, through close relatives, or as providers of labor. This is particularly true in the case of households that practice rainfed farming and/or shallow-well irrigation. No matter what the focus and the immediate and long-term goals of production, all dryland farming peasant households aspire (if there is underground water available) to dig a shallow well and to acquire a motor to put the well in use. Digging a well is a clear sign that a household is at least attempting to pull itself out from under the drudgery of subsistence cultivation that must depend upon the capricious weather.

Dryland peasant households who do begin shallow-well irrigation almost always continue to farm dry lands that are adjacent to the irrigated plot or in one or more nearby areas. Less frequent, but also very common, is for PPI households to own rainfed lands or to have lands with shallow wells on them. Also, both shallow-well and PPI peasant households are very likely to have family members, relatives, and neighbors who rely totally on rainfed farming.

Dryland Farming

Dryland farming is the riskiest and least rewarding but also the most widespread and least labor demanding of the three farming systems in Central Tunisia. Because of the variability of rainfall both in quantity and in distribution, a peasant household requires relatively large parcels of land, preferably in several micro regions, to be able to make a living. Households grow cereals, mainly wheat and barley; trees, especially olives, almonds, and apricots; and, more recently, forage crops such as spined and spineless cactus. Agricultural production is supplemented by livestock raising; the number of animals raised is a function of the household's ability to purchase them, to find grazing land (more and more difficult with the tremendous expansion of fruit tree cultivation), and to provide fodder in the dry season. It is also supplemented by wage labor in the immediate area, in more distant regions of Tunisia, or in such countries as France or Libya.

Opinions differ on how much land will sustain a household that has no access to irrigation. Some farmers assured me that as little as 15 hectares would be sufficient. The majority insist that an average size household would need a minimum of 30 hectares. All farmers, however, agreed that:

1. A household with no access to irrigation, unless it owns large parcels of land, cannot make it on cereal cultivation alone (not that households with large areas specialize in cereals); fruit trees and livestock are essential, since mature trees can survive a few years of deficit rainfall while cereals cannot.
2. The crucial factor in a household's survival is not land size per se but the quality, quantity, timing, and distribution of rain. In a good year a farm household can harvest up to 15 sacks of cereal per hectare; in a bad year the fields might produce nothing at all.

Since cereals can keep for a few years without much spoiling, households tend to stock cereals in surplus years in order to meet their food needs in deficit years. Households fortunate enough to have several consecutive good years might sell what cereal they have left from the previous year, frequently using the money to buy animals as an insurance against future bad years. Unfortunately, market forces dictate that wheat prices are lower in good years and animal prices are lower in bad years, the times when farm households are most likely to sell each.

Farmers engaged primarily in rainfed cultivation have more time to seek jobs because only minimal labor is required for dryland farming. (Plowing of rainfed land is rare; lands favored with early rains are sowed with little preparation or fertilization and left largely unattended until harvest time.) However, the availability of jobs in the immediate area, largely agricultural, is unreliable, and they are poorly compensated. Although the official minimum daily wage is about 3.00 TD, farmers confess to having paid and received as little as 1.5 TD/day. Inevitably, those who suffer most from these conditions are the poorest. They have little choice but to participate in a clearly exploitive system that sets in motion a steady process of differentiation between poor and affluent farmers.

This can be seen at three levels. First, in years of low agricultural productivity wage labor tends to be abundant because of the large number of farmers who, trying to meet household consumption needs, are looking for employment. As a result, the wages that employers, whether rich or poor, are willing to pay tend to come down. Poor farmers are as eager as more affluent farmers to exploit those who are, perhaps temporarily, poorer than they are.

Second, in successful farm years, poor farmers are less likely to seek wage labor since they are able to meet household consumption needs from on-farm production. Thus, wages increase as labor becomes more scarce. Those who do seek wage labor are naturally unwilling to work for poor farmers who can afford to pay only minimum wages, when more affluent farmers are offering the maximum. By refusing to work for the lower wages, the poor farmer, in his role as a wage laborer, is actively contributing to further differentiation between poor farmers like himself and the more affluent farmers.

And third, since shallow-well farming, the aspiration of all dryland farmers, is bound to require the hiring of labor at one time or another, starting with the digging of the well itself, poorer farmers are in a worse position to make that transition than are those with cash earnings or reserves to pay laborers.

Farmers who choose to search for work in other parts of Tunisia—for example, in Qabes, Sfax, or Tunis—or in other countries such as France or Libya, are in a better position to be adequately compensated, but the uncertainties of such a move increase with the distance traveled to find employment. The farmer must invest in transportation and living costs that may never be reimbursed should he find no work at all.

Irrigation Farming

Irrigation farming, whether via shallow wells or PPIs, is one of the measures farmers adopted to protect themselves against poor rainfall years. The integrated nature of rainfed and irrigation activities makes possible a variety of strategies to ensure a harvest. Water from shallow wells can be diverted to irrigate parts of dryland areas, a practice called "semi-irrigation"; and access to irrigation is not solely the privilege of those who have been able to construct or acquire a shallow well. It is also possible for others by way of gifts or exchanges between relatives and friends.

It is uncommon for a household to put more than 3.5 to 5 hectares under "permanent" irrigation. Irrigation of the remainder of the land depends on water availability (more available in the winter than in the summer), cropping intensity, and crop requirements.

Factors Influencing Ability to Invest in Shallow-well Construction. What enables some farm households to dig, prepare, and equip a well? The first requisite is owning an appropriate piece of land with an accessible water table that allows cost-effective well digging. Farmers who have some cash might buy a small piece of land (3 to 5 hectares) with an existing well, or specifically for the purpose of digging a well. More typically, a farmer with a larger unit of land, usually 10 hectares or more, will dig a well to irrigate part of it.

The second requisite is having the money and the connections to initiate the effort of well digging and construction and to investigate potential additional sources of funding and their various requirements. Before a farmer can borrow money he must establish proof of land ownership, preferably with a *titre bleu* (an ownership certificate signed by the *Direction de la Conservation Foncière*) or, at a minimum, with a *titre arabe* (which is prepared in front of witnesses and registered with the Ministry of Justice, but does not bear the signature of the Direction de la Conservation Foncière).

The process for those with the funds to dig and construct a well themselves is substantially simpler. Officially, a permit from the *Direction des Ressources en Eau* is required to dig a well. This necessitates having the proper papers, but many farmers who do not need digging and construction loans do not bother to obtain one. They usually borrow only for the purchase of a motor, saving the trouble of having to present ownership documents, which are not required when applying for motor loans. The loan acquisition process thus effectively discriminates against poorer farmers, who are obliged to make their way through the time-consuming and costly bureaucratic maze.

Those who do qualify for ODTC well construction loans can receive up to 65 percent of the digging and construction cost (in July 1985 the cost was calculated on the basis of 160 TD per cubic meter). Another 25 percent is given out as a grant from a special budget of the Ministry of Agriculture. The remaining 10 percent is supposed to be financed by the farmer, but the sum is usually offered to him as a grant by ODTC. Farmers have 5 years to repay the loan, but the collection rate is about 42 percent at best. A comparable arrangement is made for motor loans: 65 percent of the cost (which can range anywhere from 2,500 to 4,500 TD per motor) can be borrowed; 20 percent is covered by a grant from the special budget of the Ministry of Agriculture; and 15 percent is self financed, usually, again, covered by a grant from ODTC. The basin for water collection and the motor shelter each cost from 500 to 1,000 TD. ODTC contributes 200 TD to the cost of each and the rest is borne by the farmer.

The third and final requisite is the ability to mobilize labor, whether household or hired.

The Relative Profitability of Shallow-well vs. PPI Irrigation. With the exception of households possessing vast areas of rainfed lands, orchards, and livestock, shallow-well farmers tend to be much better off than dryland farmers. The difference in income and standard of living between shallow-well farmers and those on the PPIs is less clear cut. There are strong indications, however, that the payoffs from shallow-well farming exceed those from the PPIs, all other things (land, labor, and capital) being equal. What are some of these indications?

The first has to do with managerial decision making. Shallow wells may provide considerably less overall output of water than PPIs, but they allow greater management control. That is, farmers with their own wells have full control over their watering schedules, limited only by the output of the wells and by the scope and efficiency of the water distribution system. The farmer determines the volume, location, and frequency of watering, and can fine-tune these according to his own assessment of production needs. Farmers on the PPIs have far less autonomy over watering, and must be prepared to irrigate according to a schedule that cannot take into account the specific calendar requirements of each household on the perimeter. Appropriate labor may not be on hand, for example, at the precise moment the water arrives.

Second, farmers who have invested both capital and labor to construct or acquire a well are in general far more exacting over the maintenance of their wells than farmers on the PPIs, who have been provided with irrigation infrastructure with little or no cost to themselves. Deterioration of the irrigation infrastructure on the PPIs has been a recurrent concern of ODTC. While recent indications show improvements in maintenance, and some financial participation on the part of PPI holders, shallow-well installations are, in general, better maintained by their owners.

Third, the greater financial involvement of shallow-well farmers in the costs of installation, compared with the more passive role of PPI farmers, implies that the former are better able to meet the continuing costs of irrigated farming. They are more likely than PPI farmers to have been able to save some money for investment, either through successful wage-labor experiences in the commercial or industrial areas of Tunisia, Libya, or France, or through sales of land or animals. Their ability to support start-up costs places them in an advantageous position for sustaining operations over time. Most shallow-well farm households are not affluent, but, on average, they have more resources at their disposal than do PPI households.

Finally, shallow-well farmers, given their greater capital resources, can hire labor more readily at critical times than can PPI farmers. This ability to hire outside labor can determine the success or failure of irrigated farming, which periodically requires more labor than the household can provide, as in preparing land for tree planting, harvesting fruit, and pruning. Households capable of hiring the required additional labor, at "premium" wages when necessary, do better than the others.

The combination of clear land ownership, personal commitment of capital resources, and managerial decision making vested in the farm household itself, constitutes a mix more conducive to economic success than that found on the PPIs, despite the latter's reduced costs and, perhaps, more reliable provisioning of water.

PPI Production. Considering the great governmental emphasis on PPIs in terms of the overall budget and the provision of extension, one is struck by how small PPIs are in size, effectiveness, and number of beneficiaries. Including 360 hectares in al'Arish PPI in Kasserine North, there are a total of 17 functioning PPIs, covering an estimated area of 3,148 hectares, in the entire ODTC area. Although PPI land reform laws stipulate that the size of a PPI holding should not go below 1.5 ha and not above 8, many of the holdings are smaller than 1 ha and a few are above 10.

Production levels on the PPIs are generally lower than on shallow-well farms. Officially stated reasons for the poor performance of the PPIs include farmers' disinclination to invest in the land and their general reluctance to work hard. However, comparative experiences with publicly funded irrigation schemes in other parts of semiarid Africa and the Near East lead one to regard such "explanations" with a good deal of skepticism. Farmers on the PPIs offer several reasons for production levels below those desired: these have to do with the availability and cost of water.

Characteristic of the PPIs is the minimal control farmers exercise over water distribution. They are constrained in their choice of crops by the particular irrigation timetable adopted. Normally, water rotates once every 8 to 12 days. The number of water hours a farmer gets is a function of the size of his plot rather than of the kind of crop he may wish to grow. This bodes ill, for example, for potentially lucrative vegetable crops, since vegetables require less—but more frequent—watering than do fruit trees. Indeed, many PPI farm households that have tried vegetable production on a larger scale have had to opt out after suffering crop losses because of water scarcity. The situation is worsened if the flow of water in the deep well declines or is interrupted because of a pump breakdown or poor water allocation by the distributor. In such an event, it is not unusual to go without water for three or more weeks.

As far as water costs are concerned, government officials and some USAID personnel insist that water costs on PPIs are low—that is, highly subsidized. Farmers' complaints of high water costs are dismissed as merely signs of their miserliness and of their total dependence on the state to provide them with everything. The claim is that the actual cost of water (although how that cost is calculated is not made clear) is 70 millimes per cubic meter, while farmers pay only 14 millimes (12 in Foussana).

Farmers, on the other hand, insist that the cost of water has risen dramatically over the years, to the extent that they can no longer afford irrigation. In Sbeitla, for example, water costs have risen from 2 millimes per cubic meter in 1974–1976, to 4 millimes in 1976–1978, 6 millimes in 1978–1980, 10 millimes in 1980–1984, 12 millimes from October 1984 to March 1985, and 14 millimes starting in April 1985. Farmers who own both PPI and shallow-well farms claim that the cost of water on a PPI is almost twice that on the shallow-well farms.

Household Production Organization

Faced with such rising costs, PPI households have responded by altering their farming strategies. Typical household responses to the high cost of water include: (1) opting out of irrigated agriculture either temporarily (for one or more seasons) or permanently; (2) reducing the amount of land under irrigation in order to utilize a given quantity of water more effectively; (3) searching for a crop mix that is less water intensive; and (4) maintaining the existing production strategy. Poorer households with control over smaller plots of land are commonly the ones that opt out, though it is true that farms are sometimes abandoned by wealthier households or farmers because of the availability of more attractive alternatives to farming, especially labor migration.

Thus, by forcing some households to abandon irrigation altogether and others to reduce greatly their irrigation activities, the current high water costs and uncertainties regarding water flows have brought down overall demand for water. Water availability has thus actually increased for those who can afford it. On some perimeters, water that was available only once every 8 to 12 days is now made available both more often and for longer periods of time.

Aside from the availability and cost of water, another factor inhibits successful irrigation on the PPIs. It is the government's continued emphasis on fruit tree cultivation. Though fruit trees have the advantage of both a continuous decline in the amount of labor and water required and an increase in fruit production as they mature, they do not produce any fruit in the first two or three years, and do not come into full production for several more. This tends to discriminate against the poorest farmers and to have adverse effects on irrigation performance, as farmers without alternative sources of income are forced either to abandon the PPI plots or to pay them minimal attention in order to go out and search for wage employment. How is the farmer without alternative sources of income supposed to support himself and his family until the trees start producing? A typical official reply is, "Before, they did not have anything; now they at least have the trees, and in a few years they will forget about the bad times." Unfortunately, this knowledge does not provide people with food or clothes.

The extent to which a farm is neglected depends on the labor power that a household possesses. Farmers who have grown sons or daughters on the farm are in better positions than those who do not, since the girls can take care of the farm along with the mother, and the sons can assist the father in looking for outside employment.

Household Production

Tunisian peasant households operate as units of production, consumption, and reproduction (on both a daily and generational basis). Within this framework they are differentiated both internally and vis-à-vis other households in terms of their access to resources.

While all peasants, regardless of how wealthy they are, engage in agricultural production, the poor produce mostly for use value. The more affluent the household (affluence fluctuates for most peasants; it can change from year to year), the more its production is commoditized or exchanged. The same, however, is not true for labor, a factor of production: the poorer the peasant household, the more commoditized is its labor and the more poorly compensated, largely because of the lack of alternative employment possibilities and the paucity of skilled labor among poor households. More affluent households also engage in wage labor, but it tends to be skilled, more specialized, and much better compensated. Furthermore, while the poor sell their labor to meet the household's consumption needs, the better-off sell their labor as an investment to increase their wealth. This latter phenomenon is also evident with regard to the diversification of labor strategies: the poor generally diversify to survive from one year to the next, while the better-off diversify to increase their wealth.

The question inevitably arises as to what brings about such disparities in wealth levels and in the degree to which household production efforts are successful. Planners and government bureaucrats have usually attributed the relative success, or lack thereof, of individual peasant household production strategies, to peasants' intellectual and personality traits. In so doing, they have implicitly assumed away the importance of peasants' differential access to resources for ensuring success in household production activities. Some of these resources are material, such as land, water, capital, and livestock; others are socioeconomic and political, such as kinship and tribal affiliation, and social and political position; still others have to do with labor availability and access to markets.

Land. No matter what the farming system, the relative success or failure of a household depends, in large part, on the amount of land to which it has access. Because of the unequal and unpredictable distribution of rain in Central Tunisia, a dryland peasant household must have large parcels of land in several locations to help assure that at least one receives water. Moreover, easy access to land enables some households to shift from strictly dryland to semi-irrigated farming by digging a shallow well and putting part of the land under irrigation. Further, land may be sold to acquire capital to dig a well, or it may be used as collateral to acquire credit.

On PPIs and shallow-well farms the amount of land determines whether households can diversify production and qualify for credit and other services. In addition, on PPIs, larger plots enable households to acquire more water, since the number of hours of water a farm household receives per rotation is a direct outcome of plot size rather than of the area of the plot that is actually irrigated at one time. For example, a household that owns a 5-hectare plot but irrigates only half of it receives twice the amount of water of a household with a 2.5 hectare plot, although both are irrigating the same amount of land.

Water. Water is another resource fundamental to successful peasant household production efforts. The amount of water a peasant household has access to depends on rainfall patterns and the location of holdings, as well as on whether or not the household benefits from shallow-well or PPI irrigation.

Those peasant households who irrigate have the advantage of greater availability and control over water. The variety of crops they can grow increases, and they are permitted greater intensity of cultivation. Unfortunately, the possibility for most households of actually becoming a PPI member is remote, given the large number of dryland peasant households, the high cost of irrigating per unit of land, and the small size of PPIs.

Capital. The increasing monetization of the economy, including the commoditization of land and labor, is characteristic of most rural communities today. Central Tunisia being no different, money is required in all farming systems for a variety of purposes including tax payments, the provision of many household consumption needs, and the purchase of fertilizers, seeds, insecticides, manure, fuel or electricity (to run pumps), pump oil, and water (when pumps break, on deep and shallow wells alike). Although land sale is not very common in the area, it does occur, and capital facilitates the transfer of such lands. It is also used for financing well digging and lining and for hiring labor at peak agricultural times.

Capital, furthermore, facilitates the frequent and large-scale fulfillment of peasants' hospitality aspirations. Entertaining friends and acquaintances is an important means by which peasants get to know those in power, cement relationships, access valuable information concerning the arrival of such agricultural inputs as seeds and fertilizers, and receive in advance information related to credit availability. Entertaining may not be deliberately or calculatingly used to build influence and to obtain goods and services, but in situations where rewards such as credit are severely limited, it does not hurt an otherwise worthy customer to have broken bread with the person who is allocating the funds.

Labor. In all three production systems, farming relies mainly on household labor. Demands for labor increase with the expansion of irrigation (which calls for plowing, watering, weeding, and canal clearing) as cultivation is progressively intensified. Households that can provide labor internally (with a strong and healthy wife and grown children who reside on the farm) are in a much better position to produce more, more effectively, and earlier, than those who cannot. Not only are they unconstrained by labor shortages, but in slow periods, if their labor supply exceeds their on-farm labor demands, these households can take advantage of outside wage labor employment. Money thus acquired through wage labor can be used to hire workers in peak agricultural periods—for digging tree holes, planting trees, and harvesting.

Household labor availability is influenced by the family cycle: the most advantageous period being when the children are old enough to do the bulk of farm and housework, but too young to marry and set up their own households. The desire to insure a continuous supply of labor might help to explain the large size of peasant households. Households that are the least advantaged in terms of labor supply are old couples without any children at home or young couples with no or very young children. Various correcting mechanisms may deal with this disadvantage, including exchange labor and extended households.

Livestock. Peasant households able to purchase and maintain large numbers of livestock benefit from greater security and a wider range of production options. In addition to providing meat, milk, butter, hides, wool, and manure, livestock serve as insurance and as good sources of capital since animals can be sold to feed a household in bad years or to invest in agriculture or other household enterprises. Many well owners state that it was the sale of animals, mainly sheep, that facilitated well digging and construction. Also, raising smaller animals such as rabbits and hens provides a high-quality protein that even poorer households can eat on a more or less regular basis.

Marketing. Peasants' ability to market produce where it will receive its best price is influenced by a household's control over land, water, capital, and labor, and by its proximity to markets. Generally speaking, small farmers with minimal control over these resources are the most disadvantaged. Because of the small volume they harvest, for example, they are in no position to hire a pickup truck to transport the produce to the most attractive markets. They are thus tied down to local markets and merchants who frequently (when supply is plentiful) refuse to pay farmers the legal minimum prices. Faced with the grim alternative of taking the harvested crop back home to feed to animals or to allow to spoil, farmers are often forced to accept these illegal prices.

Kinship and Tribal Affiliation. Kinship and tribal affiliation determine access to many resources in Central Tunisia, especially land, water, animals, and labor. They help establish a household's rights to drylands, shallow-well farms, and/or PPIs. Thus, while members of kin groups, through the institutions of 'arsh and fariq, may qualify to inherit a piece of land, acquire use rights, or participate in a PPI, a stranger has very little chance of doing that except through direct purchase.

"Kin" and "stranger" are relative terms, determined by genealogical and spatial distances. A member of one's 'arsh is partially a relative but not as close as a member of one's fariq. In the same vein, a member of one's fariq can be considered very distant compared to one's own household. And, a man from ad-Doulaab, a Sbeitla sector, refers to himself and is referred to by others as a "stranger" in Shraayi', another Sbeitla sector, but compared to someone of Algerian or Libyan origin he is practically a brother.

Of course belonging to a local tribe is not in itself sufficient in gaining access to resources: the particular fariq and household within the fariq make a tremendous difference. For example, when a man from a Sbeitla PPI decided to give part of his land away, he did not distribute it arbitrarily to members of his fariq; rather, he allocated it among his three sons.

Social and Political Position. A peasant's social and political standing reinforces his control over the resources he already possesses and provides him with opportunities for acquiring more. The social and political position of household members is interlinked and determined by access to such resources as kinship and tribal affiliation, connections, land, capital, and livestock. Also important in determining social and political position are piety and religious learning.

Households' differential access to the variety of resources outlined above determines the viability and scale of production. Moreover, as this brief outline has suggested, access to particular resources is often interlinked to others. For example, an individual or household's access to capital facilitates access to people in economically and politically powerful positions, which in turn eases access to important and useful information. In this vein, presented below are field research findings related to factors enabling certain households to compete successfully for a valuable and limited resource: irrigated land.

Household Dynamics and Access to Resources

In Central Tunisia, peasants' unequal access to land manifests itself both within and among the three farming systems, ranging from those who are virtually landless to those with large parcels of land spread over several locations. A biased sample of 39 dryland farmers shows a range of from 3 to 70 hectares. (The sample was biased because it started with shallow-well or PPI farmers, all of whom own rainfed lands, who introduced me to relatives, friends, and acquaintances subsisting entirely on dry-land farming. "Pure" dryland farmers also talked about kin and friends with no land at all, but time constraints precluded interviewing them.) The range is even greater if one looks at access to irrigated land, whether PPI or shallow-well. Among an estimated 7,503 households in the Sbeitla delegation, only 310 have access to a shallow well (35 of the wells are still without motors); and only 109 households, some of which have shallow wells, have access to a PPI. Land distribution among shallow-well farmers and PPI participants is also very unequal. Since most shallow wells in Central Tunisia can irrigate a maximum of only three to five hectares, the land access differentiation among them lies in the amount of rainfed or semi-irrigated land they own. Inequality is most clearly seen among PPI farmers. In the Sbeitla PPI, which includes three zones and covers an area of 253 hectares divided among 79 households, 90 percent of the beneficiaries own only 51 percent of the land, the remaining 10 percent (8 households) owning 49 percent.

Although most of them are by no means affluent, these Sbeitla delegation households and several hundred others throughout the region have successfully competed for access to irrigated land. Why have they succeeded where others failed? What differentiates these households from relatives and friends without access to irrigation, and what differentiates them from each other? In the absence of data on pure dryland farm households, one can speculate on the factors that separate them from the others by looking at the similarities and differences between PPI and shallow-well farm groups.

To explore answers, we selected a sample of 17 households (A–Q) with access to irrigated land (12 PPI, 5 shallow-well) from the delegations of Sbeitla and Foussana. Each was visited at least three times, and each visit lasted a minimum of four hours. Information from each household was gathered through a general household survey, semiformal group and in-

TABLE 5.7
Land Ownership Among PPI Farm Households (in Hectares)

Household	PPI	Percentage	Dryland	Shallow Well
D	2.00	3.61	5+65/fariq[a]	---
E	1.80	3.25	65/fariq	---
F	1.80	3.25	65/fariq	---
G	8.00	14.45	80	---
H	1.75	3.16	13+60/3[b]	9
I	28.00	50.59	120	---
L	2.00	3.61	2	---
M	2.00	3.61	1	---
N	2.00	3.61	1	---
O	2.00	3.61	0	---
P	2.00	3.61	0	---
Q	2.00	3.61	0	---
Total	55.35	99.97		

[a] The household has 5 ha of its own and shares 65 ha communally with its fariq.
[b] It owns 13 ha outright and shares 60 ha with two other persons.

dividual interviews, informal discussions, and participant observation. Among the issues explored were: household composition and access to labor; access to cash resources and credit; presence of a well, its age, and its method of financing; presence of a motor and a motor shelter, their age and method of financing; economic diversification; labor allocation within the household; and intrahousehold differential access to household resources.

A household was defined as a kin-based corporate unit that, although not necessarily coresidential, or pooling all its resources and income, has common, though usually highly differentiated, access to the bulk of its production and labor resources and the income generated therefrom. Labor migrants who contribute more or less regularly to a household were considered members even if they were away for the entire year.

The field research findings allow us to say a few things about households' differential access to land, labor, and capital, including credit. Looking at total irrigated and nonirrigated land distribution among the twelve PPI households (Table 5.7), we note the dramatically unequal access that exists, a phenomenon that prevails on PPIs in general. Two households, or 17 percent of the twelve, own 65 percent of the area. Each of the other households, representing 8.3 percent of the number of households, owns less than 4 percent of the land. (Other PPI households, not represented in this sample, own even smaller areas of land—less than one hectare. Since they are also the ones most likely to give up on irrigation altogether, it was hard to track them down, but I hope to be able to do so in subsequent research.)

Considering the great discrepancies in land held among PPI peasant groups, we can postulate that the main requisite for becoming a PPI farmer is to have rights to a piece of land that the government selects as the site for a PPI. What need to be ascertained, then, are the factors that figure in the government's decision to choose one area over another. Water availability must be a decisive factor, since irrigation is impossible without water, but among the several sites with favorable water tables, what comes next? It is not unlikely that international, national, regional, and local political agendas play an important role; local and regional competitions and conflicts and perhaps the presence of interested influential people at the sites considered might persuade decision makers of the attractiveness of a particular area.

Access to shallow-well farms is a different story. Although government assistance in the form of loans and grants to shallow-well farmers has become common in the last few years, especially since the founding of ODTC and the involvement of USAID, many prospective shallow-well owners must still invest a good portion of their own capital into well construction. Even the households that receive considerable amounts in loans and grants cannot start the loan application process without some resources of their own. What follows are a few examples of financing arrangements adopted by the six shallow-well farmers in our sample (A, B, C, H,[1] J, and K) for the construction of their wells.

Household A received a credit of 1,782 TD for well digging, lining, and canal construction; an additional 2,856 to buy a motor; and was granted 500 fruit trees. To help cover the full expenses of well construction, motor purchase, and farm preparation, this household relied on regular remittances from a laborer son in Libya for the duration of two years.

Household B purchased its farm with a well, an old motor, and 200 fruit trees for 10,000 TD, money saved through trading and wage labor. To the goods that came with the farm the household added a new motor, financed with a 2,500 TD government loan; 400 fruit trees, also from the government; and a self-financed and constructed motor shelter.

Household C, headed by a wealthy merchant, was loaned 1,250 TD toward the digging and lining of a well, 2,960 TD to purchase a motor, and was granted 800 fruit trees. In addition to all the loans and grants received, the merchant claimed that he spent 12,000 TD of his own money to establish the farm, 6,000 TD of which he acquired by selling 150 sheep.

Household H, which, in addition to the shallow-well farm, owns a 1.75 hectare PPI plot, self-financed the initial digging of its well with a combination of household and hired labor. Once it reached water, it borrowed 130 TD toward lining the well, and 1,300 TD toward a motor. No loans or grants were offered to build the motor shelter. The household also received a total of 1,000 fruit trees and two greenhouses, financed by two loans at 1,200 and 1,700 TD respectively.

Finally, households J and K, closely related, share a well and a motor, which they acquired through government loans and grants and intensive household labor.

Stating that all households had some resources that facilitated access to a well should by no means imply that the six households were equally affluent. And, although the average shallow-well farmer is better off than the average PPI farmer, the differences between them should not be exaggerated.

Household Labor Allocation and Intrahousehold Differentiation. The preceding examples show the importance of capital and labor resources in determining how successful peasant production efforts will be. A closer view of the household reveals some additional relationships between households' differential access to resources and intrahousehold labor allocation and differentiation.

In an article on the allocation of familial labor and the formation of peasant household income in the Peruvian Sierra, Carmen Diana Deere (1983:119) observes:

> ... women in this peasant society do the bulk of time-intensive tasks of daily maintenance and participate actively in a variety of activities that generate use and exchange values for the family's subsistence. Men, in contrast, engage primarily in the production of exchange values. . . .
> As exchange values from farm production increase and an activity becomes an important source of cash income, men increasingly dominate the commercialization of the commodities that women have aided in producing.

Deere relates the economic and social roles of peasant women to the household's integration into the labor market and the commodity market and observes—as others have noted earlier (Salem-Murdock 1979)—that a woman's social class may influence attitudes about which activities are appropriate for her: poor peasant women may pursue activities that are considered unsuitable for better-off women.

What was noted by Deere in the Peruvian Sierra and by Salem-Murdock in Eastern Sudan is also true of peasant women in Central Tunisia. Like other members of a society, women are not an equally oppressed and subordinated homogeneous category. They belong to social classes and age groups subscribing to different ideals that define suitable and unsuitable behavior. Still, looking at it from an intrahousehold perspective, one notes that in all cases in Central Tunisia, women are less favored than men, and girls than boys. The inequality is translated into unequal access to resources, in that women usually are excluded from land ownership and credit, have less leisure time, and less education.

Table 5.8 and the bar graphs that follow (Figures 5.2, 5.3, and 5.4) show the number of hours that members of 15 of the 17 households, divided into three strata, spent in the performance of daily activities (house and farm work). Two atypical households (the two school teachers) were excluded, since for them agriculture is minor in terms of overall income and importance; inevitably their allocation of labor and resources is affected, and thus their inclusion in the table would bias the results. Also excluded are activities that are too seasonal to translate to daily hours—plowing and food processing. Since one is male- and the other female-oriented, their exclusion probably

TABLE 5.8
Intrahousehold Labor Allocation by Size of Holding and Age/Sex Group,
Average Hours per 15-hour Summer Day Among 15 Households

Size of Holding	Small Holders 0 - 3.9 ha (60%) N = 9					Medium Holders 4 - 7.9 ha (20%) N = 3					Large Holders 8 ha or more (20%) N = 3				
	Adult (over 15)		Children (6-14)			Adult (over 15)		Children (6-14)			Adult (over 15)		Children (6-14)		
Activity	Male	Female	Boys	Girls		Male	Female	Boys	Girls		Male	Female	Boys	Girls	
Cooking	0.0	1.8	0.0	0.8		0.0	1.9	0.0	0.8		0.0	2.1	0.0	0.9	
Collecting Firewood	0.0	1.2	0.4	0.9		0.0	0.9	0.5	0.8		0.0	0.5	0.4	0.4	
Cleaning	0.0	2.7	0.0	2.1		0.0	2.9	0.0	2.4		0.0	3.1	0.0	1.9	
Washing Clothes	0.0	1.3	0.0	0.9		0.0	1.4	0.0	0.9		0.0	1.7	0.0	0.7	
Child Care	0.0	3.7	0.2	1.1		0.0	3.5	0.2	1.2		0.0	3.9	0.5	0.9	
Animal Care	0.0	0.4	2.1	3.1		0.0	0.2	1.4	2.5		0.0	0.1	1.7	2.6	
Artisan Production	0.0	0.3	0.2	0.3		0.0	0.5	0.2	0.2		0.0	0.5	0.0	0.4	
Subtotal: Housework	0.0	11.4	2.9	9.2		0.0	11.3	2.3	8.8		0.0	11.9	2.6	7.8	
Hauling Water	0.0	0.2	1.2	1.1		0.0	0.1	1.3	1.3		0.0	0.1	1.2	1.2	
Tilling under Trees	0.9	1.2	1.1	1.7		1.6	0.8	1.6	0.9		1.9	0.5	1.6	1.1	
Planting	0.3	0.1	0.2	0.1		0.4	0.0	0.2	0.0		0.6	0.0	0.2	0.0	
Watering	3.1	0.6	1.8	1.7		3.4	0.0	2.3	1.1		3.8	0.0	2.3	1.2	
Weeding	1.1	1.2	1.1	0.9		1.0	0.8	1.2	0.9		1.0	0.6	1.2	0.9	
Harvesting	0.5	0.2	0.3	0.2		0.5	0.2	0.3	0.2		0.4	0.3	0.4	0.3	
Fertilizing	0.1	0.0	0.0	0.0		0.1	0.0	0.0	0.0		0.2	0.0	0.0	0.0	
Marketing	0.1	0.0	0.2	0.0		0.3	0.0	0.2	0.0		0.3	0.0	0.3	0.0	
Wage Labor	2.9	0.0	0.3	0.0		1.5	0.0	0.3	0.0		0.9	0.0	0.1	0.0	
Subtotal: Farm Labor	9.0	3.5	6.2	5.7		8.8	1.9	7.4	4.4		9.1	1.5	7.3	4.7	
Total	9.0	14.9	9.1	14.9		8.8	13.2	9.7	13.2		9.1	13.4	9.9	12.5	

118

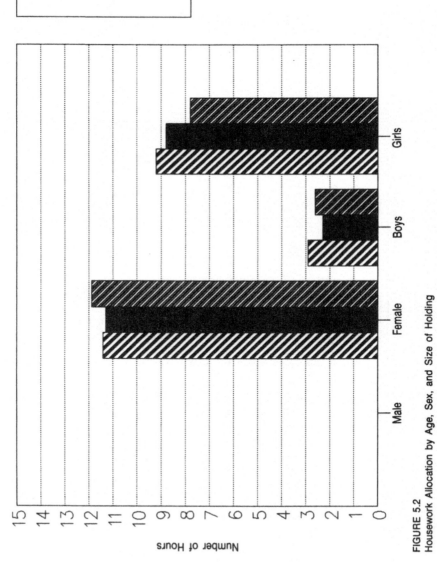

FIGURE 5.2
Housework Allocation by Age, Sex, and Size of Holding

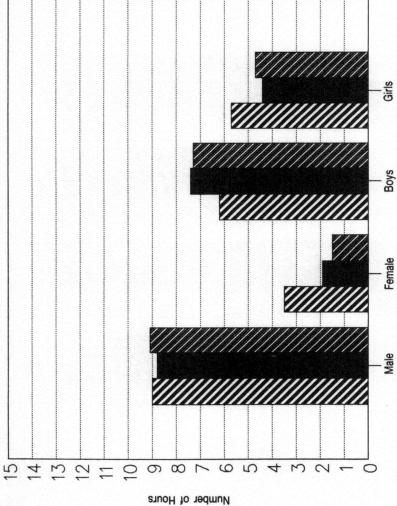

FIGURE 5.3
Farm Labor Allocation by Age, Sex, and Size of Holding

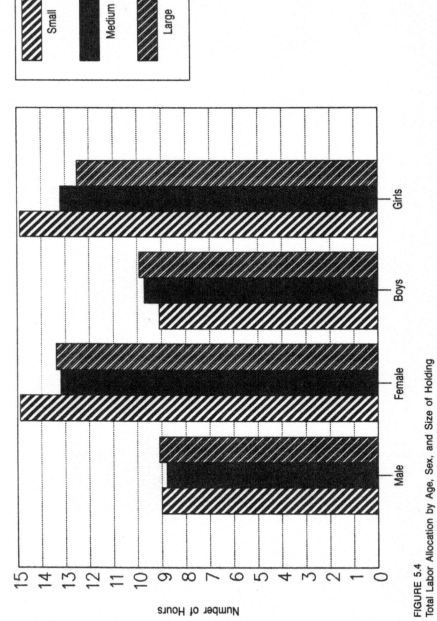

FIGURE 5.4
Total Labor Allocation by Age, Sex, and Size of Holding

balances out the male/female division of labor. Wage labor includes both skilled (such as tree pruning and motor installation) and unskilled labor.

Although a peasant woman's social position may influence attitudes about which activities are considered proper for her, none of the 15 households is rich enough to reduce greatly the number of hours that the women have to work each day. In other words, although the composition of a woman's work may vary, the duration of the work remains high. Whether they belong to small-, medium-, or large-holder households, women work from 13 (better-off women) to almost 15 hours a day (Figure 5.4). Perhaps because none of the households is rich enough to make a difference, the adult female composition of the household is often more important than the size of holding in determining the daily duration of women's work. A woman who has grown daughters at home is more likely to have some free time than one who does not. The size of holding might make a difference in the case of female children, since girls from wealthier households (generally those with larger holdings) are more likely to attend school, thereby reducing both the number of hours they spend at home every day and their work load. We were unable to test this, however, since the survey was carried out during summer vacation.

While women spend more hours working than men, and girls than boys, upper strata women spend more of their working hours in the house than do others (Figures 5.2 and 5.3). Female time, in all strata, is spent mostly in production-for-use value. The female production-for-use value and male production-for-exchange value is correlated with household access to resources; the better off a household, the higher will be the percentage of female production-for-use value of total household production. In poor families, male production-for-exchange value rises because of the necessity of treating labor as a commodity for exchange.

Production Strategies

Central Tunisian peasant households' production strategies vary according to their different access to land, capital, labor, and water; their kinship and tribal affiliation, social position, and connections; and the different farming systems in which they are involved, whether dryland or irrigated.

Dryland Strategies

Dryland farm households' strategies depend on land size and location, crops grown on the land, and the number of animals kept. Several tendencies prevail. To compensate for the scarcity of rainfall and its variability in frequency and distribution, most farmers will diversify production in terms both of crops and of areas planted, thus increasing the probability of at least some returns in some of the areas. In good years, farmers will store as much of the surplus produce as possible for the following year, and/or they may try to sell a portion of it in order to purchase animals that can be sold when the need arises. Any adult household members not taking part in agricultural activities will usually seek wage labor. Ultimately, when water-table conditions permit, those who have the cash or the connections and influence to acquire loans will dig a shallow well to enhance the security and productivity of their farm.

Irrigation Strategies

Irrigation farmers, whether on a PPI or operating a shallow-well farm, are distinguished from each other by the amount of experience they have with irrigation, the size of the holding, the availability of water and labor, and the kind and degree of support received from the various government agencies in the form of loans and grants—cash and in-kind—and extension. Because irrigation in Central Tunisia is so recent, farmers rely on extension not only for the provision of such inputs as fertilizers, insecticides, seeds and seedlings, and trees, but also for advice on methods of cultivation and irrigation. The unreliability of extension (for reasons mentioned below) tends to develop farmers who regard themselves as alone, with very little support from the outside. This is particularly true of the smallholders who form the majority of irrigation farmers in the area.

Farmers in this situation proceed carefully, especially in the beginning. They start by irrigating small parcels of land although there might be water sufficient for a larger area, sticking to crops they know well, and diversifying production to the extent that, in an extreme case, one hectare might hold over ten different crops. This conservatism, abhorred by officials and regarded as unreasonable and archaic, represents a sound minimax strategy from the operating household's perspective, limiting the possibility of high gain but also minimizing risk. Similarly, small farmers who have not been able to market their produce successfully (because of inadequate market outlets within their reach), tend to adopt a more conservative strategy the following year. Crops are diversified, with an emphasis on those crops that can be used directly by the household. Or, farmers who have lost vegetable crops, as has happened on many PPIs because of water scarcity, often reduce the area devoted to vegetables and plant only enough to meet household needs and a small surplus for marketing.

With little irrigation experience and very little of what he considers "trustworthy" support from the outside, the farmer gains from smaller plots planted in known crops the opportunity to understand the micro variations on his farm, to see what can grow where, to acquire a grip over crops' water requirements, and to avoid the risks of flooding the market with a crop that has been overcultivated, or of losing everything because his land proved unsuitable for the crop grown. Diversification also provides most of the household's subsistence needs from its own production. A clear case of small farmers' tendency to be conservative when first irrigating is the difference in farming techniques adopted by farmers of Sbeitla, where irrigation has been practiced for years, and by farmers of Foussana, where it is fairly recent.

Recommendations

At the end of the study the following recommendations were made to USAID/Tunis and ODTC.

The recent nature of irrigation in the area, coupled with the introduction of a number of new crops and new varieties of old ones, make efficient and effective agricultural extension a must if high production is to be achieved in a short time. For this to come about, a good working relationship between peasant farmers and extension staff, based on mutual respect and trust, is crucial. Although there are a few cases in each delegation where such relationships seem to exist (those are the few successful "showcase farmers" that "visiting experts" seem to meet, year after year), farmers and agents usually regard each other with suspicion. Agents regard farmers as mostly illiterate, ignorant, and archaic; farmers regard agents as mostly "green," inexperienced, uncaring, and unknowledgeable. In fact, the existing problems are normally caused neither by agents nor farmers. Any reforms in the provision of extension services, and in the implementation of development projects, should take particular care to incorporate the following changes:

1. Increase the number of extension personnel and transport vehicles.

The scarcity of extension agents (at all levels of training) is a problem to which ODTC will have to pay very close attention if it does not want its tremendous efforts at expanding irrigation and fruit tree cultivation to be wasted. Even the most skillful and totally devoted agent can do very little in the present circumstances. Everybody agrees that shallow-well farms are much more productive than PPIs. Because of personnel and transportation scarcity, however, agents usually focus primarily on PPIs, where farmer concentration is greatest, at the expense of shallow-well farms. In Foussana delegation, for example, there are two functioning PPIs, another two in progress, and 600 shallow wells, but only two ODTC extension agents (one of whom has heavy administrative responsibilities that limit the time he can spend visiting farms) with at present one vehicle, which is used primarily for administrative and political activities.

2. Improve the input supply process.

The scarcity, unavailability, and late arrival of agricultural inputs is detrimental both to farmers and to those agents who would like to maintain a good relationship with farmers. Measures should be taken to ensure that the appropriate inputs reach farmers regularly and on a timely basis.

3. Increase the availability of pump mechanics.

Despite the presence of numerous PPIs and many shallow wells in Central Tunisia, qualified pump mechanics are few, although there is frequent breakage of equipment. ODTC might consider training some mechanics, perhaps people from the farms themselves, to service the area, or encourage such activity on the part of the private sector.

4. *Target women's needs.*

Women in Central Tunisia not only perform a lot of the agricultural work along with their husbands, fathers, and brothers, they are also fully responsible for the farm when the men are away. Nevertheless, agriculture in Central Tunisia is viewed as an entirely male venture, and extension programs are almost wholly male oriented. What extension is offered to women is in the form of social services. Women's exclusion from extension is compounded by the strict adherence of rural households to the separation of their womenfolk from male strangers. Therefore, when an extension agent visits a farm that is not very well known to him, he is likely to turn around and leave without talking to anyone if the male household head is absent.

Even where male household heads are on the farm when agents arrive, a job the agent thinks of as important is likely to remain undone because the person approached is too busy. I discussed this problem with an extension agent who has a reputation for competence and hard work. He told me that he personally had faced and still faces this problem quite often. "I have been trying to get this farmer to do something; he always said he would, but he never did. I have been noticing, meanwhile, during my visits to his farm, that his wife and daughters were doing most of the farm work. One day I decided to approach his wife, an older woman. I could never have been able to do that if she were young. I told her what needed to be done and why, and she said she would see to it. I came back the following afternoon: it was done, well."

Agricultural extension for women might be achieved (a) by having extension workers talk to the older women who in turn could transmit the message to their daughters and daughters-in-law and (b) by connecting social with agricultural extension work, offering female social workers enough agricultural training to be able to advise rural women on questions and problems faced daily in agriculture, or (c) by carrying out on-farm training of several local farmers, both male and female, in each area. These farmers could then serve as extension agents for their neighbors.

5. *Incorporate women directly in development projects.*

Because of women's major contributions to household production in Central Tunisia, they should be made an integral part of all development projects in the area, and some small-scale projects should be specifically geared toward female farmers. One possibility might be a women's small ruminant project. Women could be offered in-kind credit of sheep and goats or perhaps even local cows that are well adapted to the area. The project would improve the household's nutritional status, especially that of women and children; improve the condition of the soil through manure; and contribute to female income, since wool can be converted into blankets and other woolens.

6. *Avoid interfering unnecessarily in peasants' shallow-well farming activities.*

In light of the anticipated and recommended increased focus on shallow-well farming, it must not be forgotten that the success of such ventures is closely linked to a combination of clear ownership of land, commitment of personal resources, and total managerial control—including control over water distribution. Therefore, it is highly recommended that this mix not be compromised by either vastly reducing the individual farm household's financial participation in the operation or, what is even more significant, by restricting the household's arena of decision making. Governments, donors, and parastatals are recurrently tempted to do both; they should make every effort to resist this temptation.

7. *Undertake feasibility studies prior to project implementation.*

A complete socioeconomic study should precede any final decision on where to situate a new PPI in order to avoid such situations as the one ODTC faced in Foussana, where, after the deep well was dug and the canal laid out, it was discovered that the land was *waqf* land. The studies should investigate land-tenure customs and land-use patterns, the social organization of production, and socioeconomic differentiation. They should take a minimum of three months and should be carried out by an experienced social scientist.

Notes

1. Household H has access to both PPI and shallow-well land.

References

Deere, Carmen Diana
 1983 The Allocation of Familial Labor and the Formation of Peasant Household Income in the Peruvian Sierra. *In* Women and Poverty in the Third World. Mayra Buviniv, Margaret A. Lycette, and William Paul McGreevey, eds. Pp. 104–129. Baltimore, MD: The Johns Hopkins University Press.

Salem-Murdock, Muneera
 1979 The Impact of Agricultural Development on a Pastoral Society: The Shukriya of the Eastern Sudan. Working Paper No. 17. Binghamton, NY: Institute for Development Anthropology.

USAID/Tunis
 1983 Dryland Farming Systems Research Subproject (No. 664-0312.2) and Small Holder Irrigation Development Subproject (No. 664-1212.3) of the Central Tunisia Rural Development Project. Project Evaluation.

6

Development in Hammam Sousse, Tunisia: Change, Continuity, and Challenge

Frederick C. Huxley

Introduction

General Context

Along part of Tunisia's central coast, a densely populated strip of villages, towns, and cities is called the Sahel (Arabic for "coast" or "plain"). Since Carthaginian times, villages there have produced olives, fruit, and vegetables for market, while towns and cities have specialized in craft production, commerce, and administration (Fahem 1968). More recently, the communities of the Sahel have also served a crucial political role. The Neo-Destour Party, which directed the struggle for national independence, was founded in one of them; the founder and much of the party's leadership come from the region; and relationships established there have constituted important channels of influence on the independent government from 1956 until today (Moore 1963, 1988:180; Chipaux 1986).

Hammam Sousse, a growing community near the northern end of the Sahel, is seen in Figure 6.1 relative to nearby points of interest and to the country as a whole. In addition to exemplifying the economic and political characteristics of its region, Hammam Sousse has provided a model of effective village development. This chapter will discuss change, continuity, and challenge in that community. The discussion begins by analyzing the evolution of the local political economy up to 1961. This analysis reinterprets literature on Hammam Sousse and emphasizes factors underlying the community's history of strong collective actions and sentiments. Next the chapter examines four indexes of local development—population, economy, public services, and construction—to show how they changed historically between 1956 and 1971, how they were expected to change from 1971 to 1986, and how they were observed to have changed between 1971 and 1979. The discussion then turns to how development in Hammam Sousse was likely

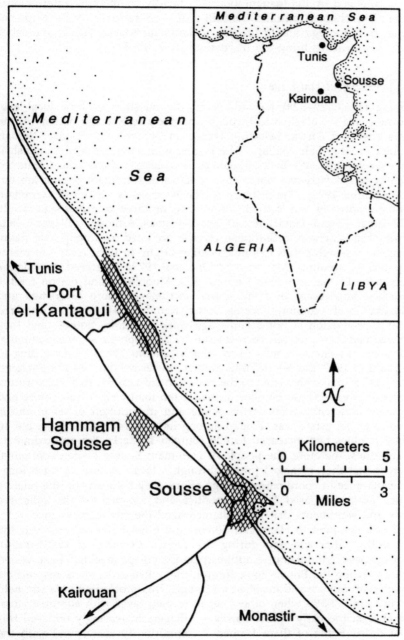

FIGURE 6.1
The Coastline of Tunisia Including Port el-Kantaoui, Hammam Sousse, and Sousse

to be challenged by the inauguration of a nearby complex for international tourism. The chapter indicates the utility of these remarks for development policies, anthropology, and the people of Hammam Sousse. Finally, it finishes with a postscript to bring the discussion up to 1988.

Local Development Until 1961

Moore (1963:527–528) has addressed the question of how local-level democracy might be achieved through one-party rule in the nations of the Middle East and Africa. Selecting Hammam Sousse as a "typical though not quite average Sahel village," he begins with factors that distinguish it from its neighbors. While local politics in nearby villages are dominated by family-based factions, Moore says, politics in Hammam Sousse are not (cf. Abu Zahra 1972). The primary reason he gives is historical: Hammam Sousse purportedly was settled "only" two or three centuries ago, while neighboring villages date from Carthaginian times. Although villager beliefs and the observations of a European traveler are cited to support this claim, subsequent research points to a much earlier origin. In 1979, local informants and published accounts (Marjan 1978:10; Qanal 1979a:50) traced the village's history back to the thirteenth century A.D. Moore's second reason for the diminished importance of family-based factions—a more diversified and productive local economy—seems better founded. Villagers emphasized vegetable production at home and wage work in nearby Sousse, and they supplemented their privately owned lands by developing a sizable communal estate some fifteen kilometers to the north (Bureau 1972a:1). According to informants in 1979, the Bey of Tunis granted this estate during the eighteenth century as an inalienable trust to the ten extended families then constituting Hammam Sousse. These families formed a ten-man council to oversee and coordinate both cultivation of the estate and distribution of its products. By the time the estate was divided among its owners in the 1930s, the 10 original families had increased to 420 (Bureau 1972a:1). For approximately two centuries, therefore, the people of Hammam Sousse owned communal resources that they managed jointly through a local institution. Such long-term experience in coordinating village efforts may help explain the relative absence of family-based factional politics and account for the collective actions and sentiments that have characterized the community since.

A factor common to Hammam Sousse and other Sahel villages was the "dual polity" that emerged during the French Protectorate (1881–1956). Under the beys, administrative authority on the village level had been vested in sheiks. When the French took control, they ousted the sheik responsible for Hammam Sousse and installed a protégé. This protégé and his son held the office until 1939,[1] when others began to gain favor with administrators. From at least the early 1930s, however, villagers increasingly opposed this official order. Some of them formed a committee to correspond with the Destour Party of Sheik al-Tha'alabi; others joined the Neo-Destour, an offshoot party established by Habib Bourguiba in 1934.

Nationally, the Neo-Destour gained prominence by building an infrastructure of party branches and associated organizations to reflect and direct Tunisian aspirations (Salem 1984:98–131). Locally, the Hammam Sousse branch of the party influenced opposition to legal authorities by building a covert organization paralleling the formal administration. From headquarters in a religious shrine near the main square of the village, the party branch gained control of the local scouting troop, a student organization, and an association for secondary school graduates (Moore 1963:533).

The growing symbiosis between local opposition and the party branch was highlighted by two events after World War II. The first was the establishment of an independent Qur'anic primary school in 1945. The leader of the movement establishing this school, Sheik Mohammed Bahri, mobilized a wide range of supporters—the party branch (clandestinely), ordinary citizens, and even the sheik who represented Hammam Sousse in the colonial administration. Taken by surprise, the French allowed the school —the only one of its kind in the region—to open, and it subsequently flourished.

The second event occurred in 1950. An election was held to choose a new administrative sheik, for the old one had been dismissed two years earlier on corruption charges. The new sheik differed from his predecessors, however, in at least two important ways: he was president of the local party branch and a grandson of the sheik originally deposed by the French in 1881 (Moore 1963:533). Thus, he manifested in his person the emerging linkage between the party and local social organization.

By the early 1950s, the Neo-Destour Party was solidly based in Hammam Sousse, and many villagers were actively opposing the French. As the "dialogue" between the liberation movement and colonial authorities entered a more violent phase in 1952, "some fifty village militants actively participated in the party's terrorist network," and three local people were killed for cooperating with the French (Moore 1963:533). Despite the extreme political discord expressed by these killings, there were local efforts to reestablish social solidarity. Informants in 1979 described how villagers sought to console the victims' families by visiting, meeting immediate material needs, and helping family members to get jobs or education. The success of these efforts is indicated by the continuing local residence of the children and other relatives of those killed. Several have married in the community and now raise their own children there.

In 1956, the establishment of an independent national government dominated by the Neo-Destour implied that the gap between the official administration and local political realities would narrow. Elections for new local governments were planned for the following year. The Hammam Sousse party branch campaigned openly in cafés and rallies, arguing that those who "had brought independence should govern the village" (Moore 1963:535). Their independent opponents campaigned mostly from house to house, promising a local government without patronage obligations to the party faithful. Since this election was the first where women could vote, the independents actively sought their support, enlisting women to mobilize their "sisters."

When the votes were counted, the independents had won by almost two to one. This surprising result—defeat of the party that had led the independence struggle and was at the peak of its popularity nationally—happened in only three of the ninety communities choosing municipal councils in 1957. Moore (1963:535-536) traces this loss to the complacency of the "clique" guiding the local party branch. Another interpretation would be that local community solidarity, which preceded the development of the Neo-Destour, was only temporarily or situationally allied with it during the independence struggle. Members of the community sought to assert its autonomy vis-à-vis their former ally when independence was achieved, appealing to women's networks to support their efforts. In doing so, they would continue to reinforce the roles of women in maintaining village autonomy, roles still manifested by their traditional dress or in their exchanges of labor and goods between households.[2]

Whatever the reasons for the independents' success, it was short-lived. Within three months, their municipal council was undermined by a combination of local and regional efforts, and village affairs were allocated to a delegate of the provincial governor.

In 1960 another municipal election was held. Heading the Neo-Destour list then was Hedi Baccouche, a villager who had recently completed university study abroad. President of the Neo-Destour Foundation in France, Baccouche became a party leader in the Sahel upon his return. Baccouche was joined by five others seeking positions in the Hammam Sousse municipal council: a young man plus four of the more popular members of the 1957 party list. Since only party candidates were allowed to run in this election (and in every succeeding one until 1980), the Neo-Destour won, but voter turnout dropped almost 30 percent to 2,362 (Moore 1963:537). During the following year, the new council put the municipality's affairs in order, and the party consolidated its position. Then, when new policies from higher echelons in the Neo-Destour streamlined the organization of local branches, the executive committee of the Hammam Sousse branch was reduced from eight members to five. In the election to fill those five seats, local leaders had to compete against each other. Baccouche ran only as an honorary president; four of the eight former leaders were reelected; and a younger protégé of Baccouche gained the fifth seat. In this way a kind of "democratic centralism" was effected: the arena for real choice (versus simple ratification) was shifted from municipal elections, where all citizens could vote, to party elections, where only members could vote.

Moore argues (1963:538-540) that the events of 1957-1961 in Hammam Sousse showed what could happen if Tunisian elections followed a quasi-Western model: they could produce autonomous municipal councils, while almost all Tunisian leaders were advocating centralized coordination and national discipline in the "battle against underdevelopment." Within the Neo-Destour Party, however, members shared a broad consensus about what was needed and how to do it, so elections could function differently there. An adept leader could judge the popular will—especially within the party but also in the community at large. Then he could eliminate candidates judged objectionable, and incorporate new people into local institutions. In this way divisions could be resolved and new forces accommodated, while the community developed in harmony with the region and nation around it.

Social organization in Hammam Sousse made Baccouche's accomplishment both possible and necessary. Several historical experiences helped form that organization. One was a diversified local economy. Another was the long-term ownership and operation of a communal estate. Still another, multi-faceted one was the struggle for independence: it included participating in political parties, inaugurating a local school, electing a new administrative sheik, and reestablishing social solidarity after villagers were assassinated.

Thus both a new political organization and a strong village community were in place by 1961. These factors have continued to influence development in Hammam Sousse.

Change and Continuity in Hammam Sousse

In the years following, the community developed within the political framework Moore described, though a good deal faster than anticipated. A new town hall, sports arena, market, and residential section were built, occupied, and functioning in 1979. Other changes were also emerging in population, economy, public services, and construction. A plan prepared for Hammam Sousse in 1972 (Bureau 1972a, 1972b) analyzes the historical development of the village during the 15 years from independence to 1971; it then projects expected changes and continuities in its development over the next 15 years. The plan thus provides a basis for comparison with observations made during field research in 1979.

Historical Development: 1956-1971

Population. According to national censuses, the population of Hammam Sousse grew from 9,435 in 1956 to 11,876 in 1966 (Bureau 1972a:43). This was an average annual increase of 2.3 percent, which was above the average rates for nearby villages and for the nation as a whole.[3] In fact, during this period Hammam Sousse was the fastest growing community of its size in all Sousse Province (Bureau 1972a:43).

During the period 1966-1971, this rate of growth accelerated further. A survey carried out for the development plan found a population of 14,692 in August-September 1971, implying an annual increase of 4.3 percent since 1966. This rate may have been artificially high, however, influenced by "temporary" factors (like immigration of persons avoiding the housing crisis in nearby Sousse) as well as by more long-term demographic trends internal to Hammam Sousse (Bureau 1972a:43). Accordingly, the development plan sought to view the population growth over a longer period, from independence to 1971. After subtracting the 420 persons counted as local residents but temporarily living elsewhere, the plan found a population of 14,272 inhabitants and an average annual increase of 2.8 percent.

Economy. The survey for the development plan counted persons residing in Hammam Sousse and working either there or in Sousse in the following sectors: industry and construction, tourism, public administration, and education. It did not enumerate persons working in agriculture, commerce, crafts, or more informal activities. Instead, the development plan estimated those sectors after adopting two assumptions: first, the labor force equalled the number of adult males who were not students; and second, the labor force constituted the same proportion of total population as it did in 1966.[4] On this basis, there were 2,711 workers and almost no unemployment in Hammam Sousse in 1971 (Bureau 1972a:73–74). The sectoral distribution of this labor force was thus: 33.9 percent in agriculture, 27.7 percent in industry and construction, 7.3 percent in commerce, 7.2 percent in crafts, 4.4 percent in tourism, 3.6 percent in public administration, 2.2 percent in education, and 13.7 percent in other occupations or unemployed.[5]

The structure of the local labor force was thus rather complex and "urban" (Wirth 1938; Fischer 1976), despite the community's long-term association with agriculture[6] and despite its designation as a "village"—a word connoting rurality—in the speech of local citizens. One aspect of this complex structure was the sectoral distribution of the labor force: almost two-thirds of all jobs were outside agriculture. This distribution is perhaps best seen as an enhancement of prior trends, the further diversification of a local economy where agricultural and nonagricultural work had been combined for a long time.

Public Services. In 1971 the number and functional specialization of public services offered in Hammam Sousse was impressive. Given the importance of education in local history, it is not surprising that the three primary schools enrolled 3,425 students (24 percent of the total village population) and operated two shifts per day. Two kindergartens also existed, enrolling some 200 children, and an estimated 479 students attended secondary schools, either locally or in the region.

The community was also served by the municipality, the administrative sheik, a detachment of gendarmes, and a branch of the postal, telegraph, and telephone service. Cultural and social activities were available at the town hall or through the party branch and several clubs. Sports and other pastimes were possible at the municipal stadium or in five cafés (including one at the municipal beach). Three Turkish baths served a clientele of about 200 persons per day. Religious services were provided by three mosques, and many villagers also visited the six local shrines of holy people, for entertainment or to celebrate rites of passage (e.g., circumcisions).

The one service where the community seemed deficient concerned health, for there was only a government dispensary to provide medical services. The lack of local doctors or pharmacies, however, was somewhat mitigated by their ready availability in Sousse, a quick taxi or bus ride away.

Construction. Perhaps the most obvious changes and continuities in the development of Hammam Sousse concerned its physical structures. In 1956, the village looked like many others in the Sahel (Moore 1963). Surrounded by gardens and orchards, the community had a dense residential nucleus crossed by narrow, twisting streets and alleys (Bureau 1972b: Carte No. SP h/4HS). Most buildings presented one wall to the street, touched other constructions on their remaining sides, and had interior open courtyards. Hammam Sousse then covered some 60 hectares, with the more recent construction generally toward its southern side. By 1963, the major village streets had been widened and straightened, and new ones were being laid out on a regular grid. By 1971, the community had expanded to 96 hectares, extending almost to the southern boundary of the municipality and moving eastward across the highway linking Sousse to Tunis (Bureau 1972b: Carte No. SP 4/HS).

Of the 2,958 physical structures in the village in 1971, 85 percent (2,511) were residences (Bureau 1972a:11). A typical house had two rooms and shared several walls with its neighbors. Owned by the persons who occupied it, the house was made of solid materials in satisfactory condition and had a kitchen, toilet, septic tank, and electricity, but no piped water, bathtub, or shower. One reason for the relative absence of running water was the lack of a sewage system in most of the village. A layer of rock underlying the community at a shallow depth (Bureau 1972a:4) made installing sewers a project of major difficulty and expense.

This picture of typical construction reflects a synthesis of data from all the zones into which planners had divided the village. Variations can be illuminated by contrasting the zone where construction was poorest with that where it was best. In both zones, most of the buildings were occupied by their owners, but the poorest zone was one of the oldest; the best zone, one of the newest. In the poorest zone, only 39 percent of construction was in good repair; in the best zone, 96 percent was. The poorest zone averaged 1.9 rooms per building; in the best zone there were 3.2, almost twice as many. In short, marked differences in construction, and especially in housing, existed in Hammam Sousse.

Historical Development: Summary and Implications. From 1956 to 1971, development in Hammam Sousse was characterized by changes and continuities in several domains. Among the changes were increases in population, public services, and construction (especially regarding the amount and diversity of housing). Among the continuities were political stability (at least since 1960) and local perceptions of a persisting community identity. Change within continuity was shown by the increasing diversification of employment in an already mixed local economy.

This local pattern of changes and continuities contrasts in some important ways with regional and national patterns of development during the period. While data are not currently available for a systematic comparison in all four domains (population, economy, public services, and construction), it seems clear that the population of Hammam Sousse grew more rapidly than that of its regional neighbors or most communities in the nation. In part, this growth resulted from immigration, as the community provided opportunities for employment and/or housing not available elsewhere (Bureau 1972a:71; see also Brown 1983, Hopkins 1977b, and Nellis 1983). Of course, these factors also helped Hammam Sousse to retain its native sons and daughters as they became adults, took jobs, and established new families. The overall effect of this pattern of development, therefore, was a rise in community importance relative to the region and the nation. That is, major social differentiation occurred between Hammam Sousse and other communities, although important differentiation was also emerging in employment and housing within the village.

Expected Development: 1971–1986

The 1972 plan projected how Hammam Sousse would develop over the subsequent 15 years by first estimating growth in the local population and then calculating what employment, public services, and construction that population would need.

Population. On the basis of the figures discussed above, it predicted that local population would grow (at 2.8 percent a year) to 21,589 by 1986, an increase of slightly over 50 percent (Bureau 1972a:47–48). This prediction, the assumptions on which it was based, and its implications for policy appeared to be vindicated in 1975. In that year the national census counted the population of Hammam Sousse as 15,812 (15,603 "urban" and 209 "rural"), less than 1 percent different from the 1972 development plan's estimate of 15,939. The plan's expectations about population growth thus seemed supported by an actual count of local residents, but a later count (discussed below) suggested that these figures were a serious underestimate.

Economy. The plan estimated there were 2,711 persons in the labor force in 1971. Since 2,821 families then lived in Hammam Sousse, this made a ratio of approximately one employed person per family. The plan figured that a total of 4,151 jobs would be necessary to maintain this ratio in 1986 (Bureau 1972a:74), but the basis of the calculation is not given and it seems to be an error. The total number of families, and jobs, in 1986 should rather be 4,267.[7] While the difference between the figures is small (less than 3 percent), it distorts subsequent calculations.

Using thereafter the assumptions employed in the plan (Bureau 1972a:74–75), one may calculate how the total number of jobs should be distributed. The plan assumed that the 2,711 jobs held by villagers in 1971 would continue to exist in 1986. When these are subtracted from 4,267, the revised total, 1,556 new jobs must be created. Assuming that the geographic distribution of these jobs would be the same in 1986 as in 1971, 1,064 (or 68.4 percent) of them should be in Hammam Sousse itself, the remainder in Sousse (Bureau 1972a:74). Inferring that industry and construction would grow in Hammam Sousse as in the past, the plan guidelines suggest that 217 new jobs should be created in that sector; 80 new jobs should be created in education to maintain the earlier ratios of teachers to students and employees to institutions; and 114 new jobs would be required in commerce to preserve that sector's share of the 1971 distribution. In crafts, greater mechanization of production and the desire for a higher standard of living were expected to keep the number of jobs at the 1971 level, and analogous factors would have a similar effect in agriculture. Installation of a perinatal clinic and a youth center, plus reinforcement of services already existing in 1971, would require 15 new jobs in public administration. Finally, and by far the most important, 638 new jobs would have to be created in tourism. In other words, 60 percent of all new employment in Hammam Sousse in 1986 would be in just one sector—a sector that constituted only 2 percent of the local work force in 1971.[8]

The plan does not discuss the procedure by which employment needs in tourism were estimated. The sector appears to be a residual category left after all others were subtracted from the total new employment expected in Hammam Sousse, but this procedure is based on questionable assumptions. For example, one of them is that the "other occupations or unemployed" sector of the labor force will be distributed exactly the same in 1986 as it was in 1971. Given the changes expected in most other sectors, why should this one remain stable?

The plan also does not detail its reasons for a tremendous increase of jobs in tourism. Instead it refers in passing (Bureau 1972a:75) to programs of the Tunisian National Office for Tourism, which favored the creation or expansion of projects on nearby beaches. One of these will be discussed below, but the example of a hotel built in the late 1960s should be mentioned here.[9] This hotel, named the Sidi Kantaoui after a nearby shrine, drew most of its employees from Sousse, not from Hammam Sousse or other villages that were physically closer. The development plan (Bureau 1972b: Carte No. 5,2) claimed this employment pattern resulted from a lack of trained personnel in the villages. The plan further warned that unless a simultaneous effort was made to train villagers, the expansion of tourist facilities would "not be able to absorb the local workforce" (Bureau 1972b: Carte No. 5,2).

Combining all this information, and assuming that the Hammam Sousse villagers working in Sousse would be distributed as they had been earlier, the 1986 labor force was expected to be structured into the following sectors: 21.5 percent in agriculture, 27.7 percent in industry and construction, 7.3 percent in commerce, 4.6 percent in crafts, 18.7 percent in tourism, 3.1 percent in public administration, 3.5 percent in education, and 13.4 percent in other occupations or unemployed.

Public Services. The plan anticipated that only a few new services would have to be created for Hammam Sousse but that many existing ones would require expansion. For instance, it advocated creating a perinatal clinic and a youth center, and included in its employment projections for 1986 the personnel necessary to staff these services. Even more, the plan expected that the village would need to enlarge its education facilities and staff: three new kindergartens, a primary school, and an academic secondary school ought to supplement the institutions already operating in 1971 (Bureau 1972a:29–33, 77).

The plan also had multiple recommendations for the municipal government. First, it should undertake several projects on its own, such as building frontage roads along the Sousse-Tunis highway to separate local from long-distance traffic, or developing a green belt and recreation centers in the area between the village and the "touristic zone" along the coast. Second, it should initiate actions enabling the village to encompass the expected increases in population and employment. Estimating that the community would need to expand by almost 70 hectares over the next 15 years, the plan recommended that the municipalities of Hammam Sousse and Sousse renegotiate their boundary (Bureau 1972a:81). Transferring 42 hectares to Hammam Sousse would have relatively little impact on the large provincial capital of Sousse, but it would benefit Hammam Sousse greatly by supplementing village lands along the southern boundary, the area most appropriate for that development.

The plan also discussed more ambitious changes. For example, it recommended establishing a sewage system for the entire village, moving the municipal stadium outside constructed areas to free more land for residential use, and shifting the national highway to bypass the community on the west (Bureau 1972a:77–85). Changes of such magnitude, however, would require decisions at levels beyond the local one and thus exceed the assumptions guiding the current plan.

Construction. In addition to the expectations relating public services to construction, the plan recommended that the local building code be changed to require foundations sufficient to support at least one additional story on all new construction. This change would help deal with the problem of housing an expanded population in a constrained area. Further, the plan recommended that the municipality encourage development by other persons or agencies of such projects as two new commercial zones, two Turkish baths, and a mosque (Bureau 1972a:77). Finally, on the basis of a 2.8 percent annual rate of population growth, a tendency toward nuclear-family residence, and the occupation of all housing then empty or under construction, the development plan expected that 1,684 new housing units would have to be created by 1986 (Bureau 1972a:67). Given the rate of construction by private parties over the preceding ten years, the national housing agencies would have to build 1,025 of the new units at a rate of 68 per year (Bureau 1972a:68–69). By 1986, this would make a density of occupation of 5.2 persons per unit, which would require the above-mentioned 70 additional hectares to be incorporated within the municipality.

Expected Development: Summary and Implications. In the period 1972–1986, Hammam Sousse was thus expected to continue growing much as it had before. Its population would increase rapidly but not explosively. Local employment would decline relatively in agriculture and crafts, remain at similar levels in most other sectors, but expand enormously in tourism. Public services would expand moderately, both in the amounts and types of activities provided. And housing was expected to keep pace: new residences would be built, mostly on the southern side of the community, and they would have fittings, densities of occupation, and construction similar to those already in place.

The major trend of social differentiation would thus continue to be between Hammam Sousse and other communities, as the former grew faster and in a more diversified manner than its neighbors. Differentiation would also increase within Hammam Sousse, however, as the structure of employment changed and newer housing became a larger percentage of the total in use.

Observed Development: 1979

In 1979, Hammam Sousse was halfway through the period of expected development just described. While in the community to investigate informal political organization (Huxley 1978, 1981, 1986), I observed that another topic was a major concern to local people. This topic was Port el-Kantaoui, a nearby complex for tourism that was entering service that summer. This complex triggered several events that illuminated how the community had actually been evolving since publication of the development plan. Let us now consider that evolution in terms of the domains discussed above.

Population. On 7 May 1979, Hammam Sousse and a small area around it were raised to the administrative status of a district. Approximately one month before the change, an official rehearsal took place to ensure everything was ready. A number of displays describing the growth of the community were put up in the municipal office; the Minister of Interior and other national dignitaries made a brief visit; and school children and adults lined the street in front to clap, cheer, and make a proper celebration.

Among the displays was one listing the growth of Hammam Sousse in population and in housing. Most of the population figures accorded with those discussed above, but the last one was a surprise: 1978—20,381! This was an increase of nearly 29 percent over the 1975 census cited above; if it were true, the community had grown more during the last seven years than it did during the previous fifteen. A local official said that the 1978 figures had been gathered during a house-to-house census before the last municipal election. Questioned about the size of the increase since the national census, he maintained that the 1978 count was probably more accurate. It had been done by local people who were able to correct any errors of names, addresses, or numbers found in the national census. He also acknowledged, on the other hand, that the municipality had an incentive to accept the higher figure: population growth was among the factors favoring establishment of Hammam Sousse as a new administrative district.

If the 1978 count was correct, the 1972 development plan had been wrong. It considered the rapid rate of 1966–1971 (4.3 percent) as "temporary"; however, an even higher rate—4.6 percent per year since 1966—would have been necessary to produce an overall population of 20,381 by 1978. An increase of this magnitude might indicate that immigration was playing a more important role in growth than was anticipated. Furthermore, such an increase would call into question all the subsequent projections of the development plan, which had based its expectations about employment, public services, and construction on the lower rate of population growth.

Economy. As part of the research on informal political organization, a sample of 100 residences was drawn at random from municipal property-tax rolls. The households occupying these residences included property owners, renters, and persons with other forms of tenure (e.g., dependents of property owners). In 1979 there were no homeless people in Hammam Sousse, according to municipal officials, other local residents, and researcher observation. Time and funding limitations ultimately prevented reaching all 100 households, but 66 were contacted by the researcher or one of six local associates, and 59 interviews were completed.[10] The most common reason for nonresponses was lack of time.

In each case, the acting head of household was visited at home and asked a standardized schedule of questions in Tunisian colloquial Arabic. First, the age, sex, education, language, occupation, and income of household members were ascertained. Then the household's access to property, visiting patterns, history of descent, and health practices were surveyed. Finally, the household head's daily activities, religious attitudes and behavior, and political attitudes and behavior were examined.

On the basis of data collected by this survey, the geographic and sectoral distributions of employment may be sketched for 1979, then compared with those determined in 1971 or expected in 1986. To facilitate these comparisons, the development plan's assumptions about the work force will be adopted here: the work force is composed of men between 15 and 60 years of age who are either employed or actively seeking work.

In 1979, 57.1 percent of the local labor force worked within the village; 31.9 percent in Sousse city and province; and 11 percent in other parts of Tunisia or Europe. This differed significantly from the geographic distribution of employment that had been determined in 1971 or that was expected by 1986. In both those cases, 68.4 percent of local jobs were in the village; 31.6 percent in Sousse city. By 1979, however, the percentage of local workers employed in the village had dropped by about one-sixth; the share of those working in Sousse remained about the same (if the 29.4 percent in the city are combined with the 2.2 percent elsewhere in the province); and a significant number of workers were migrating farther afield. This geographic distribution, then, implied a growing dispersal of local workers as the community was becoming more tightly integrated into the national and international labor markets.

The sectoral distribution of the labor force in 1979 also differed considerably from both the one determined in 1971 and the one expected by 1986. Table 6.1 shows these differences by placing the 1979 figures between the other two sets.

Overall, these figures express a shift in employment from the primary and secondary economic sectors to the tertiary one. For instance, the percentage of jobs in agriculture dropped by more than four-fifths between 1971 and 1979, while it had been expected to decline only about one-third

TABLE 6.1
Distribution of the Labor Force by Sector

Sector	Percent Determined in 1971	Percent Observed in 1979	Expected by 1986
Agriculture	33.9	6.6	21.5
Ind. & Constr.	27.7	23.1	27.7
Commerce	7.3	33.0	7.3
Crafts	7.2	0.0	4.6
Tourism	4.4	7.7	18.7
Pub. Admin.	3.6	15.4	3.1
Education	2.2	6.6	3.5
Other Occ. or Unemp.	13.7	7.7	13.4
	(N=2,711)	(N=91)	(N=4,267)

Sources: for 1971 and 1986, Bureau 1972a and author's calculations; for 1979, author's sample survey.

over the whole period 1971–1986. Crafts also declined much more rapidly than expected, though the 1979 results may be skewed.[11] The relative number of jobs in industry and construction, which the development plan had expected to increase, was trending downward. Finally, the percentage of "other occupations or unemployed" also declined more rapidly than anticipated.

In contrast, tertiary-sector employment increased, and in some cases skyrocketed. The increase in commerce was greatest, both in the absolute number of new jobs and in relative expansion from the 1971 distribution. This increase is all the more striking when compared with the expectations for 1986: the development plan projected *no* relative growth of jobs in commerce over the period 1971–1986. The next most important expansion was in public administration, where the percentage of jobs more than quadrupled over the 1971 percentage, even though the development plan had expected a relative decline over the whole 15-year period. The fraction of employment in education had tripled in eight years, while only a modest increase had been expected between 1971 and 1986. Finally, the relative number of jobs in tourism also had increased, but at a considerably slower rate than predicted by the development plan.

Accordingly, all the increases in percentages of employment were in activities providing services; all the decreases, in activities producing goods. The cumulative effect of these changes was to accelerate trends toward a service-oriented economy. Such trends would not necessarily produce a poorer local economy, but they have helped to make a less diversified and autonomous one. The diminished diversity and autonomy, in turn, have made the economy more vulnerable to forces and processes beyond the control of local people. They also reflect and reinforce the growing integration of the village community into the national and international political economy.

Public Services. Many of the increases in public services recommended by the development plan—such as the perinatal clinic, a youth center, or several new schools—had not occurred by 1979. Then a pharmacy was opened and the first private doctor's office officially inaugurated. The most important addition to public services that year, however, was the establishment of Hammam Sousse as a district (Arabic, *mu'atamadiya*), headed by a delegate (Arabic, *mu'atamad*) of the governor of Sousse province. Of the several reasons advanced for this change, one was that it officially recognized the strength of local society (speech by Minister for Education Mzali, 19 March 1979). Another was that it would enable closer coordination of national interests (as represented by the delegate) with local ones (as represented by the municipality and the *omda*, formerly called the administrative sheik). Some local people argued, however, that the change was directed mainly toward the Port el-Kantaoui complex.

In studying another Tunisian village raised to district capital, Larson (1975) argues that the change integrated that community into the nation in such a way and to such a degree that local politics were stultified. That is, the penetration and domination of the local society by the national government and associated organizations was so complete that the local political processes were "largely monopolized and coopted by political personnel and structures operating above the local level" (Larson 1975:179). As a result, the community became "bureaucratized," with ordinary citizens acting like the most subordinate workers in a highly centralized, hierarchical organization: they adopted overtly obsequious but covertly manipulative behavior to protect their personal interests and to achieve their private goals (Larson 1975:119–178).

Without commenting on the applicability of this model throughout Tunisia (cf. Huxley 1983:110–113), one may nonetheless explore its relevance for Hammam Sousse in 1979. Parts of the situation there seem similar to that described by Larson. For example, making the community a district capital brought a higher-level set of administrative structures and personnel into the village. Furthermore, several of the national organizations generally associated with district capitals—e.g., the Institution for Social Solidarity, the agricultural workers' cooperative, and the farmers' union—already had opened local branches in Hammam Sousse. They probably contributed to the more-than-quadrupled employment in the public services since 1971; the addition of personnel to staff the district administration could only further this trend.

On the other hand, certain other factors differentiated Hammam Sousse from the community described by Larson. First, Hammam Sousse had a long history of local solidarity and collective action in managing economic assets and opposing colonialism. Second, citizens of Hammam Sousse had participated actively in the political and economic life of their community, as evidenced by the first election for municipal council and by development efforts since. And third, some local citizens had become important officials in the national political economy—ministers, advisers, ambassadors, and presidents of state companies. They could, therefore, influence the goals and operations of national institutions. Moreover, many local people had personal ties with these officials and with other powerful personalities, ties that could become informal channels for influencing the formal political organization at local or higher levels (e.g., see Huxley 1978, 1981, 1986; Moore 1988:176-180; Portes 1983).

Accordingly, Hammam Sousse probably had greater autonomy within the national system than did the village studied by Larson. As with that village, however, the degree of this autonomy was produced by an ongoing interaction between members of the community, on one hand, and the government and party, on the other. Thus, it could change markedly over time, depending on the actions and interests of the parties concerned.

Construction. As noted earlier, Hammam Sousse contained 2,511 residential units in 1971, and a total of 4,195 was expected by 1986. In 1978, however, there were 4,562 local dwellings, according to the same municipal census that had indicated a tremendous surge in local population. As with population, so with housing: the national census had counted 3,007 dwellings in 1975 (Chief of the Regional Bureau of Statistics in Sousse, 10 March 1979, personal communication); the municipal census, 4,562 in 1978. Dividing the municipality's figure for population by its one for residences indicates an occupation density of 4.5 persons per unit, which is well under the nearly 6 determined in 1971 or the 5.2 expected by 1986.

If both the national and municipal censuses were correct, more than one-third of all local housing would have been created in just three years. This seems implausible, although much construction was evident in 1979. On the southern side of the community, new houses were replacing the clay quarries; within built-up zones, many big old houses around courtyards were being subdivided into smaller units; and the market for housing was active.

Observed Development: Summary and Implications. By 1979, Hammam Sousse had reached a particular juncture: change with continuity had characterized its development for a long time, but the changes were becoming rapid and more varied. Population growth, which had surpassed that of all similar communities in the province, may have accelerated even further. Local housing also seemed to have grown more rapidly than projected and even more rapidly than population. The continued high level of employment and a growing number of public services perhaps augured well for local development.

Several changes, however, indicated that development was getting beyond local control. Despite a relatively weak expansion into tourism, employment was shifting increasingly (and increasingly rapidly) toward a concentration in services. If the expected growth took place also in tourism, this shift could become a stampede. Further, more workers were finding employment outside the community, even at distances that precluded commuting, indicating a growing dependence on the national and international labor markets. Finally, the change in administrative status brought the national government into a more direct and larger role in the management of local affairs, with a potential for the "bureaucratization" of local society.

The trends that had been favoring social differentiation, both within the community and between it and other communities, were continuing and intensifying. They threatened Hammam Sousse's long tradition of strong collective action and identity. This danger came from within, as access to employment, public services, and housing encouraged the process of differentiation within the village. And it came from without, as the local society became increasingly integrated into the national and international political economy and thus subject to forces over which Hammam Sousse had little control.

Challenge: The Port el-Kantaoui Tourism Complex

In the summer of 1979, the first phase of Port el-Kantaoui officially entered service. The plan for this tourism complex, whose nucleus is located near the older Sidi Kantaoui hotel, called for hotels, time-share condominiums, and beach houses with 13,000 (Qanal 1979b:47; Sharp 1981:90) to 15,000 beds (Harris 1983:626). When completed, it would stretch some three kilometers along the coast, featuring many shops and restaurants, a casino, a yachting harbor, tennis courts, an 18-hole golf course, and a school training students for jobs in tourism (Qanal 1979b:47). Port el-Kantaoui was expected ultimately to cost 100 million dinars (about $250 million at 1979 exchange rates), with funding mostly from the Tunisian government, the International Finance Corporation of the World Bank, and the Abu Dhabi Fund for Arab Economic Development (Harris 1983:626; Qanal 1979b:46-67). At completion it was projected to employ 6,000 (Quanal 1979b:47) to 7,000 (Sharp 1981:90) workers directly, with still more supplying it with goods or services.

Port el-Kantaoui is a major project in size, services, financial investment, and employment. How is this project for tourism[12] relevant to development, and how does it articulate with the changes and continuities in the evolution of Hammam Sousse, as discussed above?

Governments of developing countries often promote tourism "to earn more foreign exchange, to increase national income and employment, and, sometimes, to achieve regional development of backward areas" (de Kadt 1979:20-21). The Tunisian government has been promoting tourism since 1962 (Groupe Huit 1979:286), and for several years it was the country's largest source of foreign exchange. Despite losing that position to the oil sector in the late 1970s, tourism has remained important: in 1983 it was estimated to have earned the equivalent of 350 million dinars, ranking after sales of petroleum and petroleum products but before worker remittances (Financial Times 1984:v).

Tourism has also been an important source of employment for Tunisians. First, it has created jobs directly by requiring people to staff hotels and restaurants, to furnish transport within the country and abroad, to handle governmental formalities, and to produce and market crafts (Smaoui 1979:102–

103). These functions generate approximately one job per hotel bed (given an average hotel occupancy rate of 40-56 percent). Second, tourism has created jobs indirectly, either by activities supplying tourist facilities (e.g., selling fish to restaurants) or activities establishing and maintaining the basic infrastructure for tourism (e.g., constructing hotels). These activities generate from 3.6 to 4.3 jobs (depending on occupancy rates) for every job created directly by tourism (Smaoui 1979:104-105; cf. Financial Times 1984:v). Tourism, therefore, has benefited Tunisia by earning foreign exchange and creating employment.

Geographically, 96 percent of tourism employment is concentrated along the coasts, "since the basic attraction of tourism in Tunisia is the beach resorts" (Smaoui 1979:108). As average annual wages in hotel work were higher than those in agriculture, construction, or textile manufacturing (Smaoui 1979:106), tourism has favored migration of workers from the interior and from agriculture. "Regular personnel" and "service staff" have constituted more than 70 percent of jobs in hotels, and more than 50 percent of jobs in other activities directly generated by tourism. Simultaneously, tourism has also "helped create and strengthen a clearly defined class of entrepreneurs" (Smaoui 1979:109). Tax laws and other state policies have encouraged the emergence of this group, whose newer members have more education and technical competence than their predecessors. Increasingly, then, workers in tourism are becoming differentiated into an employee group, on one hand, and an owner-manager group, on the other. Such tendencies toward class formation are reinforced as members of each group see themselves as having common interests, and form or join organizations to assert those interests (Hopkins 1977a:454-456, 1977b:628-631, 1981:389-390). This presumably occurred when unions representing hotel workers signed a collective agreement with the entrepreneurs to stabilize job tenure somewhat and to establish wage rates and uniform social benefits (Smaoui 1979:107). Tourism therefore has fostered unequal regional development and increased stratification in the Tunisian labor force.[13]

Causing concern on the national level, hotel occupancy rates have been declining since 1982, partly because of heavy competition from European resort areas. Land speculation in areas important to tourism is another problem, and water allocation has become a sensitive issue (Financial Times 1984:v). Finally, more broadly phrased complaints have been raised about socially disruptive aspects of tourism like topless bathing, rising prices, and European attitudes (Financial Times 1984:v).

Many of these benefits, handicaps, and concerns have also appeared on the regional level in Sousse province and city. While tourism has provided important financial support and employment, and was the original reason for establishing many public services there, it has unfortunately fostered a "chaotic" expansion of Sousse city and "could exert an adverse effect on other sectors of the economy" (Groupe Huit 1979:285-295, 303). Competition for water has become a critical problem: "the average per capita consumption in Sousse is approximately 60 liters per day and the average consumption per tourist is 300 liters per day" (Groupe Huit 1979:296; cf. Sharp 1981:92). Noting that "circumstances in Sousse could deteriorate rapidly," the Groupe Huit report calls for immediate implementation of a development plan that will harmonize tourism with other aspects of local economy and society (1979:304).

How then is tourism relevant to the development of Hammam Sousse? Tourism has employed significant numbers of villagers at least since 1971. Although the growth of this employment to 1979 was not keeping pace with expectations, the Hammam Sousse development plan had anticipated a surge of new jobs resulting from projects like Port el-Kantaoui. Such a surge would reinforce strong trends already present toward a service-oriented economy, and it could contribute toward greater increases in population, as immigrants were drawn by the expanding labor market. In turn, increased population would call for new housing and public services to meet material and other needs. All these changes would promote a tighter integration of the local community with the national and international political economy.

But how was tourism perceived locally? What were villagers' views on the likely effects of the development of Port el-Kantaoui? A local notable expressed the benefits in this way:

> To buy tractors or autos we need foreign currency. To get foreign currency by selling olives, for example, we have to sow them, cultivate them, pick them, package them, and send them abroad. But for tourism, we only give the sun, the clean sand, and the fresh air, which we don't have to pay for, either in work or in money (personal communication).

When it was pointed out that other villagers complained about the complex—how the government had nationalized land for it (cf. Sharp 1981:93), how jobs there were being allocated, etc.—the same man had this to say:

> The problem has several aspects. The government paid only 400 millimes [0.4 Tunisian dinar] per meter because the land was zoned for agricultural use, but it wasn't really good for most agriculture because the water is salty from the sea and the soil is rocky. If the land had been rezoned as building land and the government paid one dinar per meter, people would have said "Thanks be to God!" And for the complaints about mostly outsiders getting jobs on the project, everyone wants to make a lot of money but not everyone has the education, intelligence, and capacity.

In addition to dissatisfaction about job distribution and prices paid for nationalized land, other complaints were that the project was monopolizing the local workmen and that the hotels were getting first pick of local produce and fish. Villagers sometimes concluded by saying that it would all lead to more *biznez*. This word, derived from the English word *business*, denoted chasing after foreign women, who often used English to talk with their Tunisian pursuers. Many villagers saw the "chase" as corrupting, and as an index of how their community might change with continued tourism.

Apparently aware of discontent about Port el-Kantaoui, the municipal and provincial authorities, in conjunction with the management of the complex, organized a Kantaoui Festival on 20-21 July 1979. On the first day, citizens and various officials watched a parade of village schools, associations, and companies. The next day, a number of events were planned at the complex, including enactment of a traditional wedding ceremony. A local person who attended came back complaining. His friend responded by saying: "What do you expect? It's not for us Hammamis; it's for tourists, and that's why we have no schedule of what's happening and why you don't see anyone you know if you go."

Given the 1979 situation—these local opinions, and the size and importance of the complex—what outcomes might be inferred for the development of Hammam Sousse? One possibility is that Port el-Kantaoui will have little effect on the development of Hammam Sousse. The center of the complex is about three kilometers from the main street of the village, and a relatively open space separates them. Also, the complex is an inwardly focused unit, with its own restaurants, shops, and entertainment. Its clientele is likely to be affluent, perhaps older, and seeking comfort more than new experiences. Accordingly, the complex may become a social enclave, as well as a geographic one.

This outcome seems unlikely. Three kilometers is hardly a long distance, and the 1972 development plan already called for establishing a green belt and recreation centers between the village and the coast (Bureau 1972a:84-85). Furthermore, direct and indirect employment possibilities in the complex will attract local workers, some of whom already have jobs there. Public services with offices in the village will have to deal with matters in the complex. In short, even if tourists do not come to Hammam Sousse, local people will go to Port el-Kantaoui.

A second possible outcome is that linkage with the complex will intensify trends toward social differentiation within the community. Change in local employment and housing will be influenced by tendencies toward class formation emerging in tourism on the national level. If this occurs, the likely scenario is that the community will fragment, as different families or even individuals adopt roles and identities of either the owner-manager group or the employee group. In this way, Hammam Sousse would replicate the experience of Hammamet (Boukraa 1976): local society would divide into those members with the wealth, political connections, and/or training to profit from the possibilities offered by tourism, versus those members who lacked such attributes and were thus relatively worse off. In failing to build on the existing strengths of the local community, such an outcome would also resemble results of the development projects discussed by Horowitz and Painter (1986:4) and deplored by Horowitz (1986:268-271).

A third possible outcome is that local criticism of the development of Port el-Kantaoui will be dealt with as was the aftermath of the first municipal election. That is, responsible political leaders will follow the lead of Hedi Baccouche: they will revise and attenuate some of the more troublesome aspects of the project, while they seek also to incorporate local people who were formerly excluded or disadvantaged. If that creative and effective example were built upon—so that local community, local government, and central government find sufficient overlap to work cooperatively—then Hammam Sousse might move into another era of growth with positive popular participation (cf. Cochrane 1983: 45–50; Hopkins 1979:325; Southall 1979: 221–222; Trabelsi 1979:302).

Conclusions

In this chapter I have examined the development of Hammam Sousse by combining documentary, behavioral, and attitudinal evidence. I began by reinterpreting an earlier study of political organization in the community to 1961. Then I considered subsequent development, focusing on changes and continuities in four domains—population, economy, public services, and construction. This consideration followed a plan (Bureau 1972a, 1972b) that described the status of those domains in 1971 and projected how they might develop by 1986. Next I discussed the changes and continuities observed in the four domains in 1979, halfway through the 1971–1986 period. Finally, I analyzed the Port el-Kantaoui complex as a challenge to Hammam Sousse's trajectory of development, and evaluated three possible outcomes of this challenge.

These remarks provide a useful illustration for development policies. They show how intensive analysis of a well-documented case can be combined with appropriate field research (Horowitz 1986:268) to trace the evolution of a community in a strategic political and economic position. The chapter also details different levels, types, and interlinkages of social organization relevant to that community's development (see Cernea 1986:xv), be they local families, national administrations, or national parties operating through local branches.

For anthropology, this chapter has both methodological and conceptual utility. With reference to methodology, it shows how information gathered by participant observation, informal interviews, and a survey of a sample of households can test, refine, and supplement documentary evidence on the historical evolution of social organization. With reference to concepts, it illustrates how some kinds of development foster social differentiation within and between communities, and how this differentiation may articulate with class formation on a national level in Tunisian tourism.

For the people of Hammam Sousse, this chapter documents some of their accomplishments. Now facing an important challenge, they have so far amassed an impressive record. Their community has changed profoundly, yet it has also retained or reproduced a vibrant local society. The people of Hammam Sousse thus provide one local example of how popular participation in development has been and may again be achieved.

Postscript

The preceding sections of this chapter were originally written in 1986 for publication in 1987. The time frame of the discussion was established, in part, by field research in 1979 and the development plan's projections until 1986. Given that discussion, how does the analysis of change, continuity, and challenge in past community development correspond to Hammam Sousse today?

A more adequate response to this question will require new field research. However, while working on another project in Tunis during July and August 1988, I visited the community twice. In the remarks following, I will first note apparent trends in its population, economy, public services, and construction since 1979. Then I will consider how the Hammam Sousse of 1988 relates to the three possible outcomes of development that were inferred above. Finally, I will mention how further research in the community may illuminate present and future actions by national leaders.

Changes, Continuities, and Challenge Since 1979

The population of Hammam Sousse appears to have grown markedly. On different occasions, five local residents estimated it at about 26,000 in 1988. If accurate, this estimate would imply a 2.5 percent annual rate of growth from the municipal census in 1978, a 3.6 percent annual rate from the national census in 1966.

The local economy seems to have expanded. For example, commerce is thriving. Most of the stores and services present earlier are still active, and many new ones have been established along the main commercial axes. The central food market has been enlarged, and a weekly market, where vendors bring merchandise for display and sale in an open-air setting, now operates on Saturdays.[14] Local employment in education also seems to have grown, as an academic secondary school has been preparing students in Hammam Sousse since the mid-1980s. Tourism has probably become more important because all the hotels of the Port el-Kantaoui complex are finished and functioning during a banner year for the Tunisian tourist industry (Ouerghi 1988). The perceived success of the complex is among the factors that have led to a new project for revitalizing tourism in Sousse city. Generally speaking, all these economic changes appear to continue tendencies revealed by the household survey in 1979, such as the trend toward greater tertiary-sector employment.

Employment in administration seems consistent with this trend, as more public services are now available locally. The district administration is fully staffed, and the national tax-collection agency and traffic police have established local branches. The national highway has been shifted west of Hammam Sousse, allowing the old roadway to become a business route. A sewer system is being installed throughout the community, and a water-treatment plant is operating near the coast. This plant processes sewage from Hammam Sousse and nearby communities, and the treated effluent irrigates the golf course and other areas of the Port el-Kantaoui complex. The summertime Kantaoui Festival has become more popular. It now alternates presentations between the community stadium, where the audience is mostly local, and an open-air theater in the complex, where the audience is more mixed. These changes in public services also appear to continue trends evident earlier, such as the greater penetration of local life by national institutions and the growing regulation of social relations by formal, public agencies.

Construction in Hammam Sousse seems to have accorded with the increases in other domains. Most of the vacant areas within the community's perimeter in 1979 have now been filled, and multiple stories are being added to buildings in more congested areas. Land formerly cultivated between Hammam Sousse and the sea has been increasingly converted into new streets, houses, and shops. A special zone has been created near Port el-Kantaoui (Journal Officiel de la République Tunisienne 1988); all construction there is highly regulated to assure no clash with the complex.

Population, economy, public services, and construction in Hammam Sousse thus seem to have changed importantly since 1979, although many of the changes have continued trends that were already present. For example, population has continued to rise, economy and public services to expand, and construction to keep pace. A local opinion about these matters was expressed during an exchange I had with a small group of friends. I began a sentence with "the village of Hammam Sousse," which was how local people had referred to the community in 1979. This time my friends laughed. Then one said, to general approval, "Hammam Sousse is not a village now; it has become a city, a small city."

Possible Outcomes and Apparent Outcome in 1988

During the earlier discussion of Port el-Kantaoui, I inferred three possible outcomes resulting from the impact of the complex on local development after 1979. Each of those outcomes will now be considered in relation to the community today.

The first possible outcome was that Port el-Kantaoui would have little effect on local development. This outcome seems disconfirmed by events so far. For example, the complex has apparently favored greater employment in tourism and expanded public services in administration and sanitation. It has also affected local construction, fostering the creation of a zone in the community where more restrictive regulations now apply.

The second possible outcome was that linkage with Port el-Kantaoui would intensify trends toward social differentiation within Hammam Sousse. With time, and in the absence of any countervailing factors, the emerging class structure in Tunisian tourism would articulate with local trends in employment and housing, leading to fragmentation of the community and class stratification of its members. Such a process is not pronounced in Hammam Sousse today, but the creation of the affluent, specially restricted zone near the complex reflects and reinforces the tendencies toward greater differentiation in community housing. When combined with apparent trends in employment and public services, it may become the dominant trajectory in local development.

At present, the trajectory seems to be more like the third possible outcome projected earlier. It suggested that political leaders would seek to revise and attenuate more problematic aspects of the linkage between complex and community, and that they would also try to incorporate local people who formerly were excluded or disadvantaged from participating in it. Perhaps the clearest illustration of this outcome is the linkage between sewers in the community, the water-treatment plant, and irrigation for the complex. Discussion earlier in this chapter noted that competition for water was a critical problem in Sousse city, where the average per capita consumption by tourists was five times greater than normal consumption. Sousse city also provides drinking water for most of Hammam Sousse, where the supply situation is aggravated by a disposal problem. As noted earlier, Hammam Sousse lacked a sewage system. The 1972 development plan supported local requests for one, but it did not project the construction, because of the cost and difficulty involved. In 1988, however, the municipal council is building such a system with national funding. Parts of the system now in place carry used water to a treatment plant between the community and Port el-Kantaoui. According to local people, the treatment plant was also built with funding from the national government to process waste from several nearby communities. Thus, the linkage between the complex and its neighbors has been revised so that irrigation is provided to Port el-Kantaoui without diminishing the water supply to Hammam Sousse or other localities. The revisions have also drawn more Hammam Soussans into a relationship with the complex by furnishing a sewage system they wanted but could not afford on their own. Changes in the Kantaoui Festival offer another illustration of the third outcome. Regularly alternating presentations between the community and the complex signifies that both are important to the festival's success. That alternation may also increase local participation by making it easier to know when and where presentations will occur and who is likely to attend. Finally, rerouting the national highway may provide still another illustration of the third outcome. Long-distance transport can now bypass both complex and community; access to both is still easy via the business route and feeder roads; and more people participate in the benefits because Hammam Sousse has become safer for pedestrians and other local traffic.

Apparently, then, the Hammam Sousse of 1988 has developed in accord with elements of both the second and third possible outcomes. Correspondence between complex and community seems the dominant tendency at present, but this assessment could shift if conditions change and/or different information becomes available.

Local Research and National Leaders

On 7 November 1987, Prime Minister Zine al-Abidine Ben Ali replaced Habib Bourguiba as President of the Tunisian Republic. One of the new president's first acts was to appoint Hedi Baccouche as his prime minister. In July 1988, Mohamed Djegham—then president of Hammam Sousse's municipal council and president-director general of the Port el-Kantaoui complex—was named Minister for Tourism. Thus, Hammam Soussans now fill three of the most important offices in the national government. It would be a mistake to assume that those officials will mechanically act out some script inculcated by their common background. Nonetheless, a consideration of local history may provide useful insights into how they will address such issues as political participation, religious opposition, and socioeconomic development. Perhaps this chapter can introduce that consideration as it also addresses concerns about development policies, anthropology, and the people of Hammam Sousse.

Notes

The field research on which this chapter is partly based was funded by the Joint Commission on the Near and Middle East of the Social Sciences Research Council and the American Council of Learned Societies and by the University of Michigan-Dearborn Campus Grants Committee. The author thanks these organizations, the editors of this volume, and the following individuals: P. Anderson, H. Baccouche, A. Baffoun, M. Bahri, J. Ben Smida, A. Bouaouina, H. Bouaouina, M. Bouaouina, K. Cressman, A. Dawwas, N. Hopkins, M. Khaddar, R. Mdalla, C. H. Moore, L. Michalak, F. Stambouli, and S. Williams.

1. Moore (1963) says they occupied the office until 1943, but villagers in 1979 claimed that his account confounded two different persons.

2. Miller (1985) has examined one aspect of women's statuses and roles in Hammam Sousse—how their decisions about fertility have been affected by socioeconomic development. Unfortunately, the empirical basis of this study is flawed by ethnographic errors, among other problems. A better study of women in a Tunisian village is Larson (1984), which cites additional sources on the topic.

3. The average increase for Sousse area then was 1.2 percent (Bureau 1972a:1); that for all of Tunisia during the period 1960-1970 was 1.9 per cent per year. (Nellis 1983:378).

4. Work performed by women—especially domestic labor but also that done outside the home at special workshops or in "offshore" industries whose products did not officially enter Tunisia's economy—was thus omitted. Furthermore, the plan counted secondary students as part of the labor force in 1971 (Bureau 1972a:70) but not in its expectations for 1986 (Bureau 1972a:74). To permit comparisons between the labor force at different times, the following procedures were adopted. First, the students were subtracted from the 1971 figures, and each sector's percentage of total employment was recalculated. Then students were also omitted from the employment expected by 1986 and that observed in 1979.

5. See note 4 and compare with the percentages given in the plan (Bureau 1972a:73).

6. The continuing importance of this association was shown by the position of the village in the largest agricultural market of the region: in 1971, growers in Hammam Sousse produced 49.2 percent of all vegetables sold on the wholesale market at Sousse (Bureau 1972a:2).

7. Dividing the village population in 1971 (14,272) by the number of families at that time (2,821) yields an average family of 5.06 persons (cf. Bureau 1972a:74). Taking the plan's projection of village population in 1986 (21,589), and assuming that families would be the same size then, the total number of Hammam Sousse families in 1986 should be 4,267.

8. This 2 percent had tourism jobs in the village; another 2.4 percent had tourism jobs in Sousse, making the total of 4.4 percent listed earlier and in Table 6.1.

9. According to villagers in 1979, the person most responsible for constructing this hotel was Mokhtar el-Atiri. A local man who had studied engineering in France, el-Atiri was later active politically at both local and national levels and headed the national gas and electric company in 1979. He was particularly popular in Hammam Sousse for the urban development that occurred while he was president of the municipal council. Accordingly, villagers in 1979 contrasted "his" hotel with the Port el-Kantaoui project near it: the hotel was strongly supported; the project strongly criticized.

10. The 66 households contacted provide a 1.3 percent sample of the 5,142 that should have been present in 1979, assuming that the 1978 municipal census was accurate and that all residences were occupied. While every attempt was made to obtain a representative sample, extrapolations to the total village population should, as always, be made with caution.

11. The only persons revealed by the survey to be working in crafts were women. Accordingly, the relatively small number of households surveyed, or the assumptions about the labor force, or both conjointly, may have distorted this sector of employment.

12. Nash defines a tourist as "a person at leisure (i.e., free from primary institutional obligations) who is also a traveler" (1978:135). Accordingly, tourism is "the ways of these people, as well as an industry of a local or supra-local character that caters to and profits from tourists" (1978:134). These definitions clarify distinctive attributes, so that tourists and tourism may be studied in different societies (e.g., capitalist or socialist ones) and at different times (e.g., classic or modern Greece), then compared or related to other parts of social organization.

13. Tourism probably affects stratification by gender as well as by class. Relations between gender stratification and employment, while important, are not discussed in this chapter in order to enable comparisons with the statistical data currently at hand.

14. See Michalak (1983) for the importance of weekly markets in the Tunisian political economy.

References

Abu Zahra, N.
  1972 Inequality of Descent and Equalitarianism of the New National Organizations in a Tunisian Village. *In* Rural Politics and Social Change in the Middle East. R. Antoun and I. Harik, eds. Pp. 267–286. Bloomington, IN: Indiana University Press.

Boukraa, R.
  1976 La problématique de la communauté rurale au Maghreb: quelques observations sur le changement social dans la communauté de Hammamet. Revue Tunisienne de Sciences Sociales 45:11–48.

Brown, L. C.
  1983 Tunisia: The Record since Independence. American-Arab Affairs Quarterly No. 6:79–87.

Bureau (Bureau Régional d'Aménagement de Sousse)
    1972a   Ville de Hammam Sousse: plan d'aménagement. No. 1: Rapport. Sousse: Bureau Régional d'Aménagement de Sousse.

    1972b   Ville de Hammam Sousse: plan d'aménagement. No. 2: Fiches des cartes. Sousse: Bureau Régional d'Aménagement de Sousse.

Cernea, M.
    1986   Foreword: Anthropology and Family Production Systems in Africa. *In* Anthropology and Rural Development in West Africa. M. Horowitz and T. Painter, eds. Pp. xi–xv. Boulder, CO: Westview Press.

Chipaux, F.
    1986   Intrigues et disgraces au palais de Carthage. Le Monde Sélection Hebdomadaire No. 3943: Janvier 23.

Cochrane, G.
    1983   Policies for Strengthening Local Government in Developing Countries. Staff Working Papers No. 582. Washington, DC: The World Bank.

de Kadt, E.
    1979   The Issues Addressed. *In* Tourism: Passport to Development? E. de Kadt, ed. Pp. 3–77. New York: Oxford University Press.

Fahem, A.
    1968   Un exemple de relations villes-campagne: Sousse et le Sahel Tunisien. Revue Tunisienne de Sciences Sociales 15:275–296.

Financial Times
    1984   Tourism Faces Major Challenges. Financial Times Survey: Tunisia. March 16:v.

Fischer, C.
    1976   The Urban Experience. New York: Harcourt Brace Jovanovich.

Groupe Huit
    1979   The Sociocultural Effects of Tourism in Tunisia: A Case Study of Sousse. *In* Tourism: Passport to Development? E. de Kadt, ed. Pp. 285–304. New York: Oxford University Press.

Harris, D.
    1983   Tunisia. The Middle East and North Africa: 1983–1984. Pp. 613–636. London: Europa Publications.

Hopkins, N.
    1977a   The Emergence of Class in a Tunisian Town. International Journal of Middle East Studies 8:453–491.

    1977b   The Impact of Technological Change in Political Centralization: The Case of Tunisia. *In* Arab Society in Transition: A Reader. S. Ibrahim and N. Hopkins, eds. Pp. 620–631. Cairo: The American University in Cairo.

    1979   The Small Urban Center in Rural Development: Kita (Mali) and Testour (Tunisia). Africa 49(3):316–328.

    1981   Tunisia: An Open and Shut Case. Social Problems 28:385–392.

Horowitz, M.
1986 Ideology, Policy, and Praxis in Pastoral Livestock. *In* Anthropology and Rural Development in West Africa. M. Horowitz and T. Painter, eds. Pp. 249–272. Boulder, CO: Westview Press.

Horowitz, M., and T. Painter
1986 Introduction: Anthropology and Development. *In* Anthropology and Rural Development in West Africa. M. Horowitz and T. Painter, eds. Pp. 1–8. Boulder, CO: Westview Press.

Huxley, F.
1978 *Wasita* in a Lebanese Context: Social Exchange among Villagers and Outsiders. Anthropological Papers No. 64. Ann Arbor, MI: Museum of Anthropology, University of Michigan.

1981 Intermediation in Lebanon and Tunisia: Two Cases and Commentary. Manuscript. Files of the author.

1983 Informative Abstract of "The Impact of National Government on Local Life and Politics in a Tunisian Village," by B. Larson. Development in Tunisia: Bibliography and Informative Abstracts of Selected Research, 1970–1982. Berkeley, CA: Development Research Services.

1986 Political Organization in Lebanese History: Formal and Informal Sectors. Manuscript. Files of the author.

Journal Officiel de la République Tunisienne
1988 Arreté du Ministre de l'Intérieur du 28 janvier 1988 portant création d'un arrondissement communal dans le périmètre communal de Hammam Sousse. No. 10.

Larson, B.
1975 The Impact of National Government on Local Life and Politics in a Tunisian Village. Ph.D. dissertation, Anthropology Department, Columbia University.

1984 The Status of Women in a Tunisian Village: Limits to Autonomy, Influence, and Power. Signs: Journal of Women in Culture and Society 9(2):417–433.

Marjan, M.
1978 Min Ta'rikh Hammam Susa [from the History of Hammam Sousse]. Madrasati No. 6:9–15.

Michalak, L.
1983 The Changing Weekly Markets of Tunisia. Ph.D. dissertation, Anthropology Department, University of California, Berkeley.

Miller, C.
1985 The Effects of Socioeconomic Development upon a Model of Women's Fertility Decision-Making in a Tunisia Community. Ph.D. Dissertation, University of California, Irvine.

Moore, C. H.
1963 Politics in a Tunisian Village. Middle East Journal 17:527–540.

1988 Tunisia and Bourguibisme: Twenty Years of Crisis. Third World Quarterly 10(2):176–190.

Nash, D.
  1978   An Anthropological Approach to Tourism. *In* Tourism and Economic Change. Pp. 133–152. Studies in Third World Societies No. 6. M. Zamora, V. Sutlive, and N. Altshuler, eds. Department of Anthropology, College of William and Mary.

Nellis, J.
  1983   A Comparative Assessment of the Development Performances of Algeria and Tunisia. Middle East Journal 37:370–393.

Ouerghi, N.
  1988   Que prépare la Tunisie pour développer le secteur après . . . 1992? La Presse 16:17 (Juillet).

Portes, A.
  1983   The Informal Sector: Definition, Controversy, and Relations to National Development. Review 7(1):151–174.

Qanal
  1979a   Hammam Susa: Baladat 'al-'insijam wa 'al-Wa'i 'al-Hadari wa 'al-Tadamun [Hammam Sousse: The Community of Harmony, Civilized Consciousness, and Solidarity]. Qanal No. 73:50.

  1979b   Marsa 'al-Qantawi: Tajriba Siyahiya Jadida wa Farida min Nu'aha [Port el-Kantaoui: A New Tourism Experiment Unique in Its Type]. Qanal No. 73:46–47.

Salem, N.
  1984   Habib Bourguiba, Islam and the Creation of Tunisia. London: Croom Helm.

Sharp, J.
  1981   The Port el-Kantaoui Tourist Complex and Its Regional Consequences. *In* Field Studies in Tunisia. R. Harris and R. Lawless, eds. Pp. 88–96. Durham, Great Britain: Department of Geography, University of Durham.

Smaoui, A.
  1979   Tourism and Employment in Tunisia. *In* Tourism: Passport to Development? E. de Kadt, ed. Pp. 101–110. New York: Oxford University Press.

Southall, A.
  1979   Introduction: Results and Implications of the Preliminary Enquiry. Africa 49(3):213–224.

Trabelsi, M.
  1979   The Problem of Drinking Water in Small Agglomerations and Its Implications for Regional Development in Siliana, Tunisia. Africa 49(3):302–307.

Wirth, L.
  1938   Urbanism as a Way of Life. American Journal of Sociology 44:1–24.

7

An Anthropologist's Contribution to Libya's National Human Settlement Plan

John P. Mason

Introduction

In recent years, anthropologists have had relatively infrequent opportunities to do extensive field research in Libya. I had the good fortune to carry out basic socioeconomic research there in the late 1960s and early 1970s, during the period that included the end of King Idris' regime and the beginning of Colonel Mu'ammar al-Qaddafi's revolutionary reign. I returned almost a decade later to apply this experience while working as a social planner for the UN Physical Planning Project, whose purpose was to design the national "physical perspective" plan for Libya in the year 2000.

In this chapter, I focus on the planning activity in which I participated during 1977–79 drawing on my anthropological research in rural Libya, mainly in a small, isolated oasis community in the east Libyan Sahara (Mason 1969, 1971, 1974, 1975, 1976, 1977, 1978, 1981, 1982). My empirical knowledge of the rural, desert oasis where I lived and researched for a year during 1968–1970 served as an important part of the initial data base for the subsequent planning assignment. This combination of fieldwork experience in eastern Libya, including residences in both the oasis and the Cyrenaican city of Benghazi, plus my later national-level planning work while based in the capital, Tripoli, in the west, provided a broad foundation for understanding the national development process of Libya.

Libyan Geography and the General Pattern of Human Settlement

Libya, a geographic label used by Herodotus and other classical authors, refers historically to the large land mass stretching between Egypt in the east and ancient Carthage in the west (near present-day Tunis). Lying on the southern coast of the central Mediterranean, Libya thrusts wedgelike deep into the Sahara Desert. Possessing nearly 1,900 km of coastline, it comprises an area of about 1,090,000 km^2, making it the fourth largest country in Africa (see Figure 7.1).

The key physical descriptor of Libya is the ever-present desert. The Sahara is part of the great North African plateau, which stretches eastward from the Atlantic coast in Morocco several thousand miles to the Red Sea in Egypt. Born of the Sahara, Libya is made up predominantly of desert wasteland, with a strip of desert steppe, the northern highland, and a broad plain that abuts the Mediterranean (Blunsum 1968:93).

In the absence of major technological infrastructure, the geography of Libya rigidly constrains the types of settlement possible. Where rivers flow only seasonally, communities are restricted to desert oases that support date palms and horticulture, steppe zones that support pastoral nomadism, highland pastures and fields that sustain a mixed herding-planting economy, and the broad coastal plain that permits large-scale agriculture and the growth of cities. Oasis dwellers, desert and steppe pastoral nomads, and highland urbanites thus comprise the principal inhabitants dispersed over the Libyan landscape. People also move and trade back and forth across zones, linking the different environments.

Libyan Human-Settlement Policy

An explicit Libyan policy concerning the distribution of people and resources was essentially nonexistent during my first stay, from 1968 to 1970. The oasis where I lived—the Arabized Berber settlement of Augila in the east Sahara Desert in Cyrenaica—was itself a good example of the resulting problem as well as of general rural underdevelopment. A major reason for Augila's difficulties was its poor linkages to the national economy, which also suffered from underdevelopment. In turn, poor regional and national linkages were partly a result of a minimally articulated settlements policy.

The growing national income from oil, commencing in the early 1960s, did not affect Libyan national and regional development until the late 1960s to early 1970s. This lag was due to several factors: (1) only a few years before the discovery of oil, Libya was the second poorest country in the world (as ranked by the World Bank [1955]), and thus required some catch-up time to make a dent in the low per capita income and poor standard of living of the majority of Libyans; (2) even given the relatively rapid generation of national funds, considerable capital investment was needed to build the regional and national infrastructure required to promote growth and development in a geographically large country with a small and highly dispersed population; (3) neither the institutional structure nor national policy were sufficiently well developed to direct national development activities; and (4) the conservative regime of King Idris did not favor the injection of large investments into areas with low-income populations, from resources that in any case were not available until the final years of Idris' rule.

FIGURE 7.1
Libya. *Source:* United Nations. Adapted. Map prepared by Mark Cassell.

With Qaddafi's ascension to power in the bloodless coup of 1 September 1969, while I was in Augila Oasis carrying out my fieldwork, a new set of policies for national, regional, and local development began to evolve. Following the enactment of the "Islamic Socialist Revolution," Libya's poor were to be enfranchised and brought into the "mainstream of national development."

Some of the policies articulated by Qaddafi were new to the Libyan people. Embodied in *The Green Book* (1976, 1977), Qaddafi's "Third Universal Theory" depicts a form of democracy that transcends the capitalist order and advocates what is labeled "Islamic Socialism." The "Third Theory," presented in bits and pieces beginning in 1973, was effected through the enactment of Revolutionary Command Council Law Number 78. That law served as the formal impetus to the formation of popular committees and congresses all over Libya. As a result, national revenues became available to local populations, no matter how small. These revenues were used to carry out development schemes of various kinds, some ambitious, some good, some bad, but—above all—local in their origin.

UN Physical-Planning Assistance to Libya

In 1976, Libyans representing the Ministry of Municipalities requested technical assistance from the UN for the design of a national physical-perspective plan for the year 2000. For a number of months, Libyan planners and UN officials from the Center for Building, Housing, and Planning in New York (now Habitat, headquartered in Nairobi) had been negotiating a project of technical assistance. Funded by the government of Libya, the physical-planning project team recruited by the UN would assist Libyan planners in evolving a national plan.

The team of planners included a team-leader/architect (British), a regional-economist (Canadian), a civil-engineer (Danish), an architect/urban planner (Polish), and a social planner (myself, American). The job description for the position of social planner provides a sense of the role as defined by the UN and Libyan Ministry of Municipalities (UN/NPPP:1976a). The Government of Libya requested a social planner to assist in the physical planning for one year (extendable) in Tripoli. The social planner was to be a member of the UN physical-planning team assigned to the Urban Planning Department of the Ministry of Municipalities, to work under the general supervision and guidance of the UN Project Manager and in consultation with the Director General of the Department. Specifically, the social planner would:

1. Examine existing planning documents, reports, official statements, etc., for their social-policy implications; review the goals of development in the social sectors; and give a preliminary written assessment of the findings.
2. Relate preliminary findings to the work of the United Nations team through detailing technical studies, social surveys, community design,

and urban structure, with a view to evolving a coherent social-planning policy responsive to people's needs that would be reflected in the technical reports, plans, and recommendations of the UN team.
3. Determine and specify the studies and surveys in the sociocultural field that should be carried out within the framework of the project, consistent with its technical aims and objectives, and draft a work program.
4. Under the guidance of the Project Manager, and in consultation with the Director General of the Urban Planning Department, organize and conduct such surveys in the social field at the local, regional, and national levels as may be required by the project to achieve its major objectives and to implement specific urban planning and development projects.
5. Advise on the selection of persons for training in the social field, as an integral part of physical development.

A critical ingredient absent from the social-planner's terms of reference (TOR), as well as the TORs of the other team members, became evident only in time. Missing was a general socioeconomic development plan to the year 2000, with the necessary data that could serve as the basis for the physical plan. Instead, the physical plan was to be predicated on the framework and socioeconomic projections of the National Development Plan for 1981–1985, which was not yet available. The existing "Transformation Plan" for 1979–1980 (Ministry of Planning 1977a), which theoretically took the country to 1990, did not provide sufficient information on national policy or socioeconomic planning to devise strategies going beyond that date. Thus, a long-term planning framework and projection, the province of another ministry and another UN planning team, was unavailable to the physical-planning team, obliging it to attempt its own national and regional socioeconomic forecasting in order to shape projections for the evolution and development of a Libyan human-settlement plan some two decades and more down the road.

Determination of Key Factors in Evaluating Libyan National Resources, Year 2000

In the absence of adequate socioeconomic data, the team decided to select and analyze the key factors around which the national physical plan would be designed. Fifteen factors were selected as critical to the evolution and development of Libya's human-settlements strategy for the year 2000 (UN/NPPP 1978a). These factors included economic, sociological, spatial-demographic, infrastructural, and technological variables as follows:

Economic Variables

- Economic models of future development

- Scale and location of economic activity
- Central place concepts and their economic appraisal

Sociological Variables

- Social goals in the context of Libyan policy and society
- Role of women and family in the development process
- Migration, social change, and development policy for rural areas

Spatial-demographic Variables

- Functional and spatial structure of the country
- Settlement network and future population distribution
- Population problems of the wet coastal belt

Infrastructural Services Facilities Variables

- Housing patterns and social facilities
- Settlement patterns as facilities governed by water resources
- Influence of motor transport on future development
- Future demands on infrastructure
- Maintenance as an "equal partner" to development
- Possible impact of future technological development on Libya

Discussions and analyses of the key factors among team members and with our Libyan counterparts in the Urban Planning Department over several months' time produced a clear consensus about the potentials and problems for Libyan development (UN/NPPP 1978b). For instance, the geographical division of the country into coastal, oasis, and desert regions, along with the distribution of such critical resources as oil, arable land, and rainfall and underground water, gave overall shape to the nature and location of the most important economic activities. At the same time, sizable oil revenue had generated a demand for highly sophisticated technologies. Since the Libyan population was too small and too poorly educated to use these technologies, alien labor and management had become important. Finally, existing Libyan social and economic policies were having deleterious effects on the use of national resources, resulting in the rapid depletion of oil resources.

A primary objective of Libyan policy was to create conditions of equity on a national level. The government had outlined clear policy directions concerning a more balanced urban-rural development that would, in general, bring the many isolated, spatially distant rural populations into the "mainstream." For the physical-planning team, these policies raised serious questions about the cost to the government of delivering services, providing the necessary infrastructure, and, in so doing, potentially depleting valuable resources. The reports on the key factors represented the team's attempt to assist the Libyan government to achieve a compromise on this conflict.

As the social planner on the team and the only member with prior field knowledge of Libya—or of the Arab world—I was in a strategic position to influence significantly the outcome of the analysis. At the same time, the interdisciplinary composition of the team meant that considerable exchange of information was essential to a successful analysis of the critical features of Libyan development. In addition to encouraging an interdisciplinary approach, I endeavored to mediate substantive as well as personality differences among team members. It is worth noting that an important influence in coalescing the team was its opposition to the not-so-hidden agenda of the project manager to impose a Western-style urban and regional model on the Libyan human-settlement planning exercise. The net effect of this difference between the project manager and the rest of the team was that the team joined arms to create a plan that reflected Libyan needs and not the exigencies dictated by some Western model.

Social-Policy Issues in an Anthropological Light

As part of the task of formulating guidelines for the plan, I analyzed the following social-policy topics (UN/NPPP 1978c), each of which in turn subsumed several relevant issues: social soundness (equity), agriculture, land and water use, population, work and manpower (including womanpower), nomads, villages, cities, rural-urban migration, new settlements, housing and physical standards, values, and tourism. I considered each of these issues in the light of existing policy, national law, and discussions with Libyan officials, all in the context of my knowledge of the sociopolitical landscape. The analysis included a systematic review of dozens of documents, including the Libyan-UN project document (UN/NPPP 1976b); Libyan national planning documents such as the 1973–75 *Economic and Social Development Plan* (Ministry of Planning 1974) and the 1976–80 *Transformation Plan* (Ministry of Planning 1977a); Libyan laws enacted by the Revolutionary Command Council concerning social-equity issues (e.g., RCC 1972); earlier consultants' work on human-settlement planning, *Italconsult National Report* (Italconsult 1976), which some Libyan planners had found unacceptable; the same consultants' regional and master plans (Italconsult 1977); the Libyan report to the UN Habitat conference on human settlements held in Vancouver (UN/Habitat 1976); and a Libyan study on enhancing the role of women in economic development (Ministry of Planning 1977b).

The following questions present a sampling of the issues considered in the policy analysis:

Social Soundness

- Does the policy of balanced redistribution of socioeconomic resources ensure equal access to an improved quality of life?

- In pursuing the policy of reducing discrepancies of local opportunities and living conditions, how easily transferable are resources in this society of dispersed settlements?
- In a climate of newfound wealth, how is it possible to curb the consumer appetite and achieve the goal of development as investment—not consumption?

Agriculture

- Given the rapid depletion of water resources and the heavy dependence on foreign food imports, how can the policy of national food self-sufficiency be best achieved?
- How much financial and human investment should be placed in developing desert areas, given the problem of groundwater depletion?
- Given the importance of such high-water-consumption vegetables as tomatoes as a cash crop, what is the effect of crop-control policy on income and the living standard in areas of unreplenishable water?

Land and Water Use

- How can the policy of maximum water use be justified, given the unreplenishable character of much of the supply?
- How can the land-use law of 1977, which permits land of small farmers to be "acquired" by larger farmers, be juxtaposed with the likelihood that small farmers will not easily accept expropriation of their land in the name of economies of scale?

Population

- Given the policy of resettling segments of the population and establishing new settlements, what specific criteria should be used?

Work and Manpower

- With a policy of optimum utilization of manpower through redistribution of population, what are the presumed impacts of such a redistribution?
- How can the present large alien work force be reduced or replaced by Libyans?
- How does a policy of female participation in contributing to the GNP fit with the valued "traditional" family role of women?

Nomads

- How does a policy of integrating nomads through resettlement harmonize with the benefit of the nomads' continued use of a productive range of eco-zones and the Bedouin embodiment of important, preservable values?

Villages

- Given the policy of developing the rural marketplace as an economic force, what are the financial and logistical implications of placing infrastructure in Libya's many remote villages?

Cities

- Since a policy of developing polar growth centers is in place, how can such centers be made effective in fostering urban-rural linkages?

Rural-Urban Migration

- Does the policy of decelerating rural-urban migration place priority on improving rural desert settlements, starting new rural settlements, or otherwise enticing emigrants back?

New Settlements

- Does the present ecological balance of desert and nomadic communities, given problems of desertification and water depletion, offer an adequate planning model?

Housing and Physical Standards

- Under a policy for improving the living standard of rural and desert inhabitants, how are salient sociocultural features best determined and designed into housing and human-settlement plans?

Values

- Given that social development requires a sound definition of economic and social progress, how are Islamic and Libyan values to be integrated into a definition of progress?
- Since the "rectification of values impeding social development" is integral to the national plan, how are such values reflected in a physical plan?

Tourism

- How would tourism as a potential long-term economic goal, given rich historical and recreational possibilities, be promoted in the face of a strong, deep-rooted xenophobia?

Following my analysis and write-ups of these and other social-policy issues, discussions were held among planning-team members and Libyan officials of the Ministries of Municipalities and Planning to arrive at recommendations for specific planning strategies. What follows is a consideration of some of the social-planning recommendations made to our Libyan counterparts in the Department of Urban Planning and eventually included in the national Physical-Perspective Plan.

Implications of Social Analyses for the National Plan

One fairly obvious but critical factor for the planning team was the low level of development of Libyan rural areas—the hinterland behind the much better endowed and more developed coastal belt. Thus, an important focus of the overall plan was the relationship of rural settlements to the urban centers. The team noted, however, that the proportion of total population in rural areas was and would remain small. If the scale of growth were to become a problem, Libya's large cities would be affected more severely than the hinterland. Feeding and servicing cities without depending on imports, for example, was a potential difficulty, and to minimize it, the team recommended that Libyan planners focus on slowing growth in existing cities and directing the flow of rural migrants to new urban and rural growth centers.

In general terms, the team found the Libyan national policy of a balanced spatial and social distribution of resources to be sensible. From the socio-spatial perspective, however, achieving the goal of equitable distribution was more complex, mainly because environmental boundaries in Libya are sharply defined, particularly as one moves from the coastal strip to the interior.

This division along environmental lines had been crucial over the centuries in shaping the three fundamental types of settlement patterns. Pastoral camp, agricultural village, and commercial center make up the fabric of Libyan society, which for centuries had effectively linked tribesmen, villagers, and townsmen for purposes of trade and other kinds of exchange—including marriage. Taken together, the factors of environment, work, and social organization provide Libya with the ingredients that integrate the society. Moreover, despite the more recent introduction of the oil-extraction industry and its enclave communities (oil camps) in numerous places in the desert, this time-tested division along lines of place, work, and organization has held up well. Because the three-way division was fixed both in nature and in history, I felt that the physical-perspective plan would do well to capitalize and improve on it. In coordination with the regional economist and regional planner/architect on the team, therefore, I strongly recommended the achievement of the national goal of balancing resources through a socio-spatial strategy that emphasized societal integration (see Figure 7.2). The integrative aim would contribute toward a better standard of living, the use and

Libya's National Human Settlement Plan

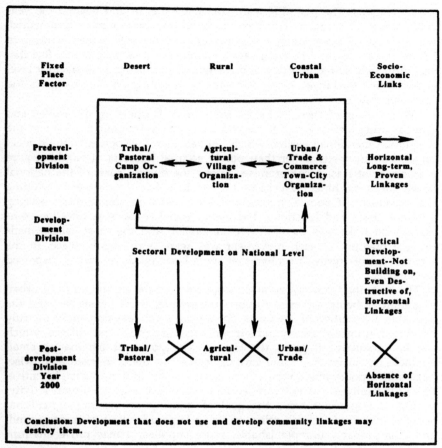

FIGURE 7.2
Potential Breakdown of Community Linkages as a Result of National Sectoral Development

conservation of a wider range of the environment, and the preservation of Libyan values.

Dramatic political changes, increased revenues from oil, and the introduction of strong national-planning policy guidelines in Libya had culminated in a development program of ambitious proportions. Industrial and agricultural development projects, a massive housing program, and a vast increase in educational, health, and social services highlighted the thrust of Libya's aspirations for present and future well-being. Much of this development had been shaped so as to fulfill major policy aims of distributing resources. The shaping, however, had not always taken place in ways compatible with the existing social structures, which were already well adapted to production and commerce and had generally provided a network for settlements and social relations. The planning team concurred that in and beyond the year 2000, when oil revenues will have declined and development diminished, the division of labor along ecological lines could well remain crucial to Libya's advancement. The team saw a planning and development effort that was ultimately self-supporting and capable of producing a satisfactory level of well-being for Libya's future generations as resting on the linkage of the three subsystems.

Development of these linkages required both operating principles and implementing institutions. Of the two basic principles defined, one was the integration mentioned earlier, which implied that development should meet broad, human needs rather than purely sectoral interests. It would require a union, or at least a compromise, among the diverse parts of the national development machinery. The second principle is that of movement, including the movement of people, goods, and ideas between communities serving different needs and functions. The use of social contacts as effective communication links was therefore recommended, and the most salient institutional medium of such movement was seen as the marketplace, in the sense of service/growth centers that serve basic needs of widely dispersed settlements.

The planning team saw rural development and the curbing of rural-urban migration as being achieved through integration, fiscal incentives, and the equitable distribution of resources. For Libyan rural development to be truly integrated, it must draw on and support existing agricultural villages, which can be productive if given the chance. The policy of eliminating small landholdings in favor of large agribusinesses was therefore seen as unwise. First, such a policy might reduce both labor demand and individual incentive, given the family-based, entrepreneurial mode of existing agricultural activity; second, it might not serve the goal of drawing on existing agricultural activity; and third, since it relies on using large quantities of underground, and thus probably unreplenishable, water supplies, it may prove environmentally unsound.

For Libyan rural areas, economy and environment impinge forcefully on each other to limit change. The major long-term economic goals for the agricultural sector considered by the team were: (1) self-sufficiency in basic foodstuffs, (2) preservation of natural resources, (3) elimination of small landholdings, and (4) development of agroindustrial units. When these goals were examined in the context of environmental conditions in the interior, certain contradictions emerged. For one, as stated earlier, replenishable water supplies are limited and variable across the geographical face of Libya. Thus, water conservation would most likely have to be rigidly enforced in the interior within several years, simultaneously with attempts to promote economic growth. So, too, economic and social goals for rural development were seen to impinge on one another. The elimination of small landholdings to create agroindustrial units, while perhaps economically justifiable, was socioculturally as well as politically unworkable because historically farm holdings have been small in much of Libya and most farmers depend on such holdings for their livelihood. Of equal importance in our objecting to an agroindustrial approach was the disjuncture it would cause in the sociocultural patterns of rural families and kin groups.

The team tried to envisage a development program that significantly ignored or underplayed social and cultural conditions. It was almost impossible to play out this scenario, given the importance of the organization of Libyan society around the extended family, village community, or tribe, and the Libyan pride and dignity that derive from and reinforce this organization. Were these characteristics not taken into account in the rural-development program, the end result would be several unsustainable, unconnected projects or programs dotting the countryside, with few links to proven, successful lifeways.

Related to the question of adapting development programs to existing social and cultural conditions was the historically important role of pastoral nomadism in Libya. Pastoralism was examined in terms of both the utilization of natural resources and the goal of preserving traditional values. Pastoral nomadism uses some otherwise unusable parts of Libya's physical environment, and it might be reorganized—without being destroyed—along the lines of modernized range-management and dry-pasture animal industry. Even though range-management programs have generally been unsuccessful, one proposed model (based on Moriondo 1977) appeared to have some potential for use in parts of Libya. The planning team did not carry out further work on the question, however, as it did not have the requisite expertise.

Libyan Societal Development and a Question of the Necessity to Change

All of the above development policies, their analyses, and the changes in Libyan society they implied, had to be carefully qualified by the social planner and his colleagues to present reasonable and socially sensitive alternatives for the country's physical evolution. In following through some of the recommendations based on the social analyses, it was important to keep in mind several general, though crucial, points about Libya's recent development. First, as recently as two decades ago, the country had been one of the poorest in the world; second, Libya had been a feudal monarchy up until 1969, with tribes as a major political force; third, substantial national development programs were suddenly thrust on the society, in many cases with little thought given to the discontinuities they might create with traditional work, living patterns, and values; and fourth, innovative political reforms and structures had been introduced that theoretically gave Libyans the chance to use development resources in ways directly benefiting themselves.

While two of the important barriers to change—poverty and monarchy—were no longer present, the other two required some careful channeling. The expanded political power that enabled access to the new economic resources was not tied to longstanding, effective social institutions. Even though the original intention of Qaddafi's socialist Islamic pronouncements had been to turn power over to the people and to give them responsibility for their own actions, the organization for doing this had little continuity with traditional decision-making patterns, nor was the society rooted in a technical tradition that would foster the effective use of new economic resources. In fact, societal forms and organizational structures severely lagged behind the new high technology. It became clear that in the absence of alien workers and managers, notwithstanding the mandate to replace them eventually, long-term strategies for Libya's national development would have gone begging.

Linked to this gap between society and technology was a factor recognized by some, though not all, Libyan planning officials: the oil wealth with which their country had been gifted and by which it could develop, had come without the need to change its values, attitudes, and motivations concerning work. That was not to say that the Libyans did not continue to work hard at what they traditionally do well—small-scale, family-oriented enterprises—nor that the use of modern technology had to mimic the Western model. There is much more to development than technical-material changes. Politicians were making concerted efforts to promote the adaptation by Libyans to the new or impending conditions wrought by development. The problem for Libyans, however, as for people everywhere, was (and is) that they are most likely to change only when they clearly perceive beneficial consequences of change.

The Anthropologist's Influence on the Plan

The time and effort I devoted to detailed planning in the formulation of the Libyan national physical-perspective plan was less than that spent assembling socioeconomic data and analyzing social policy in order to develop guidelines for the planning exercise. This lack of emphasis on detailed planning was due to the following factors: (1) a national physical-perspective plan is one that provides basic, generalized guidelines for developing a national human-settlements plan; (2) planning beyond two decades in the future makes certain kinds of details impractical, especially in the absence of necessary socioeconomic data; (3) the balance between detailed planning and design studies, on the one hand, and the need to obtain data for baseline analysis and general planning purposes, on the other, was never clarified by either Libyan authorities or UN representatives in New York; and (4) even if detailed physical plans were required, they would have to be evolved in five-year periods for several regions and hundreds of large and small settlements, representing an impractical, inappropriate use of the team's resources and time. The third reason—the contradiction between detailed planning studies and guidelines for overall physical development—was the cause of certain disagreement and strife among the team members, who found the mandate from Tripoli and UN/

New York unclear. The crux of the disagreement can be characterized in part by the following, purposely exaggerated, scenario.

Assume you are a physical-planner/architect who has arrived in a developing country such as Libya from a Western nation, knowing little about the national development process in general and even less about Libya in particular. Assume it is technically easy to impose a fairly detailed physical plan on Libya. Assume also that you have the tacit support of government officials for your ideas, since they understandably—though secretly—admire Western planning standards. You sincerely believe that Western physical-planning standards—ranging from the grand scheme based on growth poles, all the way down to grid patterns for neighborhoods and design standards for single-family residences—can be transferred anywhere, that the same blueprint can apply to Saudi Arabia as, for example, to Sweden. While such a characterization may exaggerate the actual situation, the planning exercise for Libya's national settlements scheme nevertheless seemed always to be in danger of having that kind of mentality thrust upon it.

Given my ethnographic knowledge of Libyan society and lifeways, it seemed that the most valuable contribution I could make to the plan was as mediator between the intended beneficiaries and the government and project personnel. This function appeared to me more important to the planning process than that of providing detailed specifications for a nationwide perspective plan based on English or U.S. town-planning standards, which was the project manager's conception of what I should be doing. I saw myself at least partly as a kind of protocol officer or agenda clarifier, (e.g., WAPA 1984), to assist in mediating certain technical differences concerning the scope of the project as well as the cultural differences among international planners, Libyan authorities, and—the presumed focus of all this—Libyans living their lives in a variety of socio-spatial contexts. This task was necessarily complex. It should be remembered that the role of anthropologist in protocol and agenda clarification or as "sorcerer's apprentice" (Belshaw 1976) is relatively recent in its origin. So, too, is the part played by the anthropologist in analyzing policy for international development organizations. Despite the newness of the enterprise, I attempted to play that part, sometimes admittedly at the risk of alienating two sides of the mediation—UN team members and Libyan planners/politicians alike.

Some years after the project had ended and prior to writing this piece, I seriously pondered my part in it. I realized that the project had turned out to be much more politicized than I had originally envisioned. I had frankly underestimated the political abilities of certain members of the planning profession, especially the project manager, who brought with him over four decades of experience in town-council bureaucratic machinations and was a master of bureaucratic intrigue. Thus, in a practice not discovered for several months, he would send cables to UN/New York in the name of the unknowing Deputy Minister, issuing formal instructions on critical policy and management issues.

Also, in retrospect, I did not at the time realize the full implications of the inconclusive instructions or scope of work rendered to the team by UN/New York and Libyan authorities. The gaps in the instructions, both technical and policy-related, left too much play in the delicate balance of political, bureaucratic, and technical decisions. Those lacunae created a situation in which the project manager played both sides (Libyan Ministry officials and UN/New York officials) against the middle (the team).

I used these gaps to a limited degree myself by sensitizing the rest of the team to local, regional, and national sociopolitical and economic conditions and issues. While unable to provide the complete, detailed planning standards desired by the project manager, I was able to address physical-planning issues appropriate to a national settlement plan for the year 2000. Thus I proposed planning standards for new settlements, including educational and health facilities and considering community and neighborhood design factors, and commenced a survey of community user needs and perceptions in cooperation with University of Libya sociology students to arrive at standards of house and residential-cluster design. One of my main regrets is that I was unable to spend much time getting out to local communities, although I did spend about one-quarter of my time traveling in the countryside. The bureaucratic machinations of the Ministry office where I was located seemed to chew up an inordinate amount of time, as did my four-month-long search for a residence for my family, a problem related to the serious housing shortage in Tripoli brought on by the politically motivated dismissal of thousands of Egyptian construction workers.

On the institutional development side, in my role as social planner I worked with counterparts, mainly department planning heads in both the Ministries of Municipalities and Planning, to incorporate sociocultural dimensions into the planning process. (A few of these officials were my former students from the 1968–70 period at the university in Benghazi.) As part of this collaborative effort I formalized a "Social Planner's Manual," which included a methodological framework for analyzing social policy and socioeconomic data relevant to human-settlement planning in Libya. This manual was incorporated in my final report to the Project, Ministry, and UN/New York (UN/NPPP 1978d).

As to the final product, my key-factors papers were incorporated in the body of the final report (UN/NPPP 1980) and made part of the inevitable accompanying documentation, i.e., annexes. The actual implementation of the final plan by the Ministry of Municipalities has unfortunately been difficult to ascertain, given the uncertain communications in and out of Libya over the last few years. Even the UN was unable to verify the progress of implementation, if any. It seems doubtful that much progress could have been made in implementing the plan, given severe financial constraints in Libya due to its cutback in oil production and the declining market price of oil; the enormous funding of the Libyan military, which reduced the availability of funds for socioeconomic development; and the fact that the country has virtually been in a state of war with Chad over the last decade.

Conclusions and Lessons Learned

This glimpse of an anthropologist in the role of social planner underscores several lessons for the practice of anthropology. My earlier fieldwork in a Libyan rural-desert context provided me with knowledge that could be used in the applied setting. From the physical-planning perspective, that meant knowing the environmental opportunities and constraints, as well as the articulation and composition of Libya's ecological zones. Libyans' habits of movement within and across the eco-zones were also important to understand. The mosaic pattern of desert, steppe, hill, and coastal people and their unique set of interactions historically and in the present was significant to the economic and physical planners. It was useful to them in organizing their ideas and making their projections about the nature of the linkages between the country's different local, regional, and national types of human settlement.

Libya proved to be an almost perfect laboratory for observing the impact of new national wealth on cultures and traditions that die hard. Concepts of modernization and change may have their theoretical usefulness, but they can be understood only in the light of such cases as Libya, where much of the old and valued has persisted alongside the new. On top of these coexisting old and new traditions, ideas, and values, Qaddafi imposed what seemed at first to be a radical political ethos, rooted in a rather traditional conception of Islam. Whatever the impact of the imposed ideologies and structure, Qaddafi's regime has generated new policies and posed new and difficult issues and problems to be resolved in national-planning activities. The exercise in which I participated offered the unique challenge of getting physical conceptions "right" in response to those largely new social policies.

The UN international team assigned to meet this challenge had both strengths and weaknesses. Four of the five members had significant experience in developing countries, but only I had previous work in the Middle East. The most serious problem, however, was the unavailability of the proposed socioeconomic development plan for the first five-year period of the two decades the physical plan was to address. In addition to this absence of adequate data, imprecision in the project's mandate left too much room for manipulation of ideas and personnel. To fill the data gap, the team evolved the key-factors approach, which provided a useful division of labor as well as an important analytical framework for the plan. By establishing clearly specified areas of responsibility, it also removed some of the potential for manipulation.

The particular key factors that were selected by the team members and Libyan planners in concert permitted us to raise important issues about the physical-planning implications of a far-reaching social policy based on the principle of equity. Such areas as rural development, agriculture, and nomadism thus came under scrutiny with respect to balancing their requirements against the needs of an ever-growing urban population. The evidence of the past concerning Libya's ecosystems and local environments became useful for framing the planning response to this potential disjuncture.

Overriding many of these concerns was an issue that had enormous implications for future change in Libya: material changes were occurring in the absence of changes in the population's basic values, attitudes, and motivations. The resultant lag between technology and culture created a certain disruption in the lives of the people: in a sharp break with the past, much of the physical labor was left to alien workers. This is generally the case for small-population oil-exporting countries, especially those that place their young men in large standing armies.

The unclear mandate for the planning team, combined with the absence of a relevant socioeconomic plan for the period to be covered, hindered all the team's members. In this situation it seemed appropriate for me as an anthropologist to help clarify the agenda and mediate the differences among the various actors. My inexperience, together with the seasoned political savvy of other parties to the project, diminished my success.

The rewards of the applied experience described here included opportunities for me to get around the country to enhance my ethnographic knowledge, to return to Augila Oasis, and to work with Libyan professional planners. For the last, it was unfortunate that I could not have been assigned a counterpart, but there was no trained social scientist in the department to which I was assigned, and Libyan authorities did not encourage such relationships with expatriates.

I could, perhaps, have more persistently sought out Libyan professionals to work with, but there was a dearth of professionals, and furthermore, the project manager discouraged such behavior. The project office thus developed an unfortunate insularity and a habit of working by itself. Coupled with the professional and personality conflict between the team and the project manager, this created a pattern antithetical to a collaborative learning/problem-solving approach to development work. Although I tried to step out of the cultural rut in which the team was mired, to transcend our being stereotyped as Libyan hired labor, as well as to mediate the office conflict, I was not terribly successful in these endeavors. On balance, however, my part as an anthropologist, as a social planner, and as a team member was modestly influential in shaping the national physical plan and in contributing to that elusive process called development.

References

Belshaw, Cyril S.
    1976 The Sorcerer's Apprentice: An Anthropology of Public Policy. New York: Pergamon.

Blunsum, Terence
    1968 Libya: The Country and Its People. London: Queen Anne Press.

Italconsult
    1976 National Report on Human Settlements (Libya). Rome: Italconsult.

    1977 Regional and Master Plans (Libya). Rome: Italconsult.

Mason, John P.
1969 The Culture History of Augila Oasis. Bulletin of the Faculty of Arts 4:(1). Benghazi: University of Libya.

1971 The Social History and Anthropology of the Arabized Berbers of Augila Oasis in the Libyan Sahara Desert. Ph.D. dissertation. Anthropology Department and African Studies Center, Boston University.

1974 Saharan Saints: Sacred Symbols or Empty Forms? Anthropological Quarterly 47(2):390–405.

1975 Sex and Symbol in the Treatment of Women: The Wedding Rite in a Libyan Oasis Community. American Ethnologist 4(2):649–661.

1976 Desert Strongman in the East Libyan Sahara (c. 1820): A Reconstruction of Local Power in the Region of Augila Oasis. Revue d'Histoire Maghrebine 6:180–188.

1977 Island of the Blest: Islam in a Libyan Oasis Community. Athens, Ohio: Ohio University Center for International Studies.

1978 Petroleum Development and the Reactivation of Traditional Structure in a Libyan Oasis Community. Economic Development and Cultural Change 26(4):763–776.

1981 Oasis Saints of Eastern Libya in North African Context. Middle Eastern Studies (18):357–374.

1982 Qaddaffi's "Revolution" and Change in a Libyan Oasis Community. Middle East Journal 36(3):319–335.

Ministry of Planning
1974 Economic and Social Development Plan (1973–75). Tripoli: Ministry of Planning.

1977a The Transformation Plan (1976–80). Tripoli: Ministry of Planning.

1977b Revised Resumé of the Report of the Committee for Study of Increasing the Contribution of Women to Economic Activities. Tripoli: Committee for the Study of Promoting Productivity.

Moriondo, Ezio
1977 Pastoralism in Libyan Society: Present State and Development Prospects. Rome: Italconsult.

Qaddafi, Mu'ammar
1976 The Green Book, Part I: The Solution of the Problem of Democracy, 'The Authority of the People.' London: Martin Brian & O'Keefe.

1977 The Green Book, Part II: The Solution to the Economic Problem, 'Socialism' (in Arabic). Tripoli: General Company for Publishing, Distribution, and Advertisement.

RCC (Revolutionary Command Council)
1972 Libyan Law Number 130, Source of Policy on Eliminating Social and Economic Gaps. Tripoli: Revolutionary Command Council.

UN/Habitat
1976 Libyan Report for the United Nations Conference on Human Settlements. Vancouver.

UN/NPPP (United Nations National Physical Planning Project)
    1976a Job Description for Social Planner, Assistance to the Libyan Arab Jamahiriya in the Field of Physical Planning.

    1976b Project Document, Assistance in the Field of Physical Planning (LIB/76/x01). New York.

    1978a Key Factors in Evaluation of National Resources, Year 2000. Tripoli.

    1978b Key Factors Conclusion. Tripoli.

    1978c Social Policy Issues to be Considered in the Formulation of Guidelines for the National Physical Perspective Plan. Tripoli.

    1978d Social Planning Contribution to the Project and the Plan: Pt. 1) Social Analysis, Pt. 2) Key Factors Papers, Pt. 3) Social Planners' Manual. Tripoli.

    1980 Final Report: The National Physical Perspective Plan. Tripoli.

WAPA (Washington Association of Professional Anthropologists)
    1984 Conference Handbook: Anthropology Career Conference 1984. Washington, D.C.

World Bank
    1955 World Bank Annual Review. Washington, D.C.

8

Developing Egypt's Western Desert Oases: Anthropology and Regional Planning

Douglas Gritzinger

Introduction

Virtually all Middle Eastern countries produce national plans, and most do some form of regional planning. Typically, a development anthropologist is engaged in regional planning either to do preplanning baseline studies, or, as a member of a multidisciplinary team, to help produce a special-purpose, often donor-funded, plan. My focus here is on the latter.[1] After some introductory remarks about anthropology and regional planning, I discuss a special-purpose plan made for Egypt's Western Desert New Valley in the early 1980s. In the last section I wield the wisdom of hindsight to point out how better use of the team's social scientist (in this case, a sociologist) could have improved the plan.

I am a regional planner and not an anthropologist, so this chapter differs from others in this book by looking at the anthropologist's role in interdisciplinary developing-country work from the other side. I will argue two main themes. The first is hardly new, but not yet much accepted in practice: interdisciplinary studies should be more than just different experts tackling the same problem in their own ways. Good things can come from orderly involvement in each others' work. I shall illustrate this by dwelling on the extreme case where the planning is dominated by numerical modeling, a methodology seldom associated with anthropology. Anthropologists can have much more influence in this esoteric enterprise than they might imagine, and to play a part, they do not have to fathom in detail how linear programming and other modeling techniques work. In truth, many modelers themselves have forgotten precisely what transpires inside their programs when they push the "compute" button. The anthropologist's local knowledge about such matters as household income earning strategies, farmer perceptions of new agricultural technologies, and the actual role of agricultural extension agents, can help to improve numerical models and to anchor a regional plan in the actual region at hand—rather than the imagined region in the planners' minds.

My second point is that getting this targeted, up-to-date local knowledge requires some form of field research concurrent with the plan-making—something that planning project designers, feeling time and budget constraints, would rather omit. One might suppose that if any variant of regional planning were to include field research it would be the most elaborate, comprehensive planning, which aspires to prescribe to all the region's socioeconomic sectors.[2] Typically, even writers of terms-of-reference for comprehensive plans view concurrent surveying and first-hand primary data gathering as: too expensive, incapable of being timely for a plan that must be completed in a year or less, and unnecessary when there appears to be a wealth of secondary data on the region. Nevertheless, such research is not only feasible but in fact essential to good plan making, and anthropologists are typically the best equipped to do it.

Plan-directed field research and interdisciplinary collaboration can be two sides of the same coin. Planners, engineers, and technical specialists are usually bound by the nature of their duties to their desks in the capital city, and spend their careers working for short periods in many different countries. Hence, they unavoidably come to depend on stock images of small farmers, cooperatives, extension agents, and the like, that may not always apply to the country at hand. Even though the technical people may appear well informed and awash in secondary data, they very often lack crucial pieces of information and insights into the region's socioeconomic life vital to drafting a sensible agricultural development plan or making workable recommendations for housing and services standards. Anthropologists, using both the formal and the more ad hoc research techniques they are accustomed to, are best equipped for sharpening the information at hand on key issues. Gathering precisely targeted socioeconomic data can form one basis for real collaboration with their teammates in devising the key plan recommendations and programs—a process that, in my experience, anthropologists seldom join as full partners.

Since 1981, I have participated in three Middle East regional planning projects, two in Egypt, both commissioned in the early 1980s by the Egyptian Ministry of Development and Reconstruction as plans for the country's remote regions: the Sinai Development Study (1980-1982, with Dames & Moore, Inc., the prime contractor) and the Regional Development Plan for New Valley (1982-1983, by the Dutch firm, Euroconsult); and one in Iraq, which included a plan for Iraq's Central Region: Baghdad 2001, Integrated Capital Development Plan of Baghdad (1985-1986, by the Japanese Consortium of Consulting Firms). All were nominally comprehensive, implying some egality of concern for the several disciplines and their respective experts, but in practice each was organized around a single overriding discipline and methodology. The New Valley Plan, for example, focused foremost on irrigated land development. Groundwater simulation modeling dominated the plan making.

In these planning projects, the various experts could not avoid learning something of each others' findings, but many factors beyond simple disciplinary chauvinism, such as non-overlapping work schedules, conspired to keep them from becoming much involved in each others' work, or even from taking it fully into account in their own writings. Integrating the many separate pieces of work with each other and with the predetermined central concern was a problem, even at the most rudimentary level of getting the main report and the annexes mutually consistent. For all three projects, the social science was not well integrated into the final plan, and the social scientist worked on the plan-making periphery. For New Valley, team members who did not do groundwater simulation modeling operated closer or farther from this core activity depending on their specialties, months on the project, and personal inclinations.

In all three studies, the scopes of work of the social scientists paralleled those of the other long- and short-term experts, amounting to drafting a portion of the plan. For New Valley, the sociologist was charged with constructing a scheme for "community social development." This became one of eleven annexes generated by the cast of supporting specialists, a list including: soils, groundwater, land reclamation, mining, industry, agriculture, tourism, population, administration, and services and infrastructure. Before this final writing chore, the social scientist was expected to establish (or validate) his of her local knowledge by some variant of rapid rural appraisal: an abbreviated program of interviews, small surveys, and possibly extended visits to one or another case-study community. He or she shared the assorted findings through working papers.

In the discussion below, my aim is to illustrate that orderly involvement of social scientists and technical-specialist planners in each other's work is worth striving for, and to offer the reader a bit of the texture of regional planning for arid lands. I hope to convey that regional planning is at once among the most useless of pursuits, for anthropologists or anyone, since plans are seldom implemented in toto or even in part—but yet quite useful if the drafters perceive their acts as regional scenario making and policy advising. Planning requires a different attitude than does project design where concrete execution can be only a few months and signatures away. To get beyond merely convincing readers of what might strike them as truisms and to show what this means in practice require probing a region and its plan in some detail.

The Region

Introduction

The oases of Egypt's Western Desert would have no place at all in the Nile-bound Egyptian psyche were it not for the huge Nubian Aquifer beneath them. The four groundwater-fed oases of El Wadi El Gedid, or New Valley, occupy depressions scattered over an area roughly 250 km west of the Nile between the latitudes of Idfu and Minya, a north-south distance of 450 km (see Figure 8.1). Although these oases have been occupied continuously since the time of the pharaohs, modern interest in them was sparked by the burgeoning of Egypt's Nile Valley population and the dream that groundwater could sustain a whole new civilization in the Western Desert: a second "new" valley, as Nasser dubbed it in the late 1950s. For thirty years, politicians and visionaries have proposed grandiose schemes for the region, even including diverting Nile water to it. After some modest successes with land reclamation in the early 1960s, the government ran out of money and patience, and left the region to stagnate from the late 1960s until 1982, when the regional planning study began.[3]

Since a single road links the four oases and all four depend on a single underground water resource, viewing the area as a distinct, functional region does make sense. But in the early 1980s, the government hardly treated it as such. Administratively, Bahariya was attached to Cairo Governorate rather than to New Valley Governorate, which had the three more southerly oases. Likewise, the Ministry of Planning put Bahariya in the Greater Cairo Planning Region, even though it is 334 km distant, while New Valley Governorate was lumped with Assiut Governorate to form the Assiut Planning Region. The Ministry of Development (MOD), which bore responsibility for designing and implementing major region-level projects such as new towns and Suez Canal cities reconstruction, had a third geographic slicing. Given the various administrative overlaps, coherent, ongoing planning was not being done for the region. The plan discussed here was a special-purpose plan made for the Ministry of Development by an expatriate-led team with Dutch foreign assistance. The work, completed in 1983, was done in part to develop and provide the MOD with a state-of-the-art groundwater simulation model of the region's Nubian Aquifer.

The Physical Setting[4]

The Western Desert's climate ranks among the world's hottest and driest: at Kharga, summer high temperatures approach 50° centigrade, and annual rainfall does not exceed 5 mm. In some places, rain may not fall for a generation. An incessant wind dominates the ultra-dry landscape: in lieu of rain, the desert's storms bear dust in high winds severe enough in April and May to destroy ripening winter crops. Temperatures and relative humidity moderate somewhat from south to north, causing the calculated annual potential evapotranspiration rate of northernmost Bahariya to be only 57 percent of Kharga's. This turned out to be important for the regional plan.

Geomorphically, the Western Desert is a plateau consisting of Tertiary carbonate rocks underlain by Secondary deposits that include the water-bearing Nubian Sandstones. The one elevation of note—Jebel Abu Tartur, between Kharga and Dakhla—also happens to be the site of a major phosphate deposit. Huge dune fields populate the area, threatening roads and whole villages (El Baz 1982:203). In four major depressions (formed mainly by wind erosion) 100–200 meters lower than the plateau, the exposure

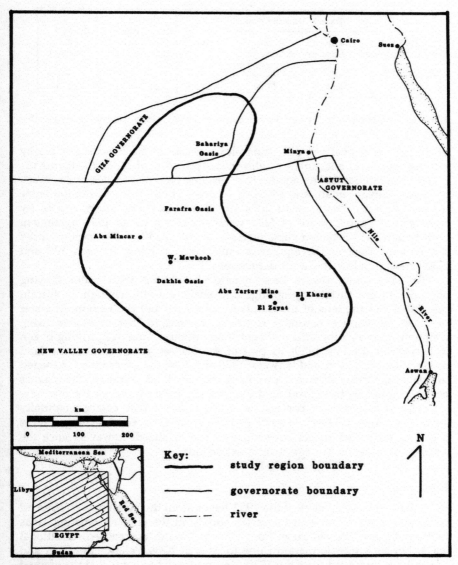

FIGURE 8.1
Egypt New Valley Study Area. *Source:* Euroconsult/Pacer Consultants (1983)

TABLE 8.1
Overall Groundwater Balance for New Valley in 1980 (MCM/Year)

Total Discharge				Total Recharge Through Boundaries	Change in Storage
Well Extractions	Natural Losses	Flow Through Boundaries	Total		
323.8	114.5	21.4	459.7	317.0	-142.7

Source: Euroconsult/Pacer Consultants 1983, Main Report, page 15.

of deeper water-bearing rock strata allows water to flow to the surface by artesian pressure, and, in turn, allows the prospect of human settlement.

The Nubian Sandstone aquifer that sustains New Valley lies under much of Egypt, Libya, Sudan, and Chad. It contains about 50×10^6 million cubic meters (MCM) of water, with 20×10^6 MCM under the study region. By comparison, Egypt's share of Nile water according to its 1959 agreement with Sudan is 55.5 billion cubic meters—about 1/360 of the amount under the Western Desert. The aquifer is multi-layered, lying between 100 and 2,000 meters below the wadi depressions.

The oases have always been generously blessed with water flowing naturally to the surface by springs and shallow wells, enough to sustain populations in the tens of thousands for centuries, but the amount of water reaching the surface naturally is tiny compared to that accessible using twentieth-century tubewells and centrifugal pumps. Tubewell drilling began in earnest in the late 1950s as part of the Nasser government's new land reclamation initiatives, and between 1960 and 1980 the government managed to double the irrigated area. Developing the new land permitted the region's native population to expand, and allowed the influx of at least a few new agricultural settlers.[5] In contrast to artesian flows that balance naturally against recharge, tubewell extractions have always exceeded recharge (Table 8.1). The untoward effects have mainly been localized, however, since the amount of water in storage dwarfs extractions.

Population[6]

In the early, heady days of the 1952 Revolution, the Nasserists envisioned creating a modern, vanguard agrarian society in the land reclamation areas that would lead the old areas from their backward, entrenched, traditional ways. No such transformation came to pass in New Valley. Education and health have improved since the 1950s, but progress has paralleled the gradual advances occurring in the "old" Nile Valley. New Valley's high fertility and low literacy rates mirror those for rural Egypt as a whole. The 1976 census reported for New Valley Governorate an average of 6.3 live births for women by the end of their childbearing years. Male literacy in 1976 was 76 percent for urban areas and 53 percent for rural; for females, 45 percent urban and

TABLE 8.2
Estimated 1982 New Valley Population

	Rural[a]	Urban	Total
Kharga	14,000	31,000	45,000
Dakhla[b]	44,000	10,000	54,000
Farafra	2,000	–	2,000
Bahariya	14,000	2,000	16,000
Total	74,000	43,000	117,000

[a] Settlements of fewer than 8,000 people.
[b] Includes West Mawhoob and Abu Tartur.
Source: Euroconsult/Pacer Consultants 1983, Main Report, page 12.

24 percent rural. These numbers approximate those of Egypt as a whole, as do New Valley's household sizes of 5.5 urban and 6.3 rural. This similarity of social indicators implies that if the government did not transform New Valley in the last 30 years, it at least provided the region with comparable levels of services.

The study team estimated the region's mid-1982 population at 117,000, of which 63 percent were rural, living in settlements smaller than 8,000 (Table 8.2). Eighty-five percent of the people resided in the southern two oases: Kharga and Dakhla. The population was young, with nearly half under 15 years old, and it was growing briskly, at about 2.6 percent per year. The dependency ratio was concomitantly high, exacerbated in the rural areas by a heavy outmigration of working-age males.[7]

A striking feature of the 1976 census was the high ratio of men to women in urban areas, contrasted with a very low one in the rural areas. The former reflects the influx of male government workers to Kharga and Dakhla, and mineworkers to the iron pits at Bahariya. The rural areas were undergoing an opposite outmigration of males. This must have been due mainly to the "push" of the poor agroeconomy, since by 1976, the time of the census migration data, the exodus of Egyptian workers "pulled" by the booming Gulf economies was not yet in full swing.

According to the 1976 census, roughly half of New Valley's economically active population was working in agriculture, and about 25 percent in government. Participation in the formal labor force was negligible for women, and about 53 percent for males over 6 years old. The employment structure differed sharply between oases. Kharga, being the governorate capital and headquarters of the New Valley Development Authority (NVDA), had a large government payroll. These government workers comprised the larger share of the region's nonnative and educated residents. Dakhla is the region's major agricultural center. The most remote oasis of Farafra stands by itself: small, self-contained, and agricultural. Bahariya's iron mine employed 85 percent of its urban males, although agriculture still dominated this mainly rural oasis, overall.

TABLE 8.3
New Valley Cultivated Land, Winter 1981-1982 (Feddans)

	Native Lands		Reclaimed Lands	Total Cropped Area
	Deep Wells	Shallow Wells		
Kharga	2,500	1,200	6,020	9,720
El Zayat	-	-	30	30
Dakhla	6,000	5,300	10,180	21,480
West Mawhoob	-	-	3,470	3,470
Abu Muncar	-	-	1,000	1,000
Farafra	-	110	150	260
Bahariya	500	5,000	-	5,500
Total	9,000	11,610	20,850	41,460

Source: Euroconsult/Pacer Consultants 1983, Main Report, page 18.

Agriculture

As mentioned, agriculture employs about half of New Valley's population. Even if mining eventually proves to be the most lucrative use Egypt makes of its Western Desert, farming has long been the dream. Unfortunately, despite two decades of upbeat press releases and the drilling of hundreds of tubewells, New Valley in 1981 was not the promised desert granary. It was just as dependent as the rest of Egypt on outside food, even though its balance of cropped land to population was far more favorable than the crowded Nile Valley's. New Valley Governorate's 1981 wheat imports totaled 132kg/capita; the value of food imports totaled £E 3.1 million, while exports reached only £E 666,000. The government had succeeded in doubling the cropped area, but not in making either the new or the old cropped areas very productive.

Flying over the four oases gives one a sense of agriculture's precarious state in the Western Desert: the cropped areas are minuscule compared to the surrounding desert. Cultivation is patchy rather than contiguous: green areas are strung along the narrow wadi floors encircled by sand dunes, patches of rocky unusable soils, and salt marshes where irrigation runoff accumulates. The old lands tend to be narrow ribbons of fields and date palm groves commanded by free-flowing artesian wells. In stark contrast, the deep tubewell-based areas have more regular, rectangular fields with windbreak trees for borders. Nevertheless, modern tubewells and surface irrigation have yet to turn the tide in the struggle to cultivate: surveys of land around the new wells reveal nearly as much fallow and abandoned land as productive (Beller Consult/ACI 1982:Annex 7.1).

In 1981, New Valley's cropped area was divided almost evenly into native old lands and new reclaimed lands (Table 8.3). Modern deep wells were installed for about half the old lands, as increased pumping had dried up many of the old artesian and shallow wells. Landholdings on the old lands

TABLE 8.4
New Valley Governorate Cropping Pattern 1980-1981

	Area (feddan)	Percent
		Perennial Crops
Date palm	5,760	20
Fruit trees	980	3
Alfalfa	5,625	20
Total	12,365	43
		Winter Crops
Wheat	7,214	25
Berseem	6,419	22
Broad bean	2,007	7
Onion	398	1
Vegetables	397	1
Total	16,435	57[a]
Total Perennial and Winter	28,800	100
		Summer Crops
Rice	3,199	11
Watermelon	397	1
Vegetables	243	1
Others	794	3
Total	4,633	16

[a] Does not add to total because of rounding errors.
Source: Euroconsult/Pacer Consultants 1983, Annex F - Agriculture, page 16.

were highly fragmented, mainly because of inheritance practices. High mud walls partitioned plots—less than 0.1 hectare—typically planted densely with date palm. Nevertheless, only 15 percent of the farms were less than one feddan (1 feddan = 0.42 hectare), with 75 percent between one and ten feddans. The policy that distributed reclaimed land in 5–7 feddan parcels pulled up the New Valley average, making its farms somewhat bigger than the overall Egyptian average, although the Nile Valley's cropping intensity of about two crops per year is higher than New Valley's one and a half and less.

Table 8.4 presents New Valley Governorate's cropping pattern in the early 1980s. Low-valued wheat and fodder crops dominated, reflecting the conservative orientation of the farmers, as well as market constraints to producing more lucrative crops. Vegetables, onion, and watermelon—the region's major potential high-value crops—are scarcely grown. Date palm and fruit trees occupy about a quarter of the total winter and perennial cropped area. Few annual crops can be found growing in the summer months aside from rice at Dakhla, grown as much for soil leaching as for food.

Date palm has long been a major oasis crop, but yields are low compared to what is possible with good care and use of fertilizer—regrettable, since even at middling yields date appears to be a lucrative crop. Most of the date trees occupy the old lands, growing close together on small plots, interplanted with fruit trees, fodder, and vegetables. They receive little fertilizer or pest protection, and are poorly pollinated. Consequently, yields are low and insects damage the ripening fruit.

New Valley farmers, despite being free of mandatory crop rotations and being permitted to grow alfalfa,[8] still had much in common with their Nile cousins: small farms of 5 feddans and less dominated, livestock was central, and crop yields were similar—in both cases well below agronomic potentials. New Valley should not be lumped with the struggling reclaimed areas elsewhere in Egypt, for its yields were much higher than those of the miserably performing Delta-fringe reclaimed areas (Gotsch and Dyer 1982). The planning team's analyses revealed, however, that production of low-valued fodder and grain crops at yields far below agronomic potentials, using high-cost groundwater, still made New Valley a losing economic proposition for Egypt.

The Plan

This section contains a summary of the New Valley Plan results and the methodologies used to obtain them. The material here is meant to lay the groundwork for the following section, where I explore how better-integrated anthropological inputs could have improved the plan.

The Results

Since the New Valley Plan was made outside Egypt's established planning cycle, it was never likely to be implemented chapter-and-verse, although the client and consultant instinctively maintained that fiction. Above all, the New Valley Plan is a political document: the product and property of one agency, the Ministry of Development, to use in its ongoing budgetary and turf battles with Parliament and other agencies. The plan reflects the MOD's mission to develop Egypt's remote areas—Sinai, the Red Sea Coast, the North-West Coast, and New Valley—mainly to absorb the country's burgeoning population growth. On the issue of resettlement of Nile Valley residents to New Valley, the planning team had no choice. The MOD would not have accepted a plan lacking resettlement, but the planners constructively tempered the MOD's grandiosity by saying unswervingly that, dreams aside, New Valley's present population was ill-served and growing fast. Improving its conditions and absorbing its own growth would by itself be a challenge.

The terms of reference stipulated that the New Valley Plan be made using available secondary data sources only. The client was mainly concerned about the expense of collecting soils and water data, but the provision

TABLE 8.5
New Valley Target Population Distribution Year 2010

Area	(1) Present Population (1982)	(2) Future Population with Autonomous Growth	(3) Potential (Target) Population	(4) Resettled Migrant (3) - (2)
Kharga	44,900	92,100	39,600	-52,500
El Zayat	n.a.	--	5,300	5,300
Abu Tartur	450	--	37,800	37,800
Dakhla	51,500	111,600	97,200	-14,400

applied to social data as well. In fact, one small-farm survey was done with the help of Asiut University, but most of the agroeconomic data used came from secondary sources: the NVDA, the 1976 census, and old consulting reports.

The plan has two parts: a short-term plan (1983–1987), and a long-term plan (1988–2010). It has a blueprint-like quality, giving the impression that it could indeed be directly implemented. The plan is *comprehensive*, setting down what should be done sector by sector: agriculture, mining, industry, tourism, housing, and infrastructure. It is *consistent*, proposing goals and targets, and an administrative organization, policy, and budgets to achieve them; it is *rational*: with cost-benefit calculations to "prove" that it pays to invest in New Valley; and it is *realistic*: the short-term spending proposals do not exceed amounts tentatively designated for the area, and Egypt certainly has the means to do all that is called for. Unfortunately, comprehensiveness, consistency, rationality, and realism, teamed with the resettlement constraint and the restriction to secondary data sources, guaranteed the plan's unimaginativeness and conservatism. I shall say more on this in the final part of this section: "Shortcomings of the Long-term Plan."

The plan calls for a year 2010 population of 353,300, of which 130,550 results from the natural increase of the 1982 figure of 116,850, and the balance of 105,900 from in-migration (Table 8.5). Agriculture is the key sector. Land reclamation would increase the cropped area from the 1982's 42,300 feddans to 142,300 (Table 8.6). Mining is next in importance. A new phosphate mine at Abu Tartur would have a direct employment of 4,000, and the iron mine at Bahariya was expected to expand. Industry is unimportant, and tourism modest. Housing and infrastructure absorb large sums.

A careful reading of the annexes reveals the consultants' diagnoses of the region's present ills, and the short-term plan offers numerous nuggets of generally good advice on everything from the kinds of tourist visits that should be offered to what should be done about Kharga's date-processing plant. All of this probably had an impact, but a comprehensive plan, being required to say something about everything, is not the place to find acute

TABLE 8.6
New Valley Proposed Irrigated Land Development Program

	Potentially Suitable New Land	Recommended for Expansion	Agricultural Land in 1982[a]	Agricultural Land in 2010
	(feddans)			
Kharga	43,000	--	9,700	9,700
El Zayat	4,500	1,500	1,000	2,500
Dakhla	29,000	29,000	21,500	50,500
West Mawhoob	2,000	2,000	3,300	5,300
Abu Muncar	4,500	4,500	1,000	5,500
Farafra	12,500	12,500	300	12,800
Karawein	30,000	30,000	--	30,000
Bahariya	20,500	20,500	5,500	26,000
Total	146,000	100,000	42,300	142,300

[a] The figures here differ from those in Table 8.3 because of rounding and because the land at El Zayat was then under reclamation, not yet cropped.
Source: Euroconsult/Pacer Consultants 1983, Main Report, page x.

analyses of particular problems. In fact, most of the study team's man-hours were consumed by the in-house task of modeling the aquifer to determine how much water could be reasonably pumped from where, and laying out a plausible schema for doing so. No one, not even the social scientist, spent much time in New Valley.[9] Some of the general policy recommendations were probably sound—despite their resulting from intellectual cogitation rather than real field study—such as liberalizing the agroeconomy and turning over to farmers reclaimed land still being held by the state and rented out. Other proposals were probably misguided: for example, the expectation that cooperatives and agricultural extension would play important roles reflected the planners' ideals of these organizations more than their actual nature in Egypt.

Community development (CD) was treated perfunctorily in the plan Main Report and in a short annex. The New Valley Plan regarded community development as inducing traditional, passive peasants to think better (more modern) thoughts and to fix up their villages—under the guidance of government CD workers. The study diagnosed poor social development as being due to government staff lethargy stemming from the workers' low salaries and sense of powerlessness. The cure was elitist and top-down: hire more CD workers, manage them better, and pay them more. The CD workers' missions were to promote cottage industries and noneconomic activities, such as village cleanup campaigns and the planting of shade trees. In short, the plan's community development was conceptually misguided, and a sideshow to the major transformations diagrammed for the region.

The plan calls for developing new lands entirely by gravity-fed irrigation, to be cultivated exclusively by smallholders who receive five feddans each.

TABLE 8.7
New Valley Proposed Cropping Pattern

Crop	Winter	Summer
	(Percent of Cropped Area)	
Date Palm/Fodder	10	10
Fruit Trees	10	10
Onions	20	
Winter Vegetables	20	
Beans	20	
Wheat	10	
Cucurbit	10	10
Rice		20
Total	100	50

Source: Euroconsult/Pacer Consultants 1983, Main Report, page 67.

It proposes a cropping pattern that the analysts found to be consistent with the postulated small-farm labor supply and cash needs, and, more broadly, to be profitable enough to justify irrigation development. Not surprisingly, the proposed cropping plan (Table 8.7) calls for growing considerably more higher-valued crops, and less wheat and fodder than the current pattern (Table 8.4).

Methodology

Three models were used to devise the centerpiece of the regional plan, the scheme for irrigated land development: (1) a linear programming (LP) farm model; (2) an optimum well-field design (OWFD) model; and most important, (3) a region-wide groundwater simulation model (GSM). Calibrated to past data, the GSM computed changes in the pumping head for varying amounts of water extracted from different locales. Regarding the OWFD model, the planners deemed it necessary because pumping costs typically vary from place to place, even for the same head, since varying aquifer properties mean that different numbers of wells are needed to achieve the same water output for a given unit of land.

The modelers intended to produce an irrigation development plan for the region in a four-step fashion:

1. From the available soils data, identify unused land suited for irrigation at eight sites in the region. (A total of 146,000 feddans was identified [Table 8.6]).
2. Determine a suitable cropping plan with the LP model. For each of the eight sites, calculate a marginal return to water for the recommended cropping pattern.

3. Using the OWFD model, calculate pumping cost as a function of water lift for the eight locations. Find for each site the water lift at which the marginal return to water equals the average cost of production.
4. Use the GSM to test various combinations of new, irrigated land acreages for the eight sites. Calculate iteratively until an implementable schedule of land development is found that maximizes new land development region-wide and whose average cost of pumping water does not exceed the marginal return at any site within 100 years.[10]

In reality, the planning did not proceed as planned. The following four points can be gleaned from carefully reading the plan and studying its tables.

First, the proposed cropping plan is basically the modelers' concoction, rather than something rigorously determined by the LP model. Given the severalfold difference between returns to high-valued crops versus those to the prevailing grains and fodder crops, an LP-derived "optimum" plan would contain far more cash crops than common sense allows, so the planners tinkered with it until they found a more "reasonable" one. The planners used this single crop plan (Table 8.7) in the models for all eight sites. In fact, they could have used a simple spreadsheet of the proposed crop plan to compute economic returns, water use, employment, and the like, instead of more mystifying linear programming, since no optimizing was being done.

Second, irrigation water requirements are extremely high, just over 16,000 m^3/ha for Kharga, basically because the planners chose surface irrigation instead of a more water-conserving technique such as drip, and because of the region's extraordinary evapotranspiration potentials. The reader knowledgeable about alternative irrigation methods should wonder about the wisdom of recommending continued use of water-intensive surface irrigation in such an evaporative climate.

Third, the cost of pumping water as a function of depth does not differ greatly between oases. In spite of the OWFD model's sophistication, and differences between oases for needed pumping capacity, the cost of pumping water from 50 meters varies narrowly between 48 and 53 £E/1,000 m^3 for all sites, except Bahariya where it costs 62 £E/1,000 m^3.

Fourth, since the same cropping pattern is used at each site and water pumping costs are about the same, the pumping depth at which marginal water cost equals marginal farming return varies between sites simply with the water requirement. The potential evapotranspiration for Farafra is only 62 percent of Kharga's, so, no surprise, its maximum economic pumping depth is much greater: 122 meters, compared to Kharga's 38 meters. It is simply this maximum pumping head and the present volumes of water being pumped at the different sites that determine how much more water can be pumped and how much new land irrigated.

Thus, the modeling results follow from one central feature of the area—the increasing evapotranspiration potential north-to-south—conditioned by many assumptions made by the planners. Not a great deal was gained from using two of the models, the LP and OWFD models, although admittedly the planning team had to crunch the numbers one way or another for the simplicities to be revealed. Adorning the LP and OWFD models with great mystique in the reports only obscures the simple nature of the relationships actually at hand.

In any case, calling guesstimates and value judgments scientific, and mystifying simple findings with esoteric methodologies, are routine sins of the trade; but common sense and interdisciplinary modeling can overcome obfuscation, as the section, "Anthropology and the Plan" endeavors to illustrate.

Shortcomings of the Long-Term Plan

Calculation intrigues aside, the New Valley Plan fell short mainly in the 5–30 year component. Special expatriate-led planning teams often seem to forget that, in reality, they are producing not socioeconomic blueprints for real execution, since their work falls outside the routine (usually poorly functioning) planning and implementing machinery, but rather development scenarios and policy option analyses dressed in the guise of plans. A long-term, 5–30 year "perspective" regional plan, particularly a special-purpose plan, serves best as a general orienter of policy, spelling out a region's limits and potentials, and the best sociotechnical direction to be heading. Such a plan fails by either over- or understating a region's potential, and, in turn, by pitching development programs that are either overly ambitious or too conservative. The too-ambitious long-term plan is usually a blatantly political document with transparent flaws and motivations behind it; plans that are too conservative are more subtle. They can result when planners are too concerned with being consistent, rational, and realistic in their advice, and actually think Parliament will certify their wisdom and adopt the plan. Planners may tout obsolescence-bound current technologies because they and their costs are well known and easily projected forward, and because they are safe choices, less open to criticism than the new and different.

The planners made New Valley's long-term plan too conservative mainly by assuming continued exclusive use of surface irrigation for the next 30 years, and by not offering alternative scenarios for adoption of precise-delivery, water-efficient irrigation methods such as drip. They did so because of (1) personal biases about which irrigation technologies are suited for small farmers; (2) the greater defensibility of surface irrigation at a time when irrigation alternatives were being loudly debated in Egypt; and (3) the ease of calculation with well-documented surface irrigation. As a result, the region's development potential is grossly underestimated. Table 8.6 shows that the plan calls for developing within 30 years all suitable lands, except at Kharga and El Zayat. That is, with the exception of Kharga and El Zayat, irrigable land, not water, is the limiting resource. However, "suitable" lands in the New Valley Plan are flat fields with finer textured soils where surface irrigation can be used.[11] Since hillier areas and rockier soils can be cropped with drip-and-sprinkle irrigation, the area potentially irrigable is much larger. Combining more available arable land with different irrigation methods and cropping plans would generate entirely different development scenarios.

The planners would have served their client better by presenting not just one cropping plan and one farming technology, however tidy it might have been for number-crunching purposes, but offering instead a limited number of longer-term agricultural-development scenarios (three or four) with their implications, probable interventions required to achieve them, and likelihood of occurrence. A long-term plan should indeed recommend one particular course of action, but the clients' capacities for exercising their own good judgment are enhanced by a more thorough exploration of alternatives than was offered in the New Valley long-term plan.

Anthropology and the Plan

Planning fails partly because the planners, being either expatriates or from elsewhere in the country, have no tangible sense of life in the region at hand. Concurrent, focused anthropological field research can help avert difficulties such as those of the New Valley Plan—ineffective mathematical modeling and misguided long-term planning—by more lucidly revealing a region's priorities, potentials, and constraints. It can also constitute the basis for anthropologists' full participation in the planning process, rather than consignment to drafting marginally useful community development plans. In the following, I explore three areas in which anthropological research and interdisciplinary collaboration could have improved the New Valley Plan.[12]

1. Mathematical Modeling

As mentioned, the New Valley planning team used three mathematical models: an optimum well-field design model, a groundwater simulation model, and a linear programming agricultural development model. While the modeling enriched certain sorts of knowledge, such as aquifer behavior, it cast a straightjacket on thinking about long-term agricultural change, among other things. An anthropologist could have helped improve the results with fieldwork in some specific ways to be discussed below. More broadly, a spirit of dialogue between the modelers and their teammates, particularly the social scientist, about the goals and process of the modeling, and about how the results should be presented, could only have helped.

Mathematical models are used: (1) to simulate the behavior of actual systems to better understand them; (2) to predict outcomes given certain conditions; and (3) to determine "best" courses of action.[13] As the case of New Valley illustrates, systems modeled in regional planning can range from purely physical ones, such as aquifer behavior or water flow in a river basin; to systems with mixed human and physical elements, such as an urban traffic flow model; to more purely human phenomena, such as a family-planning behavior model. The creativity of modeling is finding just how much of reality needs to be captured to get acceptable results, and how to do it. The more points of view and contrasting disciplines brought to mathematical modeling, the better the result.

Interdisciplinary modeling results mainly from enlightened project management and an intellectually flexible staff. If, as is usual, another party has drafted the planning-study terms of reference, the contractor may, for example, have to: convince the client to allocate more months to the anthropologist, if possible making him or her a full-time, core team member; drop, or modify, assignments for the anthropologist to produce such things as community development plans; assure that the modelers with their computers share the same offices with their team members; and make certain there is a budget for socioeconomic field research. The final plan document should be produced by a mix of specialists who work on the project from start to finish, rather than patched together in the final months by a few planner-generalists long after the others have left town. The team's interaction should be assured by recruiting the right kind of people, and by writing individual terms of reference that make them interdependent.

2. Devising Model-Farm Plans and Long-Term Agricultural-Development Scenarios

Of the three New Valley models, the one with most significance for the long-term agricultural plan and that would have benefited most from concurrent anthropological field research is the linear programming farm planning model. Its key element is model (or, as they are sometimes called, "pattern") farm plans. Despite their clumsy depiction of small-farming reality, model farm plans carry extraordinary weight in estimating settlement potential, total regional investment costs, and suitability of particular farming techniques, among other things. They are similarly important in project appraisal (Gittinger 1982). In the case of New Valley, and probably often as well in agricultural project appraisal, the planners' crop budgets, labour-use coefficients, and the like, amounted mainly to ministry estimates and working figures found in other consulting reports. Analyses of interventions contemplated to cost in the tens and hundreds of million dollars deserve better data.

Although referring to project appraisal, Gittinger identifies the importance of the social context of proposed cropping patterns for model farm plans:

> One must assess the attitude of the family to proposed cropping patterns that involve more days of labor, to patterns that increase cash crop output and reduce food crop production below household requirements, to patterns that change the work responsibilities of men and women, and to patterns that require the family to run a considerable market risk. . . . Backed by this understanding of the particular cultural environment, the analyst will prepare the farm investment analyses as realistically as possible to determine what the family gains by participating in the project (1982:90–91).

As Gittinger suggests, economists typically assume both the tasks of assessing the ground reality of alternative farm plans and of doing the investment analyses. An anthropologist, especially one experienced with the language and the people of the region, however, could deal much more competently with farmers than the economist.

The main distinction to remember between well-focused project appraisal and broad forms of agricultural planning is that the latter may also make use of model farm plans in long-term scenarios. Such long-term farm plans, with their attendant uncertainties, can incorporate curious compromises. For example, the long-term New Valley cropping pattern (Table 8.7) has a symbolic quality, expressing a logical relation between the plan's resettlement and profitability goals, and the general conformation that the region's agriculture must take to achieve them—conditioned by the planners' views on what sorts of technologies are suitable for small farmers. With their cropping pattern, the planners implicitly assured the MOD that new, smallholder agriculture could indeed be successful, as the Ministry fervently wished. But detractors have good grounds to respond: don't bet on it; the farmers would have to become horticulturalists, and do so using horticulturally second-best surface irrigation rather than drip. Even granting the plan's proviso that achievement of the long-term crop plan requires liberalizing the region's agroeconomy and supporting its export of fruits and vegetables, successful "high-yield" production of these crops using surface irrigation in New Valley is implausible considering the region's high evaporation potential and soil salinity problems.

A long-term regional agricultural-development plan/scenario should be more than a single model-farm plan multiplied by the number of farming households year by year. Examining a region's long-term agricultural development alternatives should be a broader exercise than was the New Valley Plan's, and should include: (1) field study of the region's existing farm systems—their constraints and possibilities—in part, to generate meaningful model-farm plans; (2) study of farming systems at comparable locales, in this case, places such as the Sinai, Israeli Negev, and Jordan Valley; and (3) study of the literature on agricultural change in new lands projects (see, for example, Scudder 1981).

Regarding (1), concurrent field study might best consist of detailed case studies of 10–15 farms, and other structured and unstructured data collection. The growing literature on rapid rural appraisal and farming systems research may be tapped to devise a methodology specific to the occasion.[14] Longer-term planning needs to gain an understanding from farmers, not only of their immediate constraints and potentials, but their likely direction of change a decade hence if, for example, a marketing constraint were removed, or a new technology made widely available.

As for (2), the potential for crops and methods not yet found in the study region can be learned in part by assessing their occurrence in analogous regions. The client is not served by arguments that a technology such as drip irrigation is too complicated and expensive for small farmers when smaller farmers are using it successfully in other parts of the same country. Simply acknowledging that small farmer drip irrigation does occur elsewhere, and thus cannot be ruled out a priori would have been a giant improvement for the New Valley Plan. Analysis should include searching for explanations of differing adoption by contrasting the socioeconomic settings, an excellent way, in general, of exposing development constraints in the region at hand. But planners seldom venture, intellectually or otherwise, outside their study region of the moment. Brief tours of other regions, and even of nearby countries, focused on assessing potential new crops and farming technologies should be made, possibly by all team members, but certainly by the anthropologist.

Finally concerning (3), the application of broad historical experience with particular development strategies and tactics is a hit-and-miss affair in regional planning. Had the New Valley planners been more cognizant of world experience with new-lands settlement and development, they might have understood it more clearly as a dynamic process and made models and plans better reflecting that process. The anthropologist, wearing the hat of resident social theorist, can benefit model making and long-term plan making by seeking ways of incorporating the broad historical lessons of agricultural change and land resettlement into the plan.

3. Anthropology and Planning Standards

Planning standards for liters of household water, square feet of housing, kilometers of roads, and numbers of schools and clinics translate a predicted population growth into infrastructure investment budgets. Planners, bureaucrats, and politicians make much ado about standards because they symbolize what the state would at least like to do for its people, even if, alas, it lacks the wherewithal to make good on the deal. Standards should be more than mere conversion ratios, however, since trying to implement standards set beyond the government's long-term means can result in such things as building high-quality public housing and hospitals that serve only a fraction of the people.[15] Problems can arise in part because planners and engineers often feel bound by normal, acceptable figures used in their profession that bear little resemblance to the real wants and needs of the people, not to mention the government's capacity to supply. Since a long-term plan should point policymakers in the direction of what realistically can be achieved in infrastructure and social facilities, and identify what in fact will satisfy needs in the region at hand, planning standards are important. Anthropological micro-studies on how the present population meets its housing, health, water, and waste disposal needs can help make planning standards more realistic.

The New Valley study used planning standards produced by an earlier study (PADCO 1982) that had the singular virtue of having been accepted by the MOD. The plan presents a physical and social infrastructure program that is internally consistent but bears little relation to actual living levels. Through the prism of the present, the plan seems miserly with housing (only 36 m² per household), lavish with water (village household hookups and 160 liters/capita-day), and absurd with waste disposal (central sewage systems for even the smallest villages). Planners can dissuade governments from building unaffordable infrastructure by presenting standards and budgets in direct comparison with present levels, and by identifying more affordable, incremental approaches to improvement. Anthropological case studies and small surveys can help cast light on present material living levels, identify desired levels, prioritize them, and reveal inexpensive ways of meeting them—ways possibly already being used by the region's people.

Summary

Since lagging, isolated regions often attract special, comprehensive planning studies, development anthropologists can find themselves on teams planning regions much like Egypt's New Valley. Through the details offered on the Egypt New Valley region and plan, I have endeavored to show that special-purpose planning, particularly making long-term plans, is better conceived of as identifying plausible development scenarios, than as producing a real blueprint that might actually be followed precisely. Blueprint plans are often conservative and unimaginative, offering policymakers a poor feel for a region's possibilities.

My themes concerning anthropology and regional planning were two. The first was that planning should be interdisciplinary, and anthropologists should be fully involved. With the New Valley Plan, three venues of collaboration could have been: (1) broad participation in the mathematical modeling, (2) specific lead-taking involvement in the devising of model farm plans and long-term agricultural plans, and (3) the setting of realistic planning standards. Theme two was that good regional planning should include at least some concurrent socioeconomic field research. Anthropologists are best suited for doing this research, and, moreover, it can be structured in a way that assures interdisciplinary planning with full participation of the anthropologist in the process.

Notes

1. A recent example of the former is a 1987–88 multisector study of the Kismayo Region of Somalia, funded by the U.S. Agency for International Development and done under the Clark University/Institute for Development Anthropology Settlement and Resource Systems Analysis Cooperative Agreement (Little 1988). The work was deemed a necessary prelude to planning and larger-scale interventions since even routine forms of secondary data were scarce.

2. I will not argue here the merits of comprehensive regional planning in developing countries, which, more often than not, in the spirit of comprehensiveness calls for unimplementable integrated rural development programs and nebulous settlement growth theories, such as growth poles. Bendavid-Val's (1987) proposals for analyses and programs that focus narrowly on a region's primary economic activities are commendable both for their implementability and attention to first-hand research.

3. See F. Bliss (1984) and G. Meyer (1980) for an overview of New Valley development until 1980. S. Voll (1980) offers a broad review of Egypt's land reclamation programs since the 1954 revolution.

4. Unless otherwise noted, the descriptions and data in this section come from Euroconsult/Pacer Consultants (1983).

5. Far more important has been the large influx of government workers sent to look after the wells and the various other development programs.

6. The data in this section are taken from Euroconsult/Pacer Consultants (1983): Annex H - Population.

7. The age dependency ratio is the number of those younger than 15 and older than 64 divided by the 15–64-year employable age bracket. The ratios found by the 1976 census for the region were 90.4 for urban areas, and 107.8 for rural. Thus, 47.5 percent of the urban population and 51.9 percent of the rural were under 15 years of age or over 65. These were among the highest rates in Egypt. See Euroconsult/Pacer Consultants (1983): Annex H - Population, page 34.

8. Alfalfa, an alternative host for a cotton pest, is banned in the cotton-growing Nile Valley.

9. The team "social scientist" was a male, Western-trained, Egyptian university professor of sociology.

10. Recall from Table 8.1 that water use already exceeds recharge, but the amount of water in storage is large. Pumping at a particular rate causes a gradual increase in the pumping head, which may continue indefinitely if the pumping rate is high, or stabilize at a new equilibrium level. The latter is possible because increased pumping from an area causes the local recharge to increase.

11. For El Zayat, the water needs projected for the nearby phosphate mine at Abu Tartur were deemed to restrict full development of available agricultural land.

12. Another often-cited planning role is the anthropologist as advocate, facilitating the participation of a region's people in the planning process. For lack of space and want of focus, I give this role short shrift here.

13. By finding the best course of action, I mean calculating the levels of controllable variables that maximize or minimize a single decision variable; or, if there are two or more conflicting decision variables, finding a "best-compromise" solution.

14. See, for example, Khon Kaen University (1985), and Jones and Wallace (1986).

15. An early 1980s national urban policy study, which questioned the wisdom of Egypt's long-term policy of absorbing its population growth in new, expensive, free-standing cities, amounted to an elaborate wrangle over planning standards and their implications (PADCO 1982).

References

Beller Consult/ACI
 1982 Water Resources and Soil Potential Development Project: New Valley. Freiburg/Siegen, Federal Republic of Germany: Beller Consult/ACI.

Bendavid-Val, A.
 1987 Assessing Rural Regional Patterns. *In* Patterns of Change in Developing Rural Regions. R. Bar-El, A. Bendavid-Val, and G. J. Karaska, eds. Boulder, CO: Westview Press.

Bliss, F.
 1984 Traditional Society, Regional Development and the National Context in Egypt. Sociologus 34(2):97–120. (In German.)

El Baz, F.
1982 Arid Egypt Looks to a Green Bounty in the Sands. National Geographic 161(2):190–222.

Euroconsult/Pacer Consultants
1983 Regional Development Plan for New Valley. Cairo: Ministry of Development.

Gittinger, J. P.
1982 Economic Analysis of Agricultural Projects. Baltimore, MD: Johns Hopkins University Press.

Gotsch, C., and W. Dyer
1982 Rhetoric and Reason in the Egyptian "New Lands" Debate. Food Research Institute Studies 18(2):129–147.

Jones, J. R., and B. J. Wallace
1986 Social Sciences and Farming Systems Research: Methodological Perspectives on Agricultural Development. Boulder, CO: Westview Press.

Khon Kaen University
1985 Proceedings of the 1985 International Conference on Rapid Rural Appraisal. Khon Kaen, Thailand: Siriphan Press.

Little, P. D.
1988 Preliminary Observations of Rural-Urban Linkages in Southern Somalia. Development Anthropology Network 6(1):4–10 (Spring). Binghamton, NY: Institute for Development Anthropology.

Meyer, G.
1980 Effects of the New Valley upon the Development of the Egyptian Oases. Applied Geography and Development 15:96–116.

PADCO, Inc.
1982 Egypt National Urban Policy Study. Cairo: Ministry of Development.

Scudder, T.
1981 The Development Potential of New Lands Settlement in the Tropics and Subtropics: A Global State-of-the-Art Evaluation with Specific Emphasis on Policy Implications. Binghamton, NY: Institute for Development Anthropology.

Voll, S.
1980 Egyptian Land Reclamation since the Revolution. Middle East Journal 34:127–148 (Spring).

9

Agricultural Development and Food Production on a Sudanese Irrigation Scheme

Victoria Bernal

The increase in food insecurity and the collapse of the supply/demand relationship in Sudan are undoubtedly of catastrophic magnitude. Such calamities amid enormous resources and potentialities do not just happen; they are man made.
—Zahlan (1986:3)

Drought alone does not explain famine. Government policies along with communal and regional economic and political systems have much to do with it (Abdulla 1988; Franke and Chasin 1980). The 1984–85 food shortage dramatically revealed the failure of current agricultural policies and development projects to provide food security for the Sudanese population. The centerpiece of Sudan's agricultural development strategy is its irrigated schemes, yet their role in the famine and their potential to increase the national food supply have received little attention from government or researchers. There is a food crisis on the irrigated schemes themselves resulting from policies that maximize cotton production. This crisis not only hurts the scheme populations but contributes to the national food shortage.

This chapter examines conditions of food production on Sudan's irrigated schemes through a case study of the village of Wad al Abbas on the Blue Nile Schemes. Scheme management limits farmers' food production capacities at the household level by controlling credit, technical services, and extension, and by restricting the labor and land farmers may allocate to food crops. As a result, most farmers produce well below their grain needs and thus, far from contributing to national food markets, must purchase much of their basic subsistence grain. The case of Wad al Abbas is unfortunately not unique on Sudan's irrigated schemes; literature on other schemes shows that these policies are widespread and their effects similar.

This study has significance beyond the boundaries of Sudan since Sudan's irrigated schemes, especially the Gezira Scheme, are seen by some as successful projects to emulate, and the emphasis on export crops rather than on domestic food supplies in agricultural development strategies is common. The World Bank has supported such policies for Africa with the argument of comparative advantage (World Bank 1981). This study also has implications for agricultural development planning, which often focuses on macro-level conditions with little understanding of the perspectives of agricultural producers (Little and Horowitz 1987). More generally, it contributes to the growing body of theory that addresses the constraints faced by smallholders arising from their position in a larger system rather than from the social organization, cultural values, or subsistence orientation of smallholders themselves. It contributes to the study of the political economy of development that sees agricultural development in terms of struggles over land, labor, and other resources and in terms of the changing relations between peasants and other groups in society, rather than as a technical or biological problem.

The first section of this chapter provides an overview of the organization of irrigated schemes in Sudan. The second focuses on scheme policies regarding food crops. The third exposes the gap in research on food production on the irrigated schemes. The fourth is a case study of Wad al Abbas on the Blue Nile Schemes. It presents data on farmers' food needs and yields and analyzes the impact of scheme policy on farmers' food-producing capabilities. The fifth and last section explores the implications of this study for policy and research.

The Irrigated Schemes

Sudanese irrigation schemes vary, but all are patterned after the oldest and largest, the Gezira, which began operating in 1925, after some experimentation with smaller irrigation projects, as a partnership of British government and private interests. The other schemes followed, in a pattern of expansion that continues. Well over a million Sudanese live or work on such schemes (Keddeman and Ali 1978). By one estimate, the schemes require a million seasonal laborers in addition to 200,000 tenants who, with their household members, easily comprise another million people (Shaaeldin 1986). The schemes cover 4 million feddans[1] (1,680,000 ha) and are expected to reach 6.4 million by the year 2000 (Ibrahim 1984). They comprise 25 percent of Sudan's cultivated area and produce 50 percent of agricultural output (Ibrahim 1984). The main irrigated crop, cotton, accounted for over 50 percent of Sudan's export earnings from 1970 to 1981 (Zakaria 1986).

While the British set up the Gezira Scheme in 1925 to supply their textile industry with cotton, the expansion of pump schemes along the White and Blue Niles was carried out by private Sudanese capital during the 1950s, when cotton production offered great profits at unusually high world market prices. Most of these were nationalized in the 1960s. Sudanese governments have carried out further expansions of irrigated agriculture from the mid-1960s to the present. Today the schemes provide the Sudanese state with its major source of foreign exchange, cotton.

Tenancy is a key feature of all the schemes. The state appropriated the land and offered landowners smaller irrigated tenancies as compensation, while allocating the remaining tenancies to other people. Thus the schemes incorporated existing communities and created new ones. Khalafalla argues that the land tenure regulations of the Gezira Scheme "amount[ed] to nationalization of land by the colonial administration" (1981:67). Saeed writes that "the Gezira Scheme marked the beginning of the alienation of a large number of Sudanese peasants (cultivators and herdsmen) from the means of production they hitherto owned" (1982:88). A basic condition of tenancy on all the schemes is cotton production on a specified portion of the land, generally one-third. The other crops allowed in rotation and the number of fallow periods vary among schemes and have changed over time. Failure to cultivate cotton can result in eviction. Cotton operations are rigidly scheduled and scheme inspectors ensure that farmers have completed them on time. Schemes provide managerial and technical inputs to cotton including seeds, fertilizers, aerial pesticide spraying, plowing, transportation, storage, and insurance, and they control the ginning and marketing of cotton (Barnett 1977; Ali 1983). Farmers provide the labor. On some schemes wheat and peanuts are produced in addition to cotton, under similar arrangements.

Until 1981, on most of the schemes tenants and management produced cotton under a profit-sharing plan, bearing many of the technical costs jointly. After management sold the crop and deducted these costs, it divided the proceeds with farmers. In 1981 a new accounting policy was instituted whereby farmers are charged for irrigation and land in addition to the other services and are paid a fixed price for their cotton. Farmers also pay for land and water for any other crops they grow. Perhaps in recognition of the fact that many farmers are cash poor, the schemes do not require payment in cash but rather in a minimum cotton yield, paying tenants only for cotton produced above this minimum.

Under the former system, a tenant received profits only after all the scheme's production costs had been covered, whereas under the new system each tenant's yield must only cover his or her individual production costs.[2] The current system also eliminates the delay between harvest and payment that had spanned years on many schemes. This reform has not changed the production process, however, nor has it altered the structural relations between farmers and management in terms of decision making and control over resources.

Overall, the basic framework of the irrigated schemes has changed little over time. Reforms on the Gezira in the 1960s allowed some tenants to grow wheat, rice, peanuts, and vegetables, but a "rehabilitation" plan of the International Monetary Fund has since limited this (Quarterly Economic Review of Sudan 1985). Such newer schemes as Suki and Rahad produce peanuts as a cash crop in addition to cotton, while the New Halfa Scheme also produces wheat, but cotton remains the primary crop on all the irrigated schemes. A much-vaunted rehabilitation program for the schemes, begun in the early 1980s and still under way, addresses only such technical problems as machinery and irrigation canals. It does not alter management priorities or production relations between tenants and management.

The schemes remain highly centralized in organization, and successive policies of expansion, nationalization, intensification, diversification, and rehabilitation have done little to change that. Nowhere is the negative impact of this more clearly revealed than in the detrimental effects of mandatory cotton production on farmers' efforts to produce their staple food crop.

Lack of Support for Food Production on the Irrigated Schemes

After cotton, sorghum, the main dietary staple in Sudan, is the most widely cultivated crop in the irrigated areas (Shaaeldin 1986). Its production is wholly at the discretion of the individual farmer, and none of the irrigated schemes provide services, credit, or incentives for it. They provide only irrigation for sorghum, and since 1981 have charged the farmers for that. As Ali notes with reference to the Gezira Scheme, "cotton and wheat are regarded as crops of national importance and so are eligible for credit facilities" (1986:349). When one considers that virtually all of the cotton is for export and that wheat is a traditional food only of Nubians in Sudan, and is otherwise a luxury consumer good, it is clear that "national importance" is defined in terms other than the food needs of the majority of the population. As Mohamed observes, "government interest has focused on cotton, which does not necessarily match tenant interest"(1984:5).

In 1900 Wingate wrote that "if a system of irrigation were feasible in the Gezireh it would become a huge granary capable of supplying not only the whole Soudan but other countries as well" (Gaitskell 1959:36). Pressures from the Lancashire Cotton Growing Association in Britain, however, led to the development of the Gezira as a cotton- rather than grain-producing region (Gaitskell 1959:52). Gaitskell writes of the Gezira:

> The tenants' food and fodder crops were simply permissive adjuncts. Neither money nor staff time was allocated to improving these and to encourage the tenants to develop mixed farming interests as a subsidiary to the main cash crop (1959:26–27).

The neglect of food crops was "a hallmark of colonial agricultural policy" throughout Africa (Davis 1986:162).

Neither the Gezira Scheme, nor the pump schemes, nor the subsequent schemes were designed to improve the welfare of local inhabitants or to enhance *overall* agricultural productivity. The first priority of the British, Sudanese merchants, and the Sudanese government as scheme managers has been a cheap, profitable cotton crop. Since the 1960s the government has also been interested in the subsidiary irrigated cash crops, wheat and peanuts.

Many schemes allowed sorghum production, largely because this made it possible for them simply to pay some cash to peasants for producing cotton. Early attempts at irrigated cotton production by wage labor had proven unprofitable, since hired laborers have to be paid much more and require greater supervision from management (Gaitskell 1959:52). Sorghum production is thus integral to the functioning of the schemes.

Nevertheless, neither private nor public managements attempted to improve the sorghum crop.[3] It was never part of the profit-sharing arrangements between tenants and management, but belongs solely to the farmer. No extension work is connected with sorghum. The irrigation that schemes provide to the sorghum crop is subject to the watering needs of cotton, which has priority. Schemes provide cash credit for cotton but not for sorghum cultivation. By one estimate, 75 percent of the cost of cotton production and 90 percent of the cost of wheat production are financed by management on the Gezira Scheme (Mohamed 1984:26). No financing is available for sorghum production. "Almost all the materials, machinery, and labor inputs are provided by the tenants, either from their own or from outside sources, and the produce is privately marketed" (Mohamed 1984:24). Farmers receive cotton seeds from the scheme, but they must purchase sorghum seeds through private channels, where purity and quality control are poor (Mohamed 1984:124). While records are kept of cotton production detailing inputs, costs, and productivity, and extensive reports are compiled on the basis of these figures, tenants' sorghum yields are not even recorded.

The Gezira Scheme actually forbids some of the more nutritious varieties of sorghum because they require more water (Tait 1978:168). Such schemes as New Halfa, Suki, and Rahad (established in 1964, 1971, and 1977, respectively) deviated from this pattern to the extent of forbidding tenants to cultivate any sorghum at all. Rahad and Suki gave sorghum rations to tenants, thus institutionalizing food dependence among the farming population. On New Halfa, tenants produce wheat, a staple of the Nubian tenants there, and some farmers produce a rainfed sorghum crop outside the scheme (Salem-Murdock 1984). Even though Suki and New Halfa legalized sorghum production in 1981, the New Halfa management continued to regard it as contrary to the goals of the scheme and in some cases has refused to provide irrigation for it (Salem-Murdock 1984). Many tenants from pastoralist backgrounds keep animals off-scheme as part of their subsistence production. The irrigated schemes have also been destructive of pastoral production (Horowitz and Salem-Murdock 1987), but this is beyond the scope of the present study.

Such conditions are not unique to Sudan. Throughout Africa, colonial and postcolonial governments have favored export production over food production. In the Ivory Coast, "improved and intensified techniques have been applied almost exclusively to cotton and have ignored food crops, creating a hierarchy of products, differences in productivity, conflicts in the agricultural timetables, and competition between crops for labor time" (Campbell 1984:163). In Morocco, irrigated, mechanized farms, largely the product of state investment, produce fruits and vegetables for export, while food for the majority of the population is produced by "dryland farming of cereals through primitive techniques," resulting in chronic national food shortages (Payne 1986:154).

Some diversification has occurred as a concession to tenant demands (Tait 1978); this has not meant sorghum, however, but rather such elite food crops as wheat and rice (O'Brien 1985:29), unfortunately largely at the expense of land devoted to sorghum. Furthermore, the World Bank, arguing that Sudan has a comparative advantage in cotton production (O'Brien 1985), has recommended the reallocation of land from food crops back to cotton and peanuts (Hansohm 1986:152).[4]

Those who set scheme policy face constraints imposed by Sudan's position in the world market as "Africa's most extreme example of debt problems" (Lofchie 1986:6). The World Bank, having funded much of the rehabilitation of the schemes, influences policy. Evidence suggests the Bank is less sensitive than are local officials to the food needs of the Sudanese population. According to the director of the Blue Nile Agricultural Corporation that manages the Blue Nile Schemes, the World Bank's plans for these schemes initially entailed the elimination of sorghum. He and other Sudanese, he said, argued against this on the grounds that sorghum is the staple food of local farmers. "They [the World Bank] said dura [sorghum] can be grown on rainfed land, but we said rainlands are too far for this. And, Rahad and Suki have already done this and were not successful, and Suki has had to introduce dura now."

There are a few positive signs. Rehabilitation plans for the Blue Nile Schemes now include the development of an extension program for sorghum. The latest annual report for these schemes (covering 1985–1986), however, presents extensive data and analysis on cotton production but nothing at all on sorghum, reflecting where official interest continues to lie. The legalization of sorghum on Suki and New Halfa is another step in the right direction, but most farmers on Sudan's irrigated schemes continue to produce sorghum under extremely difficult conditions.

Lack of Research on Food Production on the Irrigated Schemes

Sorghum and cotton accounted for 26 and 33 percent respectively of the total cropped area under irrigation in Sudan in 1981–1982; 639,000 feddans (268,380 ha) of irrigated land in Sudan were under sorghum, while 822,000 feddans (345,240 ha) were under cotton (Shaaeldin 1986:23). Yet, research on the schemes has produced a distorted picture by devoting very little attention to sorghum. While the Sennar and Kinana agricultural research substations do some work on sorghum (Saeed et al. 1986), the main research center on irrigated agriculture in Sudan, the Gezira research station, is "engaged in research on cotton, rice, groundnuts, wheat, barley, sugar cane, forage crops, and vegetables" (Saeed et al. 1986:390), in short, everything but sorghum. In fact, "(e)xcept for cotton, little has been done in the Gezira in plant breeding and selection" (Mohamed 1984:124).

Anthropologists and other social scientists have generally shared managements' focus first on cotton and secondarily on the other government crops, wheat and peanuts. Ebrahim (1983) provides yields for cotton, peanuts, and wheat from 1965 to 1976 on the Gezira but does not include data on sorghum. Oesterdiekhoff (1980) focuses on cotton and wheat and devotes little attention to sorghum production, although he acknowledges its importance to tenants. The irrigated schemes are often evaluated solely in terms of cotton productivity and profits. A recent example is the assertion that the Gezira Scheme is a success, following one year of good cotton yields (Quarterly Economic Review of Sudan 1985).

The International Labor Organization (ILO) (1976) discusses Gezira cotton yields and their possible improvement but does not cite sorghum yields or conditions of sorghum production. The ILO report does suggest, however, that the scheme should charge for land and water on sorghum and share in the proceeds of all crops grown by tenants, including sorghum. Furthermore, its section on planned diversification on the Gezira, under which wheat and peanuts would be grown, addresses the reduction of land under cotton and fallow, but not sorghum. The information provided, however, shows that sorghum land would be reduced by 50 percent under the plan. Since sorghum is the farmers' primary food crop, this element of diversification merited careful consideration. Similarly, ILO (1976) ignores sorghum in discussing the expansion of the Agricultural Reform Schemes (the various smaller pump schemes under government control). Yet the plans whereby "half [the land] will be under cotton, a quarter under wheat and a quarter under groundnuts . . ." (ILO 1976:261) would eliminate sorghum cultivation altogether.

Tait (1983:93) describes the Gezira Scheme before diversification as consisting of a capitalist sector for cotton production and a "non-capitalist sector for the production of subsistence crops." This dualist conception is misleading, however, because the sectors are intertwined in reality regardless of the official concern with cotton alone. All crops compete for farmers' labor and cash resources. Furthermore, management profits from the sorghum crop. That tenants are its sole beneficiaries is a fiction that has been maintained by management and unquestioned by some researchers. The sorghum crop benefits management because it contributes to the reproduction of labor on the irrigated schemes and thus subsidizes cotton production. It also ties tenants to the scheme, since if they leave they forfeit irrigated land on which to produce their food. This is especially significant since most tenants own no land outside the schemes.

Tait's (1983:113) discussion of "non-capitalist reproduction," which he estimates as dominant in 70 percent of Gezira villages, focuses on labor relations to the neglect of food production. His primary interest is cotton productivity in spite of his finding that cotton contributes "approximately only between 9 percent and 15 percent of the tenant's net profits" while it "consumes most of the tenant's [cash] outlays and most of his own labour" (1983:119). As Tait (1983) and others (Said 1968) have found, for many tenants cotton is a net loss. Yet researchers continue to focus their analyses primarily on cotton. Tait's final recommendations for "a principal restructuring of the whole scheme" (1983:121) are limited to peanuts and cotton and do not even mention sorghum.

O'Brien (1985) has dealt specifically with food production in Sudan. He contrasts private rainfed mechanized agricultural schemes, on which sorghum is the primary crop, with the irrigated schemes, but he considers the latter solely in terms of cotton production. Yet, as stated above, much of the irrigated land is devoted to sorghum. O'Brien also considers subsistence production by pastoralists and off-scheme peasants but ignores subsistence production on the irrigated schemes. As Osman and Suleiman (1969:439) point out, however, in Sudan, "much of the output produced by traditional techniques is for the market, and . . . much agricultural output produced in the modern sector is for subsistence." Not only is sorghum produced as a commercial crop on the irrigated and mechanized schemes, it has been a main item of trade and a source of commercial capital in Sudan for generations (Issawi 1966:467; Barnett 1977:61–72; Bernal 1985:78–88).

While little research has been done on sorghum production on the irrigated schemes, it is commonly assumed that, if nothing else the schemes provide tenants with subsistence. Beer asserts that, "For many years the tenant received only a few score pounds, but his living off the land was assured" (1955:42). Gaitskell writes that, though profits were small "[the tenant] got the guaranteed food crop" (1959:157). Yet there has never been a guaranteed food crop, only access to irrigated land on which even the water is not guaranteed. Furthermore, where researchers include some data on sorghum, they generally consider it in terms of profitability if all sorghum were sold, and provide no indication of how well it meets farmers' subsistence needs (e.g., Said 1968:161–162; Tait 1983:124).

The lack of research on sorghum on the irrigated schemes in terms of subsistence consumption and the possibilities for expanding production for the market not only shows a lack of sensitivity toward farmers' concerns but has left an important gap in the knowledge needed to plan Sudan's agricultural strategies for the future. While it is true that most of the country's sorghum is produced outside the irrigated schemes, sorghum production is vital for the hundreds of thousands who live on the schemes. Moreover, with a shift in policy, the irrigated schemes could be a great source of sorghum for the nation. According to Sudanow (cited in Tait 1983:113), research results on the Gezira Scheme show that sorghum yields can be trebled, given appropriate agronomic inputs.

Sudan's performance in all its major crops is below potential and poor compared to other countries', but this seems particularly true of sorghum. For example, from 1977 to 1982, Sudan's average cotton yields per acre were 67 percent of American yields, while average sorghum yields in Sudan were only 16 percent of those achieved in the U.S. (Abdel Salam 1986:411). These low yields are due to poor conditions in traditional rainfed cultivation off-scheme and to the neglect of sorghum in the most developed sector of Sudanese agriculture, the irrigated schemes.

The neglect of sorghum in agricultural development research on the schemes is not unique. The irrigated schemes and much of the research on them fit the pattern Brokensha describes as "the old orthodoxy (top-down, high-tech, capital-intensive, research station trials, neglecting subsistence crops, emphasis on individuals, usually male, rather than on households, etc.)," which, he notes, "has failed to produce the results expected" (1987:22).

Barnett's (1977:175–180) work on the Gezira Scheme, which stands out for its attention to tenant concerns, suggests that subsistence production is inadequate to meet tenants' needs. My own research on a Blue Nile pump scheme reveals very poor conditions in food production and heavy dependence on purchased food. I argue that these conditions are traceable to scheme policy that directs key inputs to cotton and, through mandatory cotton cultivation, places demands on farmers' labor and land resources that limit their capacity in sorghum production.

A Case Study of Wad al Abbas on the Blue Nile Schemes

Methods

The primary fieldwork at Wad al Abbas was carried out from June 1980 to June 1982 with a brief follow-up study in January 1988.[5] In 1982, survey data were collected from a random sample of 53 households, out of a total of approximately 1,000 households in the village. Forty-four households (83 percent) had tenancies on the Blue Nile Scheme. Because one of these did not complete the interviews, the sample of tenant households on many questions is 43. Male and female household heads were asked about their 1980–81 and 1981–82 crops, yields, expenses, profits, and grain consumption. The quantitative analyses in this chapter are based on this sample.

Wad al Abbas households are not always self-bounded units of production and consumption in agriculture. The separate households of a polygynous man share an interest in his land, while households containing an uxorilocally resident couple may include more than one unit of production because male affines generally farm separately. For these reasons the 44 tenant households comprise 38 agricultural production units.[6] Twenty-nine are households, while nine do not coincide exactly with the boundaries of a single household. (Again due to one incomplete questionnaire, sample size is 37 production units on most questions.)

The Wad al Abbas Scheme

The irrigated scheme at Wad al Abbas was established in 1954 by two merchants from outside the village. It incorporated nearly all the land villagers had traditionally cultivated by rainfed agriculture, giving tenancies as the only compensation for this expropriation. It was part of the "cotton rush" of private capital precipitated by high world cotton prices. While financed by private capital, such schemes were supported and regulated by the colonial and later national government, which allocated land rights (scheme licenses) and set the terms of production relations between scheme owners and tenants (Ali 1983). Along with most of the privately owned schemes, the Wad al Abbas Scheme was nationalized in 1968, but the shift from private to public management brought little change in organization. It is now administered by a parastatal, the Blue Nile Agricultural Production Corporation (BNAPC), as part of the Blue Nile Schemes, which cover an area of 300,000 feddans (126,000 ha).

In 1984–1985 the scheme at Wad al Abbas had 1,170 tenants and comprised 11,500 feddans (4,830 ha) (BNAPC 1987).[7] A tenancy at Wad al Abbas is 15 feddans (6.3 ha), of which 5 feddans (2.1 ha) are under cotton, 5 under sorghum (or any crop of tenant's choice), and 5 fallow, in yearly rotation. The actual holdings of individuals and, more importantly, of households vary widely. There are thus differences in the size of holdings both within and between schemes. The standard tenancy can only give a limited picture. Holdings range from one-third of a tenancy to seven tenancies among the 38 production units in the sample.

Cotton and fallow are mandatory under scheme regulations. Most tenants choose to grow their main subsistence crop, sorghum, on the other third of their land. Cotton operations follow a schedule set by management, and inspectors insure that farmers have completed them on time. Management can revoke tenancies for failure to cultivate cotton properly. In 1981 the profit-sharing arrangement on cotton was replaced by the new system of individual accounting and land and water charges described earlier. For many tenants the new accounting procedures made little difference, however, since their cotton production continued to run at a loss as it had under the earlier system.

Importance of Sorghum Production to Tenants

The majority of Wad al Abbas tenants have not received cotton profits in years and are actually in debt to the scheme. During the 1980–81 cotton harvest, I asked an inspector when the tenants would be paid. He remarked casually, "Maybe we'll pay them in March or April; but here they have no money coming to them." (As it turned out he was referring to payment for the previous year's crop.) In fact, of 1,597 tenants under the administration of the main Wad al Abbas office in 1979–1980, only 6 received any cotton profits. The remaining 99.6 percent were in debt to the scheme at the end of the year, according to the bookkeeper. Scheme personnel and tenants alike stated that 1979–1980 was not a particularly bad year, but an average one. Debts are cumulative from year to year making farmers' chances of profits slim even when a good year comes along. Tenants at Wad al Abbas have received few profits since the early sixties. In 1981 some had accumulated debts of over £S500 (US $625)[8] according to scheme records. This would take years of good yields to pay off. Such indebtedness is common on Sudanese irrigated schemes. Sørbø (1977) reports a high rate of indebtedness to the scheme among New Halfa tenants. The most recent figures show a somewhat better picture, with 448 out of 1,170 tenants receiving profits for the 1984–85 crop, but the majority (62 percent) are still in debt (BNAPC 1987). The reduction of the tenant population by over 400 in these five years should also qualify this success since it indicates that it was achieved in part by the expropriation of land from some producers. As it takes money to farm successfully on the scheme (Bernal 1985), those most vulnerable to eviction for negligence in cotton production are the poorer tenants.[9]

By 1980 when fieldwork began, Wad al Abbas farmers had abandoned any hopes of cotton profits. As one explained: "They take all the services out and the credit, and that eats it all." Another said, "If you produced 50 *kantar*[10] they wouldn't pay you." A third stated, "Even those who produce a lot get nothing for it." When others told this man, "The government takes 40 percent and gives the farmer 60 percent" (an exaggeration), he looked surprised and said, "Sixty percent! It doesn't give the farmer a thing, not a penny!" Farmers did not see cotton production as a joint effort by themselves and the scheme. Rather, they spoke of cotton as "belonging to the government" [*beta' al hukuma*]. Finally, not only do farmers not profit from growing cotton, some actually spend money to produce it because the credit provided by the scheme is insufficient to meet their labor bills.[11]

Tenants were so bitter about the profit-sharing by which they got nothing for cotton that when some were given wheat in 1981 as part of an effort at diversification, they just dismissed it, saying "it belongs to the government."

Wad al Abbas tenants cannot support themselves from cotton profits since most of them receive none. Thus, for most tenants, access to irrigated land for the production of food and, less commonly, other crops, is their primary reward for participating in scheme agriculture.

Sorghum production, institutionalized at Wad al Abbas since 1954, is one of the ways in which tenants and their households actually subsidize cotton production by their efforts to insure their own survival. (I have dealt elsewhere with two other ways—trade and wage-labor [Bernal 1988b].) The sorghum crop helps reproduce the tenant family labor force and represents the only benefit tenants receive besides cash credit for cotton cultivation. Sorghum keeps farmers from abandoning the scheme altogether.

While tenants see cotton as the government's crop, they see sorghum as their own. They regard cotton production as a futile effort but one they must carry out to avoid the complete alienation of their land. Researchers have found similar conditions on the other irrigated schemes. Said (1968:132) writes that the Gezira tenant: "looks upon cotton production largely as a cost of getting the Dura [sorghum]." He adds that the attitude of the tenant

> (who is apt to say to government and Board representatives: my Dura and your cotton) stems on the one hand from the original subsistence outlook of the tenant, as well as his long experience with low and, at times, even negative remuneration from cotton; on the other hand, it is the result of the disinterest of the government and the successive managements in these other crops since they do not share in them (Said 1968:132–133).

Although Wad al Abbas villagers are integrated into a cash economy, they value the sorghum they produce for home consumption. Tenants face rising costs of food, clothing, and other necessities. Unofficial reports put the inflation rate at 50 percent during 1980 and 1981, when much of this research was conducted (Quarterly Economic Review of Sudan 1982). As one villager put it, "Before, people here had few things and they were cheap. Now, we have many things but they require a lot of money." An old woman, remembering the time before the scheme, lamented, "The land no longer belongs to us, and the cows have become few. It was better before and things were cheap. Now they're expensive."

Whatever food villagers can produce for themselves conserves scarce cash resources and offers protection against the unpredictable grain market. One farmer explained, "Everyone plants *aesh* [sorghum] because it is expensive." Another said, "We need the aesh. We have all these small children and aesh has become expensive."

Sorghum prices vary from place to place and from the preharvest to postharvest season. Furthermore, while the government controls prices of many basic commodities, actual sorghum prices have been found to be 95 percent higher than official prices (ILO 1976:27). Barnett (1977:80) reports that in the early seventies Gezira shopkeepers would buy sorghum for £S4 to 5 per *ardeb*[12] at the harvest and sell it for twice as much before the next harvest. O'Brien (1980:259) reports that a sack of sorghum (94.5 kg) went for £S3 in the postharvest season at Um Fila on Gezira in 1976–1977 and rose to £S5.50 the following year. Duffield (1978) reports an ardeb in the 1977 harvest selling at £S10 in Maiurno near Sennar and rising to £S15 in the preharvest period of 1978.

At Wad al Abbas sorghum sold for £S11/sack in July 1980. This was up from £S3/sack only a year earlier, according to one villager who may have been quoting the low harvest price for 1979. By the preharvest season of October 1980 a sack cost £S17. Prices dropped again after the harvest. In January 1981 the sack price was £S14. By October 1981 sorghum was selling for £S23/sack; an increase of 35 percent over the previous October. These figures indicate that dependence on the market for grain is both costly and risky.[13] It is not surprising then that villagers consider it extremely advantageous to produce their own supply of sorghum. Not only do sorghum prices fluctuate greatly, but they rose at Wad al Abbas between 1980 and 1981.

When Wad al Abbas households run short of grain before the harvest, prices are at their peak, and they often buy grain little by little, by the *kayla* (12.6 kg). A kayla cost £S2.20 in October 1980 and rose to £S2.50 before the harvest, dropping to £S2.00 as the harvest began. In October 1981 a kayla was selling for £S4, a 60 percent increase over the peak price of the previous year, dropping to £S2.50 after the 1981 harvest. At £S4/kayla, a sack would cost £S30. In this sense every sack a family harvested in 1980 that saved them from buying sorghum in October 1981 was worth up to £S30 (US $37.50) in terms of money saved.

The figures show how valuable the sorghum crop is to tenants. They may seem to exaggerate the monetary value of subsistence produce (cf. Chibnik 1984:562; Hart 1982:129), but insecure subsistence producers like Wad al Abbas farmers may be strongly influenced in their assessment of the crop's value to the household by the high prices of the preharvest period, because that is when they habitually make grain purchases. In fact, since villagers are never sure how high prices may rise, they may impute an even higher value to their sorghum than is reflected in actual prices. As one villager commented on a case where cash compensation was paid for livestock damage to sorghum, "What is money? Grain is better than money."

Crop prices fluctuate, and markets in basic commodities cannot be predicted from the preharvest to the postharvest season. McCorkle (1988) describes similar instabilities in the grain market in Burkina Faso. Significantly, while the Burkina Faso farmers McCorkle describes could respond to changing tradeoffs between food prices and cash returns from cotton by cultivating more food and less cotton, Wad al Abbas farmers and those on Sudan's other irrigated schemes are restricted in their ability to withdraw from cotton production or expand food production.

Sorghum is the staple food in every Wad al Abbas household. To cut back on its consumption is to threaten health and lives. A 1978 study revealed that over 50 percent of tenant families lived on sorghum and *waika* (dried okra) alone, 55 percent consumed no fresh vegetables, and 60 percent consumed no milk (cited in Oesterdiekhoff 1980:308). What tenants do not grow they must purchase, and thus the value of sorghum is clearly greatest for those households with the least cash.

The Impact of Scheme Policy on Food Production

Management-Controlled Inputs. Sorghum production has never received attention from any management since the scheme's inception in 1954. The current administration provides no credit, services, or any other inputs besides irrigation for sorghum cultivation. Furthermore, as on all the irrigated schemes, the timing and number of waterings each crop receives are decided by management. Cotton's watering needs have priority over sorghum's, and cotton requires much more water. The priority of irrigation to cotton, along with fuel shortages, old pumps, and the deteriorating conditions of the irrigation system at Wad al Abbas, mean that the water supply to sorghum is unreliable and often untimely.

While careful records are kept of tenants' cotton yields, which are weighed in the fields after picking, no data are collected on sorghum yields at Wad al Abbas. The annual report of the Blue Nile Agricultural Production Corporation for 1981–1982 states, in reference to sorghum, "The Corporation gives little attention to the production of that crop" (BNAPC 1983).

Average sorghum yields are low, and the rate of crop failure is high. By the corporation's own account, yields are poor due to poor tillage, poor "cultural practices," low-yield varieties, and shortages of fertilizers, herbicides, and insecticides (BNAPC 1983). Conditions are similar on the Gezira Scheme, where "[s]orghum yields are generally low because the crop is grown with minimal land preparation and without herbicides, insecticides or fertilizers" (Mohamed 1984:24). Scheme policy not only neglects, but negatively affects sorghum production. Enforced cotton production limits the amount of land and labor tenants can allocate to food crops, pitting farmers' food needs against the corporation's interest in cotton.

Labor. Sorghum competes with cotton for labor since its growing season is encompassed by the longer season of cotton. It also competes for farmers' cash inputs, which primarily go for hired labor. Mandatory cotton cultivation, checked by inspectors and enforced by threat of eviction, limits the labor tenants can devote to sorghum at the expense of cotton. They are forced to seek some balance between the two crops even if they do not hope to reap a profit from cotton. Sometimes for lack of money or labor tenants cultivate only cotton, simply to retain rights to land.

Cotton is a much more labor-intensive crop than sorghum, and it has become increasingly so over time on the irrigated schemes. On the Gezira long-staple cotton required 65.63 person-days/feddan/year (156.26 days/ha) compared to 25.43 (60.55 days/ha) for sorghum in 1973–1974 and 82 person-days/feddan (195.24 days/ha) compared to 13 (30.95 days/ha) for sorghum in subsequent years (ILO 1976:259, Table 19). Cotton thus requires over six times as much labor per feddan as sorghum on the Gezira. These crops are cultivated under similar conditions on the Blue Nile Schemes, so labor requirements should be comparable there.[14]

Labor shortages and dependence on hired labor have plagued all the schemes, partly because labor demands are not spread evenly over the year but peak at certain periods. Weeding is the second most labor-intensive operation for both sorghum and cotton, after harvesting, and sorghum is weeded concurrently with cotton. Weeds can cause losses of up to 80 percent of the potential yield of sorghum on Sudanese irrigated schemes (Koch and Bischof 1982:7). At Wad al Abbas, labor is in short supply. If farmers are hard pressed and must cultivate cotton or lose their land, they may be unable to weed their sorghum properly.

During August, September, and November, the months of highest labor demand aside from cotton picking, both cotton and sorghum are weeded and sorghum is harvested. Table 9.1 compares production units' labor resources with the labor required to cultivate their holdings on the scheme in 1980–1981 (with one third cotton, one third sorghum, and one third mandatory fallow). Labor resources were estimated at 26 person-days/month for a man and 13 for a boy. Estimates were calculated on the basis of the demographic composition of units of production, not on the actual allocation of family labor. The latter would entail fewer labor resources in virtually all cases, since many villagers engage in other productive activities. Women and girls generally participate only in cotton picking at Wad al Abbas. The more conservative 1973–74 labor figures for which the ILO provided a monthly breakdown are used. Of course, labor requirements of crops vary

A Sudanese Irrigation Scheme

TABLE 9.1
Shortages of Family Labor Resources Required to Cultivate Holdings, 1980-81

Percentage of Labor Shortfall	August # units	percent	September # units	percent	November # units	percent
None	20	54.1	26	70.3	11	29.7
Up to 25	6	16.2	5	13.5	7	18.9
26-50	5	13.5	1	2.7	8	21.6
Over 50	6	16.2	5	13.5	11	29.7
Total	N=37	100	N=37	100	N=37	100
With Shortage of Labor	17	46	11	30	26	70

Note: Labor resources are estimated at 26 person-days/month for a man and 13 for a boy. Cultivation requirements are based on ILO (1976:259, Table 19), assuming one-third of holdings under cotton, one-third fallow, and one-third under sorghum.

from year to year and from one tenancy to the next depending on weather, soil, irrigation network, and pest conditions. Different varieties of cotton and sorghum also affect labor requirements differently. The average figures are useful, however, in providing a standard basis for assessing the adequacy of tenants' labor supply.

Table 9.1 reveals severe labor shortages. Since September has lower labor requirements than August or November, the production units short in that month are also short in the other two months. Eleven of 37 production units are thus short of labor in all three months. This is 30 percent of the sample or almost one in every three production units. Twenty-six (70 percent) of the 37 face labor shortages at some period during the three months. Seven out of 10 production units surveyed, then, do not possess sufficient labor to cultivate their cotton and sorghum properly even if all labor were devoted to that task. The magnitude of the shortages is also important. A considerable number of production units face shortages of over half the labor required to cultivate their land during these months. Considering the importance of weeding to sorghum yields, the labor demands of cotton at this crucial time threaten farmers' ability to produce a food crop.

Research shows comparable conditions on Sudan's other irrigated schemes.[15] On the White Nile Schemes "at certain peak points during the annual cycle, and especially during weeding and the cotton harvest, labor requirements are high and few tenant households are able to satisfy them from internal resources" (Horowitz and Salem-Murdock 1987:98). Furthermore, one of "the major bottlenecks for increasing sorghum production in the Gezira Scheme is the scarcity of labor during the planting season" (Mohamed 1984:117-118).

In practice, households do *not* devote all their labor to farming, but also engage in trade and wage-labor. Actual shortages of family labor are thus much greater. Farmers make up these shortfalls to the extent they are able by hiring paid workers. Here again, cotton production and sorghum production compete for scarce resources.

Such competition between export crops and domestic food crops is widespread, but it is particularly acute in the case of cotton. During the colonial period, cotton-producing areas of Africa often experienced severe food shortages, since cotton "interfered with the cultivation of foodstuffs because of the intensive labor demands of the crop, and because it generated very little income for the producers" (Davis 1986:162). As McCorkle found in Burkina Faso:

> under current farming-system and other constraints, there is a direct trade-off between cotton and cereal as farm managers proportionally allocate their finite supplies of land, labor, capital, technological knowledge, and inputs to one crop or the other. More investment in cotton seems to mean less cereal, and vice versa (1988:105).

In the Ivory Coast, where cotton similarly competes with other crops for labor, "[o]ne of the most serious consequences of labor constraints is the shrinking of time devoted to weeding food crops, which often leads to a drop in their output" (Campbell 1984:164).

Land. Farmers are allowed to devote only one-third of their land to food crops. The mean size of holdings at Wad al Abbas in the sample of 38 production units, several of which serve two or three households, is 1.67 tenancies or 25 feddans, of which only 8.3 feddans (3.49 ha) can be under sorghum. For the 44 households represented by these production units, the mean holding comes to 21.2 feddans allowing 7 feddans (2.94 ha) of sorghum land per household under scheme regulations. Putting the problem of crop failure aside for now, the mean yield among 18 farmers who harvested a crop in 1980-1981 was 1.97 sacks/feddan (443.25 kg/ha). The mean yield the following year was 2.9 sacks/feddan (652.5 kg/ha).

At the 1980-1981 average yield of 1.97 sacks/feddan, 7 feddans would produce 13.79 sacks (1.30 t) of sorghum; at the 1981-82 average of 2.9 sacks/feddan it would yield 20.3 sacks (1.92 t). Mean sorghum consumption among Wad al Abbas households is 15.5 sacks (1.46 t)/year. Thus, in only one of the two years would the mean holding of sorghum land produce enough to sustain the average household at average yields. In reality, due to crop failure and variation in landholdings and family size, grain shortfalls were common even in the better year.

At the 1980-81 average yield, an average household would require 7.9 feddans (3.32 ha) of sorghum or more than 1.5 tenancies to meet its needs. Yet of the 44 households surveyed, only 12 (27 percent) had more than 1.5 tenancies (if polygynous mens' holdings are divided equally between their households), while 24 households (55 percent) had one tenancy or less.

O'Brien reports that in a Blue Nile community off-scheme, farmers cultivate about 3 feddans of (rainfed) sorghum per person to meet consumption needs plus an additional 50 percent to allow for yield fluctuations (1980:370).

Given the evidence of fluctuating yields and crop failure at Wad al Abbas, tenants' food security would be enhanced if they had such options.

In fact, some farmers do have access to more land, either through ownership or through purchase, rent, or sharecropping of additional tenancies, but because of scheme regulations, farmers can only gain sorghum land proportionally with cotton land.[16] Thus, for all but the wealthiest farmers, who can afford to hire labor, this option is not viable. For production units with one tenancy or less, the land for sorghum may be inadequate; those with larger holdings face increased pressures from the labor-intensiveness of cotton production.

These calculations suggest that many Wad al Abbas households do not have access to sufficient sorghum land to meet their grain needs. Scheme regulations that insure that no more than a third of their land can be under sorghum restrict farmers' food production capacity to a level below subsistence. Furthermore, in 1982 some Wad al Abbas farmers were simply told that they would only get 2.5 feddans (1.05 ha) of irrigated land for sorghum instead of 5 feddans per tenancy, due to a water shortage.

Yet researchers have called for further reductions in tenancy size (ILO 1976:52; Olsson and Keddeman 1978:23). These recommendations are motivated by the desire to reduce tenants' use of hired labor on cotton. For example, Olsson and Keddeman argue that "a standard tenancy size of 10.7 feddans . . . would have been sufficient to eliminate the need for outside labor" (1978:23). Such recommendations are made without considering the size of tenancy required to support a household. By contrast, one of the few researchers to take tenants' living conditions and subsistence needs into account recommends increasing the size of tenancies (Said 1968:188).

A considerable amount of irrigated land is devoted to sorghum production on the schemes, but this does not mean that the majority of tenant households have sufficient land for their needs. Furthermore, as Barnett points out, tenant's holdings are not geared to their family size or consumption requirements (1977:168). In a sample of Gezira tenants, 80 percent "expressed a preference to devote more feddans to sorghum" (Mohamed 1984:65).

Strategies for increasing tenants' food security could facilitate production of surpluses for the market. Farmers at Wad al Abbas perceive sorghum as a profitable cash crop, but under present conditions only a minority have the resources to produce surpluses. Gezira farmers are similarly interested in selling sorghum. One of their reasons for wanting to plant more sorghum is the ease with which the crop can be marketed locally (Mohamed 1984). However, under present conditions many farmers are unable to produce the grain consumed by their families, let alone a commercial surplus.

The Crisis in Sorghum Production

The subsistence crop at Wad al Abbas is far from secure. In fact, during 1980–1982 the majority of sorghum producers experienced food deficits. Twenty-seven of the 37 production units surveyed planted sorghum in 1980–1981. (Four of the remaining ten units let relatives use their land, a way of providing for poor relations, three had it cultivated by sharecroppers under an agreement where they claimed no part of the sorghum crop, one planted peanuts as a cash crop instead, and two left the land fallow for lack of labor or cash.) Wealthy traders and labor migrants tend to move out of agriculture through transferring their land rights or engaging sharecroppers (Bernal 1985; see Salem-Murdock 1984 for a discussion of economic differentiation among New Halfa Scheme tenants).

Perhaps the most striking finding was the prevalence of crop failure. Nine (33 percent) of the 27 production units harvested nothing at all. Farmers cite water shortage, pests and livestock, weeds, and labor shortage as the main reasons. The crop failure rate remained high in 1981–1982; 8 units (31 percent) of 26 that planted sorghum that year experienced total crop failure. Thus, for two years in a row nearly one in three units obtained no sorghum crop at all. If crop failures are included, the mean sorghum yield in the sample for 1980–1981 was only 1.4 sacks/feddan (315 kg/ha) with yields ranging from 0–6 sacks/feddan (0–1.35 metric tons/ha). The following year, 1981–1982, the mean yield was 2 sacks/feddan (450 kg/ha). Excluding crop failures (as was done in the section on land, above) brings the average yields to 1.97 and 2.9 sacks/feddan, respectively (443.25 kg/ha and 652.5 kg/ha). These yields are quite low. Sorghum is said to yield approximately 700 kg/ha under poor conditions and two or three times as much under better conditions (Hiebson and O'Hair 1986). In general, sorghum production at Wad al Abbas is characterized by low productivity and high risk and does not regularly meet farmers' subsistence needs.

Sorghum Consumption and Yields. In terms of subsistence, average yields provide less information than households' actual harvests in relation to their consumption needs. Sorghum consumption for a family of six was estimated at 0.5 kayla (6.3 kg)/day in a 1949 Gezira tenants' report (cited in Versluys 1953:45). This amounts to roughly 4 sacks (383.25 kg)/capita/year. Bacon (1948) reckons Sudanese sorghum consumption needs at 0.9 kg/day for adults and 0.45 kg/day for children. A family of six with two adults and four children would thus consume 3.6 kg daily. Yearly consumption would range from 164.25 kg for a child to 328.5 kg for an adult, averaging 219 kg (2.3 sacks) per capita for the family of six. A Wad al Abbas farmer and head of household estimated that to feed a family of ten requires 2 sacks (189 kg) per month. That comes to 2.4 sacks (227 kg)/capita/year or 0.62 kg/capita/day. Recent CARE rations for Western Sudanese were set at 0.5 kg/capita/day (ILO 1986). For the 35 Wad al Abbas households that provided this information, annual sorghum consumption ranged from 4.5 to 60 sacks (425.25 kg to 5.67 t). Mean household consumption was 15.5 sacks (1.46 t)/year. With mean household size at 7.4, mean per capita sorghum consumption is 2.09 sacks (197.5 kg)/year or 0.54 kg/capita/day.

Wad al Abbas households consume less sorghum than did those of Gezira tenants in 1949 partly because labor migration reduces the number of people who actually eat in the village year-round, and partly because in the 1980s many households supplement sorghum with wheat and bread, which was

TABLE 9.2
Degree of Self-Sufficiency in Sorghum Production (Reported Consumption)

Yield as a Percentage of Consumption	1980-81 # units	percent	1981-82 # units	percent
100 or more	4	21	6	32
50-99	5	26	5	26
0-49	10	53	8	42
	N=19	100	N=19	100

Note: Two units in 1980-81 and one in 1981-82 employed sharecroppers who would normally receive half the crop; the entire yield is included here. The 19 units represent 21 households in both years.

not true in the 1940s (Versluys 1953:45). Recent research on scheme agriculture has not addressed tenants' consumption needs, although nutritional studies unfamiliar to this author may have dealt with this subject.

Table 9.2 shows the degree to which units of production were able to meet their sorghum consumption needs from their holdings in 1980-1981 and 1981-1982. Where production units include more than one household, their grain needs are added together. Of the 27 units that planted sorghum in 1980-1981 and the 26 the following year, 19 provided the necessary grain consumption information each year. In 1980-1981, 53 percent (10 of the 19 production units) produced less than half of their stated sorghum needs. Only 21 percent (four units) produced the amount they needed. In 1981-1982, 42 percent (eight units) produced less than half the sorghum they consumed. Only 32 percent (six units) produced what they needed or more. These 19 units represent 21 households. Sixty-two percent (13 of the 21) purchased more than half their sorghum in 1980-1981. Eighty-six percent (18 of 21 households) produced insufficient grain to cover their basic consumption. In 1981-1982, 52 percent (11 of 21 households) purchased more than half their sorghum. Seventy-six percent (16 of 21 households) produced insufficient sorghum to meet their needs that year.

These figures make it clear that sorghum production levels on the scheme are far below household needs.[17] Over half the households purchase most of the sorghum they consume. Only a small minority of farmers produce sufficient grain to feed their families. Very few actually sell sorghum for profit. Others may sell sorghum when pressed for cash, but they later buy it back at higher, preharvest prices. The minority of households able to produce grain surpluses draws attention to the importance of differentiation among tenant households that is largely based on access to off-scheme resources, but is reflected in agricultural performance on the scheme (Bernal 1985).

An alternative measure of self-sufficiency in sorghum production is to compare sorghum yields with consumption figures based on standardized

TABLE 9.3
Degree of Self-Sufficiency in Sorghum Production (Standardized Consumption)

Yield as a Percentage of Consumption	1980-81 # units	percent	1981-82 # units	percent
100 or more	5	18.5	8	30.8
50-99	3	11.1	3	11.5
0-49	19	70.4	15	57.7
	N=27	100	N=26	100

Note: Three units in 1980-81 and two in 1981-82 employed sharecroppers who would normally receive half the harvest; the entire yield is included here. The 27 units in 1980-81 represented 32 households; the 26 units in 1981-82 represented 31 households.

per capita averages. This has the advantages of allowing a larger sample size and of eliminating variation in household grain consumption whether due to differences in standards of living or to reduced consumption (because of the absence of migrant household members). Versluys' figures put per capita yearly consumption at roughly 4 sacks (383.25 kg), Bacon's at 2.3 sacks (217.35 kg) and the Wad al Abbas farmer's at 2.4 sacks (227 kg). I will use the farmer's estimate since it is contemporary with the data and from the same area. It is also close to Bacon's.

Table 9.3 shows the degree of grain self-sufficiency in the sample when these figures are applied to their sorghum yields. Seventy percent, 19 of the 27 units, that planted sorghum in 1980-1981 produced less than half their annual per capita needs. Only 19 percent (5 units) met or exceeded their needs. In 1981-1982, 58 percent, 15 of 26 units, that planted sorghum produced less than half their per capita needs. Thirty-one percent (8 units) met or exceeded their needs that year. In terms of households this means 72 percent (23 of 32 households) fell short by more than half their grain needs in 1980-1981, and 58 percent (18 of 31 households) did so in 1981-1982.

These findings show the inadequacy of food production on the scheme and the dependence of villagers on purchased food. The people of Wad al Abbas are profoundly affected by high food prices. Those without a secure cash income try to produce as much of their food as they can, but at present only a minority of farmers meet their families' sorghum consumption needs each year. Far from contributing to Sudan's food supply, they are unable to feed themselves from their farms.

These data are not unique. Culwick found that the Gezira was a net importer of sorghum in the 1950s (in O'Brien 1980:136). Recent research on Gezira notes food supply problems: "Due to low production and apparent inadequate supply from other dura-producing areas, local dura prices have increased rapidly during the last few years" (Magar 1986:154). Oesterdiekhoff and Wohlmuth (1983) cite research showing that 72 percent of household consumption expenditure among tenants went for food in 1967-1968. New

Halfa tenant families cannot survive on their tenancies alone (Sørbø 1977; Salem-Murdock 1984). The average Gezira tenant is "highly dependent on purchasing food . . . because the Scheme . . . has removed from him . . . the possibility of producing for his own subsistence and that of his family" (Barnett 1977:180), even though sorghum yields reported for the Gezira are higher than those I found at Wad al Abbas (Oesterdiekhoff 1980:295; Tait 1983; Shaaeldin 1982).

Even higher average sorghum yields mean little, however, if rates of crop failure remain significant. Furthermore, the larger the sample, the more the risk is spread out and therefore minimized. Farmers consume their own yields, however, not the average. Figures based on aggregated yields in the Gezira, which encompasses millions of feddans and thousands of tenants, conceal the degree of risk in sorghum production and give no indication of crop failure rates.

Dependence on the market for their staple food means vulnerability to hunger, for people may be outpriced in the market and unable to buy what they need. In 1977 Kiss found that Sudan was self-sufficient in sorghum but that productivity would have to rise to maintain this. She further warned that "this does not mean that the nourishment of the population is satisfactory: with the high level of poverty in the country. . . meeting the food requirements of those who can pay is not equivalent to satisfying the population's food requirements" (1977:16).

The food crisis of 1984 and 1985 revealed just how precarious Sudan's food supply is. Poor harvests in areas of rainfed sorghum production resulted in exorbitant sorghum prices throughout Sudan. O'Brien reports a bowl of sorghum selling for £S6 near Gedaref at the end of the 1983 harvest; by January 1984 a sack of sorghum was selling for £S140 (1985:31). Wallace reports grain prices in eastern Sudan rising from £S30 in 1984 to £S140 in January 1985, though she does not specify the amount of grain that sold for these prices (1985:65).

Wad al Abbas villagers said sorghum was selling there for £S20 per kayla in 1985.[18] While their own yields were not particularly poor that year, such high prices threaten the ability of all but the wealthy to make up food deficits through purchases. The wife of a well-to-do trader who is also a tenant said, "People saw the rains were bad and those who had money bought aesh and stored it. Only the poor who couldn't buy really suffered." Villagers were fortunate, however, to receive substantial amounts of food aid that was made available at low prices through the local government. They were thus able to make necessary grain purchases.

Villagers who produce cotton that generates state revenues should not need food aid. That they do is an indictment of the scheme. Not only are Wad al Abbas farmers vulnerable to hunger because they do not produce enough sorghum to meet their needs, their untapped food production potential along with that of farmers on the other irrigated schemes could contribute to national food supplies in Sudan.

The Failure of Policy. This case study of food production at Wad al Abbas on the Blue Nile Schemes shows that sorghum production is far below potential. Average yields are low and crop failure is common. Most farmers are unable to produce enough to meet their household needs, let alone surpluses that could be marketed. There is little to suggest that these conditions stem from a lack of incentives on the part of farmers, since sorghum production is the main agricultural priority for them. Nor can Wad al Abbas farmers be accused of a narrow subsistence mentality that causes them to set low production goals. Villagers are heavily engaged in commercial activities and exchanges. Furthermore, there is an active market in sorghum in the area and farmers, well informed about prices, regard it as a profitable commercial crop. Under present conditions, however, the majority of villagers are net buyers rather than sellers in the food-grain market.

Scheme policy is largely responsible for shortfalls in food production on the scheme because it constrains farmers' choices in the allocation of crucial resources—land and labor—to the disadvantage of food crops, and because the resources under management control—credit, irrigation, pest control, plowing, fertilizers, improved seeds, and agricultural research and extension— are concentrated on cotton and unavailable for sorghum.

The study indicates that the food production crisis on the schemes is largely the result of policy. In light of the recent famine, Sudan can no longer afford to ignore food production on the irrigated schemes.

Implications for Policy and Research

Policy

The most pressing policy reform for Sudan's schemes is to transfer greater control of production decisions and productive resources to the farmers. The negative food policies that have persisted on the irrigated schemes since the 1920s would have been altered long ago if farmers had had a voice in scheme operation. The need for change in this direction is not limited to Sudan's schemes. It applies generally to development planning and implementation on the African continent. Centralized, authoritarian models may appeal, among other reasons, for their apparent simplicity. It appears simpler to force people to behave in a certain way than to understand why they behave as they do, and "more efficient" to leave important decisions to a few experts rather than to a large, diverse group of people such as farmers. In practice, African bureaucracies have grown and developed complexities of their own, while results, in terms of increased agricultural productivity and the satisfaction of basic needs, have remained limited.

The nature of large-scale irrigation systems may mean that the enfranchisement of farmers is most feasible through a management composed of representative farmers, or some kind of cooperative system (as President Sadiq al Mahdi reportedly has suggested), or a flexible system allowing farmers to pick and choose from a range of government services for crops of their own choice. At any rate, a variety of options are available beyond the present structure.

Mandatory cotton cultivation must be ended. Forced labor on threat of eviction cannot be a basis for development. Realistically, it is unlikely that a plan eliminating cotton altogether would be acceptable to policymakers, given cotton's role as foreign exchange earner, but some of the land now under cotton could be set aside for its production by the parastatals solely on the basis of wage labor. Eliminating the tenant relationship in this crop would raise production costs in terms of labor expenses, but the greater assurance of proper and timely performance of agricultural operations might yield gains in productivity to offset this.

At the minimum, the neglect of sorghum in terms of agricultural research, extension, and services on the schemes should be remedied. A reconsideration of the role of irrigated agriculture in Sudan, in terms of production for export and production of subsistence foods for the domestic market, is called for.

Research

This study exposes the danger that management's priorities and problem definitions may inadvertently shape research on development projects. Studies of Sudan's irrigated schemes have been strongly influenced by the orientation of scheme management and narrowly defined national interests, rather than by the farmers who live on these schemes. Most studies start with the institution as their focus and see villagers only as they interact with the scheme. As a result, tenants' voices are largely absent from the research. Researchers' preoccupation with cotton and disregard of sorghum is a prime example of the resulting bias. Furthermore, this bias toward management is not limited to the applied anthropologist hired by an institution but is also evident among independent researchers.

Some of the bias toward management's priorities appears to be due to heavy reliance on data provided by scheme management and other government agencies. Much of the research on the schemes is based on such data. For example, seven of Tait's sixteen tables are derived from scheme management or government data (1983). Out of nine tables on the irrigation schemes in Oesterdiekhoff, six are derived wholly or partially from such data (1980). The ILO's "technical paper" on irrigated agriculture includes eight tables, only one of which is not from a Sudanese government source (1976). Researchers seem unaware that their findings may be affected by the way questions are framed and data collected by the agencies on whom they rely.

Many adopt the individual tenant as their unit of study. This is how tenants appear in scheme records, but tenants live and farm in household units. From their standpoint, therefore, it is household landholdings and yields that are crucial. Had these researchers gathered data directly from farmers, this would have immediately become clear. Significantly, household holdings, on which there is no scheme limit, show much more variation than do individual holdings, which are limited to two tenancies. Reliance on management data also may be partly to blame for the concentration on cotton, as management compiles much more data on cotton than on sorghum.

The importance of collecting data from farmers as well as management is further illustrated by reports from Sudan Plantations Syndicate (SPS), the original management of Gezira, and from the Tenants' Representative Body (TRB), cited by Versluys (1953:42). The SPS's calculations of costs and profits from a Gezira tenancy present a much more positive picture than the TRB's.

Many studies of the irrigated schemes either are evaluation studies or are patterned after such studies. A common approach in evaluating a development project is to assess the degree to which it has achieved its goals. This initial phrasing of the research problem omits the question of whether the goals themselves were appropriate and remain so. In the case of Sudan's irrigated schemes, cotton production was the primary goal, and the other sponsored crops, wheat and peanuts, the secondary goal. The schemes have had at best only qualified success in achieving even these goals, but even where objectives are fulfilled, policies must be critically examined in light of their wider consequences.

The research that formed the basis of this chapter was not designed around the Blue Nile Schemes and was not intended as a project evaluation study. It was a broad study of rural development in a village community. Interest in the scheme grew out of the realization of the great impact it had on villagers' lives, and the scheme was examined within the larger context of village and regional economic and social organization. This community-based approach revealed the irrigation scheme from a new perspective.

The study is based almost entirely on data collected from villagers themselves, and data were collected during long-term residence and participant observation in the community without the aid of research assistants. The author alone conducted every household survey and every interview. While such methods have their own limitations in terms of time requirements and sample size, they yield high quality data and provide the researcher with much more in-depth information than is otherwise possible. For the independent anthropologist, the dissemination of findings represents a special problem. The applied anthropologist is hired by an institution that pays for the results and presumably will therefore read or disseminate them. People value what they pay for, and the institutional affiliation gives the anthropologist in such a situation legitimacy (in the eyes of authorities at least). Lacking such a connection, it is harder to draw attention to one's results.

This problem is even greater for the anthropologist who is critical of current policy. For example, one of my findings is that the scheme does not benefit farmers because its management has interests largely opposed to those of the villagers. If I believe my own findings then I must recognize that information made available to management is unlikely to result in positive change. During the course of fieldwork, however, I did discuss problems such as farmers' labor shortages and lack of profits with scheme personnel in various offices. I met with indifference. This apathy may have been a reflection of the despair many Sudanese seemed to feel about development in the early 1980s. In any case, personnel did not feel responsible for improving scheme performance. Furthermore, because of the hierarchical structure of scheme administration, few people are in a position to introduce changes. In contrast, farmers are acutely aware of the scheme's shortcomings and concerned about performance. Unlike bureaucrats, farmers receive no salary and their welfare is tied to the productivity of the scheme, but they lack the power to implement the necessary changes.

I have no complete solution for this problem and its many implications. As social scientists we can try to develop theories and methods that are sensitive to the experiences of less powerful groups, such as small farmers, and produce a body of knowledge that can foster and inform broader policy debates.

Notes

The research on which this chapter is based was supported by grants from the National Science Foundation, the Social Science Research Council, the American Council of Learned Societies, the Kirkland Endowment, and Hamilton College. I am also grateful to the editors of this volume for their valuable suggestions as well as to Frank Cancian, Ronald Cohen, Nancie Gonzales and several others who commented on an early version of this material. My greatest debt is to the people of Wad al Abbas and many other Sudanese whose help made this research possible, and, at times, enjoyable.

1. One feddan = 1.038 acres = 0.42 hectare.
2. Few tenants on any of the schemes are women. For an examination of scheme policy toward women see Bernal (1988a).
3. Tait (1983) mentions improved sorghum on the Gezira, but provides no information about it. No effort to improve sorghum production on the schemes is reported elsewhere.
4. An exception to this is the case of the New Halfa Scheme where the World Bank argued for the legalization of sorghum as a substitute for wheat production. Significantly, their recommendation was prompted by water supply problems, not by tenants' concerns or food needs (Salem-Murdock 1984).
5. The results of the 1988 study are not fully analyzed as this work goes to press.
6. While the distinction between households and production units is cumbersome, it provides a more accurate depiction of a complex reality than either concept could alone. A number of researchers have pointed out the importance of critically examining the degree to which households are units of production and consumption (Guyer 1981; McMillan 1986; Bernal 1985).
7. Administrative units on the schemes do not correspond to village boundaries. Therefore these figures include tenants in neighboring villages as well as residents of the village of Wad al Abbas.
8. The dollar value of the Sudanese pound (£S) varies and has been declining with progressive devaluations of Sudanese currency. In January 1980 £S1 was officially worth US $1.25. By June 1982 it had dropped to $1.11. In January 1988 the Sudanese pound was officially worth US $0.22.

9. Since households may contain more than one tenant and individual tenants can own up to two tenancies, eviction does not always mean landlessness, but at the very least it reduces a household's productive base.

10. One kantar = 308 rotl = 312 lbs. = 141.5 kg unginned cotton; and 100 rotl, 101.30 lbs., or 46 kg ginned cotton.

11. At 1980–81 agricultural wages at Wad al Abbas, £S2 (US $2.50)/day, the credit of £S136 for a standard tenancy would cover only about one-fifth of the work on cotton. Five feddans of long-staple cotton require between 309 and 410 person-days per year (ILO 1976:259–260). If a standard work day is taken as equivalent to a person-day, £S136 would pay for only 68 of the 309–410 person-days required, or between 17 and 22 percent of the labor.

12. One large ardeb = 2.5 sacks = 236.25 kg. One small ardeb = 2 sacks = 189 kg.

13. While grain prices have risen, the dollar value of the pound has declined. Dollar equivalents are not included in this discussion because they do not reflect the increase in prices experienced by Sudanese consumers. For dollar values of the pound in the early 1980s and 1988 see note 8.

14. Both long- and short-staple cotton have been grown at Wad al Abbas in different years; the 1980–81 crop was long-staple cotton.

15. An assumption that labor shortages are the result of tenants' refusal to farm and their involvement in off-farm work (Voll 1980; Warburg 1978) is belied by these figures. In fact, to some degree, labor migration is *reflective* of the poor conditions on the scheme rather than the cause of them, because villagers are compelled to seek other sources of income since they cannot survive by farming alone.

16. Sale and rental of tenancies are prohibited under scheme regulations but nonetheless occur, although there is far from an active market in them.

17. Since many of the grain consumption figures here are low due to the absence of labor migrants, they do not reflect the amount of grain that would be required to sustain an entire farming household.

18. Prices were half that in January 1988 (£S10/kayla).

References

Abdel Salam, M. M.
1986 Agricultural Policy Formation and Administration. *In* The Agricultural Sector of Sudan: Policy and Systems Studies. A. B. Zahlan and W. Y. Magar, eds. Pp. 409–424. London: Ithaca Press.

Abdulla, Ismail H.
1988 Drought and Famine in Western Sudan. Paper presented at the conference on Sudan Studies: Past, Present, and Future, University of Khartoum, Sudan. January 5–9.

Ali, Ahmed Humeida Ahmed
1986 Finance and Credit. *In* The Agricultural Sector of Sudan: Policy and Systems Studies. A. B. Zahlan and W. Y. Magar, eds. Pp. 332–351. London: Ithaca Press.

Ali, Taisier Mohammed
1983 The Road to Jouda. Review of African Political Economy 23:4–14.

Bacon, G. H.
1948 Crops of the Sudan. *In* Agriculture in the Sudan. John Douglas Tothill, ed. Pp. 302–400. London: Oxford University Press.

Barnett, Tony
1977 The Gezira Scheme: An Illusion of Development. London: Frank Cass.

Beer, C. W.
1955 Social Development in the Gezira Scheme. African Affairs 54:42–51.

Bernal, Victoria
1985 Household Agricultural Production and Off-Farm Work in a Blue Nile Village, Sudan. Ph.D. dissertation, Northwestern University.

1988a Losing Ground—Women and Agriculture on Sudan's Irrigated Schemes: Lessons from a Blue Nile Village. In Agriculture, Women, and Land: The African Experience. Jean Davison, ed. Pp. 131–156. Boulder, CO: Westview Press.

1988b Continuity and Contradiction: The Maintenance of Peasant Production— The Destruction of Peasant Economy in a Blue Nile Scheme Village. In Economy and Class in Sudan. Norman O'Neill and Jay O'Brien, eds. Pp. 157–185. Aldershot: Gower Press.

BNAPC (Blue Nile Agricultural Production Corporation)
1983 Reports and Accounts 1981–82. Khartoum.

1987 Annual Work Program July 1, 1986. June 30, 1987. Khartoum.

Brokensha, David
1987 Local Management Systems and Sustainability. Paper presented at the annual meeting of the Society for Economic Anthropology, Riverside, CA. April 3–4.

Campbell, Bonnie K.
1984 Inside the Miracle: Cotton in the Ivory Coast. In The Politics of Agriculture in Tropical Africa. Jonathan Barker, ed. Pp. 143–172. Beverly Hills, CA: Sage.

Chibnik, Michael
1984 A Cross-Cultural Examination of Chayanov's Theory. Current Anthropology 25(3):335–340.

Davis, R. Hunt
1986 Agriculture, Food, and the Colonial Period. In Food in Sub-Saharan Africa. Art Hansen and Della E. McMillan, eds. Pp. 151–168. Boulder, CO: Lynne Rienner.

Duffield, Mark
1978 Peripheral Capitalism and the Social Relations of Agricultural Production in the Village of Maiurno Near Sennar. Khartoum: Economic and Social Research Council, National Council for Research, Bulletin No. 66.

Ebrahim, M. H. S.
1983 Irrigation Projects in Sudan. Journal of African Studies. 10(1):2–13.

Franke, Richard W., and Barbara H. Chasin
1980 Seeds of Famine. Totowa, NJ: Rowman and Allenheld.

Gaitskell, Arthur
1959 Gezira: A Story of Development in the Sudan. London: Faber and Faber.

Guyer, Jane
1981 Household and Community in African Studies. African Studies Review 24(2/3):87–138.

Hansohm, Dirk
1986 The "Success" of IMF/World Bank Policies in Sudan. *In* World Recession and the Food Crisis in Africa. Peter Lawrence, ed. Pp. 148–156. London: James Currey Ltd.

Hart, Keith
1982 The Political Economy of West African Agriculture. Cambridge: Cambridge University Press.

Hiebson, Clifton, and Stephen K. O'Hair
1986 Major Domesticated Food Crops. *In* Food in Sub-Saharan Africa. Art Hansen and Della E. McMillan, eds. Pp. 177–206. Boulder, CO: Lynne Rienner.

Horowitz, Michael M, and Muneera Salem-Murdock
1987 The Political Economy of Desertification in White Nile Province, Sudan. *In* Lands at Risk in the Third World: Local-Level Perspectives. Peter D. Little and Michael M Horowitz, with A. Endre Nyerges, eds. Pp. 95–114. Boulder, CO: Westview Press.

Ibrahim, A. M.
1984 Development of the River Nile System. *In* The Nile Valley Countries: Continuity and Change. M. O. Beshir, ed. Pp. 87–122. Khartoum: Institute of African and Asian Studies, University of Khartoum.

ILO (International Labor Organization)
1976 Growth, Employment and Equity: A Comprehensive Strategy for the Sudan. Geneva: Imprimeries Populaires.

1986 After the Famine: A Programme of Action to Strengthen the Survival Strategies of Affected Populations. Geneva: ILO.

Issawi, Charles
1966 The Sudan. *In* The Economic History of the Middle East 1800–1914. Charles Issawi, ed. Pp. 463–508. Chicago, IL: University of Chicago Press.

Keddeman, Willem, and Ali Abdel Gadir Ali, eds.
1978 Employment, Productivity, and Incomes in Rural Sudan. Khartoum: Economic and Social Research Council and ILO.

Khalafalla, El Fatih Shaaeldin
1981 The Development of Peripheral Capitalism in Sudan: 1898–1978. Ph.D. dissertation, State University of New York at Buffalo.

Kiss, Judit
1977 Will Sudan be an Agricultural Power? No. 94. Studies on Developing Countries. Budapest: Institute for World Economics of the Hungarian Academy of Sciences.

Koch, Werner, and Friedrich Bischof
1982 Weed Problems in Irrigation Schemes in the Sudan. *In* Problems of Agricultural Development in the Sudan. Gunter Heinritz, ed. Pp. 5–22. Gottingen: Edition Herodot.

Little, Peter D., and Michael M Horowitz
1987 Subsistence Crops *Are* Cash Crops: Some Comments with Reference to Eastern Africa. Human Organization 46(3):254–258.

Lofchie, Michael F.
1986 Africa's Agricultural Crisis: An Overview. *In* Africa's Agrarian Crisis. Stephen K. Commins, Michael F. Lofchie, and Rhys Payne, eds. Pp. 3-18. Boulder, CO: Lynne Rienner.

Magar, W. Y.
1986 Farms in the Gezira. *In* The Agricultural Sector of Sudan: Policy and Systems Studies. A. B. Zahlan and W. Y. Magar, eds. Pp. 145-160. London: Ithaca Press.

McCorkle, Constance M.
1988 "You Can't Eat Cotton": Cash Crops and the Cereal Code of Honor in Burkina Faso. *In* Production and Autonomy: Anthropological Perspectives on Development. John Bennett and John Bowen, eds. Pp. 105-123. Lanham, MD: University Press of America.

McMillan, Della E.
1986 Distribution of Products and Resources in Mossi Households. *In* Food in Sub-Saharan Africa. Art Hansen and Della E. McMillan, eds. Pp. 260-273. Boulder, CO: Lynne Rienner.

Mohamed, Abdel Halim Hamid
1984 Resource Allocation and Enterprise Combination in a Risky Environment: A Case Study of the Gezira Scheme, Sudan. Ph.D. dissertation, Oklahoma State University.

O'Brien, John James III
1980 Agricultural Labor and Development in Sudan. Ph.D. dissertation, University of Connecticut, Storrs.

1985 Sowing the Seeds of Famine. Review of African Political Economy 33:23-32.

Oesterdiekhoff, Peter
1980 Der Agrarsektor Des Sudan. *In* Der Sudan Probleme und Perspektiven der Entwicklung. Rainer Tetzlaff and Karl Wohlmuth, eds. Pp. 257-382. Frankfurt/Main: Alfred Metzner Verlag.

Oesterdiekhoff, Peter, and Karl Wohlmuth
1983 The Breadbasket Strategy of the Sudan: A New Option of Development? *In* The Development Perspectives of the Democratic Republic of Sudan. Peter Oesterdiekhoff and Karl Wohlmuth, eds. Pp. 7-52. Munich: Weltforum Verlag.

Olsson, Lars, and Willem Keddeman
1978 Cotton-Picking Labour. *In* Employment, Productivity and Incomes in Rural Sudan. Willem Keddeman and Ali Abdel Gadir Ali, eds. Pp. 15-26. Khartoum: Economic and Social Research Council and ILO.

Osman, Omer Mohommed, and A. A. Suleiman
1969 The Economy of Sudan. *In* The Economies of Africa. Paul Robson and D. A. Lury, eds. Pp. 436-470. Evanston, IL: Northwestern University Press.

Payne, Rhys
1986 Food Deficits and Political Legitimacy: The Case of Morocco. *In* Africa's Agrarian Crisis. Stephen K. Commins, Michael F. Lofchie, and Rhys Payne, eds. Pp. 153-172. Boulder, CO: Lynne Rienner.

Quarterly Economic Review of Sudan
   1982   Third Quarter.
   1985   Annual Supplement.

Saeed, Abdel Basit
   1982   The State and Socioeconomic Transformation in the Sudan. Ph.D. dissertation, University of Connecticut, Storrs.

Saeed, Hassan Mohamed, Arif Jamal Mohamed Ahmed, and Mohamed El Hussein El Tahir
   1986   Agricultural Research and Extension. *In* The Agricultural Sector of Sudan: Policy and Systems Studies. A. B. Zahlan and W. Y. Magar, eds. Pp. 381–408. London: Ithaca Press.

Said, Yousif Hassan
   1968   The Role of Agriculture in the Economic Development of Sudan. Ph.D. dissertation, University of Wisconsin.

Salem-Murdock, Muneera
   1984   Nubian Farmers and Arab Herders in Irrigated Agriculture in Sudan: From Domestic to Commodity Production. Ph.D. dissertation, State University of New York at Binghamton.

Shaaeldin, Elfatih
   1982   The Controversy Over Land-Water Charges and Decentralization in the Gezira. Sudan Notes and Records 63:97–112.

   1986   The Role of the Agricultural Sector in the Economy. *In* The Agricultural Sector of Sudan: Policy and Systems Studies. A. B. Zahlan and W. Y. Magar, eds. Pp. 17–43. London: Ithaca Press.

Sørbø, Gunnar M.
   1977   Nomads on the Scheme: A Study of Irrigation Agriculture and Pastoralism in Eastern Sudan. *In* Land Use and Development. Philip O'Keefe and Ben Wisner, eds. Pp. 132–150. London: International African Institute.

Tait, John
   1978   Divisifizierung, Mechanisierung und Kapitalisierung der Produktion im Gezira Scheme. Auf dem Weg zur Uberwindung kolonial deformierter Agrarstrukturen? Afrika Spectrum 13(2):165–178.

   1983   The Modernization of the Colonial Mode of Production in the Gezira Scheme. *In* The Development Perspectives of the Democratic Republic of Sudan. Peter Oesterdiekhoff and Karl Wohlmuth, eds. Pp. 81–135. Munich: Weltforum Verlag.

Versluys, J. D. N.
   1953   The Gezira Scheme in the Sudan and the Russian Kolkhoz: A Comparison of Two Experiments. Economic Development and Cultural Change, part one 2(1):32–59, part two 2(2):120–135, part three 2(3):216–235.

Voll, Sarah
   1980   The Gezira Development Project in the Sudan. Research in Economic Anthropology 3:265–290.

Wallace, Tina
   1985   Refugees and Hunger in Eastern Sudan. Review of African Political Economy (Briefings) 33:64–68.

Warburg, Gabriel
   1978 Slavery and Labour in the Anglo-Egyptian Sudan. Asian and African Studies 12(2):221–245.

World Bank
   1981 Accelerated Development in Sub-Saharan Africa. Washington, DC.

Zahlan, A. B.
   1986 Introduction. *In* The Agricultural Sector of Sudan: Policy and Systems Studies. A. B. Zahlan and W. Y. Magar, eds. Pp. 1–7. London: Ithaca Press.

Zakaria, Ahmed Bedawi
   1986 The Supply and Demand Factors for Agricultural Products in Sudan. *In* The Agricultural Sector of Sudan: Policy and Systems Studies. A. B. Zahlan and W. Y. Magar, eds. Pp. 71–93. London: Ithaca Press.

10

Advocacy in a Bedouin Resettlement Project in the Negev, Israel

Emanuel Marx

Introduction: Anthropology and Advocacy

In 1979–1980 I became deeply involved in the politics of a program to resettle the Bedouin in Israel's Negev. This experience yields insights on a theme that has recently aroused growing concern: the anthropologist as advocate. The story tells about the sociology of advocacy and about some of the difficulties attending the advocate's work. These are the difficulties in coordinating the efforts of numerous agencies of a centralized state; the problems resulting from the adoption by the parties involved of a particular view of reality; and the conflict between the advocate's need for power in order to carry out his or her function, and the restraints on that power required in order not to weaken the clients.

Advocacy involves action "on behalf of the people among whom we pursue our anthropological research" (Paine 1985:xiii). It may take the form of writing reports, petitions, and representations in order to influence one or more of the parties. It may also involve the anthropologist in planning and implementation. He or she may come to play an increasingly active role in negotiations between parties, either as mediator, "a third party who is not himself a disputant" (Gulliver 1979: 209), or as an ally of one or more of the parties. As Gulliver rightly observes, the advocate "does not necessarily . . . adopt a single strategy and then stick to it throughout the negotiations. Most commonly, he changes his strategy to fit the changing circumstances and requirements of both the disputants and himself" (1979:226). It is useless, therefore, to ask whether the advocate is still acting as an anthropologist; the answer depends on the time, place, and situational aspects of the negotiations. In the course of negotiations, the anthropologist draws on a store of specialized knowledge which, one might as well admit, is not necessarily superior to or less biased than that of other participants. Sometimes he or she may, due to training, perceive connections between events that have escaped others. Perhaps having elaborated a complex model of the social field in which the negotiations are taking place, he or she then as an advocate will engage in numerous activities that may affect the negotiations, no longer recording and evaluating them as an anthropologist. At such times, the moral aspects of the enterprise become more explicit and dominant, and analysis recedes into the background.

The advocate, then, may not always remain strictly within the confines of social anthropology, but whether or not anthropologists make "proper" use of their skills, they are eminently qualified to become advocates. First, they have learned to develop contextualized models of the social field, to understand rapidly changing shifts in power, to pay attention to the maintenance of communication networks, and to be sensitive to symbols used in communication and to the changing themes that dominate discourse. These capacities may provide a sound basis for the formulation of plans and for the conduct of negotiation. Second, their training prepares them for deep involvement in the field, permitting them to collect fresh detailed information as it develops and to maintain a steady flow of communication with the participants. Third, as members of universities or research institutes, they hold a relatively secure and perhaps satisfying position, so that when the time comes to leave the field and to relinquish the power that has accrued to them, they are likely to do so without much regret. They will resist the temptation to augment this power at the expense of their clients, whether deprived minorities or powerful bureaucracies. Because of their secure position, of course, they may hesitate to enter the fray in the first place, as in my own case.

Several interesting points emerge from the material to be discussed below. First, the process followed several stages in which the mediator initially succeeded against entrenched official resistance, but then the project faltered and failed. It went through a full cycle: from its inception and its conceptual development, to the setting up of an organization to negotiate and implement a contract, to the loss of momentum, and finally to the disintegration of the project with only part of the work accomplished. A process of bureaucratic entropy caused this failure. I argue, in fact, that both the initial success and the subsequent failure are two sides of the same coin, in which an interest group promotes and finally brings about a policy change, but is then gradually pushed aside or absorbed by the bureaucracy, so that there is no longer any pressure to hold the authorities to the policy.

This is a phenomenon peculiar to societies such as Israel that are dominated by a powerful state. In such a society very few autonomous interest groups manage to survive; they are usually either subsidized (or otherwise "supported" by the state), or eventually starved out of existence. Interest groups typically take the initiative in stimulating and promoting policy changes in every sphere of public life, and they may exert organized and continuous pressure on government to implement and to adhere to policies. In a sense, the government "rules" by adjudicating and balancing the conflicting demands of rival interest groups. In the absence of such pressures, government often finds it difficult to develop and adhere to policies. Its attention veers from one burning issue to the next, and it tends to make decisions on specific issues without an exhaustive exploration of their wider implications. In this near vacuum of policy-making, an interest group that is determined and tenacious enough to remain autonomous is likely to overcome the government's resistance and to gain its objectives, at least for some time. Once the group's objectives have been adopted, however, it is gradually drawn into closer collaboration with the authorities and loses its independence and strength. I have examined the process in detail elsewhere (Marx, in press).

A second point that emerges from the analysis is that the views of reality that are adopted and the themes that are singled out for discussion by participants seriously affect the development of the negotiation. Specifically, the fact that land ownership was considered to be the central issue for negotiation by all the parties involved in the case discussed here—the Bedouin, the representatives of the state, and the anthropologist—had far-reaching results.

Third, advocates accumulate a great deal of power, given more or less willingly by their clients. It may increase to a point where the advocates think they know best, and may become impatient with a recalcitrant client. Thus, while advocates need the power to represent their clients efficiently, they may also weaken them to the extent that they become disorganized and unable to resist their adversaries, official or unofficial.

The State and Bedouin Land: Background

These points are illustrated by the events surrounding the evacuation of some 5,000 Bedouin in the northern Negev in order to make room for a military airport. I shall briefly discuss the background to these events and then examine the evolution of the project in which I participated initially as an advocate and later as an interested observer. Formerly, the Bedouin were pastoral nomads who exploited communal ranges and who also cultivated privately owned land. Ever since the establishment of Israel, there has been a dispute between the Negev Bedouin and the Israeli authorities over ownership of this land. The Israel Lands Authority claims that the Ottoman Land Code of 1858 defined the Negev as uncultivable state-owned land (*mewat*). A Mewat Land Ordinance of 1921 prohibits all means of alienating such land, even by cultivation (see Granott 1952:95); therefore, the land belongs to the state. The Israeli authorities adopted these land laws and partly relied on them in their efforts to nationalize land. The Bedouin, for their part, claim that not only did they possess rights of occupancy on cultivated land, but also that the British Mandatory authorities collected land tax, thus recognizing at least their right of occupancy. In the 1930s some of the Bedouin sold land to the Jewish National Fund, which was officially registered as privately owned, thus implicitly confirming the rights of the previous owners. Nevertheless, in effect, the Israeli authorities have used the legal argument in order to obscure the stark reality, which involves the forcible removal of most of the Bedouin and the takeover of their land.

In the fighting that accompanied the founding of the state of Israel in 1948, most of the 75,000 Negev Bedouin fled the country or went into hiding. The approximately 11,000 Bedouin who remained or returned were confined to a reservation in the eastern Be'ersheva Plain. It comprised only a fraction of their cultivated land, estimated at 1,200,000 dunams (120,000 hectares). After its establishment in 1950, the Israel Lands Authority took possession of almost all the land in the Negev, including the areas formerly cultivated by Bedouin. It continued to expropriate Bedouin land in the reservation, so that by 1967 only a small area of about 250,000 dunams (25,000 hectares) of cultivable land remained in the hands of its original Bedouin owners (Marx 1967:56). Those Bedouin without land were allotted family plots of about 150 dunams (15 hectares) each, sufficient to eke out a living. The land was leased for one year at a time, so that the Bedouin should not acquire rights of occupancy.

The authorities occasionally switched around the plots in order to assert their control, but most Bedouin stayed on the same plot year after year, gradually coming to view themselves as permanent occupants. At first, they merely set up tents on the land. Later, they constructed flimsy wooden huts or tin shacks, and eventually they felt secure enough to build houses of concrete blocks.

Since the early 1960s, social and economic conditions in Israel have changed radically. Today's Bedouin have entered a wide range of occupations in industry, construction, trucking, the professions, the civil service, and the military. This economic diversification would have caused the majority of Bedouin to settle in towns had they not felt it necessary to live on their land in order to protect their rights of ownership or occupancy.

By the 1970s, the Negev Bedouin derived only about 10 percent of their cash income from cultivation. Pastoralism, which had until then been the second major source of income in most households, declined in importance, and sheep raising was now practiced by a small number of Bedouin who owned relatively large flocks (several hundred head). Most Bedouin men had become wage earners in factories, farms, and offices, and some had done well in business—mainly as road construction contractors—and yet most of them remained on their land in small hamlets of agnates, cultivating their fields assiduously. Only a few moved into towns where they would be close to their source of employment. This pattern was the unintended result of inconsistent government policies toward the Bedouin. On the one hand, the Lands Authority attempted to take over the land that still remained in Bedouin hands. Since its establishment, the state has sought to nationalize all land; it now owns 93 percent of the country's total area and continues to increase its holdings. It still tries to expropriate Bedouin land, now mainly by legal requisition. To forestall this policy, Bedouin settled on their land, calculating that if the government was so anxious to acquire it, then their land must have great value. By working the land and by settling on it, they hoped to safeguard their rights. On the other hand, the Bedouin who leased land from the Lands Authority were securely installed on their plots. As long as they remained there, they could count on not being evicted. So they, too, cultivated the land and built their homes on it.

Many of the Bedouin who found work in town did not hold secure jobs. The Employment Service did not favor them, and during the early years of Israeli statehood sought to keep them out of the labor market. But since the early 1960s, Israel has enjoyed long periods of full employment. The two mild recessions, one in the mid-1960s and the other in the 1980s, were not attended by great waves of unemployment. The Bedouin have profited from the situation, although their limited schooling and vocational training have forced many of them to take the less permanent and lower paid jobs. Land provided these people with some basic security: a man could settle on it, in proximity to his relatives, on whose help he could rely, and he could earn a living by cultivating it. Moreover, the state sporadically subsidized Bedouin dry farming by paying drought compensation (until 1962) or by supplying cheap seeds (from 1978 onward).

Throughout the period, the efforts of the Lands Authority to establish control over Bedouin land never slackened. The result was a gradual displacement of the landowning Bedouin. Only the legal ownership of land was still being contested. For many years the state even refrained from taking the issue to court. Only in 1975 did the Lands Authority win some test cases in district courts, but even these cases are still under appeal to the High Court.

Both the Bedouin and the authorities acted on the assumption that before long the remaining land would be taken over by the state, and were therefore reluctant to invest in improvements. As a consequence, the Bedouin area was developed very slowly. While the situation of the landowning Bedouin became more precarious, the Bedouin who leased land from the Lands Authority gradually acquired a stronger hold on it. Bedouin in both categories cultivated the land and built their homes nearby also in order to reinforce their claims. The authorities considered these dwellings to be illegal because their owners had not received planning permission (there was no way for them to obtain it) and occasionally took "offenders" to court. At the same time, it did provide some services to the population, such as schools and health clinics, and some hamlets even gained access to piped water.

In 1975, the government made a first attempt to compensate the Bedouin for the expropriations. As the legal situation was unclear, it argued, the Bedouin and the authorities had an equal claim on the land. Therefore, the authorities would compensate them for half the cultivated land. The proposed formula was that Bedouin would be given freehold land amounting to 10 percent of their claims, and would receive a cash indemnity for 40 percent of their claims. All the Bedouin, including those still owning land, took the opportunity to register their claims and to obtain official confirmation of their rights. The conditions offered being unattractive, only a few Bedouin settled their claims, but the new policy indicated that the government was prepared to recognize the Bedouin's rights; it opened an avenue for further negotiations.

The 1979 Expropriation Crisis: Advocacy, Bedouin, and Bureaucracy

Under the 1979 peace treaty between Egypt and Israel, the Sinai peninsula was to be returned to Egypt, and Israeli forces were gradually to withdraw. As a result, the Negev assumed new significance. As most of it is arid, with an average annual rainfall of less than 200 mm, it was not densely populated. Now it provided the "empty space" needed for army units to regroup and for air bases to be established. The Ministry of the Interior's planners expected that much of the new development would be concentrated in the northern Negev, from the Hebron Mountains in the north to the Tsin River in the south. The eastern Be'ersheva Plain, in particular, was to become a center for relocated industries, and a civil airport was to be built there. Land that lay unused, or was not used intensively, was now to be exploited fully. The Bedouin occupants were considered to be nomads, not firmly attached to the land, who could be moved elsewhere. The development plans for the eastern Be'ersheva Plain sought to hasten the dispossession.

With the Sinai gone, the Air Force required three new air bases in the Negev. One of these was to be built in the eastern Be'ersheva Plain on a site previously earmarked for the civil airport. The government authorized a number of officials who had hitherto dealt with the Bedouin to make the necessary arrangements. The outcome was a draft law to expropriate an area six times that needed for the air base. It would effectively have taken over all the land still remaining in Bedouin hands. The proposal did not allow the occupants of the expropriated land recourse to the courts. Compensation for the land was to be nominal, but each Bedouin household, whether it had owned land or not, would be entitled to a fully developed building site in one of seven Bedouin towns in the Negev. Two such towns had already been founded, and others were in the planning stage.

The officials and the planners did not consult or negotiate with the Bedouin, who heard of the project through rumors and garbled newspaper reports. Their anxiety increased as the months passed, and in response they closed their ranks around their tribal chiefs. This new determination was first tested in April 1979, when the Lands Authority tried to build a road to Laqia, one of the projected Bedouin towns. The bulldozers tore through the land of several families while a police unit was standing by. The area had been expropriated, but the Bedouin were still contesting the decision in the High Court. The Bedouin tried to stop the workmen and fought with the police; several persons were hurt on both sides. Public opinion in Israel and abroad reacted with sharp criticism, and the government agreed to reconsider the issue.

It was at this stage that I became involved. In the early 1960s, I had carried out an anthropological study of the Abu Jwe'id tribe of the Zullam Bedouin in the eastern Be'ersheva Plain (Marx 1967), and I had maintained contacts with the Bedouin. In February 1979, the chiefs of the Abu Jwe'id tribe, whose lands were threatened by the proposed airbase, asked me to intervene with the authorities on their behalf. At about the same time, I was invited by a planning team for the Negev to suggest ways to solve the "Bedouin problem." The team had been set up by a small group of concerned academic and professional regional planners who sought to forestall a wholesale takeover of the Negev by army units. They had gained the support of officials in the Ministries of Defense and Agriculture. Armed with these two mandates, I first tried, unsuccessfully, to persuade several of the officials who had planned the expropriation law to shelve the law and to negotiate a settlement with the Bedouin. Then, as a result of extensive discussions with Bedouin and officials working in the field, I devised a plan that would allow the setting up of the air base and would also be responsive to the needs of the Bedouin. This plan was modified in discussions with the members of the Negev Planning Team and finally accepted and published in their report (Wachman et al. 1979:131–136).

The plan was based on several premises: that only a negotiated agreement was likely to succeed; that the Bedouin should be treated as if they were owners of the cultivated land and be compensated to the full market value (but in an out-of-court agreement so that the issue of land ownership could be avoided); that the project was to be viewed as a pilot scheme which, if successful, would gradually extend to all those Bedouin whose land the state had expropriated since its establishment and who had never been compensated. Without the last provision, the program was bound to fail, because the Bedouin would firmly oppose any piecemeal settlement that left their general problem unsolved. In particular, they would not allow anyone, including other Bedouin, to settle on land that they still considered theirs. It was also proposed that, because the loss of land would deprive the Bedouin of their economic base, they should be provided with secure livelihoods and compensated in productive resources of their choice, such as irrigated farms, shops, workshops, or taxi licenses, to be purchased with the proceeds from the land. Compensation should be commensurate with the average standard of living in the country and not with the low income derived from dry farming. Every Bedouin household should be able to acquire one to three developed building sites in a Bedouin town at cost; no longer would they receive them as "gifts" from the state. If the compensation received was not enough to pay for the building site, then subsidized loans should be made available. Every Bedouin could build a house according to his wishes and requirements. The Bedouin towns were to be large and closely built up, so that they would provide a full range of services and a variety of employment opportunities; instead of seven small towns, there would only be three large ones, with a projected population of 20,000 each, including one to be specially built for the evacuees. By the year 2000 two-thirds of the 100,000 Negev Bedouin would reside in the towns.

The plan was conceived as a commercial transaction: Bedouin were to be compensated at market value for the property surrendered and were to pay the market value of the commodities and properties acquired. This did not necessarily raise the cost of the operation for the state, but it changed its character. Instead of leaving the Bedouin with a sense of having their land taken away without proper compensation and being compelled to receive a gift without commercial value from the state, they now got the message that both their land and property and the building plots in the new towns were valuable commodities. More importantly, the transaction acquired a new meaning: it was no longer a coercive measure, but a negotiated deal, and it gave Bedouin the choice of how to invest their indemnities. Eventually, they all preferred building plots and farm land (that could perhaps later be converted into building sites), but they knew that other options for investment were available.

The Negev Planning Team first got together as an unofficial group of people concerned about the future of the Negev under the new conditions created by the peace. One of its members, an eminent academic whose main interest is in regional planning, now saw a chance to translate his ideas into practice. Two members were urban planners interested in the prospects for exciting work. One of them had for many years worked for the Israeli administration in the Sinai. Another member had as a civil servant been concerned with planning and implementation of development projects in the Sinai and was looking for new fields of activity. When the government's Water Commissioner joined the group, he inevitably became its leader, since he had access to senior officials and politicians. He strengthened the group's links with the powerful Ministry of Defense. The anthropologist was at the outset marginal to the group; only when the Bedouin resettlement scheme loomed larger in the work of the team did he come to be considered a full member.

The official agency responsible for physical planning, a division of the Ministry of the Interior, not willing to give up its prerogatives, tried for many months to boycott the team. As a result, the Planning Team became militant; its members canvassed and persuaded government officials and saw to it that its recommendations were accepted and carried out. As outsiders they could disregard official channels and could communicate with officials at every level and in any department. As they were protégés of high-ranking government officials, one had to reckon with their influence. This was important in a country in which political currents change rapidly, and where officials live in constant fear, not so much of being removed from their jobs, as of their jobs being changed, causing loss of power. To counteract such a possibility, each official works hard to maintain close relations and reciprocal support with other officials and with outsiders, in his department and elsewhere. Therefore, even the opponents of the Planning Team treated its members as potential allies. The Planning Team thus succeeded in several instances in creating almost unanimous support for its ideas and in isolating those who held conflicting views. In short, the team acted as a regular pressure group.

In the early stages of the project, the members of the Negev Planning Team established a close rapport with Bedouin leaders. The Bedouin realized that the Air Force was committed to beginning the construction of the airport by a specific date, and they feared that events would overtake them. The land issue concerned not only those who were to be resettled, but all the Bedouin of the Negev. For once they united and set up a leadership of tribal chiefs, elders, Bedouin officials, and professionals. Sheikh Hamad Abu Rabi'a of the Zullam became the leader and spokesman of the group; he was a member of the Knesset, and the resettlement project concerned his and the neighboring tribes. Some of his own land was involved.

At last, the Ministry of the Interior, the authority responsible for physical planning, relented and agreed to take the Negev Planning Team under its wing on the condition that the group should no longer work on the question of Bedouin land. Now that they were established on an official basis, the members hoped to increase their influence. The lay members, who had been volunteering their time, would from now on work on contracts and be able to devote more time to the project. The government appointed the team as the official planning group; it was to work under the guidance of the Planning Division of the Ministry of the Interior. The Ministry drew up detailed instructions as to what the team was to do and how to do it. The team quickly lost its independence and with it, all its influence on the overall planning of the future of the Negev. Its final report was published a year later and shelved.

The conditions under which the Negev Planning Team labored influenced its approach to the Bedouin land question. When the team was formally appointed by the government, it lost its liberty to negotiate with various organizations and was reduced to the preparation of documents whose recommendations no one was obliged to adopt. As the Bedouin land problem was outside its direct competence and not controlled by the Ministry, the team concentrated most of its efforts on the preparation of the Bedouin resettlement project. This was to serve as a model for solving the land question. The official sponsor of the group, the government's Water Commissioner, became convinced that the program offered a viable solution, and the Laqia incident presented the opportunity to suggest a new approach to the government. In August 1979, the government adopted the plan and appointed the Water Commissioner to negotiate an agreement with the Bedouin based on the team's program.

The government decision turned out to be the beginning of another entropic cycle. The members of the Negev Planning Team now, for the second time, became involved in extended negotiations with various government departments and officials, trying to convince them of the feasibility of the plan. There was always a hidden threat in these negotiations, that a recalcitrant department would find itself isolated, trying to defend a policy to which other departments no longer adhered. In some instances, the threat became serious—for example, when a department faced the possibility that it would not be invited to participate in the implementation of the project. Without persistent pressure and a continuous flow of communications with all the people concerned, the project would soon have been abandoned, for even the government ministers who had voted for the program had to be persuaded repeatedly to continue to support it. There were moments when the whole venture seemed to be at risk. One occurred when a draft law that already had passed the first reading in the Knesset (Israel's parliament), was to be redrafted; another, when the Treasury had to provide the budget for compensating and resettling the Bedouin. Ultimately, all the obstacles were overcome, and in July 1980, the Knesset passed a law that incorporated the program. Once again, however, success led to institutionalization and to a weakening of the team. The various government departments resumed control, and old policies were revived and fused with the new ones.

My part in the project also changed over the months. In the beginning, I was mostly concerned about the effects of current policies on the Bedouin and sought alternatives. In April 1979, I formulated my proposals in writing and presented the document to the members of the team and to various government officials. I hoped that someone in government would see the advantages of my approach; I was quite content to leave my involvement at that. My colleagues on the Negev Planning Team were persuaded of the usefulness of the program I proposed and not only supported it, but incorporated it into their plans. This encouraged me to work toward implementation and to continue talks with competent government officials. None of the officials I approached refused to see me, but they responded with skepticism. Nevertheless, as I continued to make the rounds, I heard echoes of my ideas. In retrospect, I realized that the conversations had made an impact, but these talks could not coordinate the activities of officials. That had to be done by the government, without whose approval no new policy could be sanctioned and no budgets would be allocated. In this respect, the Water Commissioner, who had friendship ties with several ministers, achieved the breakthrough. When the government formally decided to adopt the plan and appointed the Water Commissioner to head a committee of study and implementation, there was an immediate change: the members of the Negev Planning Team gained access to a new range of people—senior government officials, politicians, and Bedouin leaders—some of whom supported the team at various times. Wisely, the team never ceased to communicate with its opponents, the members of the Higher Bedouin Committee, a group of Jewish officials who had hitherto coordinated policies affecting the Bedouin. It discussed the resettlement plan with all these people and, in return, received new ideas and detailed suggestions as to its implementation. This interaction resulted in proposals that were assured of a good reception by the officials. After a time, the consensus was so much taken for granted that the government even hoped to persuade the opposition to support the proposals. Following many vicissitudes, two members of the Negev Planning Team, including myself, persuaded the parliamentary opposition to vote for the new policy, as embodied in a rewritten draft law. In July 1980, the Knesset passed the "Law for the Acquisition of Land in the Negev (Peace Treaty with Egypt), 1980."

My involvement in Bedouin politics grew steadily, at the expense of all other activities, including teaching and writing. I find that even the field notes taken at the time became shorter and less detailed. When the Implementation Authority was established, all the members of the Negev Planning Team had to face the decision whether to join it in an official capacity or to stand aside. The Water Commissioner was appointed as head of the Implementation Authority, and so even this sphere of his activity became "official." He urged the members of the team to make a rapid decision by offering them jobs or consultancies in this official body. Communications with high-ranking officials and decisions involving expenditures had to be approved by him. Soon the members of the team were divided into insiders and outsiders. One member of the team became the chief negotiator; two members opted to work as planners with the organization (one of them was later dismissed because he tended to follow his own inclinations). The anthropologist and the other academic on the team returned to their university jobs and, while maintaining an interest in the progress of the work, gradually reduced their involvement. The concerns and interests of the members of the team became so divergent and their routine involvement and knowledge of detail varied so much that they could no longer cooperate on equal terms. Their meetings were discontinued, and the project was left without guidance and control.

The Implementation Authority was to evacuate the Bedouin from the requisitioned area, to compensate them, and to resettle them. The various departments that had been dealing with these operations feared that some of their competences would be transferred to the new authority. Therefore they agreed to collaborate fully with it and to appoint representatives to its board.

Because the Air Force had to proceed according to a fixed timetable determined by the negotiated withdrawal from the Sinai, the Implementation Authority worked under constant pressure, its officials now negotiating with each Bedouin household about the compensation payments. Each head of a household claimed special treatment, and the Bedouin leaders who owned land in the area became private individuals who secretly negotiated with the authorities the most advantageous terms for themselves. The Bedouin leadership thus crumbled, and the officials of the Implementation Authority no longer needed to respond to organized pressure. Some individuals conducted their negotiations very astutely and managed to obtain special benefits, such as an additional building plot for a teenage son, or the cost of removal for an individual who had gone to live in town many years ago. These concessions soon leaked out and gradually drove up the level of compensation, leaving dissatisfied those Bedouin who had made their agreements earlier.

Eventually the time came to set up the new towns for the evacuees. Once more, the issue of land became central. It turned out that the authorities did not own land that the Bedouin would accept in compensation. All the land they could offer in the Negev had been taken from other Bedouin who had never been compensated. The Bedouin now feared that the former owners of the land would treat them as usurpers. Only when the Bedouin became convinced of the authorities' intention to settle all the land claims was a solution found: the Abu 'Arar group, whose land had not been requisitioned, offered it to the authorities on condition that they be treated like the evacuees from the area of the projected airfield. In fact, the authorities dealt with them very generously. On this land the town of 'Ar'ara was established. Later, other Bedouin landowners contributed large tracts for setting up the town of Kseifa, under the same advantageous conditions.

Toward the end of 1983, when the new airfield was inaugurated, the Bedouin living in the area had voluntarily evacuated the land, and many of them were now resettled in the new towns of 'Ar'ara and Kseifa, but the project then lost momentum. During negotiations, each Bedouin descent group had tried to obtain as much land as possible, and consequently the towns spread over so large an area that the provision of services and of service centers became difficult; nor was there any point in providing commercial centers, as only a few Bedouin owned motorcars, and the city of Be'ersheva, accessible by public transport, was only 25 kilometers away. The cost of the project had been so great that the Treasury felt it could not deal with Bedouin whose land had been requisitioned in the past. At this point some of the Bedouin landowners suspended negotiations with the authorities out of solidarity with their brethren. By 1984, the activities of the Implementation Authority had almost come to a halt. About half the approximately 700 households of evacuees had by then settled with the Implementation Authority; the other half either suspended negotiations or kept them going at a leisurely pace. There was no point in settling accounts with an authority that had no funds, especially when one risked being unpopular with Bedouin who were excluded from the project. The organization has not yet been disbanded, however, as of the date of this writing (mid-1987).

Conclusions

In this Israeli organization (and one suspects in others, too), projects seemed to go through a typical cycle. It began with the presentation of new ideas. These ideas did not usually originate from members but from "outsiders" such as advocates, who gained access to the organization and who were not bound by routine duties. Only ideas that were pushed hard and continuously stood a chance of acceptance. The "outsiders" presented their case forcefully; they could approach almost anyone, ignoring bureaucratic channels. The new ideas provoked debate—of which the public was not necessarily aware—among official circles, and officials took sides. The different approaches soon became transformed into struggles for power between groups of officials. Those who won the contest were entrusted with implementation, and they engaged in a series of purposeful activities, but they never gained exclusive control over a project and the resources needed for its implementation. There soon developed an entropy that gradually engulfed the project. Each person and each group in the various government departments was involved in numerous activities that required attention, and the resources allocated to the project were gradually diverted to other equally meritorious projects. As implementation proceeded, people of ideas, the "outsiders," were left behind, because bureaucratic interaction demanded more and more time. Therefore, the project lost its aim and momentum; it floundered aimlessly until finally it was abandoned, though the organization was not disbanded. Not even the former contenders for power (such as, in our case, the Higher Bedouin Committee) could revive it.

All the parties agree that the central issue in the relations between the Negev Bedouin and the Israeli authorities is land. For more than a generation the subject has been uppermost in their minds, and it still overshadows other issues that are no less important. Discourse between the Bedouin and the authorities is governed by the land issue, and this has had a series of interesting effects. First, the pattern of settlement of Bedouin in the Be'ersheva Plain developed in response to the authorities' claim to ownership of all the land. Similarly, no land was available for resettling Bedouin whose land was required for the new Nevatim airport, because no Bedouin dared settle on land taken in the past from other Bedouin. Only when a group of landowning Bedouin agreed voluntarily to hand over their land for the establishment of a new town could resettlement proceed. Because land was so important, Bedouin sought in negotiations to maximize the area of land they were to receive in compensation, although this entailed such costs as expensive water and electricity connections, made it almost impossible to provide such other services as sewage, created substantial traveling distances to service centers, and reduced projected land values. The planners reacted to the Bedouin tendency to spread over large areas by designing single, but very large, civic, commercial, and industrial centers in some of the towns—centers that are not viable, for they lack customers and entrepreneurs. The planners also showed concern about boundaries. In Rahat, a Bedouin town north of Be'ersheva, the southern boundary was fixed along the steep banks of a creek, and the others along national roads, so that the town would be contained within the well-marked border. In 'Ar'ara, they sought to surround the town by a belt of irrigated farm land owned by Bedouin, which would prevent urban sprawl.

In order to maximize their chances of obtaining larger areas of land, each Bedouin patronymic group asked to dwell in its own quarter, claiming that its women should not be exposed to the gaze of strange men. The members of each group also sought to establish physical distance between it and neighboring groups. Furthermore, they demanded that only one access road should join their quarter to the rest of the town. Thus each group managed to establish control over a compact area and maintain a reserve for future settlement at its fringes. In this manner, they postponed for many years the establishment of a full-fledged city with all its amenities.

The negotiators, including the anthropologist, had little choice but to go along with the Bedouin's conception of land as the ultimate good, well aware that this attitude was a response to the state's persistent attempts to gain control over Bedouin land. This dialectic led to developments that left many crucial matters unresolved, yet permitted a negotiated solution of the land problem in one part of the Negev. Because the model was found to be acceptable to the authorities and to the Bedouin, it will probably be used in the settlement of land problems elsewhere in the Negev, with similar results.

I did not fully appreciate the special place of land in a society whose economic and political future appeared uncertain. Land is esteemed as a major component of basic security: it provides a site for a home that can be expanded with the growth of the household, contributing to the cohesion of its members, and it provides a site on which to grow food that can be consumed and/or marketed (Little and Horowitz 1987:254). It took me some time to understand why the Bedouin all preferred land, and the more the better, to all the other options offered. I was forced to admit that in this field I was neither thinking nor acting as an anthropologist. This sober thought led me to reconsider the role of the anthropologist as advocate.

There was a time when one distinguished between applied anthropology and advocacy. Polgar (1979:260) argues that the former refers to work commissioned by powerful groups who are often in a position to influence the outcome of studies, while the latter refers to intervention on behalf of weak groups, who presumably cannot help themselves.

Judging from my experience, this is not a valid distinction. Both the applied anthropologist and the advocate can work for powerful and for weak people (and the relative power of the parties may change situationally). Both seek to accommodate conflicting interests, and both may become involved in negotiations to a greater or lesser extent. Clearly, neither the applied anthropologist nor the advocate functions specifically as an anthropologist. As they negotiate, persuade, and plead a cause, they become political practitioners, and have only diminishing recourse to their anthropological knowledge.

Both applied anthropology and advocacy become ethically doubtful when they generate patronizing attitudes toward the people and imply that the people are unable to work out their own problems or to resist interference by the state. This assumption of the clients' weakness and incapacity goes hand in hand with a negative view of the anthropologist-advocate's own influence. She or he may believe that after handing in the report there is nothing more to do, and chances are that no one will heed its arguments (Whisson 1985:138). Another element in the configuration is the view that government is powerful and knows what it wants. The missing part in this picture is, of course, that advocacy is part of the political process. This implies that the advocate takes note of the always complex and constantly changing power structure in the field, including assessing his or her own place in the structure, however modest it may be. Advocates must become even more involved in the political process if they want their recommendations to be implemented. They need power first to persuade friends and opponents and to arrest bureaucratic entropy. Their power derives from their own resources and from those of their clients. That does not necessarily mean that they become powerful at the clients' expense. On the contrary, they need powerful clients to make them more powerful. In the case of the Negev Bedouin, the negotiators' power declined not only because of bureaucratic entropy, but also because in the later stages the negotiation dealt with individual Bedouin households. This led to the crumbling of the organized Bedouin leadership which, in turn, weakened the negotiators.

The advocate here is an anthropologist (or any other person) who negotiates with a full awareness of the political process. He or she works with all the parties involved in any particular issue and seeks to achieve a workable solution acceptable to all, knowing that all the parties concerned possess power, if of different kinds, and have more or less clearly defined aims. Such advocates are persons who have an "interjacent commitment" to the negotiating parties (Gulliver 1969:62). Gulliver rightly notes that they are usually also people of influence, with resources of their own, who may often take the lead in negotiations.

The case of the Bedouin resettlement project shows that the state cannot be treated as a well-meaning, paternalistic, and monolithic organization. It is made up of numerous departments, each of which has its functional requirements, develops its own policies, and is composed of numerous officials each with his/her own goals. Also, officials do not necessarily act in accordance with official policies, because their actions are the outcome of their interaction with clients. If top-level decisions are not necessarily conclusive and are not necessarily executed, then in practice one must deal with officials at all levels. If they are not continually persuaded to conform to planned activities, they will turn their time and resources elsewhere. For this reason, the advocate must possess some power and be willing to use it. Better still, the clients concerned must exert pressure. They have an interest in the development and can thus be expected to organize. The advocate then seeks to facilitate the organization of interest groups and, above all, to avoid coercing people to comply with government policies.

Constant communication with all the parties concerned is the key to any negotiated solution to a problem, a precondition for enlisting people's willing cooperation. It facilitates agreement and the willingness to accept change. A breakdown or even an interruption in communication results in immediate, and often unexpected, difficulties and complications. The advocate maintains communication, therefore, with the various officials involved, with the clients, and, to no lesser extent, with associates.

Effective advocacy requires a long-term commitment (Paine 1985). Advocates traditionally submit reports to decision makers, who are then expected to implement the recommendations. In reality the advice is rarely put into practice, and for good reasons. Advocates usually present recommendations that have not been examined for practicality or arranged in order of importance; also, they do not usually provide a schedule for implementation that takes possible contingencies into consideration. Indeed, the only reasonable way to provide for such contingencies is to remain in the field and to participate in implementation. Advocates who choose this approach become deeply and continuously involved in the project, maintaining communication, implementing policies, and revising plans continuously to meet changing conditions. To them, the initial report is of momentary significance; it is only a baseline and becomes rapidly outdated. They hope that all the parties concerned consider them to be impartial and not a tool of the other side. They facilitate communications all around and thus create conditions for agreement and exchange. In the process, they acquire power, which they use constructively in the support of new ideas, compromise, and persuasion. They try to manipulate and change the field of power by introducing new participants, neutralizing others, and redefining issues, but they know that their success can be only partial.

For a limited period, anthropologists become politicians concerned with achieving the aims of the people they represent. Personally, I would encourage all anthropologists who have completed a detailed field study to respond to requests of the people they worked with, once they have left the field. If fieldwork is life with people, and the anthropologist becomes intimately associated with and attached to these people, then advocacy becomes a logical (though not inevitable) sequel to it. The anthropologist's training and knowledge of the field are not essential prerequisites, although they may sometimes help—and often mar—the advocacy. It is the moral obligation incurred during fieldwork that counts.

Before long, advocates are gradually made to withdraw from active participation, with the aims of the project only partly accomplished. Once they leave the field of active intervention and reenter the realm of ideas, they again become anthropologists.

Notes

An earlier version of this paper, in Galaty et al. (1981), was presented at a conference, The Future of Pastoral Peoples, that took place in Nairobi in 1980. I first revised it for a conference on advocacy in St. John's, Newfoundland, in 1983 (Paine 1985). I have continued to revise it in response to comments received from D. R. Aronson, A. Bourgeot, W. Goldschmidt, P. H. Gulliver, M. M Horowitz, E. Nyerges, R. Paine, P. Rigby, P. C. Salzman, S. Sandford, J. W. Ssenyonga, F. Stewart, and two anonymous reviewers, to all of whom I am obliged. Work on this version was supported by the United States-Israel Binational Science Foundation.

References

Galaty, John G., et al., eds.
    1981 The Future of Pastoral Peoples: Proceedings of a Conference Held in Nairobi, Kenya, 4–8 August 1980. Ottawa: International Development Research Center.

Granott, Abraham
    1952 The Land System in Palestine. London: Eyre and Spottiswoode.

Gulliver, Philip H.
   1969   Dispute Settlement without Courts: The Ndendeuli of Southern Tanzania. *In* Law in Culture and Society. L. Nader, ed. Pp. 24–68. Chicago: Aldine.

   1979   Disputes and Negotiations. New York: Academic Press.

Little, Peter D., and M. M Horowitz
   1987   Subsistence Crops Are Cash Crops: Some Comments with Reference to East Africa. Human Organization 46(3):254–258.

Marx, Emanuel
   1967   Bedouin of the Negev. Manchester: Manchester University Press.

   In press   State and Citizen in Israel. *In* Israel, An Anthropological View. E. Marx, ed. Tel Aviv: Am Oved (in Hebrew).

Paine, Robert, ed.
   1985   Advocacy and Anthropology: First Encounters. St. John's, Newfoundland: Institute of Social and Economic Research, Memorial University of Newfoundland.

Polgar, Steven
   1979   From Applied to Committed Anthropology: Disengaging from our Colonial Heritage. *In* The Politics of Anthropology. G. Huizer and B. Mannheim, eds. Pp. 259–266. The Hague: Mouton.

Wachman, Abraham, et al.
   1979   Negev Development Plan: Interim Report No. 1. Tel Aviv: Tahal (in Hebrew).

Whisson, Michael G.
   1985   Advocates, Brokers and Collaborators. *In* Social Anthropology and Development Policy. R. Grillo and A. Rew, eds. Pp. 131–147. London: Tavistock.

11

Rural Development and Migration in Northeast Syria

Günter Meyer

Introduction

Northeast Syria has changed, since World War II, from a peripheral and backward region only marginally integrated into the national economy, into the center of Syrian agricultural development. In the 1940s and 1950s large-scale grain cultivation on the plains expanded tremendously, as did irrigated cotton growing in the valleys of the Euphrates and its tributaries—both developments initiated and largely controlled by urban entrepreneurs. The 1960s saw the first massive intervention by the Syrian government in the agricultural system of the northeast as it expropriated the great landlords and introduced a cooperative system. The second massive intervention by the state began with the selection of the northeast as the site of the single largest Syrian development project, the Euphrates Scheme, planned to increase the country's irrigated area by 78 percent. The scheme, which included construction of the giant Euphrates Dam, has dominated rural development in that region since the late 1960s.

This chapter examines the social and economic impact of the Euphrates Scheme, and in particular two important migration processes attributable to it:

- the resettlement of more than 60,000 people from the upstream reservoir; and
- the increase in labor emigration from the villages in the Euphrates valley to other Arab countries.

The first section provides an historical overview of the main phases of agricultural development and social change in northeast Syria from 1940 to 1980, which culminated in the realization of the Euphrates Scheme. The second section analyzes in detail the resettlement of the reservoir people, their socioeconomic structure before the inundation of the Euphrates valley, the factors influencing their choice of different areas of resettlement, and the social and economic situation in the main regions of resettlement.

The third section deals with the problem of labor emigration. When a conversion of the irrigation system in the Middle Euphrates valley halted cultivation for several years, hundreds of peasants from the affected villages looked for work abroad. The results of an extended survey, which also included villages in the Lower Euphrates valley, revealed different reasons for the participation in labor emigration and provided information on the socioeconomic background of the migrants, the forms of migration, and the use of remittances and their impact on the economic development in the Euphrates valley during the late 1970s.

The final section speculates on the future prospects of rural development in northeast Syria. Because of the disappointing performance of the Euphrates Scheme during the first half of the 1980s, more and more people will try to get nonagricultural jobs and are likely to contribute to the increasing problem of rural-urban migration.

The significance of this study is not confined to northeast Syria alone; it invites comparison with similar subjects of research in other parts of the Middle East. Irrigation schemes, reservoir resettlement, and labor emigration are important development processes that also contribute greatly to social and economic exchange in rural communities in other countries in this region. The High Dam of Aswan, for example, caused the resettlement of more than 100,000 Nubians from the inundated villages in the Nile valley to the Kom Ombo region in Upper Egypt (Schamp 1966; Fahim 1975) and to the New Halfa Scheme in the Sudan (Heinritz 1977; Salem-Murdock 1984 and 1987; Sørbø 1985). Other examples of this kind are the new barrages in the Turkish Euphrates valley: the Karakaya Dam necessitates the resettlement of approximately 17,000 people during the late 1980s, and a similar problem arises with the closure of the giant Ataturk Dam. In the capital-poor states of the Mashreq, labor emigration is even more widespread, with far-reaching consequences particularly for the social and economic structure of the labor-exporting countries, as studies from Egypt (Amin and Awny 1985; Ged 1985; Singaby 1985), Yemen (Swanson 1979; Fischer 1984; Meyer 1986), Jordan (Keely and Saket 1984; Seccombe 1981), and Lebanon (Azzam and Shaib 1980) attest. Against this background of development-oriented research, the present study further contributes to the understanding of social and economic change in the rural Middle East.

Main Phases of Rural Change in Northeast Syria

At the beginning of the 1940s, the Syrian Jezira—the area between the Euphrates and the borders with Turkey and Iraq—was still officially classified as a "zone of nomadism" (Lewis 1987:4). The powerful Bedouin tribes of the Fid'an and the Shammar reared their herds of camels and flocks of sheep on the plains of the western and northeastern Jezira, while seminomadic tribes cultivated mostly subsistence crops along the banks of the Euphrates and its tributaries and herded their sheep on the steppe. The first important change in this pattern of land use occurred when wheat prices increased enormously during World War II. Urban entrepreneurs, particularly from Aleppo, moved into the Jezira plains with modern agricultural machinery and began to cultivate vast tracts of land (Wirth 1964; Lewis 1987:160). They rented this land mainly from the tribal sheikhs who had been able, during the French mandate, to secure the right of private property over land originally belonging to their tribe as a collectivity. The rapid expansion of grain growing began on the best land in the northeastern Jezira, where fertile soils and an average rainfall of more than 300 mm per year provided the preconditions for relatively high yields, and continued further toward the western Jezira, where poorer soils and only 200–250 mm of annual rainfall made grain cultivation a risky undertaking.

Toward the end of the 1940s, when an increasing number of sheikhs began to manage their own farming operations on the plains of Jezira, the urban entrepreneurs turned to new profitable investment activities by financing and organizing the establishment of pump-irrigated cotton cultivation in the valleys of the Euphrates and its tributaries. This development was tremendously accelerated by the upsurge in cotton prices during the Korean War in 1950, and led to a massive expansion of cotton cultivation on pump-irrigated fields along the river banks. More and more members of the seminomadic tribes—such as the 'Afadle and Welde in the western Jezira—settled permanently and began to work as sharecroppers for urban contractors or for their sheikhs, who soon followed the example of the entrepreneurs from Aleppo and other places.

There is no question who profited most from the agricultural boom during the 1950s. Urban contractors and tribal sheikhs, cultivating up to 100,000 ha in some cases, amassed enormous wealth, whereas the vast majority of the other tribesmen, who actually worked on the fields, gained little from the new developments. This situation changed through the land reform, which started in Syria in 1958, but was delayed in most parts of the Jezira until the Ba'ath (Arab Socialist Resurrection) Party seized power in 1963. Enforcement of the land reform was intended to achieve three main aims of the Ba'ath's rural policy: to weaken the power of the party's rivals—particularly the great landlords; to build a base of peasant support; and to shape a new, more productive rural social order (Hinnebusch 1986:84). According to the Agrarian Reform Law of 1963, the maximum size of private holdings in the northeastern region was limited to 300 ha of rainfed land or 50 ha of pump-irrigated land (Hosry 1981:39). Approximately 27 percent of the rainfed land and 34 percent of the irrigated area in the three northeastern provinces was expropriated between 1958 and 1969 (Wirth 1971:456). A considerable proportion of the expropriated rainfed land in the northern Jezira was cultivated by large state farms or leased to the former agricultural entrepreneurs; the rest, including most of the irrigated land in the Euphrates valley, was redistributed to tenants, landless farmers, and farm laborers in holdings with an average size of 3 ha of irrigated land or 15 ha of rainfed

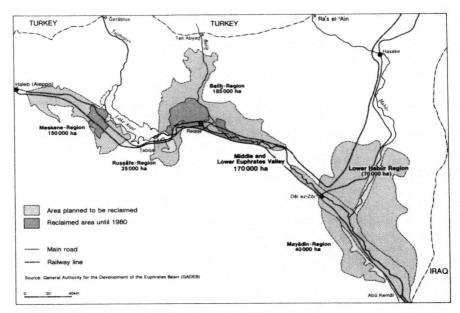

FIGURE 11.1
Reclamation Areas in Northeast Syria

land. The beneficiaries of the redistribution program were required to form state-supervised cooperatives. After the original problems had been overcome, most of the cooperatives in the Euphrates valley contributed greatly to the improvement of their members' economic situation (cf. Hinnebusch 1976:9–10). In other cases, the cooperatives failed and the former urban entrepreneurs again took over the management of irrigated agriculture (Rabo 1986:58).

The latest phase of rural development in northeast Syria began in 1968 with the implementation of the Euphrates Scheme. The first major task of this scheme was the construction of the Euphrates barrage at Tabqa. After the massive dam—4.5 km in length—had been closed in mid-1973, the waters of the Euphrates began to flood an area of about 625 km^2, thus filling the reservoir of Lake Asad. This achievement was celebrated as the most important milestone reached by the Euphrates Scheme, which had three major aims:

- reclamation of about 640,000 ha of irrigated land (cf. Figure 11.1), including some 170,000 ha of pump-irrigated land in the Middle and Lower Euphrates valley where the more efficient technology of canal irrigation was to be introduced;
- generation of electricity by a hydroelectric power station with a capacity of 800 megawatts; and

TABLE 11.1
Socioeconomic Structure of the Reservoir Population Before Resettlement

Socioeconomic Characteristics of the Heads of Households	Estimated Percentage of the Reservoir Population
Large landowners---particularly members of the sheikh families---and agricultural entrepreneurs (pump owners/contractors)	5
Small farmers, mainly cultivating 2 to 4 ha of irrigated land as:	80
-landowners	(20--24)
-sharecroppers	(28--32)
-beneficiaries of the land reform	(20--24)
-tenants of state land	(4-- 8)
Others (mainly agricultural and casual laborers and shepherds; some drivers, pump operators, mechanics, craftsmen, traders, etc.)	15

Sources: Gattinara (1973) and author's investigations.

- regulation of the Euphrates (i.e., control of floods and security from water shortage during periods of drought).

During scheme implementation, northeast Syria was affected by the vast funds being invested in the project and trickling indirectly into the regional economy, and by the restructuring of agricultural land use, the creation of new jobs, and a substantial influx of skilled and unskilled laborers from other parts of Syria. This project was also responsible for the relocation of more than 60,000 people who were forced to leave their homes and fields in the flooded Euphrates valley. What happened to these people?

Resettlement of Population from the Reservoir Area of Lake Asad

Nearly all former inhabitants of the flooded Euphrates valley are members of the Welde tribe. Of nomadic and seminomadic origin, they had settled as farmers in the reservoir area after 1949. The socioeconomic structure of the population living in the reservoir area at the beginning of the 1970s is shown in Table 11.1. The highest ranks among the economic elite were still occupied by the tribal sheikhs although their position had been considerably weakened during the previous decades. They had lost most of their political influence—with the exception of Sheikh Shawwakh Bursan, the leader of the Welde, who still represented the interests of his tribe in the Syrian parliament. The sheikh families had also suffered serious economic setbacks through the land reform. Sheikh Shawwakh Bursan, for example, had lost 250 ha of irrigated land and 1,200 ha of rainfed land, but in spite of this expropriation he remained one of the wealthiest men in the Euphrates valley, owning 50 ha of irrigated land and 600 sheep as well as 40 tractors and 10 combine harvesters, which were used for cultivating grain on rented land.

The economic situation of the sheikhs of the other 15 subfactions of the Welde tribe was similar. Although they, too, had suffered from the land reform, they still owned not only irrigated land in the Euphrates valley, which was cultivated by sharecroppers, but also rainfed fields and flocks of sheep on higher ground. Most of the agricultural entrepreneurs originated from these sheikh families or from rich merchant families in Aleppo. They organized the cultivation of cotton on rented land and provided seeds, fertilizers, motor pumps for irrigation, tractors for plowing, and 60 percent of the labor force needed for picking cotton; for these expenses they were entitled to 40 percent of the cotton crop.

The vast majority of the reservoir population was composed of small farmers who cultivated 2 to 4 ha of irrigated land on the banks of the Euphrates. Those who grew cotton on their own land relied in most cases on a supply of irrigation water through pumps belonging to agricultural entrepreneurs; this service had to be paid for by at least 10 percent of the peasant's cotton yield. Other farmers cultivated cotton as sharecroppers. They received 40 percent of the crop for performing all the fieldwork and providing 40 percent of the labor force for the cotton harvest. A third category of farmers were the so-called "beneficiaries of the land reform." They had received expropriated land, which most of them had previously cultivated as sharecroppers for the local sheikhs.

In addition to growing cotton on pump-irrigated fields, most of the farmers cultivated 5 to 25 ha of rainfed fields and reared some sheep. Through these activities—often combined with some wage-earning labor, particularly during harvest time—most of the farmers were able to secure household incomes that compared very favorably with other rural areas of Syria.

Spatial Distribution of the Reservoir-Area Population in Northeast Syria

To which areas did the inhabitants of the reservoir area move when their territory was flooded between 1973 and 1976? The Syrian authorities in Damascus and in the provincial capital of Raqqa were initially unable or unwilling to answer this question. Contacts with some members of the reservoir population, however, ultimately enabled me to locate different areas of resettlement. This was followed by a socioeconomic survey in 1979, for which 414 families were interviewed in four regions of resettlement.[1]

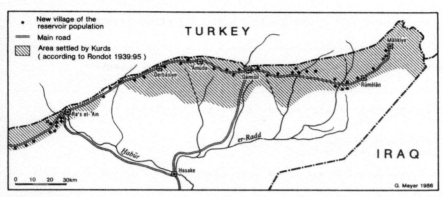

FIGURE 11.2
New Villages of the Reservoir Population Along the Turkish Border

In general, household heads were eager to answer the survey questions. Most were dissatisfied with the authorities' handling of the resettlement affair, and they were glad to meet someone interested in their situation. They freely aired their grievances, in particular about the insufficient compensation they had received for the loss of their former homes and fields. The survey revealed the following course of the resettlement process.

Originally, it was intended that the former inhabitants of the flooded area would be resettled in the newly reclaimed Pilot Project along the north bank of the Middle Euphrates valley. Here every family was promised 3.3 ha of irrigated land. After several years of preparation, however, the execution of this plan by the General Authority for the Development of the Euphrates Basin (GADEB) was stopped, only a few months before the closure of the dam. The 15 newly constructed settlements of the Pilot Project were declared to be state farms, so that the reservoir population would be able to work there only as agricultural laborers. As an alternative, the Ba'ath Party began to organize resettlement of the reservoir population in the northeastern Jezira, along the Turkish border. Here, a chain of 41 new villages was to be established in order to create an "Arabic belt" within an area of mainly Kurdish inhabitants (Figure 11.2). This policy, which took up a plan issued in 1962 (Nazdar 1978:317), was obviously aimed at preventing antigovernment Kurdish activities and any nationalistic cooperation between the Syrian, Turkish, and Iraqi Kurds in a border area with important oil resources. In this politically sensitive region, the reservoir population was offered land that had been expropriated from Kurdish landlords under the Agrarian Reform Law.

When the reservoir population was first informed of the new resettlement scheme, nearly all objected strenuously. It seemed inconceivable to them to move so far away from their familiar tribal area and settle in a region with a long history of Arab-Kurdish rivalries and hostilities. In order to find enough families prepared to migrate to the Turkish border, the Ba'ath Party

TABLE 11.2
Distribution of the Reservoir Population After Resettlement in 1979

Area of Resettlement	Percentage of Households
Official resettlement scheme along the Turkish border	33
State farms of the Pilot Project in the Middle Euphrates valley	9
Plateau along the shores of Lake Asad	54
Raqqa	3
Aleppo	0.4
Residences in the official resettlement scheme and in Raqqa	0.4
Residences in the official resettlement scheme and along the shores of Lake Asad	0.2
	100
	(N = 13,117)

Source: Author's investigations. The information was gathered by asking the resettlers included in my survey where the other households of their former village were living, and by an evaluation of the household registers on the state farms and in the new villages along the Turkish border.

conducted an intensive propaganda campaign and enlisted the support of tribal leaders.

In the end, one-third of the more than 13,000 households from the flooded Euphrates valley agreed to participate in the official resettlement scheme (Table 11.2). The others decided to move on their own to the state farms of the Pilot Project, the plateau along the shores of Lake Asad, or the provincial capitals of Raqqa and Aleppo.

As Figure 11.3 shows, there are substantial village-to-village differences in choices, and even among households of the same village the migration decisions were unanimous in only a few cases. How can these differences be explained? For many of the 61 villages the answer is clear. Reflecting the tribal origin and nomadic heritage of their inhabitants, most of these villages consisted of several small kinship settlements spread over a wide area (Ghirardelli 1985:5). In particular, the kinship groups who lived relatively far from the Euphrates normally owned rainfed land outside the flooded area. As they were not prepared to give up these fields, their obvious choice was to move up to the higher-elevations plateau and build new houses on their own land. For kinship groups with most or all of their land within

Rural Development and Migration

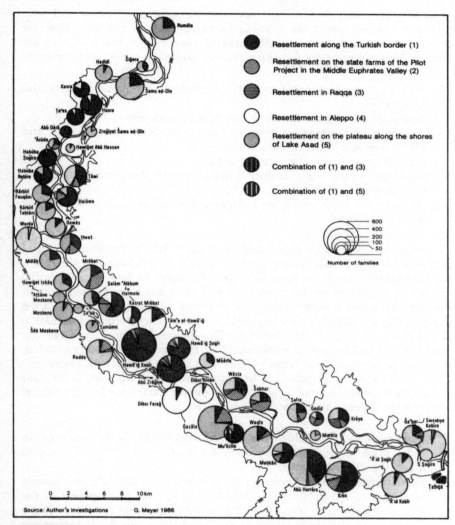

FIGURE 11.3
Resettlement of Families from Flooded Villages in the Reservoir Area

the reservoir, the choice was much more difficult. In many cases, different migration decisions were taken on a household basis, so that members of the same extended family moved to different areas of resettlement.

Factors Influencing the Choice of the Resettlement Areas

In order to determine the reasons for the different resettlement decisions of the reservoir-area population, the 414 heads of households were interviewed as to why they had chosen the respective region of resettlement and why they had rejected the other possible locations. Results indicated that the decision to migrate to the specific area of resettlement involved in most cases an evaluation of the following factors, ranked in order of importance:

- work opportunities and prospects of achieving economic security and prosperity;
- dwellings and infrastructure of the resettlement areas;
- possibility of maintaining close contacts with relatives, neighbors, and other members of one's own social group;
- familiarity with the resettlement area;
- connections with the established population in the various regions of resettlement; and
- possibility of maintaining the independence and freedom to which they were accustomed.

Several of the factors listed indicate clearly the importance of social relations, kinship networks, and nomadic values, as evidenced by the desire for independence and freedom. However, the most decisive factor was the subjective evaluation of the chances of finding suitable work conditions in the different resettlement areas. The outcome of this evaluation varied considerably and depended mainly on the individual socioeconomic situation at the place of origin in the reservoir. This becomes quite clear when we compare the socioeconomic background of the households interviewed in the different areas of resettlement. Table 11.3 shows selected socioeconomic characteristics of the populations from the reservoir area, along with their resettlement areas. Two main categories of people participated in the official resettlement scheme along the Turkish border:

- Landowners whose fields were entirely situated in the flooded area. In order to remain farmers they accepted the offer of land in the region along the Turkish border.
- Beneficiaries of the land reform who were willing to trust the propaganda campaign of the Ba'ath Party, which claimed that participation in the official resettlement scheme would be very favorable for them. These people were already indebted to the Ba'ath Party for the improvement of their economic situation in the reservoir area as a result of the redistribution of land expropriated under the Agrarian Reform Law. They were also familiar with the cooperative system they were expected to practice in the resettlement area.

The decision to live on state farms in the Pilot Project was especially favored by sharecroppers and agricultural and casual laborers. Most of them lacked the financial means to establish an independent economic basis of their own. They expected to gain permanent employment as agricultural laborers and to receive new dwellings on the state farms.

TABLE 11.3
Socioeconomic Characteristics of the Reservoir Population by Areas of Resettlement

Percentage of Households (A) and Median Size of Farms in Ha (B) Formerly Cultivated by the Households That Settled:

Socioeconomic Characteristics of the Reservoir Population	Along the Turkish Border (N = 91) (A)	(B)	On the State Farms of the Pilot Project (N = 150) (A)	(B)	Along Lake Asad (N = 69) (A)	(B)	In Raqqa (N = 94) (A)	(B)
Households that had cultivated irrigated land as:								
-landowners	35	4.0	18	3.0	25	3.2	55	12.5
-beneficiaries of the land reforms	47	3.1	29	3.2	12	3.0	7	2.5
-sharecroppers	10	3.0	41	3.2	42	3.0	8	3.1
-pump owners/contractors	6	10.0	--	--	3	7.0	13	40.0
Households that had owned or rented rainfed fields	45	14.0	66	12.5	82	35.0	41	61.5
Households that had owned more than 30 sheep	8	--	12	--	35	--	22	--
Heads of households who had worked:								
-as agricultural or casual laborers	--	--	12	--	9	--	--	--
-in other nonagricultural occupations	--	--	--	--	6	--	15	--
Heads of households								
-above 50 years of age	43	--	44	--	45	--	20	--
-illiterate	64	--	75	--	74	--	26	--

Source: Author's investigations.

The decision to resettle on the higher plateau along the banks of Lake Asad was mainly preferred by:

- farmers who cultivated rainfed fields outside the flooded areas;
- sharecroppers—often with some experience as nonagricultural casual workers—who refused to comply with the cooperative's regulations in the official resettlement scheme and who were afraid of losing their independence and freedom on the state farms; and
- owners of large flocks of sheep who wanted to continue keeping livestock.

The majority of the migrants from the flooded Euphrates valley who moved to the provincial capital of Raqqa could be divided into three main groups:

- young heads of households who expected to improve their living conditions by utilizing the income possibilities and infrastructural amenities of the urban environment—mostly literate, they wanted to offer their children better educational opportunities;
- members of the economic elite—such as owners of large irrigated areas, agricultural entrepreneurs, and owners of large flocks of sheep—who had close relationships with the provincial capital and who had sufficient financial means to establish a prosperous economic position of their own; and
- households with relatively highly qualified members who worked in nonagricultural jobs and had close personal and occupational links with Raqqa.

Socioeconomic Situation of the Reservoir Population Resettled Along the Turkish Border

Approximately 4,600 relocated households settled along the Turkish border from 1973 to 1976, the timing of their arrival corresponding mainly to the gradual rise of water in the reservoir. Many families, not believing that their houses and fields would really be inundated, delayed their exodus as long as possible. Months before the different terrace levels were flooded, army units blew up the schools and destroyed the irrigation canals to demonstrate the futility of remaining in the area. Some families stayed even after their houses had been inundated, living for a few weeks or months in tents on the higher terraces, hoping to harvest their crops on some of the more elevated fields. Other families moved first to the state farms of the Pilot Project before deciding to join the official resettlement scheme. When they finally reached the sites of their new villages, about half of them had to live in tents for up to a year before their houses were finished.

While the authorities would have liked to relocate the villagers as whole communities to minimize social tensions in the new areas, this proved organizationally too difficult. Only 9 of the 41 new settlements, with between 34 and 192 households each, are homogeneous with regard to their village of origin. In the other settlements, families from as many as seven different original villages are found. Previously accustomed to living together in small kinship groups—often separated from the neighboring group by a few hundred meters or so—their social interactions and economic cooperation had been normally limited to members of their extended families or other members of their lineage segment. In the new settlements, however, they had to live close to people with whom they often had no firm social ties. New alliances had to be formed, which proved particularly difficult between families that did not belong to the same lineage. Under these circumstances rivalries and quarrels were very common. In some villages, the different factions could not even agree about the person who should represent the interests of the inhabitants as *muchtar* to the authorities, so that every faction elected its own muchtar.

Relations with Kurdish inhabitants of neighboring villages, however, were much better than originally anticipated. No serious conflicts between the two ethnic groups were reported by either side during the first several years following resettlement.

The economic basis of the new villages is mainly rainfed agriculture with highly mechanized and mostly cooperatively organized growing of wheat and barley. In the western part of the resettlement area, where average annual precipitation is only about 300 mm, households received 30 ha of agricultural land each; one-half of this area is cultivated yearly, while the other half lies fallow (Figure 11.4). Since annual rainfall increases to about 600 mm further toward the northeast, the fallow period can be dispensed with; here, smaller plots of agricultural land were distributed to the reservoir population. In eight of these villages cotton is cultivated on pump-irrigated fields (the eight villages with "irrigated crops" on Figure 11.4). This also seems to have been planned in four other villages west of Rumélan where households received 5 ha of land each, but because no pumps were installed in these four villages until 1979, most families deserted them and resettled either on the outskirts of Raqqa or along Lake Asad.

In 1978–1979, the average annual income of the agricultural units in the new villages was £Syr 7,200 (1 Syrian pound equals approximately US $0.25), roughly equivalent to the average farm income in the flooded area of the Euphrates valley. In this respect, the Ba'ath Party's resettlement scheme has generally succeeded in providing an adequate economic basis for the participating reservoir families.

In the labor-intensive irrigated farming of the Euphrates valley, however, the possibility always existed of increasing one's income through wage labor on neighboring farms. During harvest time, men, women, and girls could contribute a considerable amount to the family income with their wages from picking cotton. Such additional sources of income hardly exist in the new villages along the Turkish border, where highly mechanized grain cultivation is dominant.

Underemployment is high in the resettlement zone, as most farmers need less than two months per year to cultivate their fields. Some of them,

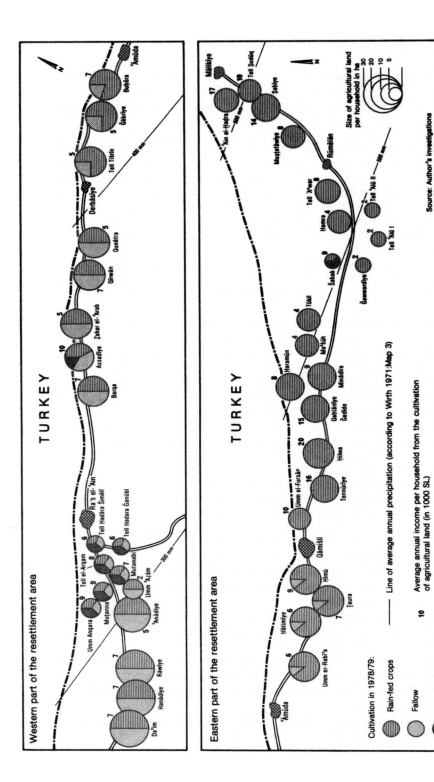

FIGURE 11.4
Size of Land, Cultivation, and Average Agricultural Income per Household in New Villages Along the Turkish Border

therefore, started to work as sharecroppers in other parts of the northeastern province of Hasake. A considerable number of families resumed their former seminomadic lifestyle: as they are allowed to keep only a few sheep in the agricultural region along the Turkish border, they spend most of the year with their flocks further south on the steppe and return to their new villages only to cultivate their fields. Other men looked for seasonal work in Raqqa, Aleppo, or Damascus. The most important source of employment outside the resettlement scheme, however, was temporary labor emigration to other Arab countries. In 1979, one-third of all resettled households had at least one member working abroad for several months of the year, mainly as casual laborers in the construction sector of Amman or in the port of Aqaba.

Resettlement of the Reservoir Population in the Middle Euphrates Valley

When the original plans to resettle the reservoir population in the Pilot Project were abandoned and the 15 settlement sites became state farms on short notice (Figure 11.5), the authorities did not bother to create a homogeneous social structure among the work force needed to run the farms. Not only people from the reservoir but also from the Middle and Lower Euphrates valley and from other parts of Syria were recruited as agricultural workers. The 260 families living in the central settlement of the state farm Rabi'a in August 1979 came from 67 different places (see Figure 11.6). Of these families, 55 percent came from villages in the reservoir area. The relationships between groups of different tribal and regional origin living close to each other in neighboring houses were sometimes so strained that even violent clashes occurred.

This was the case, for example, when a minor quarrel (over a broken tool) between a Welde from the reservoir and his neighbor, an 'Afadle from the Middle Euphrates valley, revived the traditional hostility between these tribes. (In the nineteenth century, continuing conflicts about pasture areas had culminated in a fierce tribal war during which the Welde were expelled by the 'Afadle from their former territory on the Balikh plateau.) In the particular incident on one of the state farms, other members of the Welde and 'Afadle sided with the quarreling parties. The dispute erupted into a fight that involved most members of the two opposing tribes on the state farm; it ended with the death of an 'Afadle and the intervention of the police, who arrested all Welde tribesmen.

While nearly all houses in Rabi'a, Qahtaniye, and Hittin were inhabited, between one-quarter and two-thirds of the dwellings on the five state farms east of Raqqa were empty (see Figure 11.5). On 'Adnaniye, only 10 percent of the new houses were occupied in 1979. Here, irrigation had to be stopped after breakages of the Upper Main Canal occurred because of the high gypsum content of the soil under the canal: on percolating into the ground, water had dissolved the gypsum and formed cavities under the canal, which caused the concrete lining to crack. As a result of problems of irrigation and drainage, salinity, and gypsiferous soils, only about 58 percent of the

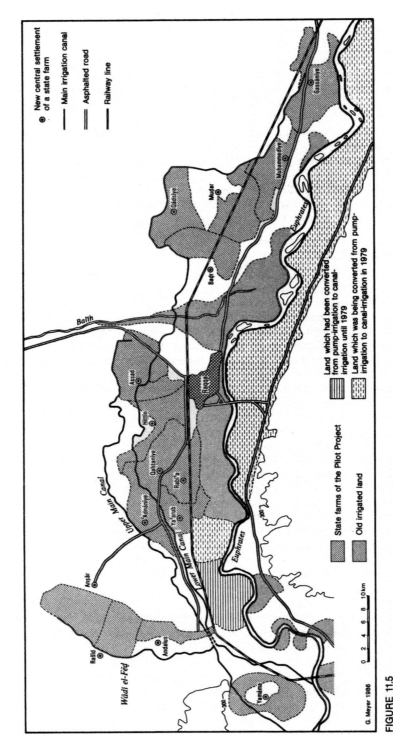

FIGURE 11.5
State Farms of the Pilot Project in the Middle Euphrates Valley

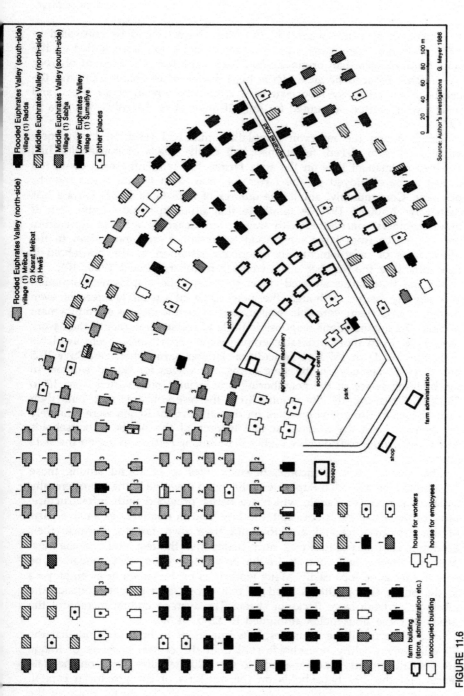

FIGURE 11.6
Origins of the Inhabitants on the State Farm Rabi'a

19,600 ha of agricultural land in the Pilot Project could be cultivated in 1977–1978; much less work was therefore available for those settled on the state-farm villages than originally had been expected. The amount of work was further reduced because of the high degree of mechanization and the emphasis on relatively labor-extensive crops like wheat, sugar beets, and maize, while cotton accounted for only 10 percent of the cultivated area in 1978.

Thus, among the reservoir population that had resettled in the new villages of Wadi el-Fed, fewer than half of the heads of households had received permanent jobs on the state farms. The remaining men could not expect to be employed on the farms for more than five to seven months per year. Consequently, about one-quarter of household heads earned less than £Syr 2,500 in 1979. A family in that situation could survive only if other members contributed with wages from seasonal work in agriculture or remittances from labor emigration to Jordan. Here—more than in the other areas of resettlement—the economic situation of the household is determined by the number of its working members (Sweet 1960:110).

On the state farms situated closer to Raqqa, the employment situation was slightly better. Although the percentage of casual laborers is even higher, most of them were able to secure seven to nine months of employment because the organizations responsible for land reclamation recruit their work force here. Even more profitable employment opportunities were available in Raqqa. While in 1979 an agricultural laborer earned between £Syr 10.5 and £Syr 12 per day on the state farms, the wages for skilled workers in the building sector of the neighboring provincial capital varied from 18 to 25 £Syr. Consequently, the families from the reservoir area who built their own houses in three new quarters on the outskirts of Raqqa were relatively prosperous. Here the average annual income of the heads of households was £Syr 5,900—considerably higher than among settlers living on the state farms.

The highest level of income, however, was to be found among those families from the flooded Euphrates valley who now live in the more centrally situated quarters of Raqqa, which are better provided with infrastructure. Most of them had sufficient capital to buy land in relatively expensive parts of the provincial capital and to build their own houses. Because their economic starting position was much better than the rest, and because most of them already had contacts in the provincial center, they tended to be able to find good jobs easily. Many worked as businessmen or as employees in the public sector. Others lived on rents from farm property outside the reservoir or from large flocks of sheep. The average annual income of the heads of these households amounted to £Syr 14,600.

In considering these examples, it is important to bear in mind that the 93 relatively wealthy households settled in the central quarters of Raqqa are a small minority in comparison to the 1,209 families living on the state farms and the 294 households on the outskirts of the provincial capital. Thus, in the Middle Euphrates valley, no more than a small group of the reservoir population was able to achieve a level of income that was the same or higher than in their former area of residence, while the vast majority of the settlers suffered a serious economic loss and a decline in their standard of living.

Resettlement Along Lake Asad

Almost 7,000 households had moved from the flooded Euphrates valley to the higher plateau along Lake Asad. About two-thirds of them lived on the southern and western sides of the reservoir where economic conditions for resettlement were much better than on the other sides, which lacked roads and other infrastructure. Most inhabitants of the flooded villages in the immediate vicinity of the barrage migrated to Tabqa. This administrative center of the Euphrates Scheme, which grew to more than 40,000 inhabitants, offered various occupational opportunities to the settlers.

Another concentration of the reservoir population is found along the main road between Aleppo and Raqqa, about 40 km west of Tabqa. Almost the total population of the flooded village Meskene and some neighboring settlements built new houses here on their former rainfed fields close to a newly reclaimed state farm.

The other new dwelling places of the reservoir population are scattered over a strip 15 km wide on both sides of Lake Asad. With the exception of a few larger villages, these settlements are in most cases small groups of houses (Seeden and Kaddour 1984:496), single farmsteads, or new quarters beside older villages.

The income of the resettled population living close to the reservoir was based mainly on sheepherding and wages from casual labor in nearby land-reclamation projects, in Syrian cities and—in most cases—in neighboring Arab countries. In addition, one out of every three households cultivated rainfed plots. In an area with an average annual precipitation between 200 and 250 mm, rainfall is often not sufficient to secure a cereal harvest. The grain fields then serve only as pasture for the sheep. The mean annual income per household was comparable to that of the settlers living on the state farms in the Middle Euphrates valley. For the majority of the male work force, the average period of employment was only three to six months every year.

Here, as in the other rural areas of resettlement, underemployment had become a major problem for the reservoir population, where it hardly existed in the flooded Euphrates valley because the combination of labor-intensive cotton cultivation, rainfed agriculture, and sheep rearing had normally provided full year-round employment. After resettlement, more and more male adults were forced to look for additional nonagricultural labor to secure their economic survival. As wages were higher abroad, the number of men leaving their families to work temporarily in other Arab countries increased dramatically. But the implementation of the Euphrates Scheme was responsible for the rise of labor emigration not only among the reservoir population: in the villages of the Middle Euphrates valley, too, the upsurge in the number of people working abroad can largely be attributed to this development scheme.

Labor Migration from the Villages in the Euphrates Valley to Other Arab States

During the 1970s, participation in international labor migration became a widespread but rather unevenly distributed phenomenon in northeast Syria. In some rural areas—particularly where labor-intensive agriculture or nearby urban centers provide sufficient work opportunities—only a few men with experience as labor emigrants are to be found. Other villages, however, largely depend on the remittances transferred home by a high proportion of the male labor force working abroad. Despite the generally accepted view that international labor migration represents one of the most important factors in the socioeconomic development of all countries in the Middle East, there have been no empirical surveys of the form and impact of labor emigration in Syria. Birks and Sinclair (1980:53), who have written extensively on contemporary international labor flows in the Arab world, state that "little is known of Syrian migration: its general outline can be sketched, but fine detail cannot be filled in."

In order to learn more about the development, structure, and consequences of this phenomenon, all former migrant laborers—and members of the families of migrants who were still abroad—were interviewed in 63 villages of the Middle Euphrates valley.[2] In addition, 21 randomly selected settlements in the Lower Euphrates valley were included in the survey. Altogether 3,079 interviews were carried out in August 1979. This was during Ramadan, when most migrants return home to celebrate the end of the fast with their families.

The Development of International Labor Migration

In the Lower Euphrates valley, labor migration to the Gulf region dates back to the late 1940s when members of a local tribe, who had settled permanently in Kuwait, invited tribesmen from their place of origin to work for them. Labor migration started a decade later in the Middle Euphrates valley and was at first directed only toward Lebanon (Figure 11.7). The outbreak of the Lebanese civil war in 1975 resulted in the redirection of the stream of migrants toward Jordan, where a booming economy and a high rate of labor emigration to Saudi Arabia had caused serious labor shortages and rising wages. After 1977 the migration flow increased dramatically, particularly from all parts of the Euphrates valley to Saudi Arabia. Between 1978, when political relations between Damascus and Baghdad improved, and the early 1980s, when Syria sided with Iran in the Gulf War, neighboring Iraq also became an employer of Syrian workers.

By August 1979, about 12 percent of the male labor force in the villages of the Middle Euphrates valley had participated in international labor migration. The highest figure was recorded in the village of Ma'adan Gedid,

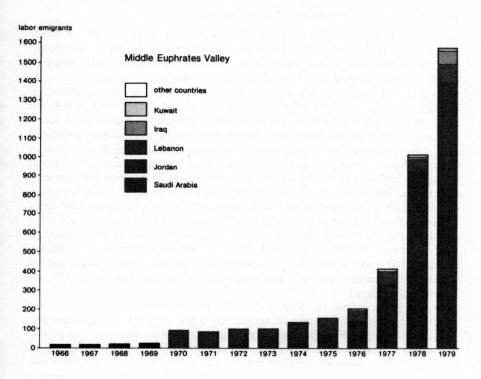
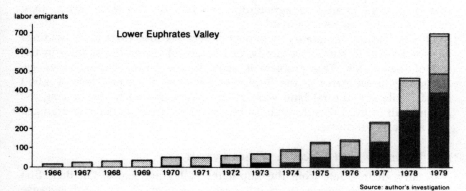

FIGURE 11.7
Development of Labor Emigration in the Middle and Lower Euphrates Valley Between 1966 and 1979

where 29 percent of the male population between 15 and 59 years of age had already worked abroad.

The Reasons for International Labor Migration

The major reason for joining the flow of migrant laborers was the much higher wage level abroad. For the same kind of work a Syrian laborer could earn twice as much in Iraq, Jordan, or Lebanon, and about eight times as much in Saudi Arabia as he would receive in his native village.

In addition to the dominant pull factor of better income opportunities abroad, the vast majority of the migrants declared that they had left for other Arab countries because they had not been able to find enough work at home. This lack of work was frequently due to agricultural problems caused by the execution of the Euphrates Scheme. In particular, the conversion from individual pump irrigation to the "more efficient system" of canal irrigation had a strong impact on the decision of numerous farmers and agricultural laborers in the Middle Euphrates valley to take up work abroad (Figure 11.8). These people had to interrupt their work in agriculture for a period of two to three years while new irrigation and drainage canals were installed and fields were leveled. As the implementation of the Euphrates Scheme began in 1977 on the left bank of the Euphrates west of Raqqa (Figure 11.5) and continued in the following year on the southern side of the river, the massive rise in labor emigration observed here since 1977 can be attributed largely to it.

A few years earlier, the implementation of this scheme had already sent a different group of migrants to search for work in neighboring countries. They were members of families who had rented state land on the higher Euphrates terraces east and west of Raqqa. When the new state farms of the Pilot Project were established here in the early 1970s, the migrants lost their pump-irrigated fields. As they were not satisfied with the low wages that they were offered as agricultural laborers on the state farms, they decided to take up work abroad.

Others became temporary migrant laborers because their farm holdings were too small to support a family, or because of increasing salinity in the soil of their fields. This problem is acute in the Lower Euphrates valley. According to estimates of the Euphrates Ministry, the equivalent of 4,000 ha of fertile agricultural land was lost in that region each year during the second half of the 1970s through salinity resulting from inadequate drainage and saline groundwater.

Age, Occupation, and Education of the Migrants

Nearly all migrants from the Euphrates valley are males. On their first trip abroad, most working in Saudi Arabia are over 25 years old, because of the difficulties involved in obtaining the necessary passport before completion of military service. Migrants aged 15 to 24 years are overrepresented in the neighboring Arab countries, which Syrians can enter on the basis of their identity cards. Before their departure, most migrants had

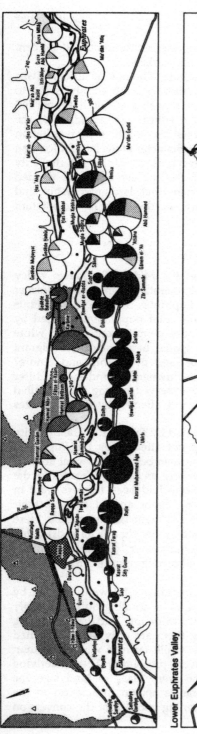
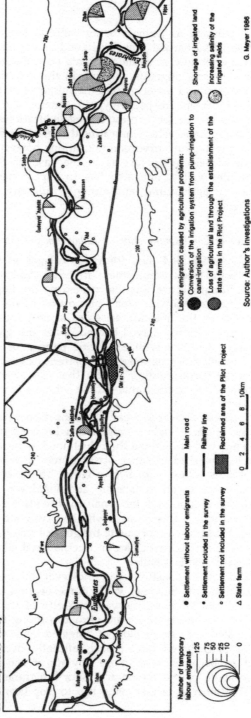

FIGURE 11.8
Extent of Temporary Labor Emigration Caused by Agricultural Problems in the Villages of the Middle and Lower Euphrates Valley

been working as farmers or agricultural laborers, while about 20 percent of them had earned their livelihood as casual workers.

Some 49 percent of the migrants were illiterate. The rate of illiteracy was higher among migrants working in the neighboring Arab countries (54 to 59 percent) and lower among the migrants in Kuwait and Saudi Arabia (40 and 43 percent, respectively). In general, the educational standard of the migrants was better than the average educational level of the male population in the Euphrates valley, indicating the selective character of the labor migration from the region surveyed. Education, however, is certainly not the only factor of selectivity. Just as in the case of the settlers from the flooded Euphrates valley, one also has to expect here that land ownership and tenure of agricultural land strongly influence the decisions of the migrant workers.

Impact of Land Ownership on Labor Emigration

Altogether, 864 men from the villages in the Middle Euphrates valley decided to seek employment in other Arab countries when their former work in agriculture was interrupted by the Euphrates Scheme. As migrants constitute a relatively small proportion of the total population affected by the project, the question arises as to why these people went abroad while the large majority stayed behind. Does the spatial behavior of the migrant workers correlate with a specific pattern of land ownership and tenure? And to what degree does their pattern of land ownership and tenure differ from the corresponding pattern that can be observed among the so-called "normal" labor emigrants—those who were not affected by the Euphrates project?

A partial answer to these questions is provided by Table 11.4. The majority of the "normal" labor emigrants, who were not affected by the Euphrates Scheme, had not gained their livelihood as farmers before they went abroad, but had worked in other occupations, especially as casual laborers in the Euphrates valley or in Syrian cities. Those who had been farmers were in most cases forced to take up additional wage labor abroad because their agricultural land was too small to provide a sufficient family income. Here we find only a few farmers who had cultivated more than 4 ha of irrigated land. Thus one can formulate the general rule that under "normal" conditions the tendency to participate in international labor migration is greater where the farm size is smaller.

Quite the opposite is true, however, for migrants who were affected by the Euphrates Scheme. With the exception of a small group of mainly agricultural laborers, the vast majority of these people had been working as farmers before they went abroad. Among them are only a few who had cultivated very small plots of irrigated land, while farmers with more than 4 ha of irrigated land are significantly overrepresented. The underlying pattern becomes even more obvious if for every class of land size the percentage of the temporary labor emigrants is shown in relation to the total number of farmers who had to stop farming because of the conversion

Rural Development and Migration

TABLE 11.4
Occupation of Temporary Labor Emigrants from the Euphrates Valley Before Going Abroad for the First Time

Occupation before the First Departure	Percentage of Labor Emigrants	
	Not Affected by the Euphrates Scheme (N = 2,215)	Affected by the Euphrates Scheme (N = 864)
Farmer (landowner, tenant, beneficiary of agrarian reform) cultivating irrigated land:	43	86
–less than 2 ha	(56)	(10)
–2 to 3.9 ha	(38)	(50)
–4 ha and more	(6)	(40)
Other occupations	57	14

Source: Author's investigations.

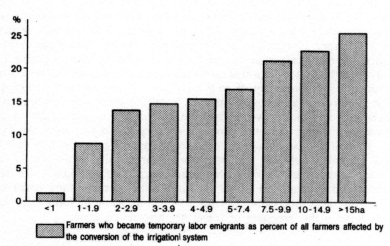

FIGURE 11.9
Rate of Participation in Labor Emigration by Size of Irrigated Area of Farmers Affected by Conversion of the Irrigation System. *Source:* Author's investigations.

of the irrigation system. As Figure 11.9 indicates, the rate of participation in international labor migration increases from only 2 percent among peasants who had cultivated less than 1 ha to about 25 percent among those who had cultivated more than 15 ha of irrigated land. Contrary to the pattern of land ownership described for "normal" labor emigrants, we are here confronted with the tendency for labor emigration to rise where the size of the formerly cultivated land is greater.

TABLE 11.5
Rate of Participation in Labor Emigration by Type of Land Tenure

Type of Land Tenure	Percentage of Farmers Who Worked Abroad (a)	Total Number of Farmers (b)
Landowners	20	1,110
Beneficiaries of the Land Reform	18	1,008
Sharecroppers	5	1,309

Sources: (a) Author's investigations; (b) Unpublished GADEB survey.

How can this discrepancy be explained? Normally farmers with larger irrigated fields are fully occupied with their agricultural work, which provides a relatively high income. Under such conditions, there is no need for them to look for work abroad. As soon as they were forced to interrupt their agricultural activities, however, they became overrepresented among the migrants, because it is easier for wealthier farmers with large plots of land to raise the money needed to travel to other Arab countries than it is for poorer peasants with tiny fields. This also explains why the rate of participation in labor emigration is much higher among landowners and the beneficiaries of the agrarian reform than among sharecroppers (Table 11.5). Members of the first two groups are in most cases in a much better economic position and can more easily afford to travel abroad than are the sharecroppers.

The pattern of land tenure and the resulting economic position of the farmers influence not only the decision of whether to participate in labor emigration but also the choice of the country of employment. As Figure 11.10 shows, the percentage of farmers going on a costly trip to Saudi Arabia increases with the growing size of farm units because it is easier for large landowners to raise the money—up to £Syr 6,000—for travel expenses and a combined Saudi visa and work permit. Many small landowners, on the other hand, can afford only to work in Jordan for lower wages because the expenses of travel are also much lower.

Migration Pattern Abroad

When they set out for the their first trip abroad, most migrants joined relatives, friends, or acquaintances who had worked before in the relevant country, were familiar with the situation there, and could help the newcomers to find a job. This kind of chain migration is a typical pattern also observed in other studies.

The cities chosen by the migrants as their place of work were in most cases the capitals of the countries of employment. In this respect Riyadh takes the lead by a wide margin, followed by Amman. The expanding Jordanian port of Aqaba also attracted a considerable number of migrants, particularly from the Middle Euphrates valley.

Rural Development and Migration

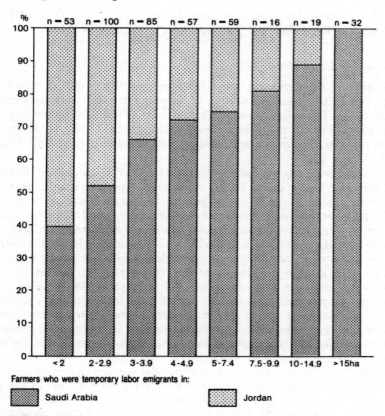

FIGURE 11.10
Temporary Labor Emigration to Saudi Arabia and Jordan by Size of Individual Farmer's Irrigated Holdings Affected by Conversion of the System. *Source:* Author's investigations.

As a consequence of the relatively low standard of occupational qualifications of the migrants, their employment opportunities abroad were limited mainly to unskilled jobs, predominantly in the construction sector, which is in general the leading sector of foreign employment in all labor-receiving countries of the Middle East (Shaw 1979:590). Fewer than 8 percent of the migrants were employed in a position higher than that of unskilled worker.

The period of work in the neighboring Arab states was in general very short, rarely lasting longer than four months. Migrants normally stayed a few months longer in Saudi Arabia because of higher travel expenses and the costs involved in obtaining a visa. Another type of migration occurs especially to Kuwait. This migration extends over a working period longer than two years and is mainly observed among populations from the Euphrates valley below Der ez-Zor, where labor migration has a very long tradition.

The flow of migrants shows considerable seasonal fluctuations, between a minimum in December and January and a maximum in June.

Economic Situation of the Returnees

Because of differences in the wage level and the length of stay in the country of employment, the savings of returning migrants vary considerably. For returnees from Kuwait or Saudi Arabia in 1978–1979, the average sum of remittances amounted to the equivalent of about US $1,600, while migrants returning from Iraq, Jordan, and Lebanon had saved on average only between US $150 and $300.

The remittances are predominantly used to cover living costs of household members and to pay debts. Of the returnees, 18 percent spent their money on building new houses, while 11 percent needed their savings to raise the bridewealth for their marriages. In this respect, the increase of labor emigration has far-reaching social consequences because the availability of large sums of cash through remittances resulted in a tremendous rise in the value of the bridewealth in the villages of the Middle Euphrates valley. From 1974 to 1979, the average amount of money to be paid to the bride's father increased from about £Syr 2,000 in 1974 to £Syr 15,000. It takes a very long time for a young man to save such a sum from his own earnings in Syria. If he does not have a chance to work in the oil-producing countries or does not have a sister who can be married off in exchange, his marriage may be delayed and his dependence on his father may continue for many years.

Productive investments to help improve the earning opportunities of the migrants in their native villages are normally regarded as one of the great economic advantages of return migration (Gmelch 1980:148–150). Such investments, however, are very rare in the Euphrates valley: fewer than 4 percent of the migrants had used their remittances for such purposes, e.g., buying agricultural machinery, livestock, or a car that could be used as a taxi, or opening a retail shop.

After returning, most migrants do the same kind of work as they did before their first stay abroad, or they remain idle until they set off on their next journey. The relatively small proportion of returnees who changed their work consisted mainly of former smallholders, who were employed as unskilled laborers in land-reclamation projects. Hardly any migrant used the occupational experience gained during employment abroad to work as a skilled laborer after his return to Syria.

The findings presented above show that the impact of international labor migration on the economic development of the villages in the Euphrates valley is limited mainly to improving the migrants' incomes and to strengthening their families' consumption power, from which regional trade enterprises and the local building sector are profiting. Only migrants who stayed in Saudi Arabia or Kuwait for several years were able to raise their standard of living significantly. For the others, who worked only a few months in Jordan, Lebanon, or Iraq because they lacked adequate work opportunities in their villages, labor emigration is a "necessary evil" just to secure economic survival. It is not surprising, therefore, that the vast majority of farmers from the villages affected by the restructuring of the irrigation system declared that they would stop working abroad as soon as they could cultivate their fields again. In most of these cases savings from labor migration covered only a minor part of the economic losses that the rural population in the Middle Euphrates valley had suffered by the interruption of their agricultural activities. But was the restructuring of the irrigation system really worth the trouble and economic disadvantage it caused? Or, to put this question into a wider context, have the tremendous funds invested in the implementation of the Euphrates Scheme really improved the economic situation of the rural population and boosted agricultural production in northeast Syria as originally planned?

The Euphrates Scheme and Prospects for Rural Development in Northeast Syria

Although it is too early for a final evaluation of the Euphrates Scheme, this ambitious and extremely costly land-reclamation and irrigation project could turn out to be a gigantic failure. The expectations of the rural population in the Middle Euphrates valley, for example, that their economic situation would be improved by the introduction of an advanced canal irrigation system were badly frustrated. The experiences from the area west of Raqqa, where the new irrigation technology had been introduced in 1979 (Figure 11.5), showed that farmers were dissatisfied with the new, centrally organized distribution of water and objected strongly to the authorities' demands for the introduction of a unified crop rotation, with small pieces of land being consolidated into larger units for efficient irrigation (Rabo 1986:36). Instead of profiting from the development project, they have to bear additional costs for repaying their share of the newly built irrigation system.

These farmers in the Middle Euphrates valley, however, have suffered much less from the implementation of the Euphrates Scheme than the families who had to leave the flooded area of Lake Asad. As outlined earlier, economic rehabilitation has not yet been achieved for about two-thirds of the settlers. These people, who were forced to sacrifice their homes and fields for the national interest of a prosperous rural economy in Syria—and who might therefore have expected to benefit first from this development—instead, in most cases, have had to face a significant deterioration of their economic position.

Concerning the contribution of the Euphrates Scheme to the improvement of the national economy, the outlook is also rather gloomy. Instead of generating about 80 percent of the country's electric power, the Tabqa power station dropped from 2,500 million to less than 1,500 million kilowatt hours per annum in 1983. In subsequent years, the turbines could work at only 30 to 40 percent of capacity, due to lack of rainfall and Turkey's increased use of the upper waters of the Euphrates (Meyer 1987:49). This problem will certainly be aggravated as soon as the vast irrigation projects that are now under construction or planned along the Euphrates in Turkey start operating (Allan 1987:30); it will also affect the newly reclaimed lands in northeast Syria. Here, only a fraction of the initial goal of completing the development of 640,000 ha of irrigated land within a 20-year period has been attained. The Five Year Plan for the period 1976–1980 targeted 240,000 ha of land to be prepared for irrigation (Manners and Sagafi-Nejad 1985:261). This goal for the first five years proved to be completely unrealistic. Mainly due to inadequate planning—leading to unexpected technical problems with gypsum subsoils in the project area—and foreign-exchange constraints, no more than approximately 70,000 ha were brought under irrigation by 1985 (IMF 1986:9).

Nor was even the newly irrigated land profitably cultivated, as optimistic cost-benefit analyses of the Euphrates Scheme had suggested (Samman 1981:337). In 1980 the agricultural revenues of GADEB, which is responsible for the cultivation of the newly reclaimed land, covered only about 45 percent of the production costs (Hannoyer 1986:34). When this disappointing result is weighed against the loss of almost 30,000 ha of profitable irrigated land in the reservoir area, the economic viability of the Euphrates Scheme becomes highly questionable.

In 1986, land reclamation continued in the Meskene region, east of Aleppo (Figure 11.1)—the only area where soils are so good that a large-scale irrigation project could be profitable. Profit is not very likely, however, along the Khabour River, where several small barrages and irrigation schemes are under construction (Hopfinger 1984:191), and in the remaining regions of the Euphrates Scheme. As only minor parts of the Russafe, Balikh, and Mayadin region were classified in a USAID study as reasonably good land for irrigation purposes, the plans for land reclamation in these areas will probably be canceled. At the same time, agricultural production in the Lower Euphrates valley continues to deteriorate because of increasing salinity.

Under such circumstances it is unlikely that agricultural production and the economic situation of the rural population will be improved. The lack of work opportunities in agriculture will mean that more and more people will be forced to look for jobs outside their villages. Most of the young unemployed men would, of course, like to work abroad, but this has become very difficult. At the beginning of the 1980s, the flow of migrants to neighboring Arab countries was interrupted by Syria's deteriorating political relations with Iraq and Jordan and the intensified military conflict in Lebanon. The number of Syrian migrants in Saudi Arabia and Kuwait has also gradually decreased because of the general reduction of foreign labor in the oil-producing countries of the Arabian Peninsula as oil revenues have declined.

It is not difficult, therefore, to forecast that the trickle of rural-urban migration to nearby provincial centers and particularly to the Syrian capital will rapidly increase and develop into the dominant stream of migration in northeast Syria. Until recently, many landless young families, agricultural laborers, sons of smallholders in the Euphrates valley, and particularly settlers along Lake Asad, had good reasons to hope for the allocation of newly reclaimed land. It was often this prospect of becoming a farmer with one's own irrigated land that prompted them to stay in their rural settlements. The hope vanished after plans to distribute newly reclaimed land in the Balikh region to 7,500 farmers (who should each receive 5.3 ha) were changed; this land is cultivated by state farms instead. Awareness is now growing among the rural population that at best the Euphrates Scheme can offer only relatively low-paid, unattractive jobs as laborers on state farms. With diminishing prospects of improving their standard of living by securing an adequate income from agriculture in their home region, more and more people opt for a life in the cities. In the past, the men worked for a few weeks or months in the cities and then returned to their villages. Now they try to find permanent jobs in the cities and settle there together with their families. The failure of the Euphrates Scheme, especially the Ba'ath Party's policy of favoring the establishment of large state farms instead of private family holdings, is unintentionally promoting rural-urban migration and thereby aggravating already-existing problems of urban expansion and congestion.

Notes

1. For details about the sampling method and further results of this survey, see Meyer 1984. The work in northeast Syria was supported by a travel grant from the German Research Foundation.
2. The author would like to thank the members of the social department of the GADEB in Raqqa as well as the director and 15 graduates from the Agricultural Institute in Raqqa for their assistance during the survey on labor emigration.

References

Allan, J. A.
  1987 Syria's Agricultural Options. *In* Politics and the Economy in Syria. J. A. Allan, ed. Pp. 22–38. London: The School of Oriental and African Studies, University of London.
Amin, Galal A., and Elizabeth Awny
  1985 International Migration of Egyptian Labour. A Review of the State of the Art. Ottowa: International Development Research Centre. Manuscript Report.
Azzam, H., and D. Shaib
  1980 The Women Left Behind: A Study of the Wives of Lebanese Migrant Workers in the Oil-Rich Countries of the Region. Beirut: ILO Regional Office for Arab States, World Employment Programme. Working Paper 3.
Birks, J. S., and C. A. Sinclair
  1980 International Migration and Development in the Arab Region. Geneva: International Labour Office.
Fahim, Hussein M.
  1975 The Nubian Settlement in Kom Ombo Region, Upper Egypt. Cairo: The American University in Cairo, Social Research Center.

Fischer, Wolfram
1984 The Economic and Sociogeographic Effects of Labor Migration in Two Villages in the Yemen Arab Republic. In Entwicklungsprozesse in der Arabischen Republik Jemen. H. Kopp and G. Schweizer, eds. Pp. 99–115. Wiesbaden: Dr. Ludwig Reichert.

Gattinara, G. C. C.
1973 Studies on Socio-cultural and Institutional Factors Affecting Resettlement of the Population from the Tabqa Reservoir and Adjacent Areas of the Euphrates River. Damascus: The Euphrates Pilot Irrigation Project.

Ged, Anne
1985 Migrations et transformations économiques et sociales en Egypte. Tiers Monde 26(103):493–506.

Ghirardelli, Gennaro
1985 Die "Hausordnung" eines Dorfes im syrischen Euphrattal. Trialog 7:5–9.

Gmelch, George
1980 Return Migration. Annual Review of Anthropology 9:135–159.

Hannoyer, Jean
1986 Grand projets hydrauliques en Syrie. Monde Arabe. Maghreb Machrek 109:24–42.

Heinritz, Günter
1977 Die Entwicklung junger Bewässerungsprojekte unter dem Einfluss gruppenspezifischen Pächterverhaltens. Ein erster Bericht über sozialgeographische Untersuchungen im Kashm el Girba-Projektgebiet/Republik Sudan. Geographische Zeitschrift 65:188–215.

Hinnebusch, R. A.
1976 Local Politics in Syria: Organization and Mobilization in Four Villages. Middle East Journal 30:1–24.

1986 Syria under the Ba'ath: Social Ideology. Policy and Practice. In Social Legislation in the Middle East. J. Salacuse and L. Michalek, eds. Pp. 61–109. Berkeley: University of California.

Hopfinger, Hans
1984 Ein neues Staudamm- und Bewässerungs-Grossprojekt am nordostsyrischen Khabour. Geographische Zeitschrift 72:189–195.

Hosry, Mohamed
1981 Sozialökonomische Auswirkungen der Agrarreform in Syrien. Sozialökonomische Schriften zur Agrarentwicklung 43. Saarbrücken: Breitenbach Publishers.

IMF (International Monetary Fund)
1986 Syrian Arab Republic—Recent Economic Developments. Washington: IMF.

Keely, C. B., and B. Saket
1984 Jordanian Migrant Workers in the Arab Region: A Case Study of Consequences for Labor Supplying Countries. Middle East Journal 38:685–698.

Lewis, Norman N.
1987 Nomads and Settlers in Syria and Jordan, 1800–1980. Cambridge: Cambridge University Press.

Manners, J. R., and T. Sagafi-Nejad
1985 Agricultural Development in Syria. *In* Agricultural Development in the Middle East. P. Beaumont and K. McLachlan, eds. Pp. 255–278. Chichester: John Wiley & Sons.

Meyer, Günter
1984 Ländliche Lebens- und Wirtschaftsformen Syriens im Wandel. Sozialgeographische Studien zur Entwicklung im bäuerlichen und nomadischen Lebensraum. Erlanger Geographische Arbeiten 16. Erlangen: Fränkische Geographische Gesellschaft.

1986 Arbeitsemigration, Binnenwanderung und Wirtschaftsentwicklung in der Arabischen Republik Jemen. Jemen-Studien 2. Wiesbaden: Dr. Ludwig Reichert.

1987 Economic Development in Syria since 1970. *In* Politics and the Economy in Syria. J. A. Allan, ed. Pp. 39–62. London: The School of Oriental and African Studies, University of London.

Nazdar, Mustafa
1978 Les Kurdes en Syrie. *In* Les Kurdes et le Kurdistan. G. Chaliand, ed. Pp. 307–319. Paris.

Rabo, Annika
1986 Change on the Euphrates. Villagers, Townsmen and Employees in Northeast Syria. Stockholm Studies in Social Anthropology 15. Stockholm: Department of Social Anthropology.

Rondot, Pierre
1939 Les Kurdes de Syrie. La France Méditerranéenne et Africaine 2:81-126.

Salem-Murdock, Muneera
1984 Nubian Farmers and Arab Herders in Irrigated Agriculture in the Sudan: From Domestic to Commodity Production. Ph.D. dissertation. Department of Anthropology, State University of New York at Binghamton.

1987 Rehabilitation Efforts and Household Production Strategies: The New Halfa Agricultural Scheme in Eastern Sudan. *In* Lands at Risk in the Third World: Local-Level Perspectives. P. D. Little, M. M Horowitz, and A. E. Nyerges, eds. Pp. 337–351. Boulder, CO: Westview Press.

Samman, Nabil
1981 Cost-Benefit Analysis of the Euphrates Dam. Water Supply and Management 5:331-338.

Schamp, Heinz
1966 Die Umsiedlung der Nubier in Oberägypten—eine sozial-geographische Studie. *In* Deutscher Geographentag Bochum 1965. Tagungsbericht und wissenschaftliche Abhandlungen. Pp. 283–291. Wiesbaden: Franz Steiner.

Seccombe, I. J.
1981 Manpower and Migration: The Effects of International Labour Migration on Agricultural Development in the East Jordan Valley. Occasional Papers Series 11. Durham: Durham University, Centre for Middle Eastern and Islamic Studies.

Seeden, H., and M. Kaddour
1984 Space, Structures and Land in Shams ed-Din Tannira on the Euphrates: An Ethnoarchaeological Perspective. *In* Land Tenure and Social Transformation in the Middle East. Tarif Khalidi, ed. Pp. 495–526. Beirut: American University of Beirut.

Shaw, R. P.
1979 Migration and Employment in the Arab World. Construction as a Key Variable. International Labour Review 118:589–605.

Singaby, T.
1985 Migrations et capitalisation de la campagne en Egypte. Revue Tiers Monde 16(103):523–532.

Sørbø, G.
1985 Tenants and Nomads in Eastern Sudan: A Study in Economic Adaptations in the New Halfa Scheme. Uppsala: Scandinavian Institute of African Studies.

Swanson, J. C.
1979 Emigration and Economic Development: The Case of the Yemen Arab Republic. Boulder, CO: Westview Press.

Sweet, L. E.
1960 Tell Togaan: A Syrian Village. Anthropological Papers. Museum of Anthropology, University of Michigan, Ann Arbor.

Wirth, Eugen
1964 Die Ackerebenen Nordostsyriens. Geographische Zeitschrift 52:7–42.

1971 Syrien. Eine Geographische Landeskunde. Wissenschaftliche Länderkunden 4/5. Darmstadt: Wissenschaftliche Buchgesellschaft.

12

Doing Development Anthropology: Personal Experience in the Yemen Arab Republic

Charles F. Swagman

Over the past three decades social scientists have become increasingly involved in undertakings of Western economic powers to promote socioeconomic development in the Third World. The initial efforts at development, or modernization as it was called in the 1950s, were organized in a large-scale format typified by such programs as Point Four. After that, development assistance tended to be scaled down and channeled through multilateral agencies such as the United Nations Development Programme and the World Bank, and through bilateral agreements between host-country governments and donor agencies such as the United States Agency for International Development (USAID), the German Agency for Technical Cooperation (GTZ), and the Netherlands Directorate General for International Technical Cooperation (DGIS). More recently, significant development assistance has been provided through increasing numbers of such nongovernmental organizations (NGOs) as the Save the Children Foundation, OXFAM, Catholic Relief Services, and World Vision.

The importance of making development projects relevant to the needs of the people and increasing local participation in them has been generally recognized by planners and administrators, particularly in the light of the many failures incurred during the fifties and sixties (Paddock and Paddock 1976). The more recent quest for appropriateness in development activities has stimulated an increased interest in the input of anthropologists and other social scientists (Hoben 1982:349), often, however, without a clear understanding of what they have to offer. Consequently, the social scientist involved in development activities frequently faces the situation where roles and expectations are not clearly defined or, in some instances, are actually in conflict with the aims and purposes of development management (Foster 1973:233–245).

An extensive corpus of literature analyzes the roles of the more academically oriented anthropologist, the processes and procedures of doing field work, and the problems often encountered (see Rabinow 1977; Wax 1971). In the more applied dimensions, however, there is as yet little literature that explores "how to do it" or "what to expect." In contrast to the independence of the academic researcher, the development anthropologist works in a context that necessitates compromise and coordination with other experts and managers who often have different agendas. Anthropologists hired to participate in development programs are also only too often left to their own devices, given little support, and simultaneously expected to come up with significant, relevant, and timely contributions. This chapter is a personal account of efforts to conduct development anthropology in the Yemen Arab Republic. The themes I address are role expectations, conflicts, and problems in performance that I encountered and that may be typical. To place the overall discussion in context, it is useful to review briefly the development situation in Yemen.

Development in Yemen: An Overview

The Yemeni revolution of September 1962, which ended the thousand-year rule of the Zaydi Imams, was a major historical turning point that terminated over a half century of isolationism. In the decade prior to the revolution, there was only limited movement towards modernization. The economic and social disruption of the civil war that followed the revolution further delayed serious efforts at development until the 1970s, when Yemen launched on a course of rapid change. In 1972 Yemen resumed diplomatic ties with the United States and the other Western countries, which had been suspended following the 1967 Arab/Israeli war. This move opened the gates for development and technical assistance that began flooding into every sector of the Yemeni economy, quickly stretching Yemen's limited capacity to absorb it.

Before the revolution and the development efforts of the past decade, Yemen was near the top of the list of least developed countries in virtually every sector of its economy. Its low level of development was primarily a problem of weak state institutions and infrastructure compounded by a shortage of productive investment opportunities. Formation of the Central Planning Organization (CPO) under the office of the prime minister led, in 1973, to the formulation of Yemen's first three-year national development plan, which emphasized the need for building infrastructure. In 1977 the first five-year plan continued the earlier plan. Development during the 1970s concentrated on strengthening the major ministries and developing such basic infrastructure as national highways, air and sea port facilities, communications, and electrification of major cities and towns. Government-sponsored development was almost entirely from "above."

During this period of national institution building, local development associations (LDAs) emerged as an expression of the need for community development. These self-help associations grew out of a recognition by rural people that the central government did not have enough resources to provide adequate services to remote areas. The central government, recognizing the popularity of these movements, granted a legal basis for their operation and allowed local resources to be used for local development. The LDAs are now entitled to use approximately 75 percent of the religious agricultural tax (*zakat*) for local development projects, and they also receive income from a cinema tax, local transport duties, and other miscellaneous taxes. In their first decade of operation the LDAs have been quite successful as vehicles for local development, building on traditional forms of cooperation, many of which are sanctioned in religious practice.

In response to the central government's priorities and requests for technical assistance, NGOs and foreign government agencies began a fierce competition for sectors in which to create development projects. The projects that were identified in the mid-seventies reached their implementation stages toward the end of the decade. The majority required participation of the local development associations, and thus provided many opportunities for applied social science research. Because Yemen's needs extended into every sector, and sociocultural knowledge of the society was lacking, many development programs sought participation by anthropologists.

The Economy

Agriculture, the principal productive sector in the Yemeni economy prior to the revolution, continues to account for 70 percent of employment today. Almost 90 percent of this production is in cereals, grown mostly for local consumption. Approximately 62 percent of the cultivated land is rainfed. Located on the northern fringe of the Indian Ocean monsoon system, Yemeni agriculture is quite vulnerable to the variable spring and summer rains (Revri 1983:14). Given the rugged, mountainous terrain of highland Yemen, most agriculture is labor intensive, and nearly half the cultivated land is in the form of terraced plots that are not amenable to mechanization and require constant care and maintenance (Swagman 1985:42). Most of rural Yemen is still a near-subsistence-level farming economy, but significant change is beginning to take hold.

The gross domestic product, which in 1960 was virtually nonexistent, rose in a little more than one decade to around $3.2 billion (World Bank 1984:222) with a 1982 per capita income of 500 dollars (YARG 1984). Because of recent wage-labor emigration to the oil-producing countries, involving up to 20 percent of the population, the individual Yemeni enjoys a relatively high standard of living (Swanson 1979:55). In fact, Yemen has recently been characterized as a "capital surplus, labor short" economy (Cohen and Lewis 1979), and the labor supply committed to the traditional agricultural base has been severely reduced. The most significant changes are in the growth of the retail and service sectors of the economy. Tied to the regional oil economy, this country of 7.25 million people has experienced a new prosperity over the last decade.

The People

In Yemen's culturally diverse society, the urban population is rapidly expanding, but over 90 percent still live in small-to-midsize villages. With over 70 percent of the total population making a living through agriculture, Yemen is a rural, peasant society. In rural Yemen, particularly in the northern and central highland areas where I conducted research, social organization is a blend of civil administration and a more traditional tribal form (Adra 1982; Dresch 1984; Gerholm 1977). Within the traditional system, local leadership is vested in the office of the tribal shaykh, whose principal duties are to represent the tribe in intertribal affairs and to settle disputes. Other local leadership offices include the village headman (*'aql*) and the community secretary (*amin*), who assists in the assessment and collection of the Islamic agricultural taxes (*zakat*). The elective offices of LDAs have become important new positions of leadership and in some instances have rivaled the importance of the lesser shaykhs.

Religious sectarian divisions also are salient features of the local sociopolitical order. In Yemen roughly half the population, residing primarily in the northern part of the country, are Shi'a, and the other half are Sunni who adhere to the Shafi'i legal school. Most of the Shi'a are followers of Zaydism, while there is a small enclave of Ismai'li Shi'a in the central part of the country near the town of Manakha in Haraz. Although recent political problems are often couched in terms of sectarian conflict, religious divisions, very prominent during the days of the Imam, are diminishing in importance today.

Doing Development Anthropology: Contrasting Experiences

The need for help in implementing the large number of development programs in Yemen gave rise to a demand for persons with a knowledge of the language and customs. With two years of experience living and working in rural Yemen while doing my doctoral research, I had very marketable skills and was recruited on a variety of contracts, including working as field officer on a German-government-financed afforestation project, and working with the Netherlands government on a health-care development project. Each project presented a different set of role expectations and experiences.

The Haraz Afforestation Project

Haraz is a rugged mountainous region in the central highlands about 50 kilometers due west of the capital city, Sana'a. The principal crops are sorghum, coffee, and *qat* (*Catha edulis* Forsk).[1] Virtually all of the agriculture in this region is carried out on terraced mountain slopes, which during the monsoon are subject daily to the scouring effects of heavy rains and thunderstorms. The steepness of the mountain slopes and absence of tree coverage promotes runoffs that destroy the ancient terraces. Abandoned terraces are usually at the greatest distance from the settlements and are often the uppermost terraces in the system. As the abandoned upper terraces disintegrate they collapse onto the lower, still productive terraces. High emigration and the correlated inflation of local wages have raised the costs of maintaining and rebuilding the terraces beyond the means of the average farmer. The result is a steadily growing erosion problem that is compounded by overexploitation of the few existing trees for cooking fuel. Furthermore, the availability of inexpensive imported wheat has reduced the incentive to keep the marginally productive terraces under sorghum production.

The Haraz Afforestation Project was designed and funded by the Federal Republic of Germany (GTZ) to control erosion in the region by promoting the planting of trees on abandoned terraces. The project entailed the construction of a nursery and an extension program. Its secondary objective was to develop a local fuelwood industry to stem deforestation and to meet the increasing demand for cooking fuel and building timber. In an attempt to employ appropriate technology, the project was to utilize only indigenous varieties.

As the first person hired to work in the rural areas, I was asked to conduct an attitude survey and assessment of the local farmers' willingness to participate in the scheme, to determine the type of trees the farmers would be willing to plant, and to evaluate local market conditions as well as household demands for building timber and fuelwood. The project management designed a basic questionnaire that I administered to local leaders in a random sample of villages in the region. In the course of conducting the surveys, I was also placed in the role of a field officer and had to explain the purposes of the project to the local community leaders. It became quickly apparent that the local community was unaware of the need for erosion control. The survey results indicated that there was some interest in planting the marginal, abandoned lands, but the overwhelming interest was in planting fruit, nut, or exotic redwoods. When the plans to propagate local species were explained, interest diminished. The project was even less attractive to the tribesmen because there would be a five- or six-year wait before the trees could be pollarded, with a harvest only every couple of years thenceforth. The villagers felt that if they were going to make the effort to plant and care for the trees, they wanted a yearly return that could be marketed widely.

A second important finding was that serious sociocultural barriers would impede the development of a new commercial fuelwood industry among the tribesmen. Firewood collection was predominantly carried out by the women, or commercially by people of lower status. Although there has been considerable movement toward a more egalitarian society since the revolution, social status nevertheless continues to be differentiated sharply in Yemeni society. A good deal of social and economic behavior is still regimented according to a caste-like system (Gerholm 1977; Stevenson 1985). The *sayyids*, direct descendants of the prophet, who traditionally were among the learned elite and often formed part of the Imam's administrative corps, form the highest rank, even though the revolution reduced their political importance. Slightly lower are the *qadis*, learned men who have either achieved or inherited the status. Like the sayyids, they mark their standing through special dress and are shown a good deal of deference by the common people. Parallel with the qadis are the *shaykhs*, or tribal leaders. The bulk of Yemeni society consists of the *qabilis*, or tribesmen, who trace their ancestry back to one of the ancient families of Yemen and who reckon their descent ultimately from Qahtan, the putative ancestor of all south Arabian peoples. Below the tribes are those without tribal ancestry, who often make their living in the marketplace as traders, craftsmen, or service renderers. Finally, the lowest levels of the hierarchy include the more disenfranchised descendants of former state servants and slaves. Firewood collection is predominantly low status and is seen as an activity beneath the tribal farmers. Thus, a fuelwood "industry" would have little appeal to the local tribesmen and, for social reasons, would not be readily accepted.

Given the original intent of the program, that is, erosion control, I recommended that the project provide a variety of the trees that were ranked high on the farmers' list (fruits, nuts, and redwoods) while at the same time encouraging the planting of the indigenous acacias, rosewoods, and other hardwoods.[2] This would demonstrate that the project was responsive to the priorities of the community, rather than fixedly intent on implementing the goals of a group of outsiders—in this case, foresters in Germany. These reports were read by the administration and the project planners in Bonn, but the recommendations were not at that time implemented. In 1986, four years after the inception of the project, however, it was modified to take into account local demands for alternative species of trees. Changes similar to the ones I originally recommended were implemented, without reference to my earlier work.

This example illustrates the important problem of how to get development planners, especially those in home offices, to revise plans once they are finalized. My original recommendations may have been ignored because the anthropologist is not recognized as having qualifications or expertise in the specific technical field. For example, because I was neither a forester nor a nurseryman I was not considered to have substantive expertise. Further, the recommendations required a fundamental shift in the original plan (away from a purely fuelwood industry and toward a mixed fruit and fuelwood program), which in turn would have required negotiations between the project and the Yemeni Ministry of Agriculture. At this stage, projects have an unfortunate tendency to be cast in iron. As Cohen has pointed out, when program policymakers and planners encounter contract research that runs against their expectations, they commonly dismiss the results (1984:145).

While the success of this research is questionable from the perspective of development anthropology, given that no attempts were made to modify the program, it was nevertheless considered successful by the project management. Within approximately three months I was able to implement and analyze an applied survey and present a series of reports that were accepted by the project management and taken to Bonn as evidence that the project was progressing.

As a development anthropologist contracted to conduct field research, I had few problems in fulfilling the role of the researcher because the expectations of the project managers were clear and unambiguous. They wanted a field survey based on a set of questions of importance to the technical experts and project management. As an anthropologist/field officer, my task was simply to carry out the research and prepare a timely report of the findings. That the results were unfortunately not in line with the original project design did not have any negative bearing on my performance.

The Dhamar Governorate Health Services Program

In contrast to my straightforward role as a field officer with the Haraz Afforestation Project are my experiences with the Dhamar Governorate Health Services Program, a very large health-care development project financed by the Netherlands Directorate General for International Technical Cooperation (DGIS), which included the construction and operation of a 125-bed hospital and a mandate to improve rural health facilities.

The Dhamar governorate, a mountainous area in the central and west central portions of the country, was one of the last regions to receive substantial development assistance. The main health facilities in the rural districts consisted of a large but understaffed health center at the district center, Dawran; a second health center built by the local development association in Madinit ish-Shirq; and about a half-dozen dispensaries and subcenters. The objective of the basic health-services segment of the program was to upgrade the services in the existing facilities by improving logistics, management, and quality of care, and by establishing preventive and mother-and-child health-care services. Additionally, the program was supposed to integrate with the national primary health-care program to establish a network of primary units in the remoter areas. The overall plan was to build up a hierarchical referral health-care delivery system in which simple problems would be treated in the villages while more complex problems would be referred to the appropriate higher level. The primary health-care program was designed to use local talent and local resources for its development.

The designers of the Dhamar Governorate Health Services Program recognized a need for some kind of social scientist, but from the beginning their expectations were vague, and they did not really differentiate or articulate the specific work required. In their advertisement for the position, they recruited for a person with at least a master's level degree in either sociology, public health, or anthropology, and experience in the Middle East. The advertisement was for someone to fill the vague role of "social researcher." This early ambiguity was an important source of the role conflict I later encountered. The practitioners of each social science discipline have different sets of theoretical and methodological assumptions that influence the kind of research conducted and that are not readily interchangeable. The main problems in implementing research for the Dhamar program were setting the agenda, the methodology, and the overall orientation.

The Research Agenda. The first priority was to set the research agenda and identify the range of topics for investigation. The initial requirements of the project management were simple, yet problematic. The research was to be conducted for the public health department and to be "project oriented," that is, directly relevant to the overall objective of developing a rural health-care system. As an anthropologist interested in social change and medicine, I had no conflict with the overall project goals. Unfortunately, the public health department was not organized and was without the service of the public health medical officer who was to set the research priorities, so topical issues were not defined by the appropriate expert. My role as the social researcher had to be defined after I was hired, for no research agenda had been set by the project. Who was to determine what research should be done and how it should be carried out? And to whom should the research be addressed? The questions needed to be worked out.

To resolve the issue I sought the advice of a senior medical anthropologist from the Royal Tropical Institute in Amsterdam, and developed a plan for an applied research program. The expatriate public health staff who were to work in the rural areas would need information on the basic mode of social organization, the structure of the rural administration, the kinds of health facilities that existed, and basic folk concepts about health and illness. Therefore, these were the topics initially selected as research foci. Folk beliefs were especially of interest because the project was to train local primary health-care workers to address the most common health problems. The research could identify common misconceptions about the causes and treatment of illnesses that could be given special attention in the training.

This research agenda, however, was met with indifference by the technical experts and some opposition by management. Medical anthropology as a subdiscipline has focused a good deal of attention on the need to understand traditional belief systems and their effects on specific medical problems that Western-trained doctors often encounter. Problems such as presentation of culturally specific symptoms or failure of the patient to comply with the prescribed medical treatment have been dominant issues in the field. Most of this type of research, however, is more theoretical than applied and is tied to semantic and symbolic analysis (see Good and Good 1982). Research on belief systems was of limited interest in the Dhamar program because most of the expatriate doctors and medical personnel lacked the language capability or cultural training to understand the symptoms that are described in self-presentation. In Dhamar, physicians and nurses rarely had time in the crowded and chaotic outpatient departments to take detailed case histories or delve into mysterious problems. Most often they simply ignored strange presentations of symptoms, and treated patients on the basis of observable indications or tests rather than on personal accounts. Consequently, since they felt no pressing need to know about local beliefs, they felt that such research, albeit perhaps theoretically interesting, was a waste of time in the context of implementing a development program. Furthermore, this kind of data was also considered a waste of money and resources by the Yemeni counterparts who would have preferred that another doctor or nurse be hired instead of the social scientist. As a research priority, these studies were quickly relegated to the back burner, and the original research agenda was discarded.

Methodological Conflicts. Anthropologists have a basic methodology that stresses participant observation and intensive fieldwork. The manager of this program had some training in public health and sociology, disciplines that emphasize survey research and statistical analysis of macro-level data. He argued that I should hire a staff of field workers to do basic data collection as well as make use of existing data. Unfortunately, there were no reliable statistics in the country to analyze and no budget to hire field staff. He assumed that Yemen would be the same as other less developed countries where he had worked, and that it was a simple matter to go to the university and recruit a cadre of students eager to work for symbolic wages. I found one student near graduation with a bachelor's degree in sociology from Sana'a University who wanted $20,000 a year, insurance, housing, and transportation. Needless to say, this not entirely unreasonable request was impossible to grant. As a consequence of different social science orientations, the manager continued to oppose field-based research, however, creating a serious role conflict and something of a catch-22 situation. Without the financial resources to conduct survey research, and without support for a field-based study, I had to chart a third course that was farther removed from traditional applied anthropology.

Research Orientation: Action vs. Applied. A third complicating factor was the distinction between "applied" and "action-oriented" research. Project management insisted that the research be "action oriented," while the original research agenda worked out in conjunction with consultants from the Netherlands was to yield results that could be applied to the project objectives. The stage was set for a confrontation over which orientation the research should follow. At the real root of the issue was who would control the project, the planners in Holland or the field management, and because the social research agenda had to be defined in the field, it became the battleground. The conflict was played out over the distinction between applied and action research, which was not clearly understood by either the planners or management. In fact, the distinction is often murky and the terms are commonly used loosely (Rubinstein 1986), particularly by those outside the discipline. While both types of research stress relevance to the needs of the people or institution studied, the action approach sees a more active role of the anthropologist in implementing the goals of the project (Rubinstein 1986:271; Tax 1975:515). In contrast to popular misconceptions, however, "action" anthropology is research oriented and concerned with the theoretical as well as the practical (Tax 1975:514).

"Action" research in the Dhamar program translated into direct work in the implementation of the program as a field officer—visiting villages, speaking with local leaders, raising interest and participation in the primary health-care project, selecting villages and candidates for training, discussing financing agreements, obtaining building sites, and the like. Research was secondary to "action." During the course of visits to site villages, some ethnographic research was possible, but primarily as an aside. My occasional attempts at applied research on issues that were germane to the program but of wider academic significance, such as research on socioeconomic barriers to efficient utilization of health-care facilities, were construed as attempts to use the project for my "personal" academic aims.

The latter point is of particular significance to development social scientists because it reflects a fundamental difference between the role expectations of researchers versus those of technical experts and management. In a discussion of the problems frequently encountered in applied research, Foster has commented that

> [an] important difference in the two fields has to do with ego gratification. . . . Each looks for basic satisfaction in the esteem in which he is held by his disciplinary or professional colleagues, according to the standards set by each field. . . . The anthropologist must feel that a reasonable part of his field research will become available to his profession and be read by his colleagues. He needs the approbation of other anthropologists, their recognition that he is contributing to the field, if he is to be a first-class anthropologist. It is not enough to have the satisfaction of knowing that his administrative superior is pleased with his work. The administrator achieves distinction by success in reaching the goals of his organization; the anthropologist achieves distinction by a creditable list of scientifically sound publications (Foster 1973:235–236, 239).

While the project management and planners further their careers by successfully implementing development projects, peer review and recognition of contributions to the general field is the important reward for professional anthropologists, even those engaged in international development (Rubinstein 1986:275). Of course, the development anthropologist may contract to conduct research without the secondary goal of producing a published research finding, as I did with the Haraz Afforestation Project. In that case there were no unmet expectations on the part of either the project management or the researcher. The problem becomes acute, however, when long-term commitment is undertaken with the explicit purpose of doing work that is at once of direct importance to the project and leads to professional advancement. Limiting the "research" activities to the direct action of advocate (Jacobs 1974:209–210) or field officer left serious expectations unmet.

In the Dhamar Health Services Project, I did demographic research to plan for primary health care, evaluated the existing primary health-care program in Yemen, drafted guidelines for selecting workers and unit locations, and mediated between people and the project, explaining the purposes of primary health care and enlisting local participation. I find it difficult to assess, however, whether these practical accomplishments constitute a successful instance of development anthropology. They were definite contributions to the Dhamar Program but did not result in a set of findings for academic analysis. In using the criteria of success recognized by technical experts and managers, the social research section successfully met its objective. From the perspective of a professional anthropologist, however, the action research orientation did not lead to results useful for professional advancement. Ironically, ethnographic studies were precisely the end products that the planners in Holland expected, and their absence raised questions about what the research section had done over the two-year period.

Lessons Learned: Role Expectations and Realities

My experiences lead me to conclude that reducing role conflicts and matching expectations with performance are the most important problems to overcome in order to function effectively as a development anthropologist. Doing development anthropology is best when the roles and expectations, which are the responsibility of the project designers and managers as well as the social scientists, are clearly spelled out from the beginning. A project that focuses on action rather than applied research can minimize role conflict and unmet expectations by stating the general nature of the agenda, methodology, and research orientation from the outset. The Haraz project was such a situation, and the research objectives were met to the mutual satisfaction of the management and the researcher. In contrast, the Dhamar experience resulted in low levels of satisfaction due to conflicting interests and a low level of collegiality. When I completed my contract and left the Dhamar program I emphasized the point that the research position was in reality that of a field officer. My replacement was recruited on that basis.

From my experiences with the Haraz Afforestation Project and the Dhamar Governorate Health Services Program, it is apparent that the development anthropologist should combine or supplement his or her anthropological training with technical training to the point at which competence becomes recognized. Combinations such as nursing and anthropology, public health and anthropology, management and anthropology, or any other professional training or experience in combination with the special training in anthropology are useful for doing the work of development, reducing role conflicts, and matching expectations with actual performance.

Notes

1. The leaves of the qat plant are chewed by the Yemeni for their mild stimulant effect and form a large part of Yemeni social life. It is a highly lucrative crop, with over ten times the profit margin of coffee (Revri 1983).

2. Among the most common trees used for firewood and building and slated for propagation were *talh* (*Acacia negra*), *tannib* (*Cordia abyssinica*), and *sidr* (*Ziziphus spina-christi*).

References

Adra, Najwa
1982 Qabayla: The Tribal Concept in the Central Highlands of the Yemen Arab Republic. Unpublished Ph.D. dissertation. Temple University.

Cohen, John, and David Lewis
1979 Capital Surplus–Labor Short Economies: Yemen as a Challenge to Rural Development Strategies. American Journal of Agricultural Economics 61(3):523–528.

Cohen, Ronald
1984 Approaches to Applied Anthropology. Communication and Cognition 17(2/3):135–162.

Dresch, Paul
1984 The Position of Shaykhs among the Northern Tribes of Yemen. Man 19:31–49.

Foster, George
1973 Traditional Societies and Technological Change. New York, NY: Harper and Row.

Gerholm, Thomas
1977 Market, Mosque and Mufraj: Social Inequality in a Yemeni Town. Stockholm Studies in Social Anthropology, No. 5. Stockholm University.

Good, B., and M. Good
1982 Toward a Meaning-Centered Analysis of Popular Illness Categories: "Fright Illness" and "Heart Distress" in Iran. In Cultural Conceptions of Mental Health Therapy. A. J. Marsella and G. M. White, eds. Pp. 141–166. Dordrecht, Holland: D. Reidel Publishing Company.

Hoben, Allan
1982 Anthropologists and Development. Annual Review of Anthropology (11):349–375.

Jacobs, S.
1974 Action and Advocacy Anthropology. Human Organization 33:209–215.

Paddock, J., and E. Paddock
1976 We Don't Know How. Ames, IA: Iowa State University Press.

Rabinow, Paul
1977 Reflections on Field Work in Morocco. Berkeley, CA: University of California Press.

Revri, Raman
1983 *Catha Edulis* Forsk: Geographical Dispersal, Botanical, Ecological and Agronomical Aspects with Special Reference to the Yemen Arab Republic. Göttingen:Institut für Pflanzenbau und Tierhygiene in den Tropen und Subtropen der Universität Göttingen.

Rubinstein, Robert A.
1986 Reflections on Action Anthropology: Some Development Dynamics of an Anthropological Tradition. Human Organization 45(3):270–279.

Stevenson, Thomas B.
  1985 Social Change in a Yemeni Highlands Town. Salt Lake City, UT: University of Utah Press.

Swagman, Charles F.
  1985 Social Organization and Local Development in the Western Central Highlands of the Yemen Arab Republic. Unpublished Ph.D. dissertation, University of California, Los Angeles.

Swanson, Jon
  1979 Emigration and Economic Development: The Case of the Yemen Arab Republic. Boulder, CO: Westview Press.

Tax, Sol
  1975 Action Anthropology. Current Anthropology 16(4):514–517.

Wax, Rosalie
  1971 Doing Field Work: Warnings and Advice. Chicago, IL: University of Chicago Press.

World Bank
  1984 World Development Report. New York, NY: Oxford University Press, published for the World Bank.

YARG (Yemen Arab Republic Government)
  1984 Statistical Yearbook. Sana'a: Central Planning Organization.

13

Land Use and Agricultural Development in the Yemen Arab Republic

Daniel Martin Varisco

The Yemen Arab Republic (YAR), or North Yemen, has received donor financial and technical assistance since the early 1970s in order to modernize its agricultural sector. Consultants in a steady stream have reiterated the litany of obstacles to development in the YAR: lack of trained manpower, a largely illiterate and uneducated population, insufficient revenues, and a poorly developed infrastructure of roads and basic services (see Hogan et al. 1982; Varisco et al. 1984; World Bank 1979). Given the range of obstacles, it is difficult to designate any one factor as most important in the persistence of underdevelopment. The majority of planners, whether from donor agencies or from the government, tend to view the problem strictly in economic and technological terms; yet in sifting through reports generated by development efforts, it becomes clear that the most fundamental link in the production system—the farmer—has been ignored. One searches in vain for an understanding of the Yemeni farmer in his or her context, a context that is not adequately framed by economic statistics of dubious value or unsubstantiated generalizations about how traditional farmers behave.

In the development process in Yemen, the anthropologist has an important role to play in bringing the farmers and their social context into focus, because it is only by extended field study in farming communities that the data can be provided for analysis of those social factors that hinder or facilitate change in agricultural production. In the last decade, a number of anthropologists have conducted fieldwork among Yemeni farmers. As these studies are now appearing in print, their results can be applied to development planning. At the very least, anthropologists can correct the simplistic and misleading characterizations of Yemeni farmers that are so common in the ever-burgeoning corpus of development reports.

In this study, I focus on an issue over which there is general confusion in the literature on Yemen, specifically, variations in land use and how these affect the introduction of change in the agricultural sector. This discussion demonstrates the positive role that an anthropologist can play in both the planning and implementation of agricultural development projects. I draw on the results of recent ethnographic fieldwork, relevant research reports, and the nationwide agricultural census of the Ministry of Agriculture and Fisheries (MAF 1983). My own field experience among farmers in an irrigated valley of the central highlands (Varisco 1982) is supplemented by subsequent consulting experience with the USAID mission in Yemen over a period of five years. A brief introduction to the Yemeni development context will preface the discussion of land use and the role of the anthropologist in development initiatives.

The Yemeni Development Context

The YAR came into existence in 1962 with a military coup that toppled the centuries-old Islamic imamate of the Zaydis. The imam, who ruled as a temporal and spiritual leader, coexisted with several major tribal confederations that retained virtually full autonomy in their respective territories. The vast majority of the population living in the central and northern highlands consists of tribal farmers, while a landlord-peasant relationship evolved in the south and along the coast. A sometimes heavily taxed mode of subsistence production predominated, although a few cash crops have periodically been important. For example, Yemen was at one time the world's major producer of coffee. The country has virtually no agricultural exports today, the main cash crop, *qat (Catha edulis)*, being cultivated almost exclusively for local use.

Few Westerners were allowed to penetrate into the Yemeni highlands in the days of the imamate. Even today the setting invokes images of medieval Arab culture, of quaint architecture and rhino-horn daggers. Beneath the superficial stereotype, however, the modern Yemeni is experiencing rapid social and economic change (Varisco and Adra 1984). The strictures of social status, previously reinforced by virtually complete class rigidity, have largely eroded. For example, several types of service providers have gained in status through the democracy instituted by the revolution. These include the traditional ritual experts (barbers, praise-singers, musicians) as well as those who worked in the market (butchers, vegetable sellers). And while the tribes remain politically significant, the former religious elite has lost the automatic prestige afforded it in the past. To a great extent, the traditional categories no longer structure the social order in modern Yemen.

The pace of change in the YAR has paralleled the oil boom on the Arabian Peninsula, because at least one-third of the male labor force works abroad, mostly in Saudi Arabia and the Gulf states. Worker's remittances have fueled the Yemeni economy, which peaked at $1.4 billion in 1978 and continued at about $1 billion per year in official estimates into the early 1980s. The remittances alone accounted for close to one-third of the YAR's 1981 gross national product of $3.8 billion. This flow of cash into the economy, primarily outside the government sector, stimulated a consumer binge and energized the construction sector. The newly available cash was channeled into building a local infrastructure from scratch; indeed, it is the private sector that has most contributed to the country's expansion in the last decade. More recently, unchecked spending along with limited economic growth at the national level has led to a recession. The recent discovery of marketable oil in Yemen is considered to be its economic salvation, but until the money flows in, the country must face a growing crisis of inadequate revenues.

The first national census, conducted in 1975, estimated a total population of 4,705,000, not counting the half-million Yemenis living or working abroad (Steffen et al. 1978; Steffen and Blanc 1982). While the annual rate of population growth was estimated at that time to be 2.4 percent, the government believes the current population is much larger than that projection. This is reflected in the 1986 national census, which indicated a population of 9,275,000. Regardless of the correct population size, the YAR is the most densely populated country on the peninsula—with some 35 inhabitants per square km in 1975. The population is overwhelmingly rural, as evidenced by the fact that 83 percent reside in communities of fewer than 500 persons. As is common for less-developed countries, levels of health are poor, with an infant mortality rate, for example, of 190 per 1,000 in 1980. In 1980, life expectancy at birth was only 42 years. Data concerning education and access to potable water show similarly poor findings (see Varisco et al. 1984).

The population inhabits several environmental zones that make up a total land area of approximately 195,000 square km (Kopp 1981). In the west, a hot and humid coastal strip, the Tihama, faces the Red Sea. About half of this zone can be used as scrub rangeland for small herds of sheep and goats as well as a few camels. With a maximum annual rainfall of 300 mm, agriculture in this region generally requires irrigation, whether the traditional spate systems (recession cultivation) along the major coastal wadis (river courses that swell after the rainy season in the highlands) or the new and increasingly numerous tube-well systems. While grain crops of sorghum and millet still predominate, the expansion of irrigation from wells has generated production of new vegetable and fruit crops.

A range of foothills begins about 50–60 km inland and rises dramatically to rugged peaks over 3,000 m in elevation in the area known as the Western Highlands. Annual rainfall may reach 1,500 mm to the south but is considerably less to the north. Winter mists supplement the two main rainy seasons of spring and late summer. Over the centuries farmers have transformed the steep mountain slopes into rows of terraces, whether watered by runoff harvesting or by springs. Sorghum, wheat, and barley dominate the production cycle, although maize is on the increase in irrigated plots. Few vegetables are grown, but coffee and qat are cultivated as cash crops. Travel is still difficult in this region, despite recent construction of roads.

About 40 percent of the country consists of a highland plain intersected by small ranges of hills and a few major passes. With a temperate climate, this region has a long tradition of dry-farming, particularly in the south.

While terraces are still found, most cultivation is carried out in broad, level fields in the basins. Grains are the dominant crops, but such fruits as grapes and apricots are also important. Recently, cultivation of tomatoes and potatoes has increased because of donor efforts in seed selection and pest control.

Further east, the plateau offers increasingly sparse vegetation in an inhospitable climate, culminating in the Empty Quarter of the Arabian desert. In pre-Islamic times, several major dams allowed for widespread agricultural systems. The most famous of these is the Ma'rib Dam, mentioned in the Quran; the demise of the dam followed the fading fortunes of the Sabaen kingdom well before the Islamization of Yemen. As a massive, state-sponsored structure, the Ma'rib Dam diverted the flow of a major wadi to an extensive system of fields downstream. The government has rebuilt the dam with foreign assistance, but it remains uncertain whether the new structure will have a significant impact on overall agricultural production.

Land Use in Yemeni Agriculture

Data on the use of agricultural land in the YAR have recently become available, but they are contradictory on several points, with major differences in estimates of the country's cultivated area. Formerly, the government's Central Planning Organization (CPO) assumed a total agricultural land area of about 15,000 square km. The recent MAF census (1983), however, recorded the amount of agricultural land as 13,508 square km, of which 10,198 are currently cultivated. Dr. Horst Kopp (1981), who has made extensive analyses of maps, aerial photographs, and field surveys, arrived at a total of 16,790 square km, of which 13,850 are annually cropped. The Landsat study carried out for USAID and the YAR by Cornell University (1983) placed the total cultivated land area at 20,600 square km with 83 percent accuracy, although this has not been cross-checked by field surveys. This last estimate represents a far greater area than previously thought, but it is unclear how much of the cultivated area may in fact be abandoned. In any given year some of the land will lie fallow, but a number of researchers have noted a steady increase in the amount of abandoned agricultural land, caused, in large part, by the migration of Yemeni men for work abroad.

Throughout the country, the dominant mode of production is dryland farming that uses either direct rainfall or runoff harvested from adjacent uncultivated land. For runoff harvesting, the farmer places his fields beneath a slope and sets up small stone walls to channel the slope's runoff into and through the fields, thus farming even where the rainfall is insufficient. Toward the south of the country rainfall increases, but periodic droughts are common in the north. The CPO estimated the amount of rainfed land as 83 percent of the total cultivated area; Kopp (1981) arrived at a figure of 73 percent; the Cornell University study estimated 75 percent; and the MAF census (1983) suggests about 77 percent. Much of the abandoned agricultural land, especially in the more marginal highland terrace systems, was dry-farmed in the past.

Ancient dams and water systems throughout the country attest to the long history of irrigation in Yemen. The major spate-irrigation systems are located in the coastal region (Halcrow and Partners 1978; Makin 1977; Maktari 1971; Tesco et al. 1971–1973), and spate is also practiced in the Eastern Plateau and other areas where feasible. In some areas shallow wells supplement spate irrigation in the nonflood season. The CPO and the MAF census (1983) indicate that about 8 percent of the cultivated area is based on flood irrigation.

Two types of perennial water flow in Yemen: springs that feed a relatively continuous basal flow in wadis, and isolated highland springs. The CPO estimated the amount of spring-irrigated land at 5 percent, while the MAF census figure is about 2.4 percent (1983). Although Kopp (1981) did not distinguish between spring and spate irrigation, it would appear from his general discussion that his estimate is similar to the CPO figure. Most highland spring systems are terraced and based on redistribution of flow from cisterns (Varisco 1982, 1983). In a few cases, such as Wadi Dhahr near Sanaa, the spring flow has been traditionally directed into a major watercourse.

Before the 1962 revolution, virtually all wells in Yemen were dug by hand and manually operated by pulleys (cf. Rossi 1953). The hydraulic pump has since revolutionized Yemeni irrigation, resulting in irrigated production on land that was previously dry-farmed. The outdated CPO estimates placed the amount of land irrigated by wells at 4 percent. Kopp (1981) found an area of 5 percent, but the MAF census (1983) identifies some 11.7 percent as under well irrigation. In 1982 wells were being drilled at the rate of an estimated 1,500 per year, mostly for agricultural use (CID 1984). The expansion of well-irrigated land has resulted in the lowering of the water table in some areas, especially the Sanaa basin.

The MAF census (1983) provides the most detailed information on cropping patterns for each of the YAR's eleven administrative divisions or governorates. Since this census was conducted over several years, the comparison of data between governorates is subject to error because of rapid changes within each area. For the country as a whole, 68.8 percent of the agricultural land is planted with field crops, primarily the major subsistence grains. Only 6.7 percent of the land has permanent crops, mainly such cash crops as qat or fruit trees. In a given year, an estimated 7 percent of the agricultural land is left fallow. Furthermore, some 16.6 percent has been abandoned; the figure reaches 49.6 percent for the austere eastern governorate of al-Jawf.

The choice of crop depends on a variety of environmental, economic, and cultural factors. In all parts of the country the dominant food crop is sorghum, whether irrigated or rainfed (Varisco 1985). The irrigated varieties yield far more fodder value from the stalks and leaves. Most of the sorghum grain is consumed within the household, although a small amount is available in the market at high prices. The fodder value of the crop is of major importance in the highlands because of the lack of other suitable fodder apart from expensive, irrigated alfalfa. The availability of cheap, imported wheat on the market has hampered the government's encouragement of wheat production. Barley, a traditional low-risk and low-profit subsistence crop in the highlands, has declined in production. Few farmers cultivated fruits or vegetables in the past, but the pattern is rapidly changing because of urban demand and government-sponsored projects. Most notable has been the rapid introduction of potatoes and tomatoes. Farmers have shown a willingness to adopt new crops, but most are unable to care for them properly, and consequently yields are low.

The YAR exports virtually no food crops, despite direct market opportunities in neighboring Saudi Arabia. The major cash crop in the highlands is qat, in some places cultivated as a tree and in others as a shrub. For the past five centuries, qat has been grown mainly for a select few who chewed its leaves as a stimulant. While qat is not a narcotic and has not been demonstrated to be addictive, it has become the focus of attention in the concern for Yemen's agricultural development. Most Yemenis now chew some qat; many even chew daily in afternoon social gatherings. The increased demand, primarily in urban centers and towns, has stimulated production to an extraordinary extent. Many planners believe that although the production of qat provides high returns to even the smallest farmers, it detracts from the increased production of food crops and potential exports (Varisco 1988). Chewing has major social importance, however, and has become a symbol of Yemeni identity (Varisco 1986; Weir 1985).

Land Tenure

Land in the YAR is officially classified according to type of ownership as defined in Islamic law. The prevalent form is clearly private possession (*milk*). Under Islamic law, a private owner may dispose of his land as he wills, except under such few cases as the right of preemption. The right or doctrine of preemption (*shuf'a*) stipulates that land owned by a shareholder in a cistern-based irrigation network, for example, cannot be sold outside the shareholding group without the consent of the other members. In effect the fellow shareholders have a right, in order of priority, to preempt the sale because of a perceived threat to the functioning of the network (cf. Varisco 1982:246–253). In tribal customary law, under a variant of shuf'a, land can be kept under the communal ownership of a tribal group (Chelhod 1975:73; Dostal 1974:3). Written deeds, jealously guarded by the owner or deposited with a trusted community leader, document almost all land ownership. Islamic law allows an individual to gain ownership of unclaimed wasteland by reclaiming it for agricultural use.

A second type of land, *miri* or *amlak al-dawla*, is under the jurisdiction of the state. In the YAR it is mainly land confiscated after the 1962 revolution from the extensive holdings of the Zaydi imams and their major supporters. Much of this state-owned land is in the coastal region, where some has been set aside for government-sponsored agricultural farms. The state also rents agricultural land to tenants.

The third major category of land is controlled by the *waqf* authority, which is responsible for overseeing religious trusts (cf. Messick 1978). It is land or other property willed in perpetuity under Islamic law for the promotion or maintenance of religious institutions and affairs. Some waqf holdings are under complete control of the present-day Ministry of *Awqaf* (pl. of waqf), while others are jointly shared by the authority and the survivors of the original owner. This institution was important in the past, but few waqf trusts are formed nowadays. Waqf land is available for rental, often on a long-term basis.

A more vaguely defined fourth type of land is under communal control for nonagricultural uses such as public roadways, public activities, or community grazing. Determination of this type is usually based on local customary law according to historical practices in the area.

Since there is no national land registration in the YAR, only rough estimates are available of the relative areas of each type of land. Most development planners have followed an estimate made in the mid-1960s by Horst Dequin, a German technical adviser to the government of the YAR. Dequin (cited in El-Akhrass 1972:1) provided the following estimates: 74 to 82 percent private, 15 to 20 percent waqf, 2 to 3 percent state, and 1 to 3 percent communal.

Several local surveys echo the rough statistics for the national level, with important regional variations. For the central highland area around Manakha, Gerholm (1977:59) found 80 percent of the land private, 15 percent waqf, and 5 percent state. For the southern highlands, a field survey in al-Hujariyya suggested that 95 percent of the land was private and 5 percent waqf (Yacoub and Akil 1971:13). For the coastal region, a UNDP-sponsored survey (Tesco et al. 1971–1973) of Wadi Zabid noted that 36 percent of the land was waqf and 10 percent state. Zabid was historically a magnet for wealthy families who sometimes made major bequests to the waqf authority. By contrast, there was virtually no waqf land along Wadi Rima' in the north (Makin 1977:56).

Sharecropping and land rental may be arranged on private, waqf, and state lands throughout Yemen. Islamic law codifies the conditions of agricultural contracts, whether for a percentage of the yield or for fixed sums of cash or a commodity. The amount of the share is a decision for the parties involved, but the prophet Muhammad forbade a contract in which the tenant received as little as a third or a fourth of the yield (al-Sayaghi 1968 [3]:650). In the spirit if not the letter of Muhammad's pronouncement, Islamic jurists seek to assure the tenant a share sufficient to maintain his family. They tend to favor percentage rather than fixed-amount arrangements, so that risk is shared between tenant and landlord. Contracts may be annual or long-term (e.g., 30 years), and a tenure relationship may in some areas be inherited.

A variety of contradictory information is available on the prevalence of tenancy in Yemeni agriculture. While the statistical data seldom indicate it, the overwhelming majority of tenants are engaged in sharecropping for a fixed percentage of the yield. The MAF census (1983) indicates that 62.0 percent of the agricultural households (covering 76.4 percent of the land area) are owner operated, 24.7 percent are operated by both owner and tenant (on 18.3 percent of the land area), and only 13.4 percent of the households are fully tenant operated (on 5.3 percent of the land). This rendering differs from an earlier and less exhaustive survey by ECWA (1980:15–16), which found 44 percent of the households to be owner operated, 35 percent operated by owner and tenant, and 21 percent fully tenant operated. Part of the discrepancy is due to the finding in the ECWA survey that full tenant operation occurs in 35 percent of the coastal or lowland households, but in only 5 percent of the highlands or uplands households. Other surveys of the coastal area indicate a relatively high percentage of sharecropping (e.g., Makin 1977:56 for Wadi Rima'), yet the MAF census (1983) does not reflect a higher rate of tenancy for the coastal region.

Several regional surveys of limited scale show important variations in the prevalence of tenancy. In Jabal 'Iyal Yazid of the northern highlands, Steffen et al. (1978 [2]:55) found that 92 percent of the households were owner operated and another 4 percent both owner and tenant operated. In Khawlan, by contrast, southeast of Sanaa, Zaman (1983:34) cited only 54.9 percent of the households as owner operated and 36.6 percent as both owner and tenant operated. In Wadi Tha, also southeast of Sanaa, some 70 percent of the households were found to be owner operated, with an additional 13 percent being households where owners only leased land. Only 10 percent of the households were both owner and tenant operated (ILACO 1983:9). While tenancy does not dominate Yemeni agriculture, it clearly has an important role in certain regions. Unfortunately, the available surveys do not provide enough information to determine the precise factors influencing tenancy in a given region.

The data on Yemeni sharecropping show several patterns, as no single system serves the entire country, but the following factors help to determine the share ratio between tenant farmer and landlord:

1. Crop grown. In al-Ahjur of the central highlands, for example, a tenant raises sorghum for a three-quarters share of the harvest; wheat, maize, and barley for a seven-eighths share; and coffee and qat for a two-thirds share.
2. Presence of irrigation. The tenant usually receives a greater share of the crop on rainfed land, although the total yield will be less than on irrigated land. For recently introduced tube-well irrigation, the split is often three ways—with one-third to the tenant, one-third to the landlord, and one-third to the well owner.
3. Who provides the production inputs such as seeds, fertilizer, tractors, and pesticides. In the highlands most inputs are the responsibility of the tenant. This has been cited as a problem in introducing new technology, because the tenant usually cannot afford it, and the landlord has no incentive to provide it (cf. Rees-Jones 1984:12). While tenants

in the spate-irrigated areas of the coastal region generally receive a smaller share (one-third to one-half), this is offset by the landlord's provision of most inputs.
4. Who pays the one-tenth tax (*zakat*) on agricultural produce. Sometimes the tax is split by taking out one-tenth of the harvest before dividing it between tenant and landlord. In most cases, however, the tenant is responsible. The zakat tax is reduced by half—to one-twentieth—on some types of irrigated land where upkeep of the irrigation system is necessary. This latter provision historically was used for systems with well or water-lift technology (al-'Alawi 1972:45).
5. Quality of soil. Sometimes the rent on less fertile land is lower or more negotiable, since the yield will be smaller.
6. Extent of clientelism. A landlord-tenant relationship is seldom a simple business relationship. While the tenant's share may at times seem low in parts of the coastal region, he or she may in fact receive other forms of aid from the landlord in a continuing relationship as client.
7. Supply and demand. The ethnographic evidence from several observers suggests that the tenant's share has been increasing with high emigration rates and the resulting decline in available male labor for farming (Swanson 1980:2; Rees-Jones 1984; Tutwiler and Carapico 1981; Varisco 1982:256–257). In many areas of the highlands where the share was previously two-thirds, the tenant may now claim three-quarters.

Fixed-price rental agreements, not nearly as common as sharecropping, often take place among relatives. In the Rada' area the 1985 standard price for cereal crops was approximately 7.5 kg grain per *habla* (81 m^2 in this context), and 200 Yemeni riyals (ca. $30.77) per habla for growing qat. In the mid-1970s in the Ibb area of the southern highlands, Messick (1978) reported a land rental price as ca. 30 kg sorghum grain per *qasaba* (64 square m in this context), although the tenant could grow any crop on the plots. The ECWA survey (1980) mentions a general pricing of 950 Yemeni riyals per ha on rainfed land, 1,000 Yemeni riyals per ha of tube-well land, and 1,500 Yemeni riyals per ha of spring-fed land. With tube-well irrigation, the water is usually sold for a fixed amount of cash per hour of flow.

In the practical application of Islamic jurisprudence, inheritance laws are as complicated as the mathematical tables used by a life-insurance salesman. This is especially true for large families with many potential inheritors. In principle, the children are to receive equal inheritances, but males receive twice the share of females. Furthermore, the eldest brother commonly claims and receives a larger share for his role in settling the family estate.

Islamic law stipulates the right of females to inherit, but tribal families may ignore it (Mundy 1979). A woman may trade her right to land for another part of the inheritance—such as a room in a house or cash. Women in Yemen may act as landlords, although usually their business affairs are handled by male relatives. Even though the female receives only half the share of a male, she always has a male relative to help her. One of the traditional justifications for the difference in shares is that the male deserves more because he has a family to look after, while the female will be provided for by her husband or brothers. The larger male share also serves to maintain land within the male descent line, an important principle in the tribal ideology of Middle Eastern societies. A Yemeni proverb says, "If land changes hands within the family, there is no regret."

Land Use and Agricultural Development

The challenge for the anthropologist as a consultant is not only to provide accurate information on the social and economic context of the farmer, but also to isolate factors that will impinge most directly on the successful planning and implementation of a project. The technicians and economists can describe the context in which development should occur, but the success of any initiative must be based on how it is received. What then are the major implications for development of Yemen's agriculture arising from existing land-use practices?

How Land Is Perceived

Land ownership is a secret jealously guarded by most Yemeni farmers. Their suspicion of anyone who asks about land use or ownership is an obstacle noted by several ethnographers (Kuczynski 1977:160; Rees-Jones 1985:3; Stevenson 1985:xx; Varisco 1982:238). The results of censuses and surveys must be tempered with the understanding that it is not in the farmer's interest to answer directly and accurately. A continuing fear in rural areas is that the government will confiscate land, a practice documented during the days of the imamate. Project planners need to be sensitized to this issue. It is generally not advisable to attempt detailed field surveys of land ownership prior to implementation of a project, no matter how desirable that information might be.

A number of Yemeni proverbs indicate the importance placed on land. "I look on my land as I do men, for men are indeed slaves to the land," says one central highland proverb. A man without land is considered poor indeed. As a result, land continues to be a major investment among Yemenis (Gerholm 1985:30). Not all land is of equal value, however. Land prices near major towns and cities have soared with the construction boom. Irrigated land is worth at least double the price of nonirrigated land (cf. Messick 1978:352). Kuczynski (1977:162) reported that cultivated land was five times as valuable as uncultivated land in the northern area around Sa'da, although this would not be the case on the fringes of expanding urban areas.

The value of land is attested in the large number of legal disputes over its use. Donor agencies who have needed to rent or have been provided land for agricultural projects have encountered innumerable problems. Land supposedly owned by the government may actually involve private owners, and boundaries are always in dispute. Donors should be wary of projects

TABLE 13.1
Fragmentation of Farm Holdings in the YAR

No. of Parcels	Percentage of Total Agricultural Land Area
1	16.3
2 - 3	37.2
4 - 5	21.2
6 - 9	17.1
10 - 19	7.8
20 or more	0.4
	100.0

Source: MAF 1983.

involving land rental—for an experimental station, for example—because of past experience with disputes over contracts.

Fragmentation of Holdings

A dominant feature of the terraced system of agriculture in the YAR is the fragmentation of field holdings, as shown in Table 13.1. Almost half the holdings are broken into four or more parcels. Fragmentation increases the potential for disputes over boundaries and over access to plots for cultivation or irrigation. Because of the many boundaries, it is often difficult to introduce new technologies that require large and uniform field areas (e.g., tractors or pipe systems). Farmers with several parcels will expend more time and energy than those with consolidated holdings. Smaller-scale technology would be more appropriate to their needs.

Fragmentation cannot be understood apart from the distribution of holding size, presented in Table 13.2. In general, the average holding is larger for the coastal region and eastern plateau than for the highlands. Rainfed holdings are usually larger than those with irrigated land, since the yield is so much lower. A survey in Wadi Rima' (Makin 1977:59) showed that the average holding size varied from 2.5 ha for perennial wadi irrigation to 10.0 ha on rainfed land. Holdings with tube-well irrigation averaged 3.5 ha. One generally finds a greater percentage of fragmentation on rainfed holdings.

Relationship of Land and Water Rights

In both Islamic and local customary law, land and water are perceived as closely related (Varisco 1982:236–255). Islamic jurists prohibit the sale of a water right from the land it is meant to irrigate in cases where a traditional allocation system has been established. An individual can sell a

TABLE 13.2
Average Farm-holding Size in the YAR

Size (ha)	Percentage of Total Agricultural Area
0 - 0.25	1.1
0.25 - 0.50	3.2
0.50 - 0.75	2.9
0.75 - 1.0	3.9
1 - 2	9.0
2 - 3	9.4
3 - 4	7.6
4 - 5	6.5
5 - 10	22.5
10 - 20	19.5
20 - 50	9.9
50 - 100	1.2
100 - 200	3.3
	100.0

Source: MAF 1983.

given amount of water, such as a specific amount of flow on a given day's turn, but the water right is attached to the land. Even in inheritance, water rights cannot be separated from the land being inherited. In the past, water rental was apparently not common in Yemen, except near urban centers with a larger number of absentee landlords. The recent expansion of tube-well systems, however, has seriously disrupted the traditional approach to water rights. In a number of cases, new wells have apparently resulted in the lessening or termination of spring flow, yet it is not always possible to prove a direct connection. Overpumping from wells will also dry up the older, shallow wells. As new, deeper wells are sunk, pipes are used to transport water across relatively long distances, with increased problems of access and boundary disputes. Indeed, neither traditional Islamic law nor customary law adequately addresses the problems created by tube wells and the associated lowering of the water table. While donors in the YAR are aware of this, the government has not yet been able to develop a national water policy.

In legal literature and customary practice, the issue of access to water is critical. Any water source must have a buffer zone (*harim*) of land for public or community access. This is partly due to the basic Islamic principle that water must never be denied for another to drink or to water his mount. The interrelationship of land and water is formalized in other legal principles. One of the primary means of reclaiming wasteland for private ownership is by irrigation, but Islamic law and tribal practice recognize the doctrine of preemption, which protects shareholders in a water-allocation system by allowing them the right to preempt a sale of land within the allocation system.

Several development projects in the YAR have directly or indirectly influenced existing allocation systems for irrigation. The construction of new barrages along the major coastal wadis has provided more water for some areas and less for others. These projects, concerned only with the construction aspects, have given little or no consideration to the confusion created in the communities involved. They have generated new legal disputes without significantly improving overall production from the increased water supply.

Importance of the Contract

Despite the lack of a national system of land registration, documentation is probably available for virtually every productive plot in the country. Deeds listing the precise boundaries, history of ownership, and often the associated water rights of land are usually kept secret until needed in a legal dispute or property transfer. Islamic law places great emphasis on the written contract, although in customary practice rental agreements may be verbal. Any project that involves the use of land, whether on a government-owned farm station or on a farmer's private fields, should include a written contract in which the obligations of each party are set out and confirmed in the presence of local community leaders.

The Mechanization Malaise

Donors and planners often assume that technology is the key to increased production. The value of appropriate machinery for facilitating the production cycle is not disputed here, yet consideration must also be given to potential side effects on the farmer's performance. Thus Yemeni farmers who obtain tractors, for example, rarely have preparation for adequate maintenance or adequate recourse to proper repair services. All too quickly a major economic investment may be relegated to the trash heap. Some farmers become doubly discouraged, unable to adapt to the needs of the new technology, and unwilling to fall back on the old.

One of the advantages of mechanization is that it fills the gap created by the labor shortage. With so many Yemeni men working abroad, there seems little choice but to shift to cultivation on consolidated holdings with modern methods and machinery. If such a shift is inevitable, it will also spell the end of the small farmer in Yemen. Most of the terraces patiently constructed over the centuries are not amenable to mechanized production. At present the abandonment of highland terraces, where the returns from dry-farming are too minimal to justify the effort, is evident everywhere. The potential for erosion damage of highland soils is considerable (cf. Collins 1987).

Male Bias

Most development planners in Yemen have overlooked the major role of women in agricultural production. Virtually all expatriate advisers provided to MAF and donor projects in agriculture are male. Where extension outreach has been provided to Yemeni women, it has tended to be in home economics rather than farm methods. The impact of high male emigration from rural Yemen has increased women's work loads in many areas, although not in all cases (Adra 1983). To a great extent, Yemeni women are maintaining the family farm. Few attempts have been made to introduce ways of reducing women's work loads by means of labor-saving technology for light agricultural work and processing of food or fodder. The need is for simple, affordable machinery rather than complicated, expensive farm technology.

The future of agriculture in Yemen is unlikely to be male centered, yet most of the large projects either assume that women have a minor role to play because of an exaggerated view of segregation in Yemeni society, or expect that once Yemeni men earn salaries women will not need to work in the fields. Anthropologists (e.g., Adra 1983; Myntti 1979) have demonstrated that women in Yemen value their economic role in agricultural production. Donors should initiate projects that recognize the importance of Yemeni women in agriculture.

Development Initiatives and the Role of the Anthropologist

Most of the donors active in development in the YAR have been concerned with institutional weaknesses, primarily the capabilities of the nascent MAF. The two most common thrusts of previous efforts have been in providing technical experts, often at the central ministry level, and in training students abroad. Several bilateral donors—as well as FAO and UNDP—have initiated agricultural projects, but these have seldom been coordinated with each other. USAID has placed its greatest emphasis on agriculture, especially under a contract with the Consortium for International Development (CID) for developing the institutional effectiveness of the MAF. American advisers have been placed in the central ministry, which provides counterparts, and have been given charge of projects in poultry, horticulture, and irrigation.

An assessment of the cumulative efforts to develop the YAR's agriculture has yet to be written. From the Yemeni perspective the results have not been spectacular. A frequent criticism by MAF officials is that donors overemphasize research. Indeed, anyone willing to sift through the plethora of reports and project papers would find a pattern of superficial observations and duplication of efforts. Many reports simply parrot statistical data from the Yemeni government; most are not translated into Arabic for use by Yemeni officials.

The role of the anthropologist in previous agricultural development efforts has been minimal. In the World Bank's (1979) country study of the YAR, one of the standard development guides for the country, the social milieu of Yemeni farmers is completely ignored. Agricultural development is defined in this study purely as an economic and technological problem. USAID has attempted to include anthropologists at the planning stages, but thus far not in the implementation of projects. The *Social and Institutional Profile of Yemen* (Varisco et al. 1984) and *Agricultural Sector Assessment* (Hogan et al. 1982) provide general surveys of the farming population with consideration of social factors relevant to project implementation. USAID also includes a social-soundness analysis for each project identification document and project paper, but these have not always been conducted by anthropologists with experience in the country. In one case—a horticultural subproject paper submitted by CID to USAID—the social-soundness analysis was simply a superficial characterization of an "Arab" society based on outdated sources and none of the relevant ethnographic research (cf. the critique in Griffin and Varisco 1984:236–255).

To be blunt, the policy planners of donor agencies and of the YAR government consider anthropological analysis, insofar as it is not directly concerned with economic variables, as a frill. While there has been a willingness to fund a limited number of research efforts, the data collected by anthropologists are seen as background rather than as a blueprint for action. An example of this is the USAID-funded study of two Yemeni communities by Tutwiler and Carapico (1981). The final publication documents trends in rural marketing and their consequent impact on agricultural production. While the volume has been cited in several reports, it has not generated any project initiatives. Since it was not translated into Arabic, the results are inaccessible to many Yemeni officials.

The relative lack of anthropological impact on development planning in the YAR cannot be blamed solely on the bias of donor personnel or government officials. The development anthropologist needs to spell out the implications of his or her findings in practical terms familiar to policy planners. Social-science jargon does not communicate social-soundness analysis to planners concerned primarily with economic and technical aspects. Thus, it is important to emphasize the practical and save the exotic or theoretical for other forums.

Anthropology and USAID's Irrigated Farming Systems Project

USAID has proposed a major development project—the Irrigated Farming Practices (IFP) Project—to improve and expand tube-well irrigation in the central highlands of the YAR (USAID 1985). The project's goal is to work with farmers presently irrigating from tube wells in order to introduce the new methods and technology needed to enhance water application and to improve production of crops suitable to the irrigation regime. A major emphasis of the project is to set up demonstrations on selected plots and to communicate through the media and local community groups.

From the standpoint of land use, the area chosen for the project has a reasonable chance of success. In recent years farmers with tube wells have consolidated their holdings while farmers on small rainfed holdings have moved out of the area. As a result of other donor efforts, farmers in the area have already tried new cash crops, especially potatoes. Since most of the tube-well systems are of recent origin, the problems of intricate, long-standing water-allocation systems are minimal. Most of the land being developed was previously dry-farmed, an option no longer viable in much of the region.

Caution must be applied in the implementation of the project. The farming-systems studies should avoid detailed cadastral surveys if the project personnel are to gain the trust of local farmers. Furthermore, since it is clear that women are actively involved in irrigated production, an effort must be made to train them as well as men in the new methods proposed. One suggestion to encourage this is to include female engineers among the technical advisers working with farmers in the area.

While the social-soundness analysis for the IFP Project contains recommendations for working with the farming families in the project area, anthropologists have no part in project implementation. This points up one of the greatest obstacles to development anthropology—the failure in most projects to create a role for an anthropologist as a cultural interpreter between the donor personnel and the beneficiaries. No matter how informative or useful the social-soundness analysis may be, there is no way to anticipate the variety of problems that will inevitably arise during its implementation. In my own experience in the YAR, I know of few projects that have failed due to faulty technical or economic data; failure is almost always due to miscommunication and misunderstanding on a personal or sociocultural level. For example, a survey team once proposed a site for an experimental farm station on privately owned land. The team members did this without consulting the farmers involved. When word of the proposal leaked back to the farmers, the credibility of the team members—and foreign experts in general—had been badly damaged.

Conclusions

I have examined the issue of existing land-use practices in order to elucidate areas of problem or promise for agricultural planning. The major implication rising from the discussion is that the farmer cannot be taken for granted. It may seem a simple task to ask a farmer to grow a new crop with new technology. On paper all that is necessary to justify the project is a prediction of economic viability, but in the field there are other factors to consider. Ultimately, the implementation of an agricultural project must address the limitations of the existing land-tenure system and land-use practices. Since system and practices are culturally framed, there is a need for the anthropologist to demonstrate that understanding the farmer's social milieu is relevant to implementing projects.

Development anthropology suffers from some of the same limitations as salvage anthropology with the bulldozers parked next to the excavation. In many cases where an anthropologist is included on a design team, insufficient time is allowed for contact with the beneficiaries, or there are difficulties in obtaining the appropriate permission for field study. While some consultants may be able to draw their conclusions from previous reports available outside the country or in the capital city, the anthropologist must be able to spend time in the field. More often than not, much of his or her time is consumed in the endless round of meetings with donor personnel and government officials. Unless the anthropologist has previous experience in the country, his or her recommendations may be so general as to be essentially useless. A superficial social analysis will reinforce the belief that such analysis is not important in development.

Having raised the issue of limitations on the development anthropologist as a consultant, I am not able to offer any definitive solutions. The very nature of the development process poses a problem beyond time constraints, restrictions on research, and general bias against social analysis. Anthropologists are not infallible by any means, but their training, experience, and language skills generally allow them to look at development from the bottom up. While anthropological input in planning has increased in recent years, administrators and government officials still largely perceive social analysis as a useless decoration. The most positive approach for the anthropologist is to focus attention on effective communication of his or her unique knowledge for the practical needs of development planners. This requires an attitude of participant observation not only in the region concerned, but also in the context of development institutions. More than any other type of consultant, an anthropologist cannot avoid the overall issue of development and his or her role in it.

References

Adra, Najwa
    1983 The Impact of Male Migration on Women's Roles in Agriculture in the Yemen Arab Republic. Report prepared for FAO.

al-'Alawi, 'Ali ibn Muhammad
    1972 Sirat al-Hadi ila al-Haqq Yahya ibn Husayn. Beirut: Dar al-Fikr.

al-Sayaghi, Sharaf al-Din al-Husayn ibn Ahmad
    1968 Al-Rawd al-Nadir. Vol. 3. Ta'if: Maktabat al-Mu'ayyad.

Chelhod, Joseph
    1975 La Société Yéménite et le droit. L'Homme 15(2):67–86.

CID (Consortium for International Development)
    1984 Irrigated Farming Practices Concepts Paper. Sanaa. Report submitted to USAID, Sanaa, Yemen Arab Republic.

Collins, Jane
    1987 Labor Scarcity and Ecological Change. In Lands at Risk in the Third World. P. D. Little and M. M Horowitz, eds. Pp. 19–37. Boulder, CO: Westview Press.

Cornell University
 1983 Agricultural Land Use Inventory. Final Report. Ithaca: Cornell University, Resource Information Laboratory.

Dostal, Walter
 1974 Sozio-ökonomische Aspekte der Stammesdemokratie in Nordost-Yemen. Soziologus 24(1):1–15.

ECWA (Economic Commission for Western Asia)
 1980 Crop-Sharing and Land Tenancy Practices in the Yemen Arab Republic. Report submitted to the Yemen Arab Republic.

El-Akhrass, Hisham
 1972 A Note on Land Tenure in Yemen. Sanaa: Central Planning Organization, Yemen Arab Republic.

Gerholm, Tomas
 1977 Market, Mosque and Mafraj. Stockholm: University of Stockholm.
 1985 Aspects of Inheritance and Marriage Payments in North Yemen. In Property, Social Structure, and Law in the Middle East. Ann E. Meyer, ed. Pp. 129–151. Albany, NY: State University of New York Press.

Griffin, Richard, and D. M. Varisco
 1984 Criteria for Establishment of the IFP Subproject. Sanaa: CID. Report submitted to USAID, Sanaa.

Halcrow and Partners
 1978 Wadi Surdud. Development on the Tihama. England: Sir William Halcrow and Partners. Report submitted to the Yemen Arab Republic.

Hogan, Edward, et al.
 1982 Agricultural Sector Assessment. Washington, DC: USAID.

ILACO (International Agricultural Consultancy)
 1983 Technical Note No. 9. Report on Farming Systems Research Survey in Wadi Tha. The Netherlands: ILACO.

Kopp, Horst
 1981 Agrargeographie der Arabischen Republik Jemen. Erlangen.

Kuczynski, Liliane
 1977 La Vie Paysanne dans un Village du Nord Yémen. Objets et Mondes 17:155–174.

MAF (Ministry of Agriculture and Fisheries)
 1983 Khulasat al-Nata'ij al-Niha'iya al-Zira'iya fi Muhafazat al-Jumhuriya. Sanaa: MAF, Yemen Arab Republic.

Makin, M. J., ed.
 1977 Yemen Arab Republic. Montane Plains and Wadi Rima' Project. A Land and Water Resources Survey. England: Ministry of Overseas Development.

Maktari, Abdullah
 1971 Water Rights and Irrigation Practices in Lahj. Cambridge: Cambridge University Press.

Messick, Brinkley
 1978 Transactions in Ibb: Economy and Society in a Yemeni Highland Town. Ph.D. dissertation. Department of Anthropology. Princeton University.

Mundy, Martha
   1979 Women's Inheritance of Land in Highland Yemen. Arabian Studies 5:161–187.

Myntti, Cynthia
   1979 Women and Development in the Yemen Arab Republic. Eschborn: German Agency for Technical Cooperation (GTZ).

Rees-Jones, Hywel
   1984 Farm Systems Survey I. Qa'Bakil. Dhamar: Dhamar Agricultural Improvement Center.

   1985 Farm Case Studies. Qa'Jahran and Qa'Bakil. Dhamar: Dhamar Agricultural Improvement Center, Publication No. 98.

Rossi, Ettore
   1953 Note sull'irrigazione, l'agricoltura e le stagioni nel Yemen. Oriente Moderno 33:349–361.

Steffen, Hans, et al.
   1978 Final Report on the Airphoto Interpretation Project of the Swiss Technical Cooperation Service. Vol. 2. Berne.

Steffen, Hans, and O. Blanc
   1982 La Démographie de la République Arabe du Yémen. In La Péninsule Arabique d'Aujourd'hui. Paul Bonnenfant, ed. Pp. 73–106. Paris.

Stevenson, Thomas
   1985 Social Change in a Yemeni Highlands Town. Salt Lake City, UT: University of Utah Press.

Swanson, John
   1980 Rural Development and Local Organization in Hajja and Hodeidah. In Local Organization, Participation, and Rural Development in the Yemen Arab Republic. Regional Baseline Study Report. Yemen Research Program, Rural Development Committee, John Lewis, director. Ithaca, NY: Cornell University.

Tesco, et al.
   1971–1973 Survey of the Agricultural Potential of the Wadi Zabid. Yemen Arab Republic. Budapest. Report prepared for United Nations Development Programme (UNDP).

Tutwiler, Richard, and S. Carapico
   1981 Yemeni Agriculture and Economic Change. Sanaa: American Institute for Yemeni Studies.

USAID
   1985 Irrigated Farming Practices Project Paper. Sanaa: USAID.

Varisco, Daniel Martin
   1982 The Adaptive Dynamics of Water Allocation in al-Ahjur, Yemen Arab Republic. Ph.D. dissertation, Department of Anthropology, University of Pennsylvania.

   1983 Sayl and Ghayl: The Ecology of Water Allocation in Yemen. Human Ecology 11:367–383.

   1985 The Production of Sorghum (Dhurah) in Highland Yemen. Arabian Studies 7:53–88.

1986 On the Meaning of Chewing: The Significance of *Qat* (*Catha edulis*) in the Yemen Arab Republic. International Journal of Middle East Studies 18:1–13.

1988 The Qat Factor in North Yemen's Agricultural Development. Culture and Agriculture, Bulletin of the Culture and Agriculture Group 34(Spring):11–14.

Varisco, D. M., and N. Adra
1984 Affluence and the Concept of the Tribe in the Central Highlands of the Yemen Arab Republic. *In* Affluence and Cultural Survival. R. Salisbury and E. Tooker, eds. Pp. 134–149. Washington, DC: American Ethnological Society.

Varisco, D. M., et al.
1984 Social and Institutional Profile of Yemen. Sanaa: American Institute for Yemeni Studies.

Weir, Shelagh
1985 Qat in Yemen. Consumption and Social Change. London: British Museum.

World Bank
1979 Yemen Arab Republic. Development of a Traditional Economy. Washington, DC: The World Bank.

Yacoub, S. M., and A. Akil
1971 A Socio-Economic Study of Hojjuriyya District, Yemen Arab Republic. Beirut: American University of Beirut.

Zaman, A.
1983 A Report on Socio-Economic Survey of West Khawlan, Yemen Arab Republic. Rome: FAO.

14

The World Bank and the Çorum-Çankırı Rural Development Project in Turkey

Zülküf Aydın

The Çorum-Çankırı Integrated Rural Development Project, the first of its kind on a large scale in Turkey, began in 1976 with World Bank funding. In this chapter, I will describe the aims and organization of the project in the light of empirical data collected in a village in Sungurlu County of Çorum Province, and analyze some of the basic assumptions of its design. I will then evaluate existing or potential contributions of social scientists to the project, contending that although social scientists may be unable to guarantee the realization of the project's aims *in toto*, they may nonetheless have an important role to play in directing attention to the contradictory nature of some of these aims. Through in-depth analysis of local structures, the social scientist will understand the mechanisms that may work against project aims and be able to point out discrepancies between the aims and the means chosen for their achievement. The final section of the chapter shows how existing unequal structures act as catalysts for further differentiation, which contradicts the project's goal of equity.

The Area and the Project

The neighboring provinces of Çorum and Çankırı are located in North Central Anatolia about 200–300 km north of the capital city, Ankara (see Figure 14.1). The project area, covering 21,270 sq km, lies between 750 and 1,000 m above sea level. Çankırı Province is mainly mountainous, while Çorum Province is mainly flat. The highest mountains, 1,500 m above sea level, constitute approximately 1,000 sq km, of which only small areas are suitable for cultivation. Cultivable lowland areas lie mainly in the southern parts of both provinces. In this area of plateaus between small hills and narrow valleys, irrigation extends the total of cultivable land from 89,000 to around 100,000 hectares. The Kızılırmak and Yesilırmak rivers and their

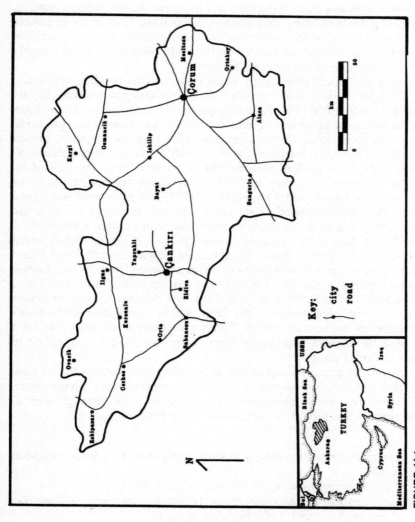

FIGURE 14.1
Çorum-Çankırı Rural Development Project Area. *Source:* State Planning Organization (1986).

tributaries enable adjacent lands to be irrigated from various small dams. With most of the proposed 5 large dams and 30 small dams not yet fully operational, only a small proportion of the potentially irrigable area is currently being irrigated from the project dams.

Approximately 850,000 people live in the two provinces, about 70 percent in rural areas. The majority, some 85,000 farming families, are small landowners with less than 75 decares, and there are 66,000 landless families. Production is for both home consumption and market. Most of the cultivable land is in wheat and barley, with smaller areas in lentils, animal food crops, and sugar beets. Animal husbandry and outside wage work make roughly equal contributions to family farm budgets.

A policy of import-substituting industrialization in the late 1960s and early 1970s left Turkey with a severe balance-of-payments problem (Keyder 1979:198; Gülalp 1983). The Turkish government's request for World Bank funds for industrial projects was refused with the stipulation that "industrial lending was conditional on the acceptance of a rural development project loan" (Nott 1983:200). Desperate to find fresh loans to offset balance-of-payment difficulties, Turkey accepted the constraint. After the visit of an IBRD/FAO mission to Turkey in 1972 to lay down the conditions of an Integrated Rural Development Project (FAO 1972:1), an agreement was signed in 1975. The initial duration of six years was later extended to expiration in June 1984 because many components of the project were unfinished.

The World Bank's insistence on financing an agricultural development project in Turkey derived from changes in its policies toward Third World agricultural development. Having been criticized severely for its bias toward wealthier farmers in the Third World, and realizing the limited success of the so-called "Green Revolution," the Bank had decided to support poorer sections of rural populations in the Third World (see Robert McNamara's Nairobi speech [McNamara 1973]). Turkey's application for loans could not have come at a more appropriate time to try the Bank's new policy of helping the rural poor.

In the project appraisal report, the stated objectives were both "to raise production and thereby incomes . . ." and "to improve rural infrastructure. . . ." These two broad objectives were to be achieved through various components of the project, which included the establishment of:

1. an intensive extension service to work along with the existing extension service;
2. agricultural credits through the Agricultural Bank;
3. new irrigation facilities for about 12,500 hectares and on-farm development for about 7,500 hectares of land;
4. new village access roads and the upgrading of some existing roads;
5. a supply of drinking water for 120 villages;
6. electricity for 233 villages; and
7. newly constructed social facilities, including village hall, bath house, and laundry, in 63 villages (IBRD 1975a:11).

Eight different government agencies were involved in project implementation, under the coordination of the State Planning Organization (SPO). The General Directorates of Agricultural Affairs and of Veterinary Services in the Ministry of Agriculture, Forestry, and Village Affairs were responsible for extension services and veterinary services, respectively. Large-scale irrigation projects were entrusted to the General Directorate of State Hydraulic Works (DSI), while the General Directorate of Soil and Water Conservation (Topraksu) was responsible for the construction of small dams and on-farm irrigation facilities. The General Directorate of Village Roads, Water, and Electricity Works (YSE) was responsible for the operation and maintenance of roads and village drinking-water systems. The General Directorate of Land and Resettlement (Toprak Iskan) managed the construction of facilities at village centers. Provision of electricity for a number of villages was the responsibility of the Directorate of Village Electrification of the Turkish Electric Authority (TEK). Finally, the Agricultural Bank of Turkey was in charge of the distribution of credit to farmers. Of the eight government agencies involved in the project's implementation, only the Project Extension Service was established especially for the purpose; the other agencies were already in existence.

The loan agreement stipulated the establishment of a National Advisory Committee, consisting of the Directors General of the eight government agencies. The State Planning Organization was to act as coordinator between the World Bank and the eight agencies. Also, under the chairmanship of the governor of each province, a Provincial Advisory Committee consisting of representatives of each of the eight agencies was established. The secretaries of each Provincial Advisory Committee were the provincial project extension directors, who were directly answerable to the project extension director. County extension agents in the district were in charge of informing, training, and supervising village agents, who in turn kept in contact with farmers.

When the crucial role of the extension service became apparent with the success of the project, an additional extension service was established. The Bank's priorities of "helping the rural poor, dampening the rate of urban migration," creating jobs, and contributing "to greater regional balance" would thus be achieved through a "direct approach" (IBRD 1975a:4). The "direct approach" meant that whereas the income of approximately 79,000 farming families would normally have been expected to rise to $980 over the period, participation in the project would raise incomes by a further 70 percent to $1,670 per annum at the end of the project period (IBRD 1975a:iii). Since the majority of families in the project area enjoyed an income of between $60 and $140, only about one-quarter of the national per capita income of $550, the area fell "within the 'target population' appropriate to a rural development project" (IBRD 1975a:iii).

Basic Assumptions of the Project

Many assumptions underlie the appraisal of the project and therefore also the project's implementation. The first is directly related to the Bank's understanding of rural development as:

a strategy designed to improve the economic and social life of a specific group of people—the rural poor. It involves extending the benefits of development to the poorest among those who seek a livelihood in the rural area. The group includes small-scale farmers, tenants, and the landless (IBRD 1975b:3).

In other words, rural development projects are supposed to benefit everybody living in rural areas regardless of socioeconomic differences. Poverty is thus isolated from its political and economic dimensions and seen as something that can be eliminated at will. Another assumption relates to how this benefit would be realized. It was believed that through the use of machinery, improved seeds, and inputs, the income of small producers would increase and their standard of living improve. Increased production alone was thought automatically to reduce poverty. Further, the use of machines, inputs, and the provision of services was expected to increase local employment possibilities, thereby reducing rural-urban migration. Thus, providing credit and inputs and offering extension services were seen as a panacea that would alleviate poverty through increasing production. The increase of production and elimination of poverty were assumed to be completely compatible, with no contradiction between them. A similar compatibility between the project aims and national policies was assumed, without any significant consideration of the possibility that national policies might limit considerably the realization of project aims. The project was designed and organized in such a technocratic fashion as to suggest that technocrats knew better than peasants, whose opinion therefore did not need to be asked. The implicit assumption was that once the more knowledgeable technocrats persuaded the ignorant farmers about the wonders of the project, its aims would be realized. Since government institutions were the most important means of spreading the benefits of the project, they did not impede this diffusion. Last but not least of the assumptions was the consideration of the target group as homogeneous—no socioeconomic analysis was undertaken during project appraisal to determine land distribution, class and gender differentiation, income distribution, or local community organization.

Many of these assumptions were false, and often contradictory. The project's implementation could not bring about all the desired results.

Extension Service

The extension system, to be carried out along with monitoring and evaluation, was to introduce improved cultivation and livestock-management practices to increase the production mainly of wheat, barley, and perennial and annual forages. It aimed also to reduce the amount of cultivable land in fallow from 46 percent to only 6 percent.

The project extension service was established for the efficient training and advising of farmers, while the already existing extension service was involved in regulatory work. The General Directorate of Agricultural Affairs in the Ministry of Agriculture and Forestry provided overall coordination. A director headed the project extension service, supported by a deputy in each province, while in each county an extension service head was charged with providing services and training village agents. Each province had a staff of subject specialists to provide the county extension personnel with information and training. Actual fieldwork was carried out by village agents recruited from among the most progressive farmers. It was thought that the village agents, being leading local figures, would have the respect and the confidence of their peers and therefore would be useful assets in the dissemination of knowledge and technology (IBRD 1975a:20). Village agents underwent extensive training and were supervised by the county agents and their assistants. It was planned that each village agent would serve 500 farmers in five or six neighboring villages.

Village agents were supposed to organize biweekly group activities in each village, including lectures, discussions, and demonstrations, as well as visits to at least 120 farmers in the villages under their jurisdiction. Each village agent was to select those farmers who would implement a package of all recommended practices and whose farms would serve as "demonstration fields" (IBRD 1975a:Annex 7:2). In their contacts with farmers, village agents were supposed to disseminate knowledge of better methods of seedbed preparation, seeding, weed and pest control, and harvesting, and, in animal production, better methods of feeding, health and disease control, and genetic improvement of animal quality (IBRD 1975a:12).

Because of financial constraints, the number of village agents never reached the target estimates. The maximum number of village agents employed was 78 in Çorum and 46 in Çankırı, only half the number proposed in the appraisal report (only one village agent per 1,000 farmers rather than one per 500).

The heavy reliance on village agents did not yield a positive impact on the project as a whole. Interviews with the extension officials in Çorum and Çankırı provinces and in Sungurlu County in Çorum, and with some village agents in Sungurlu in 1983–1984, revealed problems in selecting village agents. Extremely low pay and the short term (three months at a time) of the contracts did not attract villagers with local leadership qualities. In the project's initial stages, the far right wing National Action Party within the National Front Government controlled the Ministry of Agriculture and used party allegiance as a criterion in appointments. Doubts were expressed about the adequacy of the extension training given to village agents. High turnover, caused by dissatisfaction with pay and the insecurity of temporary appointments, led to a continual training of new staff. Owing to transportation and communication problems, village agents were not appointed to mountain villages or to any areas that lacked proper roads. In an interview, Sungurlu County's head of extension services emphasized that lack of transportation and lack of fuel, especially during Turkey's severe economic crisis in 1977–1980, made it almost impossible to control the activities of village agents. According to Sungurlu County extension officials, the World Bank's imposition of village agents was a mistake. The village agents selected "were not educated enough to understand the technical requirements of production increase themselves, let alone diffuse it to others." One of the three international consultants to the project, the agricultural extension adviser, reported in his survey of village agents' extension work that the agents were inadequately trained in practical work and were complaining about the slowness of farmers in adopting the recommendations (Grammelspacher 1979).

As a result of many complaints by agricultural engineers and subject specialists as well as other extension officials, by 1982 the Ministry of Agriculture decided to use trained agricultural technicians instead of local people as village agents. According to officials in Sungurlu County and Çorum Province, "the damage was already irrevocably done in the past six years." Similar evaluations and complaints can be found in reports by extension staff (CCRDP 1977a, 1977b, 1979).

Having been trained as agricultural engineers or agricultural technicians, most extension staff identified the basic problems to be lack of knowledge and ability on the part of village agents, poor coordination between the various agencies involved in the project, and lack of supplies. If technical and organizational problems could be solved, they felt, the project would be successful. Success was defined as increased production and the use of modern inputs (chemicals and improved seeds). Producers were blamed for their stubbornness in not recognizing what was good for them and not adopting the packages advocated by the extension agents. Left unquestioned was whether the majority of the farmers could afford to adopt these packages, whether they were in a position to use them as a whole, and whether the recommended inputs were attainable. Extension agents in counties and provinces also complained about the amount of project-imposed bureaucratic work, especially the processing of credit applications, which prevented them from having enough contact with farmers in their fields.

Monitoring and Evaluation

The project extension service was also entrusted with the task of monitoring "to determine the progress of the project, identify areas of difficulty, and to provide data on rural development" (IBRD 1975a:20). Basic data on farmers' use of project innovations and the resultant effects on crop and livestock production, income, and family living conditions were to be collected regularly by county agents.

In addition, a multidisciplinary team comprising a coordinator, an assistant coordinator in charge of evaluation, and three research officers was to carry out a baseline survey over the five-year project investment period, examining both preproject and postproject conditions. The three research officers, including economist(s) and anthropologist(s), were to carry out in-depth studies "on income distribution, migration, and the household economy using both participant observation and the survey method of research" (IBRD 1975a:Annex 10:2).

In spite of encouragement on the part of the Turkish government, the research was never taken seriously. For example, the task of the baseline survey was given to a team of Turkish academics rather than a "base study team" whose establishment was stipulated by the project agreement (IBRD 1975a:Annex 10:1). Under the supervision of the State Planning Organization, an agricultural economist, a demographer, and a statistician carried out the research on contract. University students were used for the administration of the survey, which was completed in 1976 in one month. The survey results were submitted to the project directorate more than two years after having been attained, long after they could form any basis for action. One of the most important findings of the survey was that given unequal land distribution and unequal access to resources, the project would basically benefit large capitalist farmers rather than smallholders (Özler and Peker 1979:75, and verified by our own fieldwork in a village in Sungurlu). As will be argued in the following pages, rich farmers who managed to obtain credit for buying tractors benefited most from the project. While medium-sized family farms increased their productivity, their standard of living showed no obvious signs of betterment. The project's impact on small farmers was further indebtedness and a further push for family labor to seek supplementary income from outside the farm through casual wage laboring.

The reason for not taking the results of the survey into any serious consideration must be sought in the technocratic attitudes toward development held by Turkish officials, in their doubts about the usefulness of social science research. The only social scientists with whom they had any patience were the agricultural economists. Despite the project agreement stipulation, and although a need for detailed studies based on participant observation had been expressed by the coordinator of the baseline study, no anthropologist was appointed to the evaluation team as a research officer (Nott 1983:250).

The agricultural economists abandoned several unsuccessful attempts to carry out surveys of socioeconomic conditions. For instance, in 1977 the agricultural economist in Çankırı decided to administer a questionnaire to 1,600 households in the province, covering household composition, size, education of members, land and livestock ownership, cropping patterns and production, and use of machinery and inputs. After completing only a handful of questionnaires in four months, however, he abandoned the inquiry as taking too much time. Village agents were asked to complete inventory forms about the villages where they were worked, but their data were extremely unreliable and incomplete. Furthermore, yield estimates were not related to farmers' practices, as they were prepared in towns by the extension staff who had little contact with farmers. One observer who was directly involved in the project research work stated that the extension staff members objected to their time being used for the collection of socioeconomic data. As a result, socioeconomic research was administered unrigorously and the data obtained were incomplete (Nott 1983:267).

The chaotic nature of data collection hampered implementation of the project. With unreliable and incomplete information, progress could not be monitored, nor problem areas identified, nor mitigative measures proposed.

Provision of Credit and Inputs

Along with the extension services, the provision of credits was expected to reduce poverty and increase production. Almost half of the IBRD's total lending of $75 million was assigned for this purpose. The Agricultural Bank of Turkey was to provide $22.1 million for credit, and farmers were expected to raise $10.9 million. Both short- and medium-term credit were offered, the former for cultivation expenses (seeds, fertilizer, chemicals, and other operating costs) and the latter for farm machinery and buildings. Obtaining credit from the Agricultural Bank was neither simple nor straightforward, however, for farmers had to demonstrate their creditworthiness. Real estate mortgages and guarantees of cosigners were required before any loans could be advanced. Apart from this, farmers had to convince the project extension representatives that they were able to use the short-term credit effectively to increase production and productivity, whereas for medium-term credit the extension staff had to be convinced that the projects were technically feasible, financially viable, and economically rational.

Short-term credit was for a maximum of one year, credit for machinery for a maximum of five years, and credit for buildings for a maximum of seven years. The requirement of a land title as a guarantee initially excluded a large number of small farmers who either did not have the title deeds in their names or were sharecroppers. In an attempt to overcome this, the provision of credits through membership in credit cooperatives was allowed from 1979 onwards. Whether this really helped the poorest section of the rural population is doubtful. Fieldwork in a Sungurlu village indicates that landless farmers and small landowners in most cases could not obtain credit, and when small landowners did obtain credit, it benefited the merchants and money-lenders rather than the borrowers. The exclusion of landless farmers from the project's credit system was contrary to the general aim of alleviating poverty. In an area where 33 percent of farming families (66,222 out of 199,097) are landless and where 49 percent of total landowning farming families own 25 decares or less land (KIKB 1983a, 1983b), it is impossible to discuss the alleviation of poverty without including the largest and poorest segment of society. This point was also raised by Grammelspacher, the agricultural extension adviser to the project. In various reports based on a sample of credit applications, Grammelspacher states that credit distribution was highly unequal, basically favoring large farmers (1978a, 1978b, 1978c, 1979). In particular, medium-term credit for the purchase of machinery and buildings had gone to a very small proportion of farmers (3 percent). Even then, as Grammelspacher points out, although the level of medium credit allowed the purchase of tractors, it was not high enough to allow the purchase of additional equipment or machinery. He concludes that credit loaned to farmers was unlikely to make a significant contribution to production through mechanization. Smallholders had somewhat better, though still very limited, short-term credit, but the raising of short-term credit limits in July 1978 further increased the access gap between large and small farmers, as land titles were required as a guarantee. Grammelspacher (1978b) found that farmers who owned less than ten decares were completely denied credit, and the proportion of borrowers among the owners of 50 or less decares of land declined. His analysis (1978c) of credit implementation in Çankırı showed that large farmers were disproportionally advantaged in access to credit.

The Agricultural Bank of Turkey not only extended cash to farmers but also supplied some agricultural inputs (fertilizers, seeds, etc.) as part of the credit scheme, although this provision ran into great difficulties during most of the project years. Owing to Turkey's economic difficulties and foreign currency shortages in the late 1970s and early 1980s, the importation and distribution of good seeds and chemicals was highly erratic, leading to corruption and black marketing (Nott 1983:232-233). Along with shortages and high prices of gasoline, the unavailability of good seeds and sufficient quantities of fertilizer seriously affected farm productivity. The gasoline shortage also endangered the very basic framework of training and visits, as the extension staff often could not visit the areas.

Project Performance

At the end of the project's extended duration in 1984, the following picture had emerged. The desired reduction of fallow areas from 49 percent to 6 percent of the land had not been realized, the fallow lands having been reduced from only 36.7 percent (not from 49 percent as estimated in the IBRD appraisal report) to 22.4 percent (Proje Yayım Servisi 1986).

A shift toward the production of pulses did follow the effort to introduce pulses and forage crops in crop rotation in place of a wheat and fallow cycle. As a result, the area under pulses increased from 35,500 hectares to 93,700 hectares. Although the productivity of many crops did not reach the levels estimated in the appraisal report, in addition to larger yields of pulses some increases certainly occurred in most cereals, industrial crops, fodder crops, and vegetables, although not significantly in animal products.

The amount of credit given to farmers rose from TL (Turkish Lira) 32,251 in 1977 to TL4,758,361 in 1985, while the number of credit-receiving farmers increased from 3,938 to 74,278 between the same years (SPO 1986:100, Table 32). The increase in the number of credit-receiving farmers may suggest a more equitable access to credit than I indicated earlier. Certainly with the availability of more money the number of credit receivers increased, yet more than 50 percent of the 200,000 farming families in the project area did not receive any credit. As the rules of credit allocation had not been changed since the publication of Grammelspacher's various reports based on a sample of credit applications, it can be assumed that the distribution of credits continued to follow an unequal pattern (1978a, 1978b, 1978c, and 1979).

The sum of TL3,977,825 was overdue, with legal action involving 31,316 farmers. While in the first years of the credit program farmers were able to repay their loans in time, by the last few years of the project they were highly indebted and not only were unable to repay the bank, but were even in danger of losing their mortgaged lands and machinery. Unfortunately there is no information on how credit was distributed, on the relationship between land size and amount of credit, or on the relationship between land size and indebtedness. In almost all the published and unpublished reports concerning the Çorum-Çankırı Project, facts are expressed in aggregate figures without much indication as to their social context (cf. FAO 1984; Proje Yayım Servisi 1986; SPO 1986). Production increase is identified with benefit received by the farmers without any information about how this benefit may be distributed. The State Planning Organization goes so far as to say:

> [T]otal crops value of the project area in 1984 was TL94,282,870,000. When this number is divided by the 85,300 farm units of the Çorum-Çankırı regions, a gross farm income of TL1,105,309 per farm can be expected. This number, as compared with FAO calculations of TL221,000 per farm in 1982 and Baseline Surveys' crop income calculations of TL10,358 per farm in 1977, represents a net increase, although the effects of inflation and home consumption, though marginal, have to be taken into consideration (SPO 1986:64).

This statement hardly reflects reality. First, it does not consider the fact that farmers are highly differentiated in terms of their landownership and access to resources, and that therefore not everyone would enjoy an increase. Second, the calculation ignores the unequal terms of trade between agriculture and industry. The gross income per farm was arrived at by multiplying the quantity of products by farm-gate prices, without taking into consideration rising prices of inputs and an extremely high annual inflation rate—between 80 and 90 percent.

The prices of industrial products consumed by farmers are similarly overlooked. A simple calculation of the terms of trade between the agricultural and industrial sectors reveals that there has been a transfer of resources from agriculture to industry, to the detriment of farmers. During its 65 years of history the new Turkish state has interfered in the formation of prices of agricultural inputs and produce to varying degrees. Whether this price determination favored agriculture or favored industry depended on the composition of the state and reflected the relative strengths of industrial and agrarian interests. For political considerations prices of agricultural produce were kept relatively high in the 1960s, but since the first half of the 1970s they have been kept lower (Boratav 1987; Akad 1987).[1] Table 14.1 shows the gradual working of the terms of trade against the agricultural sector as a whole. From 1977 on, prices received by farmers have declined in comparison with prices of nonagricultural commodities consumed by farmers. In other words, to be able to maintain their level of consumption and their standard of living, farmers have been forced to offer more and more agricultural products to the market. Assuming the terms of trade shifted against the agricultural sector by about 40 percent between 1977

TABLE 14.1
Internal Terms of Trade Indexes Between Agriculture and Industry

1966	100.0	1976	100.4
1967	103.1	1977	96.9
1968	103.4	1978	87.3
1969	105.4	1979	68.2
1970	109.6	1980	62.9
1971	112.1	1981	70.1
1972	107.3	1982	65.7
1973	111.8	1983	60.7
1974	111.2	1984	59.3
1975	108.3	1985	56.6

Sources: Akad 1987:148; Boratav 1987:99.

and 1984 and the inflation rate averaged 85 percent a year, real average farm income (corrected for both inflation and the shift in the terms of trade) remained almost constant—increasing by less than 1 percent a year during the seven-year period. At an annual inflation rate of 80 percent, farm income would have been about 25 percent higher at the end of the period; at a 90 percent rate it would have averaged about 17 percent lower. Again, whatever the average, it is clear that many farm households were worse off despite the overall increase in output. This counteraction of impoverishment by a continuous increase in production seems to have been the aim of the Turkish state. Through state-controlled agricultural prices the market orientation of farmers is intensified, and at the same time the provision of credit, improved seeds, machinery, and chemicals is intended to increase the quantities of agricultural commodities offered to the market by farmers. As our fieldwork shows, however, not all sections of farming communities can respond to the state incentives to increase their productivity in the way desired. Poorer farmers in most cases are not able to increase productivity because they lack sufficient resources and access to credit and markets. It was also evident from our village fieldwork that inequalities in rural areas are intensified by development projects induced by state (and international) agencies, which bring about different outcomes for different classes.

Concentrating on production aspects, the Çorum-Çankırı Project ignored the organization of marketing structures. As we shall see in our empirical study, existing marketing channels are highly unfavorable to small producers, which contributes to their exploitation by various agents. Reliance on existing marketing channels ran contrary to the project's goal of greater equity.

One consequence of the project has been an increase in the quantity of agricultural machinery. The number of tractors rose from 8,660 in 1976 to 18,381 in 1983; trailers increased from 8,190 to 19,128; tractor plows from 7,837 to 20,181; and tractor-drawn seed drills from 398 to 890 (SPO 1986:44, Table 9).

The further mechanization of agriculture counteracted one of the basic aims of the project: that of "dampening the rate of urban migration," for it encouraged the release of labor from agriculture. Although an increase in the cultivation of pulses during the project years created some employment possibilities in the area, they were not sufficient to absorb labor made redundant through increased mechanization. According to the State Planning Organization (SPO 1986:75) there was no significant change in migration between 1970 and 1980. Between 1970 and 1975, emigrants from Çorum and Çankırı provinces (74,757) exceeded immigrants (42,623) by 32,134. The corresponding figures for the period between 1975 and 1980 were 66,819 emigrants and 29,369 immigrants, a net outflow of 37,450.

The project also aimed to provide social services for villages. Some 30 home economists were employed to instruct village women concerning family planning, nutrition and hygiene, basic health, and child care. Courses were organized annually in three villages in each district, but attendance was poor, averaging 12 women and/or girls. Two home economists interviewed were not sanguine about the positive impact of their courses. One of them said, "We tell these people to keep themselves and their babies clean, but there is a water shortage; we tell them to have a balanced diet that includes protein, vegetables, and carbohydrates, but they do not have the money to buy them. Theory and practice are two different things." On the basis of the limited analysis available, we cannot assert that these courses have had no beneficial impacts on farming families, but initial impressions do not support an optimistic assessment.

Social facilities comprising village centers, public baths, and laundries have been built in 63 villages. The baths are an issue of contention because none of the 63 is used by the villagers, and no one understands the logic behind their construction. Today 11 of these baths have been converted to village bakeries, and the rest remain unused, a source of jokes among the villagers. If prior research had been carried out on their desirability and necessity, public funds would not have been wasted on building them.

Observations at the Village Level

In the summer of 1984, Demirseyh village in Sungurlu County, Çorum, consisted of 421 households with a population of 1,832. Livelihood was from agriculture, casual labor, and animal husbandry, in descending order of importance. The village, whose precise origins are unknown, is situated on the skirts of a hill, with undulating agricultural lands stretching from north to south; it is linked to Sungurlu District by a stabilized road. Most houses are built of mud bricks supported by wooden frames and roofed with red tiles, though a fair number of houses are flat-roofed, covered with earth. The village contained a post office, three grocery shops, and two coffee houses. As part of the rural development project, the village was electrified and a village center was built. There were no house hookups for water, but water was available from various fountains in the village.

Village Landownership

Table 14.2 reveals a sharply unequal distribution of landownership. A third of the villagers are landless, and an additional 42 percent own less

TABLE 14.2
Land Distribution

Land Size (Decares)	No. of Families	Percent of Families	Total Amount of Land Owned — Percent of Land-owning Families	Decares	Total Land (Percent)
Landless	138	32.77	–	–	–
0 - 25	113	26.84	39.9	2,034	10.5
26 - 50	64	15.2	22.6	2,520	13
51 - 100	66	15.67	23.3	4,810	24.9
101 - 200	31	7.36	11	4,588	23.8
201 - 500	7	1.66	2.4	2,464	12.8
500+	2	0.5	0.7	1,450	7.5
Absentee	not known	not known		1,449	7.5
Total	421	100	99.9	19,315	100

Source: Sungurlu Tax Records 1984.

than a quarter of the total cultivable lands. Some 70 percent of the land is held by only 25 percent of the owners, and an unknown number of absentee owners hold an additional 7.5 percent. The most affluent 2 percent of village households control 20 percent of the total land.

Most farmers are smallholders in the village, a situation that is general throughout Turkey (Varlier 1978) except in the eastern and southeastern regions (Aydın 1986). In dry-farming conditions, holdings below 75 decares are usually considered "small" in Turkey, and around 50 percent of landowning families in the village fall into this category. The baseline survey carried out in the project region indicates, however, that in Çorum villages farmers considered holdings in excess of 80 decares to be "large," while 40 to 50 decares were considered "medium sized" (Özler and Peker 1979:91). Of course, the size of the holding alone does not determine household income, since soil fertility and access to irrigation are also important. Nevertheless, the figures from the village suggest that the landholding pattern was unequal, with only a small number of farmers owning large farms and the majority owning small or medium-sized farms. The size of landholding influenced not only the level of incomes but also the differential access to sources of credit, inputs, and seeds.

The village's main crop is wheat, followed by barley, and, to a lesser degree, lentils, chick peas, maize, and some animal fodder. In the limited irrigated areas such vegetables as tomatoes, peppers, eggplants, cucumbers, and onions are produced. Very small amounts of watermelons, sweet melons, grapes, apples, and pears are also grown.

In dryland agriculture, tractors do most of the tilling, though traditional ox-drawn wooden plows are still used when tractor use is infeasible. Normally tractors are rented, but in 1978 and 1979 during the gasoline and foreign currency shortages when gasoline prices increased disproportionately, a large number of farmers unable to afford the rent for a tractor had to revert to ox-drawn wooden plows. This coincided with the extension agent's fruitless, albeit infrequent, visits to the village to persuade farmers to use machinery and improved technology. He was unable to advise them how to reduce the costs.

At the time of our fieldwork 15 tractors were in the village, 10 of them obtained with the help of credit received from the Agricultural Bank. These tractors were used in rental and sharecropping arrangements as well as in the cultivation of the owners' lands.

A small or medium farm relies on family labor, only occasionally employing one or two wage laborers. If the cost of renting a tractor is considered reasonable, even small farmers try to have their land tilled by tractor, which frees them to go outside the village for seasonal or casual wage labor. The smallest landowners tended also either to work others' lands on a sharecropping basis or to sharecrop out their land, either to another small owner or to a tractor owner. The rental of tractors was encouraged by the fact that small landowners were not able to buy and maintain draft animals. They would use the part of their labor freed by the use of rented agricultural machinery to earn cash to meet the cost of the rent. In many cases, therefore, the farmer was not around to supervise the tilling of the land or the harvesting of the crop by machinery, as he would be working outside the village. His wife or another relation, however, would keep an eye on the tilling. Family members, mostly women and children, would provide the labor for harvesting.

The large farms in the village all owned tractors and used family labor as well as wage labor, but with minimal involvement of children in production. On most medium and small farms women carried out the bulk of agricultural work in addition to their household tasks. The renting of machinery and the use of intensive female labor allowed small (and some medium) farmers to work outside the village for supplementary income. Were it not for the cash earned outside the village, agricultural production in its present form could not be carried out, because of the high cost of inputs and machinery. This fact is a constant source of complaints and grumbling in the village.

Sharecropping arrangements took place mostly between landowning families. Families with small holdings (for example, two or three decares of unirrigated land) had two alternatives: either to take land in to increase the size of their holding to a reasonable level, or to give their land to someone else to sharecrop if it was not worth cultivating themselves. Preference might be given to family members or people of the same kin group, but there was no great pressure to keep such arrangements among relatives. Because of inheritance laws, land had been fragmented in such a way that a small piece might be owned by a number of siblings. One of the brothers would be responsible for its cultivation, and the rest would get their due share. A recent tendency has been to give the land to a tractor owner on a sharecropping basis; in this arrangement the landowner provides the land and half of the seed, while the tractor owner provides the other inputs. The tractor owner then keeps two-thirds of the harvest, as it is believed that the use of a tractor increases productivity of the land. Some absentee landowners also give preference to tractor owners.

Only a few of the large number of landless people in the village were working as sharecroppers, because landowners preferred to rent either to another landowner or to a tractor owner who would have the necessary equipment and be able to afford production inputs. Most landless families, however, were involved in agricultural production as wage laborers or on the farms of relatives. Some of the landless were sons who worked their fathers' lands with the expectation of inheriting them. The limited availability of work outside the village tied them to the village and their parents' land as a source of security, even when they formed a separate household.

Of 138 landless families, only 21 were engaged in sharecropping arrangements. As stated previously, most sharecropping took place between landowners, and a total of 96 landowning families were involved in sharecropping arrangements. The number of families that gave their lands to sharecroppers was 62, while the number of landowning families that took on additional land on a sharecropping basis was 34. Sharecropping arrangements were not restricted within village boundaries, and it was quite common for families to sharecrop land in adjacent villages. Since the majority of sharecropping arrangements took place between landowning families and did not involve large pieces of land, there was not a strong tendency to political clientelism in the village. Cash renting was insignificant in the village, though it did exist, as people were not prepared to risk a fixed amount of rent on the possibility of crop failure due to erratic rainfall. Nobody wanted to sell land, even though incomes from small holdings were not high, for the value of land was rising both because of increasing mechanization and because of the readiness of migrant workers coming back from Germany or Holland to pay high prices for it.

About 30 families in the village had at least one member working abroad and sending back money. On the other hand, more than half the households in the village were involved in seasonal labor migration. In the long summer season especially, laborers would go to big cities like Ankara, Istanbul, and Izmir to work on construction sites or do odd jobs. For instance, a group of people in the village had a monopoly on selling fried fish from a boat in the Eminönü-Sirkeci area of Istanbul. The work involved buying the cheapest available fish from the fish market, frying it, and selling it on small boats around the Galata Bridge. In order to keep this profitable business under their control, the unmarried migrant villagers would remain in Istanbul in the winter, while the married ones would rejoin their families in the village.

Incomes earned by migrant laborers from the village directly contributed to the maintenance of agricultural production, as shown by the credit and market relations that link the village to the wider economy. The Çorum-Çankırı Integrated Development Project intensified the integration of the village economy into the national and international economy. In the following sections I will examine the credit and market mechanisms in the village.

Credit in the Village

Eighteen household heads were selected to include a range of landless, small, medium, and large farmers, some of whom were involved in sharecropping and some in wage labor. Interviews with these household heads revealed that the majority of landowning farmers in the village had borrowed money from the Agricultural Bank or from the Village Development Cooperative. In the first two years of the project small farmers were unable to obtain credit from the Agricultural Bank because of bureaucratic hassles, the requirement of collateral (land titles and merchant guarantors), and the low value attributed to the land by the Agricultural Bank in extending credit. Farmers complained that the bank underestimated the value of their land (sometimes by as much as 90 percent) in establishing credit. If a farmer's land that was worth TL100,000 was evaluated at TL5,000 in the first two years of the project, and if the farmer wanted to borrow TL10,000, he would have to find a guarantor for the second TL5,000. Thus small farmers, discouraged from borrowing from the bank, tended to borrow through traditional channels: merchants, usurers, friends, and family members. Landless people and sharecroppers were completely excluded from the credit program.

When small producers did manage to obtain short-term credit from the bank, the amounts were usually too small to be used productively in agricultural improvement, and went for such immediate necessities as food and clothing. The documents of the Agricultural Bank and Extension Service in Çankırı Province and Sungurlu District misleadingly show that short-term loans in the first four or five years of the project were repaid to the bank. The figures are misleading because quite a large number of small farmers were in fact unable to repay the credit from the first year onwards, but postponed the debt in a cumulative manner. The process works like this: at the end of the year, unable to produce the amount to be paid to the bank, the small farmer borrows the money from a merchant or usurer for a week or so, with interest. Then, having paid the bank the amount owed, he qualifies for a second year's credit, which is given to him within one or two weeks of repaying the previous loan. The farmer then takes the money to the merchant or usurer and repays that loan with interest. In all these transactions the only money produced by the farmer is the interest to be paid to the merchant or usurer. In just a few years the original credit is consumed. As the project drew closer to its conclusion farmers simply stopped paying the bank, hoping that the government might not push them as hard as the merchants and usurers for repayment.

Short-term credit was also given to farmers in the form of fertilizers and other agricultural chemicals. Under the state's monopoly of distributing artificial fertilizers in Turkey, shortages arose from time to time during the project years. These shortages led to black marketing, and merchants were quick to cash in. They would buy the sought-after artificial fertilizers from farmers who, needing the cash, were prepared to sell rather than to apply the chemicals on their own lands.

Large farmers did not encounter much difficulty in obtaining credit from the bank, though they also complained about the paperwork. In medium-term credit there was a clear bias toward larger farmers, since credit was given on condition that the farmer provide, from his own resources, 25 percent of the value of the equipment to be purchased. Four medium farmers managed to obtain credit for the purchase of tractors, using remittances from relatives working in Europe. Though most of the credit obtained from the bank was used in agriculture, in two cases it was used for commercial activities.

Another institution involved in agricultural credit provision was the Village Development Cooperative. In response to complaints that the Agricultural Bank was creating difficulties for small farmers in credit provision, it was decided that a member of a cooperative could obtain credit from the bank as long as the cooperative supported the application. The government had introduced Village Development Cooperatives in Turkey in previous years as part of a general policy of development through rural cooperatives, but most of them, without resources, did not function at all. The government sought a solution by giving a certain number of slots to each cooperative for selecting workers to be sent to Europe; these workers were to pay a monthly contribution to the cooperative, which would use the money in agricultural production. The export of workers to Europe came to a standstill in the early 1970s as a result of the crisis experienced by Western economies, and the workers already abroad stopped sending remittances. Consequently, the Village Development Cooperatives—known popularly as "Germany Cooperatives"—ceased to operate. Once there was a possibility of obtaining credit through them, however, large and influential landowners took control of the cooperative administration and influenced the distribution of credit.

The three richest families were strongly represented in the administration of the village cooperative. They made sure that members of their kin groups received priority in obtaining credit, especially medium-term credit. Though kinship ties were weakening in the village, there still existed a form of patron-client relationship between rich and poor members of the same kin group. The ideology of "being on the side of one's kinsmen" in such important matters as weddings, politics, and conflict was still strong among the villagers. Leading families, with more economic strength and education, were involved in party politics, and therefore needed their kinsmen's votes. Although they did not have a strong hold over these kin members, in return for votes they would help them in dealings with state officials. This kinship relation worked in credit allocation as well, and members of the three most influential families had better access to credit through the cooperative. These three strong kin groups were basically interested in medium-term credit and did not mind if other people obtained short-term credit through the cooperative.

With the involvement of the Village Development Cooperative in the distribution of credit, the number of borrowers among the small producers increased. Even landless people and sharecroppers managed to borrow from the credit system in the project's later years. During my last visit to the area, in the summer of 1987, I found that the Agricultural Bank and the cooperatives had taken legal action against many small farmers and landless borrowers as well as a few middle-sized and large farmers for defaulting on their debts.

The use of chemicals and other improved inputs was more widespread among medium and large farmers. Small producers tended not to use the credit they obtained for agricultural production because, first, other pressing needs took priority, and second, they were well aware that the limited amount of credit they could obtain would not enable them to buy the whole package of inputs suggested by the extension workers. It was clear to them that the use of just a few items from the package would significantly increase production. They rationally applied their small amount of credit to purposes other than agriculture.

Marketing

Everyone in the village knew that productivity increased in wheat, barley, and lentils during the seven years of project implementation, thanks to the use of machinery, chemicals, and improved seeds. All agreed that farmers were now marketing larger amounts of agricultural and animal produce. Most agricultural crops are sold according to official floor prices. The government is usually rather late in declaring the floor prices, however, and sometimes well after the harvest it adjusts them to reflect world prices. This always works against the small producers. The main buyers in the grain market were the state-owned Soil Products Office and private merchants. Producers, especially the smaller ones, prefer to sell or are forced to sell to merchants rather than to the Soil Products Office. Quite a number of merchants buy grain at the farm. Small producers sell their grain to the merchants on site at a lower price than to the state-owned soil-products office, for a number of reasons. First, for the producer who does not have a large crop, it is less cumbersome than taking it to the town center, where selling to the Soil Products Office not only entails queuing for a few days, but also the payment of rental fees for transport during queuing time. The merchants offer instant payment. Second, small producers are quite often indebted to the merchant; in such cases they may mortgage their crops against the payment of the loan at a fixed price, lower than the government-declared floor price. It also became quite common for the government to declare the floor prices and buy the produce from the farmers, then a few months later, under pressure from big landowning and merchant interests, to increase the floor price and pay the difference to those who had already sold their crops to the Soil Products Office. This works against the interests of small producers who are forced to sell their produce to merchants as soon as the harvest is over, while larger producers who can afford to store their produce obtain higher prices for it. The additional income that results from floor-price adjustment by the government thus accrues to the merchants, who store the grain until the floor-price adjustments take place.

Although large farmers are able to take advantage of price adjustments by holding on to their crops, they are nevertheless negatively affected, along with the other agricultural producers, by the movements of input prices. The constant increase in the prices of inputs prevents farmers from obtaining an increased income in real terms. Every farmer was aware of this anomaly. Government price policy worked against the aim of the project to increase farmers' incomes.

Project Facilities and Services in the Village

While villagers responded positively to the government's bringing in electricity and improving the condition of the road, they were bewildered by the village baths, which were never used. Many reasons were suggested for their remaining idle: shortage of water, high running costs, and social factors. One villager commented lightheartedly that he did not want people to know how many times a week he had sexual intercourse (in Islam one has to have complete ablutions after copulation). Villagers had no reason to prefer the village bathhouse to their own bath facilities at home. Overall, they thought it would have been a better use of public funds if the state had built canals, a health center, or a drinking water system.

Reservations were also expressed about the courses organized for village women, attempting to teach things that had no relevance in the village and were more appropriate to a town lifestyle. The claim in the completion report by the State Planning Organization (SPO 1986:7) that the project improved the lot of women in Çankırı and Çorum is hardly justified, since few village women participated in the activities designed for them. Quite the contrary, with the intensified market orientation of the village economy as a result of the project, the workload of women increased considerably. For instance, with the increasing use of artificial fertilizers, weeds of many kinds also flourish, adding significantly to the workload of women, whose responsibilities invariably include hoeing and weeding.

Feelings were mixed about the extension service. There was agreement about the uselessness of the village agent and the usefulness of the demonstrations, but the number of demonstrations was so small that their impact was very limited. Only a few medium farmers went to the extension office in Sungurlu to seek information on any issues. Obviously the organization of the extension service did not lead to frequent contact between the farmers and extension staff. The existing extension staff and agricultural technicians also resented the fact that a new extension service was established and that it relied so much on the village agents. Consequently not much cooperation or support developed between the newly established extension service and the old one.

Where Were the Social Scientists?

As in most development projects, the role of social scientists in the Çorum-Çankırı Rural Development Project was marginal, and their contribution has not had any impact, even though the concept of monitoring and evaluation is very pronounced in the rhetoric of the World Bank (see Cernea and Tepping 1977). The Bank's emphasis on monitoring and evaluation stems from the belief that project implementation and management could be improved if there were constant checks. Whether a project might be successful if it had a properly implemented monitoring and evaluation system depends on the project's aims. If the aims are not feasible, then no matter what the extent of monitoring and evaluation, success will not be high. This seems to be the case with the Çorum-Çankırı Project. On the one hand, the project aimed to increase the integration of farmers into the market economy through increasing their marketable products, and, on the other hand, it aimed to eliminate poverty. Since market forces operate within an unequal context in which farmers have different strengths in terms of their access to resources and services and their wealth, this integration tends to exacerbate existing structural inequalities. This was quite clear in credit distribution and marketing of the produce. As credit distribution was directly related to the amount of land owned, large farmers were able to utilize this facility beneficially, while small farmers were not able to obtain enough credit to maintain a self-sustaining reproduction cycle. Credit obtained was one of the reasons for their protracted indebtedness, and quite a number of them were facing such serious consequences as losing their land. The marketing of agricultural produce is also structured in such a way that it works against the interests of small producers, who end up being squeezed by merchants and gradually pauperized.

If social scientists had been employed in the project, I do not think their work could have completely eliminated its contradictory aims, but their findings, if taken seriously, might have enabled the authorities to curb the extremes of its consequences. The structures of the bureaucratic organizations responsible for implementation could have been studied to see their inner workings, their decision-making processes, the nature of their members, and the possible nature and outcomes of future cooperation between them. In this way some of the difficulties encountered by the project might have been eliminated from the outset. Appointing a social scientist to a high position with authority and responsibility might also have led to a different organization of credit allocation, as social differentiation among the farmers would have been taken into consideration.

The baseline study (Özler and Peker 1979) was full of indications showing that if carried out against a background of structural inequalities the project would intensify these inequalities rather than eliminate poverty or benefit everybody en masse. Because the contributions of the social scientists were not taken seriously by the project bureaucracy, the baseline study was carried out late (completed in 1979) and its results were considered too academic. A thorough study of the structural specificities of the region by social scientists might have led the project planners to reconsider and clarify some of the project's basic assumptions, which in turn might have led to changes in its organization and implementation.

There was no single detailed community study by anthropologists during the project years to reveal the inner workings of these communities, to help gain insights into kinship and power relations, beliefs and cultures, and behavioral patterns. Such a study would have served as a medium through which villagers could have expressed their needs and desires.

These conclusions about the role of the social scientist are not new or original and are well known to development planners in agencies like the World Bank; yet in each new development project they are not taken into full consideration. Why not? Let me answer this question with another question: are the international development agencies really interested in both increasing productivity and eliminating poverty at the same time? Or are they prepared to sacrifice one of these aims for the other, while retaining both in their rhetoric?

Notes

1. Between 1960 and the middle of the 1970s, in order to expand the internal market, resources were transferred to the agricultural sector through state-controlled prices for agricultural produce. By the 1970s, industry and commerce had overtaken agriculture as the leading sector of the economy. During the general economic crisis experienced by Turkey in the late seventies, state funds were used for the benefit of the industrial and commercial sectors at the expense of agriculture. Export-oriented industrialization policies adopted by the governments from the middle of the seventies necessitated cheapening manufactured export commodities by means of state subsidies.

References

Akad, Tanju
    1987 Kırsal Kesime Devlet Müdahaleleri ve Kooperatifler (State Intervention in Agricultural Sector and Cooperatives). Onbirinci Tez, No. 7. Ankara.

Aydın, Zülküf
    1986 Underdevelopment and Rural Structures in Southeastern Turkey. London: Ithaca Press.

Boratav, Korkut
    1987 Birikim Biçimleri ve Tarım (Forms of Accumulation and Agriculture). Onbirinci Tez, No. 7. Ankara.

Cernea, M. M., and B. J. Tepping
    1977 A System for Monitoring and Evaluating Agricultural Extension Projects. Washington, DC: World Bank Staff Working Paper No. 272.

CCRDP (Çorum-Çankırı Rural Development Project Report)
1977a   Birinci Altı Aylık Rapor (First Six-monthly Report). International Project Report. July.

1977b   Progress Report to June 1977 plus some of the Second Half of 1977. Report prepared for World Bank. Ankara, 13 December.

1979   Çorum Ili Proje Yayım Servisi Birinci Altı Aylık Çalışma Raporu (Çorum Province Extension Service: First Six-monthly Report). Unpublished.

FAO (Food and Agriculture Organization)
1972   Turkey: Central Anatolia Integrated Rural Development Project. Unpublished report by FAO and IBRD program in collaboration with the Turkish Government Services.

1984   Technical Advisory Support for the Çorum-Çankırı Rural Development Project: Project Findings and Recommendations. Rome.

Grammelspacher, Karl Heinz
1978a   The Implementation of Medium Term Credit in Çorum Province through the Çorum-Çankırı Rural Development Project. Internal Project Report (31 October).

1978b   The Implementation of Short Term Credit in Çorum Province through the Çorum-Çankırı Rural Development Project. Internal Project Report (9 November).

1978c   Credit Implementation in Çankırı Province through the Çorum-Çankırı Rural Development Project. Internal Project Report (27 December).

1979   Credit Implementation in Çorum and Çankırı Provinces through the Çorum-Çankırı Rural Development Project. Internal Project Report (5 January).

Gülalp, Haldun
1983   Gelişme Stratejileri ve Gelisme Ideolojileri (Development Strategies and Development Ideologies). Ankara: Yurt Yayınları.

IBRD (World Bank)
1975a   Appraisal of Çorum-Çankırı Rural Development Project. Washington, DC.

1975b   Rural Development: Sector Policy Paper. Washington, DC.

Keyder, Çağlar
1979   The Political Economy of Turkish Democracy. New Left Review No. 115.

KIKB (Köy Işleri ve Kooperatifler Bakanlığı)
1983a   Köy Envanter Etüdü 1981 Çankırı (Village Inventory Study 1981 Çankırı). Istanbul.

1983b   Köy Envanter Etüdü 1981 Çorum (Village Inventory Study 1981 Çorum). Istanbul.

McNamara, Robert
1973   Address to the Board of Governors. Nairobi.

Nott, Gladys Amorocho
1983   The Political Economy of Monitoring and Evaluation: The Case of the Çorum-Çankırı Development Project, Turkey. Ph.D. dissertation, University of East Anglia.

Özler, Güntaç, and Mümtaz Peker
1979   The Social and Economic Structure of Çorum-Çankırı Region. Unpublished report.

Proje Yayım Servisi
1986   Çorum-Çankırı Kırsal Kalkınma Projesi 1986 (Çorum-Çankırı Rural Development Project 1986). Unpublished report. Ankara.

SPO (State Planning Organization)
1986   Çorum-Çankırı Rural Development Project: Draft Completion Report. Ankara.

Varlier, Oktay
1978   Türkiye Tarımında Yapısal Değişme, Teknoloji ve Toprak Bölüşümü (Structural Change, Technology and Land Distribution in Turkish Agriculture). Ankara: State Planning Organization.

15

Tradition and Change Among the Pastoral Harasiis in Oman[1]

Dawn Chatty

So little social science had been conducted in the central desert of Oman that, as late as 1980, one writer had only this to say about the Harasiis: "Information about the way of life here and about the tribe of the Harasiis which inhabits the area is very limited, although it is thought that the small nomadic groups pursue camel herding exclusively and engage in periodic movements . . . but little is known about these people" (Scholz and Cordes 1980:11). In 1981 I began a 24-month anthropological study in the region, the government of Oman having instructed me to examine the felt needs and problems of that population and to design and implement practical social programs to meet those needs. The government desired to raise the standard of living of the population "without undermining its traditional way of life" (Chatty 1984:2) or forcing it to settle and join the agricultural communities of north and south Oman. The regime wanted to extend the same basic services to the pastoral populations of its central desert that it had developed in most of the rural regions since the accession of His Majesty Sultan Qaboos bin Said bin Taimur in 1971. The government did not entertain the expedient of settling these pastoral nomads, nor, for that matter, the idea of developing their pastoral marketing system, but it built a tribal center at Haima—a complex of buildings with a police station, a reverse osmosis water plant, a mosque, and a petrol station—and appointed a *wali*[2] as its representative to run it.

My preliminary recommendations were to implement immediately the same fundamental health, education, and welfare services in the Jiddat as existed in the rest of the country. Within three years (1981–1984), mobile primary health care, limited curative services, educational facilities, veterinary services, and welfare services were instituted for these highly mobile people. As these programs based at the Haima Center maintained significant outreach sectors, Haima soon became the administrative focus of the tribe. The sudden availability of petrol and sweet water alone drew tribespeople to Haima. Once they were there, the newly formed government programs and services attracted their attention. Now, access to government personnel for services and for the resolution of disputes that used to be handled exclusively among Harasiis themselves, is beginning to erode an identity based solely on tribal membership, and replace it with a broader one that also includes membership in the Omani state. In this chapter I will briefly describe the Harasiis tribe as it was before modern government services were first introduced and as it is now. I will, in this fashion, indicate how the Harasiis sense of identity has been modified in just a very few years.

The Northern Mountains, the Southern Mountains, and the Central Desert Plateau, a flat limestone slab called the Jiddat-il-Harasiis (see Figure 15.1), comprise three distinct geological zones within the land area of the Sultanate of Oman. The eastern boundary of the Jiddat-il-Harasiis is an escarpment that drops into the Huqf depression and is, in places, a hundred meters high. To the north, the Jiddat gradually changes into the gravel fan of the Northern Mountains and, to the northwest, it comes up against the southern finger of the Rub'a al-Khali sand dunes. Its western boundary is marked by a gradual transition into the rolling plains heralding the Southern Mountains. The Jiddat itself is particularly flat with very few ridges or outcrops of more than ten meters. Its most conspicuous features are the scattered depressions, called *haylat*, which vary in size from 1 to 25 hectares. The surface of the Jiddat is *hammada*, made up of rock, pebble, and coarse sand. Stanley Price (1988, IV:4-7) describes the region's central climatic characteristics.

The Jiddat's proximity to the Arabian Sea mitigates some of the extremes of climate associated with most deserts. June is the hottest month, with an average shade maximum of 43.4°C and daily extremes of 47° or 48°C. The coolest months are December, January, and February with monthly maxima of 26°C to 27°C and an average minimum of 11.4°C in January. In addition to great changes in temperature between months, there is a daily fluctuation of as much as 15° to 20°C. Relative humidity can vary between less than 10 percent and saturation in the course of 24 hours in winter or in summer. Rain tends to fall in late winter and spring and, very exceptionally, in summer.

An almost daily sea breeze between March and October can cause air temperatures to drop as much as 10°C in ten minutes, while relative humidity rapidly increases. If this breeze drops to below 8 knots after midnight, the moist cool air condenses and forms a fog bank at ground level. When the stronger sea breezes between June and September prevent the moist air mass from descending to ground level, fogs are less common.

The mean annual rainfall of 50 mm and the amount of moisture available from the fogs determine the vegetation cover. The density of trees on the Jiddat is remarkable for a desert. The *Acacia tortilis* is the most widespread tree, while in the sandy depressions and in all haylats *A. ehrenbergiana* is common. In haylats with deeper sand accumulations, single trees of *Prosopis cineraria* grow, some reaching 15 or 20 meters in height. These trees can grow on the Jiddat despite the low rainfall because of fog moisture. Even

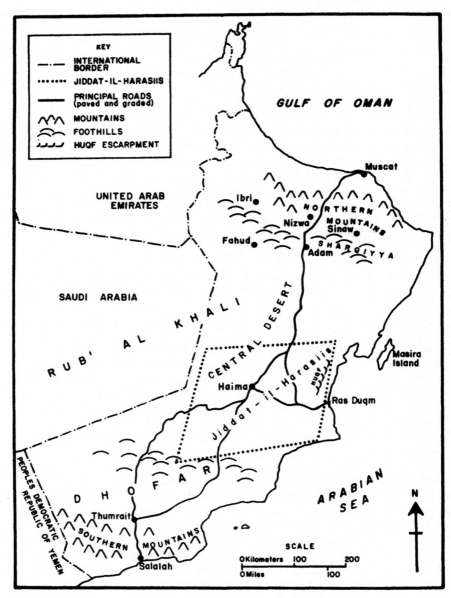

FIGURE 15.1
Sultanate of Oman. *Source:* Adapted from *Oman and Its Renaissance* by Sir Donald Hawley, Stacey International Publishers, London 1977. Prepared by Jane S. Davis.

in the absence of rain, bursts of green leaf may occur at all times of the year. When air temperatures are moderate and fogs most common, during March-April and again in September, growth is stimulated and grasses flower in response to the moisture. Thus the prime ecological consequence of the fog is that the Jiddat has a level of primary production twice a year even without rain.

A small population, the Harasiis tribe, lives on the Jiddat. These pastoralists, who appear to have been originally a Dhofari tribe, speak a modern south Arabian language known as Harsuusi. According to Harsuusi oral tradition, the original section of the tribe was Beit Afarri, living in Wadi Kadrit between Salalah and Hadramaut. Over the past few hundred years, the Harasiis have gradually pushed—and been pushed—northeast into the Jiddat. As they moved into the various wadis that mark the natural geographic borders of the Jiddat floor, they have come up against other pastoral tribes—the Jeneba to the east along the Jazir Coast, and the Wahiba to the north in the Wadi Halfayn. Unable to push farther, the Harasiis today are mainly concentrated on the desert plateau itself, although in the summer they are found sharing the Awta and Jazir Coast with the Jeneba tribe (see Figure 15.2).

They raise camels and goats on natural forage for the production of milk.[3] Migration, structured by a combination of seasonal and ecological variables in the location of pasture and water, ensures survival of both herds and herders as they move from deficit to surplus areas throughout the year. Territory is important among the Harasiis. They seek to control a region that contains sufficient resources to sustain communal life. Tending to live in haylats or wadis where trees can be found under which to shelter and where browse and graze is plentiful, they determine their territorial frontiers loosely as running along the floor of the Wadi Rawnab to the south and east of Rima, along the middle of Wadi Haytam to the northeast, up to the general region of the Harashiif dunes to the north, and across to the Ramlat-as-Sahmah to the west. They share borders with the Jeneba on the east, with the Wahiba and Duru' to the north, and the Beit Kathir on the south.

These borders are in constant flux. Over the past three decades the seasonal availability of pasture and water has undergone a pronounced geographic shift from southwest to northeast, requiring readjustment of relations with the Mahra, Jeneba and Wahiba. In the 1950s, 1960s, and 1970s various texts and oral traditions placed the territory of the Harasiis as extending from the Jiddat-il-Harasiis westward to Mughshin-al-Ayn and Bir Khasfah where they were said to have watering agreements with the Mahra and Bataaharah. Since that time, the territory has slowly moved eastward, so that during the 1980s disputes have tended to focus on water rights along borders shared with the Jeneba in the Wadi Rawnab, Wadi Halfayn, and Wadi Baw.

In the past, access to water for the Harasiis was extremely limited. Tribal tradition had it that they never drank water, but lived almost entirely on the milk from their camel and goat herds. Their cultural explanation for

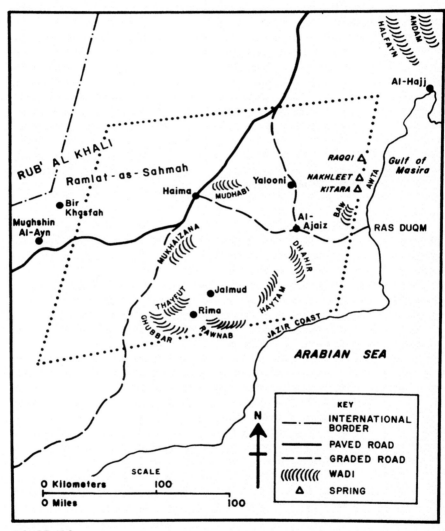

FIGURE 15.2
Jiddat-il-Harasiis. *Source:* Adapted from *Oman and Its Renaissance* by Sir Donald Hawley, Stacey International Publishers, London 1977. Prepared by Jane S. Davis.

this reflects geographic truth. Until the 1960s there was no source of sweet water on the Jiddat floor. Marginally potable water was found only along the Awta, the lowlands of the Huqf escarpment lying just along the coast of Oman from Duqm north toward al-Hajj. There, a series of springs is found (Raqqi, Nakhleet, Baw), probably recent rain runoff that has percolated through the limestone. These springs are heavily mineralized, yielding water that is barely potable even under extreme conditions, but the unique feature of a heavy, early-morning fog frequently provided the herds with sufficient moisture for their needs. These herds then provided the human population with enough milk for its nutritional requirements.

Economic Character of Traditional Life

The following information is extracted from a series of surveys and interviews of a random sample of 10 percent of Harasiis households made in 1982, prior to setting up government services for the tribe.

The Harasiis tribe is made up of approximately 2,000 people. Households are generally extended family units, the average family being composed of nine members. At the core of the household is the nuclear family of husband, wife, and children. Generally two to three adult relatives of one degree or another make up the rest of the family unit: grandparent, in-laws, cousins.[4] On average, a household keeps a hundred goats and a few sheep that are the responsibility of the women. Twice-daily milking and regular herding are undertaken by the women and older girls. Decisions over breeding and culling are generally taken by men, though sale of goats is always a joint decision—particularly as it is the women who own them. The average household keeps 25 camels of which 5 or 6 heavily pregnant or lactating females are generally kept near the homestead. The remainder of the camels are left *mafkook*, free to graze in the open desert. (Their whereabouts are carefully monitored, and an elaborate camel information exchange system operates among all the tribesmen. On meeting, tribesmen first exchange news about the conditions of the pasture, then the whereabouts of various mafkook camels, and finally news items of various family members.) Homesteads are generally moved a significant distance three or four times a year. Homesteads whose household heads are employed locally tend to make minimal adjustments to their campsite location in between the major moves. A full-time husbandman, though, will shift his homestead a few kilometers every few weeks to ensure that the family herd of goats and sheep does not exhaust what graze exists around the campsite.

Household Subsistence

Basic to the organization of all pastoral communities is the existence of sedentary communities in adjacent areas, and access to their agricultural products. In Oman, relations of interdependence bind the pastoral nomads to the sedentary communities along the Sharqiyya foothills. The pastoralists bring animals to auction in the village marketplace; pots and trays for repair at the local coppersmiths; and palm frond mats, bowls, baskets, and ghee for sale. At the same time they purchase the comestibles necessary for their families and herds. (Since 1983, during periods of drought, they have been buying dried feed, either third grade wheat chafings or hay—rhodes grass—for camels and goats.) For generations this relationship, largely uncomplicated by external factors, bound the Harasiis of Central Oman to the villages of the Sharqiyya foothills—particularly Adam and Sinaw—in an economic partnership. The cash economy of the village was reinforced by the continual influx of "capital on the hoof." Transactions were completed and money changed hands. Significantly, though, when the final purchases were made, the bulk of the money had simply moved from one end of the market to another—from the animal buyer's pocket to the merchant's till. For the Harasiis, the relationship with the villages reinforced not an exchange but a domestic economy. For example, the individual Harasiis tribesman may have sold two goats for forty Maria Theresa thalers, and then spent this exact amount for flour, coffee, tea, dates, sugar, and clothing for his family. His long treks to the village markets were motivated not by profit but by the need for some basic household item.

The Traditional Universe

The universe of the Harasiis was limited to the Jiddat floor. The long treks for supplies could take anywhere from 5 to 15 days. Adam, then Sinaw and Nizwa were the primary trading centers, with Salalah a distant third choice. On occasion, long journeys for medical care were undertaken to other Gulf States, sometimes as far as Kuwait. One individual is recorded as having emigrated to the Trucial Coast in search of an education, returning to the Jiddat twenty years later as a well-trained English-speaking nurse with the rank of colonel in the United Arab Emirates' Air Force. But such instances are rare. To the tribesmen as a whole, the Jiddat-il-Harasiis was the world. The tribe of about four hundred "arms bearing" men was organized into seven subgroups or lineages each called *buyut* (singular, *beit*). These seven lineages (Beit Aksit, Mutaira, Barho, Sha'ala, Aloob, Afarri, Katherayn) were divided into two main factions, one headed by the Beit Aksit and the other by the Beit Mutaira. The leadership of the tribe as a whole lay with the Beit Aksit, whose ancestral forebear is acknowledged to have united the disparate units into one tribe about 150 years ago. Each lineage generally recognized two spokesmen who acted on its behalf. These men were called *rashiid* (plural, *rushada'*) and represented the lineage in discussions concerning the welfare of the tribe. The pivotal position among the rushada' was that of the sheikh. He traditionally enjoyed a vast and ill-defined field of privileges and annually journeyed to Salalah to receive a gift from the sultan and, on occasion, to ask the sultan to adjudicate. For the individual Harsuusi tribesman, however, contact with others was limited, by and large, to members of other pastoral tribes such as the Jeneba, the Wahiba, the Duru', and the Mahra. The regular treks for supplies to villages along the borders of the desert were about as far a trip as the Harsuusi individual experienced. He had no knowledge of the political struggles in the north between the imam and the sultan and between the Hinai and Ghafiri, or in the south between the feuding tribes of Dhofar. The Harasiis, one of four pastoral tribes in Oman, was the only one not drawn into the several struggles to topple the sultan. The individual's identity as a Harsuusi tribesman was continually reinforced by the geographic remoteness of the homeland, its inaccessibility, and the almost total political isolation in which the tribe functioned.

Petroleum Exploration, Exploitation, and Employment

Petroleum and Politics

In 1954 an exploratory party of the national oil company, Petroleum Development Oman (PDO), made its way from the southern coast of Oman at Duqm into the Central Oman Steppes. There contact was made with the sheikhs of the Duru' tribe who agreed to allow PDO to prospect in their territory. The oil company needed to establish a system of labor recruitment and supervision effectively to exploit the oil promise in the area, but the request was completely foreign to the local people. Although tribal leaders were accustomed to acting as political mediators on behalf of their tribesmen, PDO's mixed political and economic needs were novel to them. At first, internal jealousies divided the tribal sections, and subunits or lineage leaders took to claiming the exclusive right to furnish labor for PDO, for which there was a significant reward.

In 1958 PDO began to prepare for a new drilling location at Haima. There was fear that the Jeneba tribesmen might claim the region as their own, though Haima was normally used by the Harasiis and was far from any disputable border. Four years earlier, when PDO had first landed at Duqm, Salim bin Huweila, a minor lineage leader, had been on the beach to greet the advance party. His curiosity and opportunism kept him close by, and whenever the oil company required the services of a local he was there ready to serve. After consultation with Sultan Said bin Taimur, PDO decided to search for a labor supervisor from the Harasiis, and Salim bin Huweila was appointed shortly thereafter. Following some labor unrest, both Salim and the traditional leader, Sheikh Shergi, were sent to Salalah to confer with the sultan.[5] They were to remain in Salalah for six months before being allowed to return to the Jiddat once the labor unrest had died down. Over the next decade, PDO was to play off the two men against each other, though their differences were more stylistic than ideological. The oil company found Salim to be a man of "charm and great personality," while Sheikh Shergi was pejoratively described in the same PDO field reports as a "small, greedy, little man." When Salim became too demanding or too difficult, PDO would turn to Sheikh Shergi. When Sheikh Shergi began to make "outrageous" requests—generally for water—they would ask that the sultan allow them to ignore Sheikh Shergi and return to dealing with Salim. Finally, in 1968, having had a great deal of trouble with Salim—despite his charm—PDO requested that the sultan allow it to deal with Sheikh Shergi for labor supervision. This was accepted by the sultan, but refused by Sheikh Shergi, who by this time had begun to make overtures for support from Sheikh Ahmed bin Mohammed al-Harthi, the powerful Minister of Interior. Sheikh Ahmed had a strong and growing following in the Sharqiyya region of Oman, which Sultan Said bin Taimur was unhappy about. It was reported in a number of PDO papers that the sultan was willing to allow Sheikh Ahmed his power base so long as he did not try to extend it south into the Jiddat. The underlying consideration was twofold: first, the sultan was very concerned that the traditional Hinai/Ghafiri power struggle not spill out of northern Oman and that Sheikh Ahmed's growing Hinai following be contained; and second, Sultan Said bin Taimur seemed to regard the Jiddat as well as Dhofar as his private reserve more than as a region of the country. When the sultan learned that Sheikh Shergi had refused "to act without directions from Qabil" (home base of Sheikh Ahmed), he angrily removed the sheikh from office and appointed Salim bin Huweila as the "new" sheikh of the Harasiis (PDO 1948–1975:1974:3). This arrangement worked well for the company but was never acceptable to the tribesmen nor, of course, to Sheikh Shergi, who bided his time.

In 1972, two years after his accession, Sultan Qaboos bin Said reinstated Sheikh Shergi and removed Salim bin Huweila, much to the dismay of PDO where his services had come to be appreciated. The decade of PDO and government interference in Harasiis tribal political organization had come to a close, but not without some loss of confidence by tribesmen in their authority figures. The Harasiis were suddenly exposed to a world far removed from their own reality, but of which they were reluctantly a part. They were no longer simple Harasiis pastoralists making a living in the barren and isolated Jiddat-il-Harasiis. They had become an Omani people occupying a greatly sought-after territory.

After 1970, the government of Oman and the national oil company entered central Oman with two major interests bearing on the Harasiis. First, fixed and stable boundaries had to be established. Second, permanent and reliable individuals from each tribe had to be selected to manage the hiring of laborers. The already fragile tribal political system, which had barely coped with earlier government interference, disintegrated, and Harasiis tribal authority in the person of Sheikh Shergi hardly existed. His past experience with the old sultan seems to have broken his willingness to do anything other than better himself and his own family. When, for example, the rushada' asked him to see the sultan and plead for another water tanker (in the period between 1975 and 1985), he would do so, but when the tanker arrived he would claim it for his own exclusive use. After his third tanker, in 1981, there was much muttering among the rushada'. Finally a meeting of all the tribal leaders was called in the office of the wali, to establish whether Sheikh Shergi had enough support to remain their leader. For lack of agreement on a successor, they did not replace him, but as a result of that attempted coup, Sheikh Shergi gave the next water tanker he received from the sultan to a kinsman, with the proviso that he actually distribute water among all the buyut. This accomodation did not last long, and within a few months the tanker was used exclusively for that one family. More and more individuals were going into Muscat and requesting interviews with various ministers (most often the Minister of Water and Electricity) to make requests to better their families, sometimes their beit, and only incidentally the tribe as a whole (as when the government installed reverse osmosis water plants in the region, after repeated individual requests for them). The annual trips to pay respects to the sultan continued, but to the individual tribesmen the sheikh was no longer an effective mediator or broker of their affairs with the world outside of the tribes. Traditional concerns such as pasture allocation and territorial rights remained communal issues within the beit and among the rushada' of the tribe, but the new concerns centering around paid employment with PDO and various government agencies were issues that each man handled on his own.

Pastoralism and Wage Labor

Economically the Harasiis tribe fared far better. From the moment in 1954 when oil exploration teams came ashore at Duqm, a new universe opened. Each of the oil company activities opened up new employment opportunities, and tribesmen quickly adapted to the routine—if not always the discipline—of the company. As more and more men took jobs as guides, drivers, guards, and manual laborers, their salaries became an increasingly important factor in the economic interplay between the desert and the village. In many cases, a man's salary began to replace revenues from animal sales as the main source of purchasing power. At first, animal sales declined and herd size increased, but by the early 1980s this process was checked by disease, a long period of drought, and the low carrying capacity of the Jiddat-il-Harasiis.

The activities of the oil exploration teams, the development of camps, the setting up of rigs, the opening up of wells, and later, petroleum exploitation were accompanied by tremendous infrastructural changes. Graded roads replaced tracks, and in 1981 a tarmac highway was opened, running through the center of the Jiddat and connecting the north and the south of the country for the first time. The 5-to-15-day journey across the desert by camel became a thing of the past. In 1974 the first Harsuusi-owned half-ton truck appeared on the Jiddat. Within five years nearly every Harsuusi household had one or more trucks. In our sample only one household head did not own a vehicle, but each of his three adult sons had one, and they alternated in procuring water, animal feed, and comestibles for their father's household, and in transporting his livestock to market. Journeys to town centers were no longer measured by days, but hours; six hours to Nizwa, eight to Muscat, seven to Salalah.

With the commencement of oil exploration and later exploitation on the margins of the Jiddat floor, the world for the Harasiis came to be quite radically altered. No longer was their concern uniquely with household subsistence, herd well-being, and pasture. Now wage labor came to be an important reality. The nature of employment on the Jiddat often required that the adult male household head be away from the family unit for weeks at a time. During such absences from the household, another male relative would often take over the vacant economic role, and would see to it that the household was provided with sufficient water, milk, animal feed, and other necessities. Even unrelated households camping in the same haylat or close to each other tended to help each other.

The new oil employment did not require men to migrate. Because their jobs remained within the borders of the Jiddat, they could still keep a distant eye on family and herd from their posts. Furthermore, the terms of employment were favorable, allowing men long stretches at home—two weeks on duty followed by one week off being fairly standard practice. Thus, though traditional patterns changed to keep pace with new factors in their environment, they were not yet breaking down. For example, milking camels was strictly a male preserve. Today, when the male head of the family is away at his job, a relative or close family friend will always endeavor to milk the household camels for the family's use. Only when no man is available will a woman do the milking herself.

As early as 1982, our surveys of the Harasiis population showed, 82 percent of the sampled households had some form of income beyond the sale of animals. Households where men were employed full-time had, on the average, 35 percent fewer camels and 25 percent fewer goats than did households with no outside salary. These same households revealed a surprisingly low incidence of sales of livestock, perhaps because of the demands of full-time employment as well as the distances between producer and market—easily 1,000 kilometers for a round trip. So while employment might seem to have inhibited regular sales of livestock and thereby accelerated graze depletion, the effect has been the opposite. The families whose heads are employed full-time have cut back on their herds, and thus employment has had a beneficial effect on grazing.

Probably the most profoundly altered factor in the tribesman's daily life has been his access to water. Before 1955, water was available only on the Awta. The practice of collecting water from the heavy morning fog was widespread. Water requirements had to be kept to a minimum. Four-fifths of a family's camels might be left mafkook, or on the loose to graze, with only the pregnant or lactating camels kept at the homestead. The traditional Harasiis goat, a short-haired white animal, was particularly adapted to the region, drinking no water in wintertime and very little in summer. Then, at some time during the reign of Sultan Said bin Taimur (probably during the 1960s), long-haired black goats from the north began to appear on the Jiddat, probably the result of successive human migrations north to Wadi Halfayn and Wadi Andam during droughts on the Jiddat. These black-haired goats were less suited to aridity and required greater quantities of water, but they were locally perceived as being a more marketable, fattier animal, and their meat was more widely appreciated in the market towns of northern Oman.

Over the last few decades the Harasiis had been pushed back from the coastal regions by the Jenaba tribe until they are now restricted to the Jiddat floor itself. Fortunately, their access to water has not been entirely cut off. Almost as though responding to the needs of the Harasiis, the national oil company arrived on the Jiddat in the mid-1950s and drilled water wells at Haima and Al-Ajaiz. By agreement with the government, these wells were left in operation after the exploration teams moved to more promising fields. In the 1960s, the Al-Ajaiz well served as a migratory magnet for the Harasiis. By the mid-1970s most families had purchased half-ton pickup trucks and were able to move further afield to areas of better graze particularly for their more water-dependent herds of black goats. Three times a week, and sometimes five, the household head would make a trip to the nearest well to bring water for his family and herds. The average family required 14 drums of water in winter and 21 in summer. Using half-ton pickup trucks that carry only four drums at a time—each with a capacity to hold 209 liters—a man bringing water for his family and herds could easily drive 500 kilometers a week for water alone.

The Harasiis share with other tribes several water wells located on borders, such as the well at Ghubbar, southwest of Rima, that is shared with the Mahra and the well at Rawnab that is shared with the Jeneba. But until 1984, an area of almost 40,000 square kilometers had only one uncontested source of sweet water and another of brackish water. Since then, fortunately, several reverse osmosis plants have been built by the government at such points as Wadi Mudhabi, Wadi Haytam and Wadi Dhahir for the pastoralists to use.

Since the first oil exploration teams landed at Duqm in 1954, the traditional patterns of exchange among Harasiis households have altered dramatically. The new employment opportunities have meant, in many cases, wages replacing livestock as the primary source of purchasing power. With the introduction of the vehicle on the Jiddat in the early 1970s, the economic balance was upset even further. Instead of sales of goats increasing to meet the new costs of operating a vehicle, the opposite appears to have happened, for sales decreased. Camels are sold only when a major purchase such as a wedding must be financed. Modern employment, which by its very nature removes the men from the household for weeks at a stretch, has decreased the amount of time available for managing the herd. Although men do keep a "distant eye" on the herd, they have to put off, alter, or reconsider many management decisions in the light of their work-shift obligations. Debt management seems to have replaced herd management as the answer to new revenue requirements. While increased borrowing and lending contribute to greater social cohesion within the tribe, the extension of credit to the Harasiis from outsiders has not worked—as Harasiis defaulters on installment-scheme purchases are discovering.

The arrival of the national oil company in the Jiddat, the employment opportunities on site for the Harasiis, the road network and wells dug by the company and later by the government, the rapid introduction and acceptance of the half-ton truck for transport, all these factors and events have forced the Harasiis to recognize and relate to a reality beyond their traditional borders. That reality is the national government, (*hukume*).

As few as five years ago, the term hukume and even Oman meant little more to a Harsuusi tribesman than something and someplace far away, beyond his tribal lands. Today the Harsuusi individual has come in contact with government services and with the concept of hukume as being an entity greater than himself or his tribe, from which much assistance can be extracted. Health services, educational opportunities, water, and welfare for the poor, crippled, widowed, or orphaned, all are accepted and appreciated.[6] The Harasiis are beginning to understand the hukume as representing them as well as various other populations within the country. They are coming to see themselves as not just Harasiis tribesmen but also as one of a number of peoples who make up the Sultanate of Oman. They are coming to expect that what other Omani have, they should have. Thus today it is not unusual to find Harsuusi individuals sitting in ministerial waiting rooms with petitions for increased government services: more health care, water, schools, tents, more of anything that would make life easier. The other side of the coin, service or loyalty to the nation, has not yet become part of the Harasiis frame of reference. Still today they tend to turn to the United Arab Emirates and other Gulf States when satisfaction from the hukume has not been complete. An individual unsatisfied by the hukume would travel to the UAE to receive whatever was originally demanded (most often health-related), and once satisfied, return to the Jiddat. The crude political awareness the Harasiis have developed recently leaves much to be desired, but it is early days, and time can only deepen the individual's understanding of the multisided nature of national as opposed to tribal identity.

Harasiis identity at one level is shifting from a communal to an individual one. Though the allocation of water and pasture remains an important concern at the level of households and buyut, other, new concerns are imposing themselves upon the consciousness of the individual—matters like private debts, schooling for children, local leasing contracts for water bowsers (tank trucks) and other heavy vehicles. At another level, there is an incipient shift from a tribal to a national identity, a shift toward "government" as something greater and more powerful than the tribe, something that can get things done. These two trends are part of the same process: the gradual decline in the importance of the tribe as the individual Harsuusi increasingly incorporates himself into the modern nation-state.

Notes

1. An earlier version of this chapter was published under the title, "The Harasiis: Pastoralists in a Petroleum Exploited Environment," in *Nomadic Peoples* (Chatty 1987).

2. A wali is a government-appointed administrator for a *wilayat* or region of the country. Each wali was meant to undermine and challenge the authority of the

traditional sheikhs in his region. And with the wealth and power of the government behind him, each has succeeded.

3. Young male goats and camels are either sold or slaughtered and consumed locally within the first four or five months after birth.

4. Polygynous households accounted for less than 10 percent of our sample. Though permitted by Islam, the economic realities of life make it a rare occurrence. When a Harsuusi male has more than one wife, each woman maintains her own homestead.

5. In this case, items had been found missing from PDO stores. Salim bin Huweila refused to allow PDO to search the baggage of Harasiis laborers leaving the camp on discharge. Sheikh Shergi took his side and a general strike of Harasiis laborers was threatened.

6. Negative aspects to these new benefits, such as corruption and graft, are seen as produced by individuals and are not lumped as part of the character of the government.

References

Chatty, Dawn
    1984 Women's Component in Pastoral Community Assistance and Development: A Study of the Needs and Problems of the Harasiis Population, Project Findings and Recommendations. New York, NY: United Nations.

    1987 The Harasiis: Pastoralists in a Petroleum Exploited Environment. Nomadic Peoples 24:14–22.

PDO (Petroleum Development [Oman] Limited)
    1948–1975 Uncatalogued papers on Tribes, Geology, and Labour. Muscat.

Scholz, Fred, and Rainer Cordes
    1980 Bedouin Wealth and Change: A Study of Rural Development in the United Arab Emirates and the Sultanate of Oman. Tokyo: The United Nations University Press.

Stanley Price, Mark
    1988 The Arabian Oryx in Oman: An Analysis of a Reintroduction. Cambridge: Cambridge University Press. In Press.

About the Editors and Contributors

Zülküf Aydın is a lecturer in sociology at Durham University (England), where he obtained his doctorate in 1980. He has conducted fieldwork in Turkey and Jordan on rural transformation, and has written on theoretical and empirical issues related to this transformation. He has taught at the Middle East Technical University (Turkey), London University, and Yarmouk University (Jordan). His current research interests include agrarian change, international labor migration, and state and society in the Middle East.

Victoria Bernal is an assistant professor of anthropology at Hamilton College, Clinton, New York. She received her Ph.D. from Northwestern University in 1985. She has conducted long-term fieldwork in the Sudan as well as a short study in Chad. Her work on agricultural development policy, land tenure, and peasant workers has been published in the *African Studies Review* and in several edited volumes. She is currently completing a book on proletarianization and agricultural development to be published by Columbia University Press.

Dawn Chatty received her Ph.D. in 1974 from the University of California at Los Angeles. After teaching at the American University of Beirut and the University of California at Santa Barbara, she was awarded a Fulbright teaching grant, and from 1977 to 1979 she taught anthropology at the University of Damascus. Since 1979, she has been living in Muscat, Sultanate of Oman, where, as a United Nations Technical Assistance expert, she studied the needs of pastoral nomadic populations and helped set up social programs to meet those needs.

John Aron Grayzel is a foreign service officer with the U.S. Agency for International Development serving as chief of the Regional and Resource Development Division of the agency's Bureau for Science and Technology. He is also a professional lecturer in rural development at the Johns Hopkins School of International Studies, a former visiting associate professor of anthropology at Boston University, and at present a research associate at the school's African Studies Center. He has a J.D. from Stanford University and a Ph.D. in anthropology from the University of Oregon, Eugene. He has worked in Mali, Mauritania, Senegal, Morocco, Tunisia, Egypt, and Madagascar; and has written on land tenure, pastoral systems, and law and ethnicity in such publications as *Human Organization*, the *American Bar Association Journal*, and most recently in Downs and Reyna, eds., *Land and Society in Contemporary Africa*.

Douglas Gritzinger is a doctoral candidate in urban and regional planning at Cornell University, where he also received an M.S. in agronomy in 1979. Since 1981 he has carried out assignments in Egypt, Iraq, and Tunisia for European, Japanese, and U.S. donor organizations.

Nicholas S. Hopkins is a professor of anthropology at the American University in Cairo, Egypt, who has also taught at New York University, the University of California at Los Angeles, and Princeton University. He earned his Ph.D. from the University of Chicago in 1967. His principal research experience is in Mali, Tunisia, and Egypt. He has published a number of books and articles on Africa and the Arab World, including *Agrarian Transformation in Egypt* (Westview 1987), *Arab Society: Social Science Perspectives* (edited with Saad Eddin Ibrahim), and *Testour ou la transformation des campagnes maghrébines*.

Michael M Horowitz, professor of anthropology at the State University of New York at Binghamton and director of the Institute for Development Anthropology, has carried out research among farming and pastoral peoples in Senegal, Niger, Mali, Burkina Faso, the Sudan, Zaire, Rwanda, Zimbabwe, Tunisia, Jamaica, and Martinique. He has been an advisor and consultant to the United Nations Development Programme, the U.N. Sudano-Sahelian Office, the Food and Agricultural Organization, the World Bank, the Agency for International Development, the Overseas Liaison Committee of the American Council on Education, the Overseas Development Council, the Board on Science and Technology for International Development of the National Academy of Sciences, and the U.S. Congress Office of Technology Assessment. In 1974–1975 he served as regional anthropologist and director of applied social science research for AID's Regional Economic Development Services Office for West Africa, and from 1979 to 1984 he was senior social science advisor to AID's Office of Evaluation. He coedited *Anthropology and Rural Development in West Africa* and *Lands at Risk in the Third World*. He received the Ph.D. in anthropology from Columbia University.

Frederick C. Huxley is a visiting researcher with the Center for Contemporary Arab Studies, Georgetown University, in 1988–1989. He has a doctorate in anthropology from Yale University (1975) and has taught at the American University of Beirut, the University of Michigan–Dearborn, and the University of California–Davis. Currently researching development in political-economic systems at the local and national levels in Tunisia, Dr. Huxley has published a monograph on formal and informal politics in Lebanon, a series of reports about development literature on five Arab countries, and several journal articles, book chapters, and reviews. He also has consulted with the U.S. Agency for International Development on drinking-water projects in the Yemen Arab Republic and on development literature about parts of the Arab World.

Emanuel Marx is professor of social anthropology at Tel Aviv University, and heads the Social Studies Center at the Jacob Blaustein Institute for Desert Research, Ben-Gurion University. He has studied Bedouin in the Negev and in the South Sinai, in a new town in Northern Israel, and in a Palestinian refugee camp in the West Bank. His major research interests are pastoral nomadism and bureaucratic behavior. His books include *Bedouin of the Negev* (1967), *The Social Context of Violent Behaviour* (1976), *A Composite Portrait of Israel* (1980), and *The Changing Bedouin*, edited jointly with A. Shmueli (1984). During the current year he is working at the Refugee Studies Programme, Oxford University.

John P. Mason is a senior social scientist in the Evaluation Office of the Agency for International Development, Washington, D.C. He has worked for two decades in international development, including a decade overseas in Arab, African, and Caribbean countries. Mason, who did Ph.D. research on socioeconomic change in a Saharan desert oasis community in Libya, has taught anthropology at the University of Libya (1968–1970), Rensselaer Institute (1971–1973), and the American University in Cairo (1973–1977). He worked for the United Nations in Libya (1977–1979) as a social planner on a physical planning project and for the Cooperative Housing Foundation as a development anthropologist and assistant vice president (1979–1985). Mason is a former director of the AID Development Studies Program in Washington. He has field experience in project feasibility studies; design, management, and evaluation in urban development and planning; village planning; and water and sanitation. Mason is a past president of the Washington Association of Professional Anthropologists.

Günter Meyer is professor of social and economic geography at the University of Erlangen–Nürnberg, Federal Republic of Germany. He carried out long-term field research on socioeconomic development in the newly reclaimed lands in Egypt (1976–1977); on rural development, nomadism, and labor emigration in Syria (1978–1980); and on economic development in the Yemen Arab Republic (1981–1983). Since 1984 he has engaged in various research projects in Egypt, focusing on urban expansion, the informal sector, and small-scale manufacturing in Cairo, and on industrial development in the new desert cities.

Alice L. Morton is director of Evaluation and manages three AID-funded development projects at RONCO Consulting Corporation in Washington, D.C. She has taught at American University, Manchester University, the University of California at Davis, and Rutgers University, usually in multidisciplinary social science programs. She received her Ph.D. from London University in 1976, having carried out two years of field research in Ethiopia on spirit possession and the status of women. She began working in international development in 1976, when she joined AID as a social science analyst. Since then, she has carried out project-related assignments primarily in Africa, North Africa, and the Middle East.

Henry Munson, Jr., is associate professor of anthropology at the University of Maine. His first two books, published by Yale University Press, are *The House of Si Abd Allah: The Oral History of a Moroccan Family* (1984) and *Islam and Revolution in the Middle East* (1988). He is presently writing a book on the social and political roles of Islam in Morocco. His articles have appeared in *American Anthropologist, Religion, The Middle East Journal, Middle*

Eastern Studies, The Muslim World, and several journals in Morocco. Professor Munson received his Ph.D. in anthropology at the University of Chicago in 1980.

Muneera Salem-Murdock is senior research associate and executive officer at the Institute for Development Anthropology and an adjunct assistant professor at SUNY-Binghamton. She has carried out research in Sudan, Tunisia, Jordan, South Yemen, and Senegal on irrigation, household production systems, and differentiation, and has served as consultant to the World Bank, the United Nations, the Food and Agriculture Organization, and the Agency for International Development. Dr. Salem-Murdock is the author of *Arabs and Nubians in New Halfa: A Study of Settlement and Irrigation* (University of Utah Press, 1989).

Monica Sella received her master's degree in agricultural economics at the University of Wisconsin and has carried out field research in the Senegal Valley for the Land Tenure Center and for the Institute for Development Anthropology.

Charles F. Swagman received his Ph.D. from the University of California at Los Angeles in 1985. He was a visiting assistant professor of anthropology at the University of Utah in 1986 and 1989 and has served as a consultant to various international organizations. He carried out research on development as related to local organizations and to health care in the Yemen Arab Republic from 1980 through 1984 and is the author of *Development and Change in Highland Yemen* (University of Utah Press, 1988) and of articles in *ORIENT, Social Science and Medicine,* and the *Journal of Anthropological Research.* He is currently training at the UCLA School of Public Health in the Division of Population and Family Health and is an affiliated scholar with the UCLA Institute for Social Science Research.

Daniel Martin Varisco received his Ph.D. in anthropology from the University of Pennsylvania in 1982. He has conducted ethnographic research in North Yemen, Egypt, and the Arabian Gulf. Since 1981 he has worked as a consultant in development issues related to agriculture, irrigation, social analysis, participant training, and wildlife conservation. During 1983 he was a fellow of the American Research Center in Egypt for a study of Arabic manuscripts on traditional star calendars. He has edited and translated a thirteenth century Yemeni agricultural almanac, now in press. Articles on the ethnography of the Middle East and on traditional agriculture and astronomy in the region have appeared in *Arabian Studies, Arabica, Journal for the Economic and Social History of the Orient, International Journal of Middle East Studies, Studia Islamica,* and *Zeitschrift für Geschichte der Arabisch-Islamischen Wissenschaften,* as well as in several Arabic periodicals.

Index

Animal husbandry
  in Central Tunisia, 103
  Demirseyh village in Sungurlu County, 324
  Mediterranean agriculture, 34
  in Turkey, 314
Anthropologist as broker
  Egypt, 175–177, 184, 190–195
  Libya, 155, 160, 161, 169–172
  Morocco, 15, 20, 25–27, 43, 47, 48, 61, 71, 72
  Negev, 228–230, 233, 235, 238
  Water User Associations, 74, 77, 79, 92
Aquifer, Nubian, Egypt, 177, 178, 180, 186, 187, 190
Arboriculture
  and credit, Morocco, 57
  in Egypt, 182, 183, 184, 186
  fruit trees, Yemen, 296
  Haraz Afforestation Project, 283, 284, 289
  in Mediterranean agriculture, 34
  qat cultivated as tree, 297
  tree crops in rural Central Tunisia, 75, 84, 87, 91, 98, 101, 102, 104, 107–109, 111, 115, 121–123

Banking Strategies for Semiarid Lands, 67
Barley, 34, 53, 54, 75, 98, 104, 202, 257, 294, 297, 299, 314, 316, 325, 330

Cash
cash-poor farmers pay debts to scheme in cotton, 199
  earned outside the village, 326
  economy of village, 208, 342
  expenditure, for labor, 105, 210
  expenditure, for land, 34, 106, 298
  expenditure, for water, 84, 122, 300
  expenditure, to rent tractor, 326
  flow into national economy, 293
  from charcoal making, 39, 209
  income, and gender differentiation, 116
  income, of Negev Bedouin, 231
  indemnity to Bedouin for land, 232
  inheritance, Yemen, 300
  and labor expenditure for all crops, 203
  loans to farmers, 55, 321
  need for, and blackmarketing of artificial fertilizer, 329
  paid to tenants for producing cotton, 200, 209
  remittances and rise of bridewealth, 272
  saved if food grown, 208
  system circumvented, 89
  and value of sorghum to household, 209, 215
Cash crops, 188, 191. See also Cotton
  coffee, qat, 293, 294, 297
  cotton, wheat, peanuts, 200
  peanuts, 199, 214
  potatoes, 307
  qat and fruit trees, 296
  on scheme to neglect food crops, 200
  sorghum, 213
  tomatoes, 162
Cattle, cows, 34, 75, 85, 98, 124, 208
Cereal, 21, 28, 34, 37, 54, 61, 67, 75, 91, 98, 104, 202, 212, 263, 281, 300, 321
Children
  average 6.3 live births per woman, 180
  education, 71, 132, 137, 256, 348
  family unit, 341
  health, 91, 285, 324

inheritance, 63, 69, 300
nutrition, 124, 208, 214
peasant household labor, 111, 121, 326
water users, 90
Colonial policy, 50, 64, 71, 75, 129, 199, 200, 201, 206, 212
Commerce
　Hammam Sousse, 126, 132, 135, 139, 147, 165
　Turkey, 333
Cotton
　expanded in Euphrates valleys, 245, 247, 250, 257, 262, 263
　favored over sorghum on schemes in Sudan, causing food crisis, 197, 198, 199, 200, 201, 202, 203, 204, 205, 206, 207, 209, 210, 211, 212, 213, 217, 218, 219, 220, 222
Credit, agricultural
　Central Tunisia, 110, 111, 114–116, 124
　for cotton, not for sorghum, 197, 200, 201, 207, 209, 218, 222
　Morocco, 47, 49–57, 62–72
　Turkey, 314, 315, 316, 318, 319, 320, 321, 322, 323, 325, 326, 328, 329, 330, 332
Crop choice, 102, 104, 262, 295, 314, 321, 325
　central highlands, 299
　dryland, 121
　Haraz, 282
　with irrigation, 294
　Kasserine, 75
　on linear programming model, 187, 188
　modern farmer, Morocco, 54
　of new irrigation farmers, 122
　with new technology, 307
　New Valley, 183
　on PPIs, 108, 111
　on schemes, 197
　traditional farmer, Morocco, 53
　YAR, 296, 297

Dryland (rainfed, unirrigated)
　agriculture, 16, 20, 21, 23, 28, 33–35, 57, 61, 62, 75, 95, 98, 101, 103–105, 107, 110–114, 121, 201, 202, 204, 205, 212, 217, 247, 248, 250, 252, 256, 257, 263, 281, 295, 296, 299, 300, 301, 302, 307, 326

Electricity, 81, 98, 100, 101, 111, 133, 151, 240, 248, 273, 280, 314, 315, 324, 331, 345
Environmental degradation
　Libya, 166
　NW Morocco, 42, 43
Extension, 16, 22, 23, 26, 28, 55, 72, 95, 96, 98, 108, 122–124, 175, 176, 186, 197, 201, 202, 218, 219, 283, 305, 314, 315, 316, 317, 318, 319, 320, 321, 326, 328, 330, 331, 332

Farms
　average income, 323
　management, 66
　model, 191, 194
　purchase, 115
　size, 21, 35, 47, 50, 53, 63, 166, 257, 268, 270, 326
　types, 61
Farmer strategy
　to increase food security, 213
　irrigation, Central Tunisia, 122
　medium farms, 62
　mixed, 105, 109
　modern, 53
　production, Central Tunisia, 121
　subsistence, 76
　traditional, 52, 55
Food, nutrition
　crops, 184
　imports, 166, 182
　market, 162
　needs unmet because of government policy, 197, 198, 200, 201, 202, 203, 204, 205, 207, 208, 209, 210, 211, 212, 213, 216, 217, 218, 219, 221
　qat growing detracts from, 297, 305
　requirements have always been unmet, 36
　small ruminant project, 124, 147
　sorghum dominant food crop, 296
　stocking during good years, 104
　use of credit for, 55, 65, 328
　wheat main food crop of Jbala, 33
Forage, fodder, animal food, 53, 67, 101, 102, 104, 183, 184, 187, 188,

200, 202, 296, 297, 305, 314, 316, 321, 325, 339
Forest, deforestation, afforestation
Haraz Afforestation Project, Yemen, 282, 283, 284, 285, 288, 289
and prohibition of slash-and-burn agriculture, Morocco, 30, 34, 35, 37–39, 43

Goats, 34, 40, 75, 82, 85, 124, 294, 339, 341, 342, 346, 347, 349

Households
Bedouin, 233, 234, 238, 239, 241, 242
economy, 75, 76, 81, 84, 95, 96, 98, 100, 101, 103–116, 121, 122, 124, 125, 138, 191, 197, 198, 205, 206, 207, 208, 209, 211, 212, 213, 214, 215, 216, 218, 219, 220, 221, 222, 231, 250
size, 181
survey, 138, 252, 253, 254, 256, 257, 259, 262, 263, 272, 283, 299, 319, 323, 324, 325, 326, 327, 328, 341, 342, 345
Houses
Bedouin resettlement, 231
description, Sungurlu County, Çorum, 324
empty, 259
families living in tents before their houses were finished, 256
Hammam Sousse, 141, 142, 148
new, migration wages spent on, 272
settlement pattern, 75, 82, 84

Inputs, 53, 56, 65, 68, 69, 111, 122, 123, 184, 199, 201, 204, 205, 209, 210, 212, 299, 300, 316, 318, 319, 320, 321, 322, 325, 326, 327, 330, 331
definition of modern farm, 53
Irrigation
and agricultural credit, Morocco, 57, 61, 72
canal, 82, 84, 87, 102, 111, 115, 125, 200, 248, 256, 259, 266, 273
and migration, Northeast Syria, 245, 246, 247, 248, 250, 251, 256, 257, 259, 266, 268, 269, 270, 273, 274, 275
New Valley Plan, Egypt, 176, 180, 182, 186, 187, 188, 189, 190, 192, 193
from sewage plant, Hammam Sousse, 148, 149
smallholder, Central Tunisia, 95, 96, 98, 100, 101, 103–111, 113–115, 121–123
Sudanese scheme, 197, 198, 199, 200, 201, 202, 203, 204, 205, 206, 207, 209, 210, 211, 213, 217, 218, 219, 220
Turkey, 312, 314, 315, 325, 326
of vegetables, Mediterranean agriculture, 34
and water-user associations, Central Tunisia, 75, 76, 81, 82, 84–87, 91, 93
Yemen, 294, 296, 297, 299, 300, 301, 302, 304, 305, 306, 307

Kinship
importance of, 254, 329, 330, 333
settlements, 252, 257
and tribal affiliation, 110, 112, 121
and use of wells, 89

Labor
agricultural, 52–54, 62, 69, 76, 103–105, 107, 109, 111, 115, 187, 191, 197, 198, 199, 201, 203, 205, 210, 211, 212, 219, 222, 247, 249, 250, 251, 254, 257, 266, 268, 274, 275, 281, 326
force, Hammam Sousse, 132, 134, 135, 138, 143, 144, 150, 151
household, 84, 109–112, 114–116, 121, 191, 207, 210, 319, 326
international labor market, 141, 160, 172, 203, 246, 264, 271, 274
Libya, 166
off-farm, 52
sexual division of, 121, 130, 150, 181, 210, 326
shortage, 211, 213, 214, 218, 220, 222, 264, 281, 304
wage, 62, 76, 81, 101, 104, 105, 110, 111, 115, 121, 122, 201, 207, 210, 219, 232, 250, 257, 262, 263, 268, 272, 319, 324, 326, 327, 328, 345

wage, oil company, 343, 344, 345, 346, 349
  for well digging and maintenance, 88, 91, 106, 107, 122
Labor migration, 91, 107, 115, 198, 259
  Central Tunisia, 74–76, 84, 91, 100, 101, 109, 114
  Egypt, 181, 185
  emigration, Yemen, 281, 283, 293, 295, 300, 305
  Emigration from highlands of northwest Morocco, 30, 40–43
  from Hammam Sousse, 138
  to Hammam Sousse, 134, 143, 144
  and rural development, northeast Syria, 245, 246, 251, 252, 253, 254, 256, 259, 262, 263, 264, 266, 268, 269, 270, 271, 272, 273, 274, 275
  rural-urban, Libya, 160, 161, 163, 164, 166
  rural-urban, Morocco, 52, 62, 64, 69
  rural-urban, Turkey, 315, 316, 318, 323, 324, 327, 328
  Sudan, 214, 216, 222
Land
  commoditization, 111
  communal, 37, 39, 68, 75
  expropriation, 207, 208, 231, 232, 233
  irrigated, development, 187, 188, 190, 199, 205
  nationalized at zoned agricultural rate, 144
  rainfed, amount needed for subsistence, 61, 62, 75, 104, 110
  reclamation, 177, 178, 180, 183, 185, 186, 195
  rental, 54, 203, 206, 231, 232
  rights of ownership, 231, 232
  sale, 107, 110, 111
  scarce, 104, 136, 148, 213
  speculation, 143
  tenure, 53, 61–63, 71, 76, 98, 100, 106, 107, 110, 113, 114, 203, 206, 214, 230, 232
  uncultivable state-owned, Israel, 230
  use, 102, 162, 182, 197, 202, 203, 204, 210, 212, 213, 214, 219
  values, 57
  waqf, 103, 125, 298

Landless farmers, 113, 222, 247, 274, 314, 316, 320, 324, 327, 328, 330
  and charcoal making, 38, 39
Land reform, 108
  Jbalan highlands, 34
  women excluded, 116
Lentils, 314, 325, 330
Literacy, 90, 180, 268
Local involvement in development
  anthropologist as advocate, 242
  DAARP, Morocco, 16
  Tunisia water user associations, 78, 91
  Village Development Cooperative, 330

Machinery
  credit for, 320, 322
  increase during project, 323
  and inputs, 316, 319, 320, 323, 326, 330
  introduction of, and employment patterns, 75, 247, 304
  needed for women farmers, 305
  purchase, 272
  rented, 326
Market
  access, 110, 112, 116, 122, 323, 332
  black, 321, 329
  cotton, 198, 199
  economy, 52, 104, 163, 328, 332
  food, 126, 131, 147, 150, 151, 197, 204, 213, 217, 218, 219, 296, 314
  grain, 201, 204, 208, 209, 297
  interest rates, 50, 66
  Monday Market of Bni Harshan, 30, 32, 34, 35, 38–40, 43
  oil, 170, 294
  and social contacts, 341
  and terms of trade, 322, 323, 332, 333
  value, 57
Marketing
  Turkey, 330
Marketplace, 284
  Harasiis, description, 341
  and social contacts, 166
Marriage, spouse, husband, wife
  among the Harasiis, 341
  and exchange, 164, 272
  and household labor, 111, 124, 326
  and inheritance, 63, 69, 301

Index

Migration
　human, Oman, 339, 342, 346, 347
　urban, Morocco, 30, 40
Monitoring and evaluation, 316, 318, 332

Office de Dévelopement de la Tunisie Centrale (ODTC), 77, 95, 96, 98, 100, 101, 106–108, 115, 123, 125

Plan, development
　agricultural, 198
　Egypt's New Valley, 175–178, 183–195
　Euphrates, 245, 251, 257, 259, 273–275
　Hammam Sousse, 131–140, 144–147, 149–151
　Libya's Human Settlement Plan, 155, 158–161, 163, 164, 166–172
　Negev, 228, 229, 232–238, 240, 242, 243
　Planning and Evaluation, 96
　and potable water, 78, 86
　real and ideal, 48
　State Planning Organization, Turkey, 315, 319, 322, 324, 331
　Sudan scheme, 199
　Yemen, 280, 284–289, 292, 293, 295–298, 301, 304–308
Polygyny and household units of production and consumption, 205, 212, 349
Poverty
　Central Tunisia, in contrast with the coast, 76, 91
　expectation of alleviating, 316, 320, 332, 333
　and hunger, Sudan, 217
Périmètre Publique Irrigué (PPI), 98, 100–105, 107–116, 122, 123, 125
Projet Chaouia, Morocco, 28

Religion
　and politics, 129, 150, 282
　and social position, 112, 138, 293
Religious
　agricultural tax, 281
　institutions, 132, 298
　land, 34, 35, 298
Resettlement decisions, 253

Roads, construction of, 91, 136, 147, 231, 233, 294, 314, 345

Seeds and other inputs
　for cotton, Euphrates valley, 250
　definition of success, 318
　differential access to, 325
　distribution erratic in Turkey, 321
　gift of government, 101
　and increased productivity, 330
　need for cash, 111
　and need for extension, 122
　part of Israeli subsidization of Bedouin dry farming, 232
　provided by schemes for cotton, 199, 201, 218
　responsibility of tenant, 299
　schedule of payment, 102
　seen as panacea, 316
　subsidized, 323
　supplied by Agricultural Bank of Turkey, 321
　use of credit for, 62, 65, 320
Sex differentiation and water use, 81, 82
Sharecropping
　Morocco, 21, 52, 56, 69
　Sudan, 213, 214
　Syria, 247, 250, 254, 256, 259, 270
　Turkey, 320, 326, 327, 328, 330
　Yemen, 298, 299, 300
Sheep, 34, 75, 82, 85, 98, 112, 115, 124, 231, 246, 247, 250, 256, 259, 262, 263, 294, 341
Social science
　conflicting methods and theories, 285, 287
　indigenous, 15–17, 20, 22, 24, 43, 150
　not well integrated into final development plan, 177
　opportunities in Yemen, 281
　undervalued by technocratic officials, 319
Survey
　Bni Harshan, 35, 40
　of community needs, Libya, 170
　demographic, Hammam Sousse, 132
　of farmers, Morocco, 61, 62
　of farmers, Tunisia, for WUAs, 76, 78, 96

of farmers, Yemen, 283, 284, 285
household, Hammam Sousse, 131, 138, 147, 151
household, northern Syria, 250, 251, 264, 268, 275
household, Oman, 346
household, Tunisia, 113, 121
household, Turkey, 318, 319, 322, 325
household, Wad al Abbas, 205, 211, 212, 213, 220
of migrants, northern Syria, 246
small farm, New Valley, 185
viewed as too expensive, 176, 287

Tenancy, 199, 206, 211, 212, 213, 220, 222, 298, 299
Tourism, 128, 132, 135–137, 139, 141–148, 150, 151, 161, 163, 177, 185

Urban entrepreneurs
  Morocco, 54, 56
  Syria, 245, 247, 248, 256, 264
Urban planning
  Egypt, 181, 190, 195
  Hammam Sousse, 134
  Libya, 159, 160, 161, 163, 164, 166, 171
  Negev, 235, 240
Urban poor
  Morocco, 30, 40, 41

Village agents, 315, 317, 318, 319, 331, 332

Wheat, 33, 34, 36, 39, 52–54, 75, 104, 182, 183, 187, 199, 200, 201, 202, 203, 207, 214, 220, 221, 247, 257, 262, 283, 294, 297, 299, 314, 316, 321, 325, 330, 342
Women
  and agricultural extension, 124, 305, 307, 324
  in agriculture, 69, 124, 210, 305, 326
  collect firewood, 283
  could vote, 129
  in crafts, 151
  in development, 124, 160, 161, 162
  household labor, 116, 121, 326
  labor, and social class, 116
  may trade right to land, 300
  ratio of men to women, 181
  responsible for sheep and goats, 341
  spring a "feminine" spot, 81
  unequal access to resources, 116
  and water-user associations, 89
  work loads increase with male emigration, 305
  workload increased, 331
World Bank, 28, 49, 51, 100, 142, 156, 198, 202, 221, 279, 281, 305, 312, 314, 315, 317, 332, 333